O9-AIF-289

Praise for
As Kingfishers Catch Fire

"*As Kingfishers Catch Fire* covers it all, the *A* to *Z* of Christian spirituality. It is filled with the kind of wisdom that can only come from long obedience in the same direction! It's more than a book; it's a gift. Thank you, Eugene!"

—MARK BATTERSON, *New York Times* best-selling author of *The Circle Maker* and lead pastor of National Community Church, Washington, DC

"There is no one who has done more to shape my 'pastoral imagination' than Eugene Peterson. Now, through this extraordinary collection, we see how words become pastoral work. An exegete and a poet, Peterson opens up to us not only the text but its world, welcoming us to walk with Moses, David, Isaiah, Solomon, Peter, Paul, and John. And as we do, we find ourselves keeping company with Jesus. Read it devotionally; read it as a study in sacred storytelling; read it to come alive along the Jesus Way."

—GLENN PACKIAM, associate senior pastor, New Life Church, Colorado Springs

"I can hear Eugene Peterson's warm and gravelly voice in each well-crafted chapter of *As Kingfishers Catch Fire.* I wish I could have been in a pew listening to the Word spoken for a particular time, place, and people, but reading this collection is the next best thing. Peterson's attention to biblical texts, theological concerns, and earthy applications for real people are the same threads we find in his many books. Reading just the introduction to each section is time well spent, but I promise you won't stop there."

—DAN BAUMGARTNER, senior pastor, First Presbyterian Church of Hollywood

AS KINGFISHERS CATCH FIRE

EUGENE H. PETERSON

A CONVERSATION ON THE WAYS OF GOD
FORMED BY THE WORDS OF GOD

AS KINGFISHERS CATCH FIRE

WATERBROOK

As Kingfishers Catch Fire

Any restating of the Scriptures that are not specifically referenced as biblical text are the author's paraphrases. Italics in Scripture quotations reflect the author's added emphasis.

Some names have been changed to protect the identities of the persons involved.

Brief portions of some of these sermons have appeared in other publications, including *The Message Study Bible*, © 2012, published by NavPress, and *Conversations: The Message with Its Translator*, © 2002, published by NavPress.

Hardcover ISBN 978-1-60142-967-4
eBook ISBN 978-1-60142-968-1

Cover design by Kristopher K. Orr; cover illustration by Lesha Kurbatov

Published in association with the literary agency of Alive Literary Agency, Colorado Springs, Colorado, www .aliveliterary.com.

Published in the United States by WaterBrook, an imprint of the Crown Publishing Group, a division of Penguin Random House LLC, New York.

WaterBrook® and its deer colophon are registered trademarks of Penguin Random House LLC.

Library of Congress Cataloging-in-Publication Data
Names: Peterson, Eugene H., 1932- author.
Title: As kingfishers catch fire : a conversation on the ways of God formed by the words of God : sermons / Eugene H. Peterson.
Description: First Edition. | Colorado Springs, Colorado : WaterBrook, 2017.
Identifiers: LCCN 2016058027 (print) | LCCN 2017011092 (ebook) | ISBN 9781601429674 (hardcover) | ISBN 9781601429681 (electronic)
Subjects: LCSH: Peterson, Eugene H., 1932—Sermons. | Christ Our King (Church : Bel Air, Md.)—Sermons. | Presbyterian Church (U.S.A.)—Sermons. | Sermons, American—20th century. | Bible—Sermons.
Classification: LCC BX9225.P466 A5 2017 (print) | LCC BX9225.P466 (ebook) | DDC 252—dc23
LC record available at https://lccn.loc.gov/2016058027

Printed in the United States of America
2018

10 9 8 7 6 5 4

For Rickly and Debbie Christian
and
Jon and Cheryl Stine,
faithful and skilled companions
over a lifetime of writing

CONTENTS

Part 3: "PREPARE THE WAY OF THE LORD"

PREACHING IN THE COMPANY OF ISAIAH

Part 4: "ON EARTH AS IT IS IN HEAVEN"

PREACHING IN THE COMPANY OF SOLOMON

Part 5: "YES AND AMEN AND JESUS"

PREACHING IN THE COMPANY OF PETER

Part 6: "CHRIST IN YOU THE HOPE OF GLORY"

PREACHING IN THE COMPANY OF PAUL

Part 7: "IN THE BEGINNING WAS THE WORD"

PREACHING IN THE COMPANY OF JOHN OF PATMOS

LETTER TO THE READER

Eugene Peterson. The brilliant pastor-poet behind the wildly successful The Message Bible and spiritual classics like *Running with the Horses* and *A Long Obedience in the Same Direction.* A detail you may not know is that he spent twenty-nine years as pastor of the same church in Bel Air, Maryland, faithfully sharing his heart with his congregation Sunday after Sunday and all the days in between.

Wouldn't it have been amazing to have been a fly on the wall or a person in the pew those twenty-nine years, listening to Peterson unpack "the whole counsel of God" (Acts 20:27)? What you have in your hands—*As Kingfishers Catch Fire: A Conversation on the Ways of God Formed by the Words of God*—is our attempt to make that happen.

Throughout this definitive collection of teachings, Peterson is intentional in keeping the main idea the main idea: that we, as Christians, live lives of *congruence.* Put another way, that the inside matches the outside. Or as we used to hear, that we indeed practice what we preach.

With the exception of small editorial polishes here and there, these teachings are presented in their original form, without any anxiety to update. In other words, there will be references to the moon landing, nods now and then to places specific to Peterson's congregation, and phrases like "My text for today is . . ." We believe they add a charming integrity to this work, more responsible than relevant, each page honoring real time, revealing how we can "find ourselves living, almost in spite of ourselves, the Christ life in the Christ way." We hope you agree.

Sincerely,

The WaterBrook Multnomah editorial team

PREFACE

Sixty years ago I found myself distracted. I was being tossed about by "every wind of doctrine" (Ephesians 4:14), except it was not winds of doctrines that were distracting me but the winds of the times. It was the sixties, and there was a lot going on: charismatic personalities like John F. Kennedy and Martin Luther King Jr., the civil rights revolution in the South, Timothy Leary and the drug culture, Earth Day and the flower children, Vietnam . . . There was so much going on—in the world, in the culture, in the church—so many important things to do, urgent voices telling me what had to be done. There was no one thing needful. There were many things needful, all clamoring for my attention.

I was living in a small town twenty miles from Baltimore, a sleepy colonial town that was fast becoming a suburb. I had been assigned by my denomination to gather and organize a congregation. I started out with a fair amount of confidence and much energy. I was well supported organizationally and financially. The personal encouragement was strong. The mission I had been called to lead was clearly articulated.

But as time went on, I found myself increasingly at odds with my advisors on matters of means, the methods proposed for ensuring the numerical and financial viability of the congregation but without even a footnote regarding the nurturing of souls. I was given books to read on demographics and sociology. I was sent to seminars on programming strategies for appealing to the secular suburban mind-set. Leadership was interpreted almost entirely from business and consumer models.

It wasn't long before I was in crisis: a chasm had developed between the way I was preaching from the pulpit and my deepest convictions on what it meant to be a pastor. I sensed my attitude toward the men and women I was gathering into a congregation was silently shaped by how I was planning to use them to succeed as a pastor developing a new congregation with little thought to serving these souls with the bread of life. I found myself thinking competitively about other churches in town, calculating ways in which I could beat them in the numbers game.

Then three things happened about the same time that brought me to the realization I didn't know what I was doing. It began in my pulpit. I realized I didn't know how to preach. I was not a preacher. What I was doing from the pulpit each Sunday was not preaching; in fact, it had nothing to do with preaching. I was whipping up enthusiasm. I was explaining the nature of what we had to do, while arbitrarily fitting Bible texts into key places. I was using the place of worship as a bully pulpit. I had become very American in all matters of ways and means. I never wavered in my theological convictions, but I had a job to do—get a congregation up and running—and I was ready to use any means at hand to do it: appeal to the consumer instincts of people, use abstract principles to unify enthusiasm, shape goals by using catchy slogans, create publicity images that provided ego enhancement.

And then, almost at the same time, two more things happened: I heard a lecture and read a poem. The combination of lecture and poem changed everything. The two events taught me what I needed to know to become a pastor of the gospel. The lecture was given in person by Paul Tournier, a Swiss physician; the poem was written by Gerard Manley Hopkins, a Jesuit priest, long dead.

Paul Tournier in midlife had shifted the location of his medical practice from a consulting room, with its examining table and supporting laboratories and surgeries, to his living room, before a fireplace, with him holding a pipe in his hand instead of hanging a stethoscope from his neck. For the rest of his life he used words—listened to and spoken—in a setting of personal relationship as the primary means for carrying out his healing vocation. He left a way of medical practice that was primarily focused on the body and embraced a medical practice that dealt primarily with the whole person, an integrated being of body, soul, and spirit. He wrote many books and I read them all.

Driving the twenty miles home from Johns Hopkins Hospital, the site of the lecture, my wife and I commented appreciatively on Tournier's words, in the course of which she said, "Wasn't that translator great?" And I said, "What translator? There wasn't any translator." To which she said, "Eugene, he was lecturing in French. You don't know twenty words of French. Of *course* there was a translator." And then I remembered her: a woman about his age, standing to the side and a little behind him, translating his French into English. She was so unobtrusive, so self-effacing, so modest in what she was doing that I forgot she was there, and ten minutes after the lecture, I didn't even remember she had been there.

But there was something else: Paul Tournier himself. During the lecture I had the growing feeling that who he was and what he was saying were completely congruent. He had been living for a long time in Switzerland. Precisely the way he lived and what he was now saying in Baltimore came across as an accurate and mature expression of all he had been living and writing. Just as the translator assimilated to the lecturer, her English words carrying not just the meaning but also the spirit of his French words, so his words were one with his life—not just what he knew and what he had done, but who he was.

It was a memorable experience, the transparency of that man. No dissonance between word and spirit, no pretense. And the corresponding transparency of the woman. No ego, no self-consciousness in either one of them. Later I remembered T. S. Eliot's comments on Charles Williams: "Some men are less than their works, some are more. Charles Williams cannot be placed in either class. To have known the man would have been enough; to know his books is enough. . . . [He was] the same man in his life and in his writings."[1]

That's the sense I had that day about Paul Tournier: he wrote what he lived and he lived what he wrote. In the lecture that day in Baltimore, he was the same man as in his books written in Switzerland. A life of congruence, with no slippage between what he was saying and the way he was living. *Congruence.* It is the best word I can come up with to designate what I realized I needed in my pastoral work.

I recalled Herman Melville's comment: "Yes, the world's a ship on its passage out, and not a voyage complete; and the pulpit is its prow."[2] The prow and the ship, not two different things but the same thing.

And then, not two weeks later, this poem:

As kingfishers catch fire, dragonflies draw flame;
As tumbled over rim in roundy wells
Stones ring; like each tucked string tells, each hung bell's
Bow swung finds tongue to fling out broad its name;

---

1. Charles Williams, *All Hallows' Eve* (Oxford: Benediction, 2009), introduction.
2. Herman Melville, *Moby-Dick* (New York: Dover, 2003), 43.

Each mortal thing does one thing and the same:
Deals out that being indoors each one dwells;
Selves—goes itself; *myself* it speaks and spells,
Crying *What I do is me: for that I came.*

I say more: the just man justices;
Keeps grace: that keeps all his goings graces;
Acts in God's eye what in God's eye he is—
Christ. For Christ plays in ten thousand places,
Lovely in limbs, and lovely in eyes not his
To the Father through the features of men's faces.[3]

The Christian life is the lifelong practice of attending to the details of congruence—congruence between ends and means, congruence between what we do and the way we do it, congruence between what is written in Scripture and our living out what is written, congruence between a ship and its prow, congruence between preaching and living, congruence between the sermon and what is lived in both preacher and congregation, the congruence of the Word made flesh in Jesus with what is lived in our flesh.

It is what we admire in an athlete whose body is accurately and gracefully responsive and totally submissive to the conditions of the event: Michael Jordan at one with the court, the game, the basketball, and his fellow players. Or a musical performance in which Mozart, a Stradivarius, and Itzhak Perlman fuse and are indistinguishable from one another in the music. Congruence also occurs often enough in more modest venues: a child unself-consciously at play; a conversation in which words become as movements in a ballet, revealing all manner of beauty and truth and goodness; a meal bringing friends into a quiet awareness of affection and celebration in a mingling of senses and spirits that provides something like a Eucharistic dimension to the evening.

And congruence is what we participate in as we read "As Kingfishers Catch Fire," the sonnet that gave me metaphors to identify the distinctive heart of pastoral

3. Gerard Manley Hopkins, *The Poems of Gerard Manley Hopkins,* ed. W. H. Gardner and N. H. Mackenzie (London: Oxford University Press, 1967), 90.

work. Hopkins piles up a dazzling assemblage of images to fix our attention on this sense of rightness, of wholeness, that comes together when we realize the utter congruence between what a thing is and what it does: kingfisher and dragonfly catching and reflecting sun brightness, a stone tumbling over the rim of a well, a plucked violin string, the clapper of a bell sounding. What happens and the way it happens are seamless. Hopkins then proceeds to the congruence of "each mortal thing" bodying forth who and what we are. But what kingfishers and falling stones and chiming bells do without effort requires development on our part, a formation into who we truly are, a becoming in which the means by which we live are congruent with the ends for which we live. But Hopkins's final image is not of us finally achieving what the dragonfly and plucked string do simply because they are determined by biology and physics. His final image is Christ, who lives and acts in us in such ways that our lives express the congruence of inside and outside, this congruence of ends and means, Christ as both the means and the end playing through our limbs and eyes to the Father through the features of our faces so that we find ourselves living, almost in spite of ourselves, the Christ life in the Christ way.

With Tournier's witness and Hopkins's metaphors working together, I finally started to get it: preaching is the weekly verbal witness to this essential congruence of what Christ *is* with his work that "plays" in us. Not just the preaching but prayers at a hospital bed, conversations with the elderly, small talk on a street corner—all the circumstances and relationships that make up the pastor's life. Not ideas, not goals, not principles, nothing abstract or disembodied, but the good news of the "Word . . . made flesh" (John 1:14, KJV) becoming *our* flesh, our limbs and eyes. I still had a long way to go, but at least now I was being a pastor and not staying awake at night laying out a strategy or "casting a vision."

—

One of the unintended consequences of this (I noticed it only in retrospect) was that I was beginning to treat my congregation with far more dignity than I had been treating them. Impatience began to diminish; condescension slowly faded out. I was learning to embrace the congregation just as they were, not how I wanted them to be. They became an integral part of the sermon. Preaching became a corporate act. Common worship was the context: singing and praying, baptisms and Eucharist, silence and blessings. But I soon realized our common worship on

Sundays was also developing tendrils that reached into homes and workplaces, casual conversations and chance meetings on the street.

I was discovering an imagination for developing a sense of narrative that kept our lives relationally together in something deeper and wider than anything we were individually. I began to weed out the depersonalizing stereotypes that identified the souls in my care as either problems to be fixed or resources to be exploited. I developed conversations that grew into stories that in turn developed into something akin to a novel in which all these people who were worshiping together were involved with one another, whether they knew it or not or even wanted to be. Congregation was not a collection of individuals but something more like a body with distinctive parts, but all the parts working organically with Christ as the head.

The sermons gathered here document this collaboration of pastor and congregation in acts of worship and a life together for twenty-nine years (1962–91) at Christ Our King Presbyterian Church (UPCUSA) in Harford County, Maryland. They are not selected because of any merit as my "best" sermons but because I have come to think of them as three decades of representative collaboration with my congregation.

A friend who had been a student of Karl Barth told me that Barth often spoke of the impossibility of conveying with accuracy in a book what was proclaimed from a pulpit, like attempting to sketch a kingfisher in flight or to describe a lightning strike when all we have to go on is what is left after the storm. Sermons copied into a book are like that. Much, maybe most, of what is involved in a sermon is left out of the book: the voice of the preacher, the congregation listening to the sermon, the worship in song and prayer and silence, the architecture of the sanctuary. That is why I am naming what is written here "kingfisher sermons." But maybe a prayerful imagination in the reading can supply at least some of what is lost in the book.

I have organized the sermons in seven groupings under the names of Moses, David, Isaiah, Solomon, Peter, Paul, and John of Patmos. Each name identifies a distinctive approach that needs to be included in the "whole counsel of God" (Acts 20:27) that I wanted my congregation to be on familiar terms with. To give added emphasis to the "whole" counsel, I placed seven sermons in each group: seven sermons in each of the seven groupings, forty-nine sermons in all.

I wanted to enter into the biblical company of prototypical preachers and work out of the traditions they had developed under the guidance of the Holy Spirit. When I prepare and preach a sermon, I need constant reminding that I am part of a company that has a rich and varied genealogy. I do not start from scratch. I do not make up something new. I want to develop a coherent and connected biblical imagination with my congregation, not live out of a suitcase full of cast-off items from various yard sales and secondhand stores.

Part I

"HE SPOKE AND IT CAME TO BE"

PREACHING IN THE COMPANY OF MOSES

Introduction

An enormous authority and dignity have, through the centuries, developed around the first five books of the Bible, traditionally designated the Books of Moses. Over the course of many centuries, they account for a truly astonishing amount of reading and writing, study and prayer, teaching and preaching.

God is the primary concern of these books. That accounts for the authority and the dignity. But it is not only God; *we* get included. That accounts for the widespread and intense human interest. We want to know what's going on. We want to know how we fit into things. We don't want to miss out.

The Books of Moses are made up mostly of stories and signposts. The stories show us God working with and speaking to men and women in a rich variety of circumstances. God is presented to us not in ideas and arguments but in events and actions that involve each of us personally. The signposts provide immediate and practical directions to guide us into behavior that is appropriate to our humanity in the particular place and time in which we live, and that is honoring to God.

The artless simplicity of the storytelling and signposting in these books makes what is written here as accessible to children as to adults, but the simplicity (as in so many simple things) is also profound, inviting us into a lifetime of growing participation in God's saving ways with us.

Preaching requires that we develop a Moses imagination, with stories and signposts. Using the name of Moses to identify these books does not mean he wrote them, for many unnamed Hebrew prophetic minds told and wrote what was eventually gathered and copied here. Moses, rather, represents the way of life and the way of using language that sets the tone for everything else that makes up Holy Scripture. The five books are foundational for the subsequent sixty-one. Preaching in the company of Moses keeps proclamation personal and local while at the same time breathing the clean air of creation (what God does) and the air of covenant (how God brings us into participation).

Moses is mentioned in the New Testament more frequently than any other Old Testament person—seventy-eight times. His influence is everywhere. It is impossible to exaggerate his importance. A giant in the land. The first Christians (and preachers!), living by faith in Jesus Christ and teaching others to do the same, had Moses constantly on their tongues and his example always in their vision.

Elie Wiesel, retelling the Moses story with a blend of biblical and Talmudic materials, wrote, "Moses [was] the most solitary and most powerful hero in Biblical history. The immensity of his task and the scope of his experience command our admiration, our reverence, our awe. Moses, the man who changed the course of history . . . his emergence became the decisive turning point. After him, nothing was the same again."[4]

The way of language in which Moses is our first teacher is most accurately described, I think, as a storytelling language, a language textured by the give-and-take of a life under the formative influence of God's Word, language that develops in a worshiping congregation, language that invokes God and then listens and prays. It is the language of a mixed company of struggling sinners and faltering saints, preachers and teachers, homemakers and business people—people on pilgrimage, telling their family stories, passing on the counsels and promises of God. Preaching in the company of Moses develops precisely this storytelling imagination that keeps our sermons grounded in the everyday realities of the people to whom we are preaching.

But during the last three hundred years, the name of Moses, so long identified with the Five Books, the Torah, has for many been gradually effaced from the spine of his books, much as names disappear from centuries-old, weather-scoured cemetery markers. In this case the weather did not consist of wind and rain, snow and sleet, but of historical criticism, a new way of reading the Bible.

So for many of our pastor colleagues, the long practice of reading the Bible as a

4. Elie Wiesel, *Messengers of God: Biblical Portraits and Legends* (New York: Touchstone, 1976), 181.

book of faith has played second fiddle to reading it strictly as history. The *story*—the narrative of a lived faith in God—has been obscured if not lost altogether. Those who read the Bible this way (but not all) ignore the literary context of the Bible and take it apart, looking for development and historical change. They challenge the historicity of foundational events and traditional ideas of authorship and then reconstruct the history, but they leave the Bible itself as a pile of disjointed fragments from various times and places. They have no interest in the literary and theological coherence of the text. These critics suppose that by digging underneath the Moses books they can serve us a better or truer truth. But most writers are highly offended when people get more interested in the contents of their wastebaskets and filing cabinets than the books they write. "Read the book!" The meaning is in the book, not in the information about the book.

When I was twelve years old, in the year 1944, my father bought a disreputable '36 Plymouth, drove it home, and parked it in the alley behind our house. There it died. It never ran again. I don't think my father ever went out back and looked at it again. But I put it to good use. I was a couple of years away from getting my driver's license, and I sat in that old wreck most days for an hour after school and practiced using the gear shift, shifting from first to second to third and back down again, using the brake and clutch pedals, positioning my hands on the steering wheel, imagining myself in the act of driving over mountain roads and through blizzards.

After a few months I had mastered the moves. But having used up my imagination in driving the inert machine, I thought I might as well try to find out what made it tick when it did tick. I think I had a vague idea that maybe I could make it run again. I took it apart, piece by piece, educating myself in the ways of carburetors, cooling systems, transmissions, and brake drums. After a few months I was familiar with most of the parts now laid out on the grass, but I never did figure out what made it run. And of course by the time I had completed my investigative work, there was no chance of it ever running again.

—

Is it possible to appreciate the work of the historical critics that in large part (not completely) removes Moses as the author of the Five Books and yet at the same time affirms the traditional Mosaic presence that has provided a cohesive and personal authorial voice, the story line that has kept all the parts together for both Jews and Christians for so long? Is it possible to take the Torah apart historically and then put it back together again as a book of faith with theological and literary integrity? I think it is. It is not only possible but worth any effort it might take. And pastors occupy an influential place in the Christian church from which to do it.

The world that we read of in our Bibles was essentially an oral world, although there is plenty of evidence that much of the speaking also got written. Language in itself, in its origins and in most of its practice, is oral. We *speak* words long before we write and read them. The world we live in today continues to be primarily oral. Orality does not mean primitive. Words spoken are both previous to and inherently superior to words written, even in the most literate of cultures.

Among our Hebrew ancestors, generations of orally transmitted traditions developed and seasoned their unique people-of-God memory. Here and there, now and then, the words were written down and preserved, copied and collected, honored and read. Moses is remembered as one who wrote down the words (Exodus 24:4; 34:27–28; Deuteronomy 31:9, 24). The words became books. In all that was said or sung or written, the memory and words of Moses provided the story line that kept it all together. Over time, the telling and the writing became the Five Books of Moses.

Moses's presence was profound: his leadership, his integrity, his ordained authority as the leader of the people of God out of the slavery of Egyptian bondage into the service of God, his Sinai transmission of God's revelation, his provision and instruction for recentering the life of the people in worship. His pastoral care of his flock during all those years in the wilderness shaped all the seemingly disparate stories, instructions, and directions into a coherent whole. Moses looms still as the architect of the huge, sprawling house of language that is the Torah, the Five Books, the founding document for the faith of Israel and the Christian gospel. Torah: the revelation of God written for the people of God, Jew and Christian alike. Not just *author* in a strictly literal sense, but *authority* in an encompassing literary and Spirit-inspired sense.

Jesus, who confined his language to the spoken word, and those who wrote his story for us commonly referred to the Torah ("the Law") simply as "Moses." In the early church Moses was the most prominent ancestral name, whether as leader of the people of God or as the one giving voice to the revelation of God in the Torah. *Torah* and *Moses* were virtual synonyms in both Judaism and the church.

As we preach in the company of Moses, we will nourish this storytelling imagination.

I

"In the Beginning God Created"

GENESIS 1:1–2:4
JOHN 1:1–3

A little more than a year ago, three men were orbiting the moon in a space capsule. It was Christmas Eve, and they took turns reading Genesis 1, the opening chapter of the Bible: "In the beginning God created the heavens and the earth," a most magnificent choice of texts for Christmas Eve.

The *Apollo 8* spacecraft was transformed momentarily into a Jewish/Christian pulpit. Man's most impressive technological achievement to date was absorbed in the declaration of God's creative act. Apollo, the most dashing of the pagan Greek gods, bowed down in worship to "God, the Father Almighty, maker of heaven and earth."[5] The astronauts did what a lot of people spontaneously do when they integrate an alert mind with a reverent heart—they worshiped.

One person objected stridently. The self-proclaimed atheist Madalyn Murray O'Hair noisily complained that the nation's space program had been hijacked to advance a minority religion. She said that the tax money of millions had been used to propagate the Christian faith of a few, violating the rights of the atheists. The wealth of a nation had been put in the service of a Christian witness. The conscience of the atheist was offended.[6]

She was, of course, right. It *was* unfair. You might even say it was shocking. We have gotten used to listening in on the conversations between Mission Control in

5. Apostles' Creed, www.umc.org/what-we-believe/apostles-creed-traditional-ecumenical.
6. "People and Ideas: Madalyn Murray O'Hair," PBS, www.pbs.org/godinamerica/people/madalyn-murray-ohair.html.

Houston and astronauts orbiting the earth and moon. It is a highly technical conversation using an unambiguous mathematical-scientific vocabulary. We have learned to admire the cool, unflappable consistency of the men who sit at the controls of the complex, intricate mechanisms of space travel. We are occasionally reminded that they are human by a boyish burst of enthusiasm over the view of Earth wrapped in beauty. We are even reminded once in a while that they are sinners as tempers flare or profanity slips out. We reassure ourselves, by reading interviews with their spouses and looking at pictures of their homes, that they are really humans much like we are. But that is only the diverting, anecdotal background to the big picture. The astronauts represent modern man at his scientific apogee, superbly in control, precisely trained, dominating the world with power and skill.

When these men without warning recite an ancient confession of faith, when these men openly admit they are not just the conquerors of space but at the same time worshipers of God, well, it *is* unusual. Mrs. O'Hair did well to be angry.

The fact is that the space capsule is an educational center. Millions of persons were watching images of it on TV and listening to radio transmissions of the conversations. What the astronauts said had enormous coverage and intense impact. It was one of the educational highlights in human history. The world became a classroom. An appropriate passage from Heisenberg or Einstein would be heard and repeated all over the world and through repetition would be indelibly impressed on the minds of millions.

But this text was from millennially old Genesis. Would there be laments over the wasted educational opportunity for science? Would anyone feel that this was a painful opening of old wounds? For a long period of time there had been bitter controversy between Genesis and geology, Eden and evolution. Battle lines had formed. The defenders of God used their Bibles instead of bullets. The defenders of Darwin stockpiled weapons in the form of fragments of jawbones and stratified rocks. One group looked to the Garden of Eden for the beginnings of creation; the other group was convinced you could learn far more by exploring the Galápagos Islands. Neither group seemed to be paying much attention to the other. But in recent years at least a kind of coexistence has been settled on. There aren't so many arguments. But neither are there many conversations. Each group now goes its own way, one reading Genesis, the other reading scientific journals. Would reading Genesis from the space capsule awaken the sleeping dogs of the old science-religion controversy?

It was one of those rare times when virtually everyone heard Scripture read accurately. The Bible was read at a highly dramatic moment in the history of humankind, and everyone had a stake in the event. They heard it as a word of God, a declaration of faith, an announcement about God in his action as Creator. And the evidence that the word was heard rightly is that the scientifically trained astronauts were not threatened by it and the atheist was.

Since the days of Galileo, Genesis 1 has been controversial. But the controversy is not between science and faith, not between the person who reads Darwin and the one who reads Calvin. Whenever the controversy has been conducted along those lines, it has been the wrong battle, like two brothers fighting over a woman they find out is their sister.

I grew up in a church culture that thrived on conflict. We were a small sectarian congregation and existed on the margins of what we understood as "the world"—people who didn't believe in God or who didn't believe in God the way we understood him. Or they didn't read Scripture the way we did.

I more or less took it for granted that my schoolmates were unsaved and that it was my Jesus assignment to witness to and pray for them. I had absorbed many taboos that separated me from my friends: no vulgar or obscene language, no movies, no dancing. By the time I entered adolescence, a "great chasm" (Luke 16:26, NASB)—the same that separated the rich man Dives in Hades from the beggar Lazarus in Abraham's bosom—had developed between me and my schoolmates.

Itinerant evangelists who frequently visited our little flock warned us of the dangers around us. By the time I entered high school, I was repeatedly warned of the godless evolution that was being taught by my biology teacher, Mr. Ryder, whom I rather liked but who also, I soon realized, put me in particular peril. I had no idea that twenty-five years earlier a high school biology teacher in Tennessee, John Scopes, had been arrested, put on trial, and convicted for teaching the same things. I boldly compensated for my marginal status in class discussions by pitting texts from Genesis against my teacher's citations from Darwin. Differences of opinion gradually developed into arguments with my classmates and soon degenerated into mean-spirited invective. I loved using the Bible to pick fights with evolutionists and atheists.

As the years passed, I found I rather liked having an enemy. It sharpened my sense of identity. The visiting evangelists gave me plenty of enemies to oppose—liberals, Catholics, Calvinists, evolutionists, environmentalists, Democrats, communists—exposing some of them as a front for the Antichrist.

As I edged into adulthood, I began meeting and reading the writings of Christian friends who loved science, some of them scientists themselves. Like so many of you in this congregation, they seemed to have no trouble integrating their Christian faith with the findings of science. I remember one friend telling me several months ago that science and religion are opposites, the way your thumb and forefinger are opposites: if you are going to get a grip on things, you need them both.

And then—I had wasted a lot of time by now—I began learning to read Genesis on its own terms and discovered it was a stunning piece of theological art, a beautiful evocation of this created world and the God who created it.

I came to realize that this first page in the Bible was a masterful preparation for shaping an imagination capable of entering what Karl Barth has called this "strange new world within the Bible"[7]—slowly, quietly, reverently. I set aside what I had been so vehemently arguing in my ignorant adolescent certainties and let God speak his presence and reality to me. I was gradually learning to let God tell me who he is and the way he works.

I decided to quit trying to prove God to others and instead started listening to God speak to me, not making pronouncements on God but listening, listening, listening. Instead of searching Scripture for truths I could use to bully or impress my friends, I would take my place alongside them in this God-Creation and enter into what God was creating in me and around me.

And I would not be in a hurry. There is a leisurely quality to this first page of Genesis, a lot of repetition—God as subject (thirty-five times), God in action (*created, said, made, called, saw, set, blessed, finished, rested, let there be, and it was so*). And then the verdict, the final stamp of approval placed on every item of creation: *good* (eight times) and the final *good* given the emphasis *very good.*

7. Quoted in Eberhard Busch, *Karl Barth: His Life from Letters and Autobiographical Texts,* trans. John Bowden (Eugene, OR: Wipf and Stock, 1975), 101.

The numbered days, one through seven, provide a rhythmic, ordered structure: everything in order, nothing haphazard, nothing unintentional.

The Genesis week is a workweek. God creates. God is not described as a force, an energy, an idea, a principle, an abstraction. He simply goes to work.

But this seventh day gets an emphasis all its own. The six workdays are simply cited by number. The concluding day is repeated three times: "On the *seventh day* God finished his work . . . he rested on the *seventh day* . . . God blessed the *seventh day*" (Genesis 2:2–3). And then a new verb is introduced: "God . . . *hallowed* it, because on it God rested from all his work which he had done in creation" (verse 3).

Where have you heard that verb before? Right. In the prayer Jesus taught us to pray. The first petition in the prayer is "Hallowed be thy name" (Matthew 6:9). Or, "Let your name be recognized as holy." In English we don't have a verb for *holy*. *Hallowed* is not part of our everyday speech. So it is more like "Let your name be reverenced."

The seventh day, set apart for being reverent before God, being quiet and receptive before God as we take in all that God has done across the spectrum of creation—light; earth and sea; sun, moon, and stars; fish and birds; animals of all kinds; and, the crown of creation, man and woman. We are living an existence teeming with life, and we are an integral part of that life.

And then this: Moses, after God had rescued his people from a life of slavery in Egypt and then gathered them at Mount Sinai, gave them a charter to guide them in their new life of freedom, the Ten Commandments. The fourth of those commandments is lifted from Genesis: "Remember the sabbath day, to keep it holy" (Exodus 20:8). Use this day to take into account all that God has done for you. Take nothing for granted. And do it every week. Forty years later Moses preached his final sermon to his congregation on the plains of Moab. As they prepared to enter the Holy Land, he repeated these ten commandments, which were to define the way they lived in the life of creation and salvation. The fourth is there intact, newly minted from Genesis: "Remember the Sabbath day, to keep it holy" (Deuteronomy 5:12, HCSB).

I love picturing the first sermon Moses preached from Mount Sinai now joining everything God did in Genesis with the way they are to live that everything, now bookended with the final sermon Moses preached from the plains of Moab, emphasizing the Genesis connection to the way they were to continue to live in the new land of Canaan: *Remember.* One day a week stop what you are doing and pay attention to what God has been doing and is doing. Be reverent and worshipful and grateful for the Genesis world we are placed in. Remember in gratitude and worshipful adoration. Hallow this day. Keep this day holy.

In the course of being your pastor, I have come to think of the first page of Genesis as a launching pad for shaping an obedient and reverent life of following Jesus in our daily, ordinary, working, and worshiping lives. I don't know if any of you will remember this, but a few years ago I came across some words in a sermon about Jerusalem preached by Isaiah to his congregation of exiles in Babylon that seemed to me to be written just for us. I told you about them then. But the longer I am your pastor the more important they have become. What I mentioned to you then was that the cultural and spiritual conditions in which we are living as pastor and people in America strike me as being very much like the exile conditions of the Hebrews in Babylon: the pervasive uprootedness and loss of place (only three or four families in our congregation were born in this county), the loss of connection with a tradition of worship (only a few of you were raised as Presbyterians), the sense of being immersed in a foreign and idolatrous society (in contemporary America there is very little moral consensus, no common memory, and most of us are far removed from where we grew up).

But what I have more recently noticed is that the words *create, created,* and *Creator* occur more times in the exilic preaching of Isaiah than any other place in the Bible: sixteen times, as compared to the six occurrences of *created* in the great creation narrative of Genesis 1–2.

Under Isaiah's influence, as I move from this pulpit to hospital rooms and family rooms, coffee shops and community gatherings, praying with and listening to bored or devastated men and women, the word *create* has emerged out of the background of what happened long ago in Canaan and Egypt and Babylon into prominence right here—an actively gospel word announcing what God is doing today among the exile people, which is us.

Create is a word used in the Bible exclusively with God as the subject. Men and women don't, *can't,* create. But God does. When nothing we can do makes any difference and we are left standing around empty handed and clueless, we are ready to notice what God is creating, not just "in the beginning," but now, today. When the conditions in which we live seem totally alien to life and salvation, we start looking around at what God is doing.

And that is where the seventh day of creation comes in. When God finished the work of creation (*finished* is used twice in as many verses), he "rested" (also used twice). Is that why we are twice commanded (in Exodus and Deuteronomy) to "Keep the Sabbath holy"? I think so. We are keeping company with God in the present, in the *now:* attending, adoring.

Doesn't it look very much as if Genesis points to the seventh day as the clue to the meaning of creation? There is far more to creation than *creation then.* There is *creation now.* The evidence accumulates that if we are to live out the reality and meaning of creation, we are going to be inextricably involved with Sabbath keeping. If Genesis is a text for getting us in on and participating in God's creation work, Sabbath is our point of entry.

Amen.

2

"Friend of God"

GENESIS 12:1–4
JOHN 15:13–15

Abraham is called the friend of God three times in our Scriptures. The first time, more than a thousand years after the death of Abraham, was in the middle of a prayer. The Hebrew king Jehoshaphat was threatened by an invading army. As he prayed to God for help, he identified himself with "Abraham thy friend" (2 Chronicles 20:7, KJV). A few hundred years later during the devastation of the Babylonian Exile, an Isaiah prophecy brought a word of God to the people that identified the congregation as "Israel, my servant, . . . the offspring of Abraham, my friend" (Isaiah 41:8). The third mention occurs in the New Testament letter of James that argues the unity of faith *and* works by bringing Abraham into the argument with the words " 'Abraham believed God, and it was reckoned to him as righteousness,' and he was called the friend of God" (James 2:23, NRSV).

If we went to Israel/Palestine today, we would find that the town most associated with Abraham in his lifetime, Hebron, has been named by the Muslims *El Khalil,* Arabic for "the friend." Jew, Christian, and Muslim agree on this point at least: they remember Abraham as the friend of God.

And then this: in the midst of that profoundly moving conversation Jesus had with his disciples the night before his crucifixion, he said, "Greater love has no man than this, that a man lay down his life for his friends. You are my friends if you do what I command you. No longer do I call you servants, for the servant does not know what his master is doing; but I have called you friends, for all that I have heard from my Father I have made known to you" (John 15:13–15). *Friends,* three times in as many sentences.

The person and life of Abraham is definitive for getting a feel for what is involved in being in relationship with God. And it is significant that the word that is used to define his life is this word *friend.* And it is also significant that this is the exact word Jesus picked up to identify his God-in-the-flesh relationship with his followers and their relationship with him.

In the culture we have grown up in, all of us have been exposed to a good deal of concern that we develop a healthy self-esteem so we can live whole and satisfying lives. In the process the term *identity crisis* has entered our vocabulary as a key element in self-understanding. *Who am I? What does it mean to be me?*

I understand that and appreciate the concern. But I want to replace the jargon of educators and psychiatrists and psychologists with a simple but far more accurate and comprehensive designation. And I want you to consider well the answer "friend of God" and take seriously the good news wrapped up in those three words.

—

The Abraham story is the first extended story in Scripture that brings us into a lifetime of living faith in God. The first eleven chapters of Genesis lay the groundwork, providing an orientation, a kind of map of the territory in which we live. But the storytelling that is launched in chapter 12 with Abram as the subject gives us a detailed immersion in what we can expect as we spend our lives developing a self-understanding of what it means to live out our identity as friends of God, lives of personal and God relationships with family and community, learning the language of faith, acquiring a feeling of at-homeness in this world of creation and covenant.

As it turns out, and using Abraham as a template, the term *friend* is going to be *the* key in understanding what it means "to be me."

—

Being a friend is the opposite of being an enemy. That simple contrast stands out above all else in Abraham. Abraham was on such terms with his God that he responded without suspicion and without fear. Abraham somehow knew that God was on his side, that God was for him and with him, a friend.

The dominant feeling in the country and culture in which Abraham grew up was that the gods were distinctly unfriendly. An elaborate priestly caste was at work night and day to protect people from the malicious caprice of the gods, temper tantrums from the sky, unpredictable outbursts of anger, or maybe just cold indifference. Elaborate rituals were engaged in, taboos were carefully observed, sacrifices administered. It was the biggest business in the Middle East, for the gods were mysterious and dark forces that couldn't be counted on.

Not much has changed in four thousand years. For us, the gods have been secularized, but the primary sense for probably most of the people who are driving on the roads of Harford County today is anxiety, guilt, and indifference. We are as wary as any of the Chaldeans that Abraham grew up with, living in an atmosphere of malign forces that can't be anticipated or controlled, be it cancer or accidents or guns.

In the modern West as well as the ancient East, there is an undercurrent of fear, much of it fueled by neurotic or manipulative religion that results in the apprehension of God as the enemy.

This is *wrong,* and one of my assignments as your pastor is to tell you why it is wrong. There are many things to be afraid of in this world and many persons who endanger our security, but God is not one of them. That is why we need to develop an Abrahamic imagination. Abraham stands out as a person who rose above all the commonplace terror of his times and lived as God's friend. Abraham knew that God was his friend. He lived in an atmosphere charged with divine goodness.

Abraham was not called the friend of God because he was singled out for special benevolent attention by God, a kind of teacher's pet. He did not live a charmed life. He was called the friend of God because he experienced God accurately and truly. He *lived* as God's friend. He responded as God's friend. He believed that God was on his side, and he lived like it.

To be a friend of God does not mean everything is cozy between you and the Almighty. To be a friend to someone does not mean you pamper or indulge him or her. Friendship also involves struggle and loss, tension and turbulence. One of my favorite proverbs is "Faithful are the wounds of a friend" (Proverbs 27:6). A friend, if honest and true, will tell you things you don't want to hear. A friend, if deeply serious about you, will do things that feel painful. Friends do that because they respect our dignity and honor our uniqueness.

God's friendship with Abraham meant that God told him to leave family and homeland for a long and uncertain journey west. The secure, settled, prosperous life of Ur and Haran was abandoned because God said, "Go." Abraham never had an easy life. Read the twelve chapters given to the story of Abraham when you are relaxing this afternoon, and appreciate the difficulties involved. He, together with his wife, Sarah, endured decades of childlessness, lived through a famine in Canaan and danger in Egypt, suffered the expulsion of Hagar and Ishmael from the household, endured the trauma of offering up Isaac as a sacrifice, and engaged in agonized intercession for his nephew Lot in Sodom.

God's friendship didn't install Abraham on an oasis where he slept on a hammock strung between date palms, refreshing himself with a swim in the pool between naps. God's friendship meant leaving home, long journeys, dangerous ventures, doubt-filled actions, difficult obedience. Karl Barth, perhaps our most perceptive theologian in getting inside the biblical stories, wrote concerning Abraham, "He *must* pass from a well-known past to a future which is only just opening up."[8] Through all this, Abraham knew that God was for him and with him.

Here is a sentence that is important for understanding what was going on with Abraham: "At that time the Canaanites were in the land" (Genesis 12:6). Abraham had just made a long and difficult trip and found that the country he entered was already occupied. It wasn't a frontier. It wasn't virgin territory waiting for a new way of life to be created on it. It was already full of bustling city-states, thriving places of worship, trade agreements. As one commentator said, "The gates of salvation do not swing open at all with the solemn disclosure that God would give this land to Abraham. Rather, this promise is strangely contiguous to the statement that at that time the Canaanites were dwelling in the land. Abraham is therefore brought by God into a completely unexplained relationship with the Canaanites, and Yahweh does not hurry about solving and explaining this opaque status of ownership as one expects the director of history to do."[9]

—

8. Karl Barth, *Church Dogmatics 4.2, The Doctrine of Reconciliation,* trans. G. W. Bromiley (New York: T&T Clark, 2010), 200.
9. Gerhard von Rad, *Genesis: A Commentary* (Philadelphia: Westminster, 1961), 166.

Here is another element contained in the word *friend. Friend* is totally about a relationship, not a function. There is an everyday, ordinary quality to it. We find ourselves friends with people not for what they can do for us but simply for who they are. And if we suspect we are singled out for someone's friendship because of what we can do for that person—social prestige, economic advantage, etc.—we are apt, and rightly so, to resent it. God was not Abraham's friend in order to network with him. And there is no hint in the story that Abraham considered God's friendship an invitation into a world of celebrities. Abraham found everyday, practical ways to express appreciation and loyalty to God, and God found everyday, practical ways to express appreciation and loyalty to Abraham. Abraham was not in love with a dream or aspiring after an ideal. He was God's *friend,* period. The evidence? The relationship was worked out on journeys and at water holes.

And altars. One of the architectural features of the ancient world was its grandiose statuary and temple buildings. Gigantic statues of gods. Dazzling temples, ziggurats, and pyramids dedicated to gods. Abraham built altars wherever he went. Built them with his own two hands out of the stone he found. The description is always local and detailed. "Abram passed through the land to the place at Shechem, to the oak of Moreh. . . . Then the LORD appeared to Abram, and said, 'To your descendants I will give this land.' So he built there an altar to the LORD, who had appeared to him" (Genesis 12:6–7). It was all very geographical, almost matter-of-fact. Religion wasn't an emotion he carried around with him for comfort or solace. It was one with the routines of the journey. "Remember that big oak tree just outside of Shechem? That is where I listened to God and God listened to me."

And not just at Shechem. Abraham's friendship with God was not sentimentally tied to one spot: "Thence he removed to the mountain on the east of Bethel, and pitched his tent, with Bethel on the west and Ai on the east; and there he built an altar to the LORD and called on the name of the LORD" (verse 8). He didn't keep going back to Shechem when he wanted to get in touch with God. He built an altar wherever he happened to be. Friendship was renewed and nurtured at each stage of the journey. Faith wasn't a memory of something that started in Ur and Haran. It wasn't a hope of something that wouldn't be completed until all the families of the earth were blessed. It was daily, regular, and frequent, using whatever stones he found there on the ground to mark the spot.

That is how friendship works. Friends remember one another in both common and uncommon ways. They call one another on the spur of the moment. They remember special days. They visit simply for the pleasure of the other's company. Things don't have to get done in a friendship. Friendship is not a way of accomplishing something but a way of being with another in which we become more authentically ourselves.

As we get a feel for the qualities of friendship, I think this also is important: Abraham's life seems curiously empty of accomplishment. With the exception of his intercession for Sodom, he doesn't seem to have asked his friend God for anything. His relation to God was not mercantile, not utilitarian. He wasn't taking pains to stay on good terms with God so he might get a good inheritance. His altar building doesn't seem to have been an insurance policy against disaster. His altars were spontaneous acts of friendship and gratitude, expressions of respect.

—

And get this: being God's friend didn't mean that Abraham was heroically good or above average in virtue or untainted by sin. Abraham is not conspicuous in the human qualities that we usually admire. He lied to protect his own skin in exchange for the sacrifice of his wife's reputation. He laughed at God when the divine promises sounded absurd to him. He played the coward with Abimelech.

What friendship means is that two persons are in touch with each other and share important interests. And that is what the friendship of God and Abraham is all about. Abraham was in touch with the God who was in touch with him. He accepted God's concern for him as the reality of his life, and he returned it by making God the center of his life. He obeyed, he journeyed, he prayed, he believed, and he built altars. He did none of this perfectly. But *perfect* is not a word we use to describe friendship relationships. *Perfect* is a word that refers to inanimate things—a perfect circle, say, or a perfectly straight line. With persons we talk of response, growth, listening, and acting. Abraham did all of that in relation with God, whom he was convinced was determined to be a good friend to him.

—

Significant as Abraham is to us—to the world!—do you realize how little we know of him? We are so used to measuring the significance of people by what they accomplish—the celebrity factor. But it is impossible to measure Abraham that way.

If we think of him as the star quarterback on God's salvation team, we will most certainly misunderstand both Abraham and ourselves. His life is enveloped in deep shadows. The times in which he lived are obscure and dark, little known to historian and archaeologist. What emerges out of all that is *friend.* Abraham in biblical history is like those marvelous paintings of Rembrandt in which a hand or a face is singled out of the background darkness with a single shaft of sunlight.

What we *do* know of Abraham is his quite ordinary friendship with God and God's friendship with Abraham, using the everyday stuff of the culture—hospitality, altar building, family relationships, famine, sacrifice—but using it all sacramentally, using the visible circumstances and people and things as witnesses and occasions for being in faith present to God as friend. In this he marks the very beginning of the biblical process.

It is only right that Jesus gets the last word: "I have called *you* friends" (John 15:15, NRSV).

Amen.

3

"And Sarah Conceived"

GENESIS 21:2–3
JOHN 3:3–8

Birth is a miracle. Every birth. And every new birth is a miracle. We are all participants in the miracle. We have all been born. Jesus used the birth imagery in his phrase "born from above" (John 3:3, NRSV) to introduce Nicodemus to an equivalent miracle in their famous nighttime conversation. God is in the business of making life, bringing into being what is not. *Birth* is the name of this act. It is always a miracle.

Naming an event a miracle doesn't mean we can't understand it. It means we can't anticipate it. It means we can't reproduce it. We cannot control it. There is more going on than we can comprehend. There is more to life than we can account for. *Miracle* is a word Christians use to name events, at least some of them, that God brings about.

Each birth is unique. There has never been one just like another one. The most knowledgeable of geneticists cannot tell when the child will appear, the day it will speak its first word, the month it will walk, the day he or she will die. Each birth is new. But birth is also common, both spiritually and physically. Births keep taking place all around us. Each one is a miracle. Life keeps taking place before our eyes in ways we cannot anticipate, through a process we ourselves cannot take credit for. There is always a sense of awe and wonder and gratitude in this most common of events. Birth is common. It is also a mystery. Maybe that is why men and women through the millennia have commonly believed in God or gods.

The story of the birth of Isaac is plainly and simply told. Abraham and Sarah are promised a son by God. But the son never comes. They wait and they wait. Years pass. Sarah passes the years of childbearing. They give up hoping and make alternate plans for an heir. The promise, though, is reaffirmed by God. And then, when Sarah is ninety and Abraham a hundred, Sarah conceives and bears a son. Abraham names him Isaac, which means "laughter" (Genesis 16–21).

Simple as it is, this birth story does something for persons of faith that needs to be done over and over and over again. For our tendency is to treat God in one of two ways. One is to flatten him down into an explanation, depersonalize him into the banal and the humdrum. We lose all sense of mystery. We reduce God to morals or platitudes or a genial source of good advice. We lose all sense of the transcendent, the glorious, the beyond. The other tendency is to sentimentalize God into diversion, entertainment. We fantasize him into an escape from whatever we don't like about what is happening right now. Most of us do these two things alternately. And our lives are unchanged.

The core message of the gospel is that God invades us with new life, but the setting for this is most often in the ordinariness of our lives. The new life takes place in the place and person of our present. It is not a means by which God solves problems. God creates new life. He is not a problem solver but a person creator.

These creations, these birth miracles are around you, in the person of your child or your wife or your husband or your friends or your parent or your brother or sister or neighbor. The miracle of life is before you in the mirror, the person of faith that God has managed to conceive and bring to birth in you or in your child or spouse or friend or parent.

—

What I hope happens as I set this Isaac story before you and as you worship this morning is that you will be observant and aware and in love with this life that is in you and before you. We are in training in order to enjoy and nurture and encourage and affirm every instance of life. We are determined never to be negligent of it and always aware of it. We want to avoid abusing it and instead practice celebrating it. God creates life among us. Christ's birth is the climaxing birth story that summarizes and emphasizes and continues in a sequence of miracle births.

The birth of Isaac is the first detailed birth story told to us in Scripture.

Here are some things about the Isaac story that I have found important to pay attention to, things that help me be responsive to the way God conceives and brings new life to me.

The first and maybe the most important is this: the birth miracle takes place in the most ordinary of settings. When we hear the word *miracle,* we must not imagine fireworks and drum rolls and trumpet blasts and then, presto, a piece of heavenly magic that sends us reeling. That is fun but it is not gospel.

The Chinese perfected this years ago with their fireworks, and it takes a lot of money to reproduce it. It is something to look at and talk about and applaud but not to live. The Christian faith has no time for ideas or feelings or sentiments or sideshows that don't get lived. The birth of a child is the most accessible reality we have of an event that takes place in actual life, the invisible that becomes biologically visible.

You can buy a religion of promises and wise sayings and interesting answers to big questions for fifteen or twenty dollars. The world is full of such stuff. But what most of us want to know is does it *happen*? And can it *happen here*? And is it *living*? We must ask the stubbornly practical questions when we come to God and to church. I have no patience with a truth that cannot be lived, and I don't want you to have any patience with it either.

Abraham lived by faith. He believed in a God he never saw. He obeyed a command that had no guarantees. He took the risk of traveling to a far country and living as a stranger. His life was shaped by promises and lived in risk. I would like to live like that. But before I do, I want to know how it turned out for Abraham. Did anything come of it? Was it a fantasy? Those dreams of blessing all the nations of the earth—was that just megalomania? Was he living in an unreal world, out of touch with the facts of sexual biology when he kept hearing the promises of a son to be born to him?

The answer is "The LORD visited Sarah as he had said, and the LORD did to Sarah as he had promised. And Sarah conceived, and bore Abraham a son in his old age at the time of which God had spoken to him" (Genesis 21:1–2).

Birth. Life erupting in the form of an infant in the everyday lives of Abraham and Sarah. Invisible faith becoming a visible event. It is the most spiritual act and the most visible. There are years of waiting and giving up, years of praying and doubting, years of venture and holding back. And then there is an infant that can be measured and weighed and fed and clothed. God calls. Abraham believes. God promises. Sarah conceives and gives birth. Abraham and Sarah, a man and woman of faith, have a son.

And then there is this: the birth miracle sets before us a life that is always emphatically personal. The life of faith is a life in which we discover that *persons* are brought into being by God. Every birth has to do with a person, a God person, not a thing. The miracle of birth is a miracle of personhood.

We are always drifting off into the impersonal. It is easier and less demanding. But it is also demeaning and estranging. Always and everywhere in Scripture our attention is brought back to the central fact: God is a person; God makes persons; God remakes persons. A person like you. A person like me. A person like Isaac.

It is not through nations and armies, not through movements and ideas, not through laboratories and machines and computers that God does his primary work. It is through persons. The birth miracle is a person with a name—your name.

God entered the emptied, despairing, winding-down lives of Abraham and Sarah, not with a new idea, not by sending them on an exotic trip. He gave them a child.

The emphasis on the personal is highlighted in the instance of Isaac, not because it is significant for anything he *did,* but just because of who he *was:* Isaac, "laughter." From all we know about him, he was no hero, no leader. He simply was. I think I can go further and say he was an exceptionally colorless person. Nothing is held up for admiration or adulation. He was the least of the patriarchs. But he was a person, the fulfilled promise of God born. That seemingly bare minimum was more than enough, the miracle of life that links the faith of Abraham with your life of faith.

The sheer fact of being a person outweighs everything else—whether you are a good person or a bad person, a successful person or an unsuccessful person, a happy person or a sad person, a famous person or an obscure person, a big person or a small person. God creates life, a miracle—you, me. Nothing can detract from or diminish the sheer miracle of that.

One more thing about this story. A birth miracle is a happy surprise. God creates life, and it is surprisingly better than we expected. We feel so good about it that we laugh. This child was named Isaac, "laughter." Laughter comes spontaneously when there is an unexpected turn of events that is good. A story takes a sudden turn at the end, and we laugh. Life is joyous. We laugh.

There is a great deal about God that has to do with faithfulness. God is consistent. We can depend on his character. There is solidity and continuity built into the creation. We gain a sense of ease and familiarity with the laws: moral, natural, and spiritual. We learn to live without anxiety.

But there is more to it than that. More to God than you can ever understand or anticipate. Being a Christian is not learning how to live by some rules so we are in touch with reality or getting trained in proper behavior so we will not get our fingers burned or our legs broken or our hearts broken or our consciences wounded. The great thing about living in faith with God is what we can't anticipate, can't predict. Sooner or later in the Christian way, we are going to laugh.

A birth miracle we will name Isaac, "laughter." Every birth combines the mysterious with the unknown. Birth is an everyday event but is never commonplace. It always contains elements of surprise that shock us out of our complacency and bring laughter. God does not just make us and love us and save us along lines that are clear to us in the Scriptures and history and our own experiences. He also surprises us with new life. "Sarah said, 'God has made laughter for me; every one who hears will laugh over me.' . . . And the child grew, and was weaned" (Genesis 21:6, 8). You can count on it that there was great laughter at that birthing.

We read Scripture—we read this Isaac birth story—not so much to find out what has happened but to find out what happens. We are not so much curious about the past but about who we are. The Bible is the best book for discovering the all-inclusive reality in which we exist and then for initiating us into it.

The story of Isaac's birth is about what is possible. It is promise and proof that we can live a different life than what is given to us biologically and environmentally and economically. There is something more basic than our genes and parents and country and salary and moods and IQ. Is it possible to live forgiven and not carry great loads of guilt, to participate in the salvation of the world? Is it possible to love and grow into a relationship with another person in which we are enriched and enhanced and built up? Is it possible to bless and be blessed? To give others the best that is in us and not the worst? To receive from others their best and not their worst?

Yes. It is. As everyday realities, these births are wonders, whether as a new baby in the world or as a new creature in Christ. We are launched by acts of love and promise into ways of seeing and being. Our first birth thrusts us kicking and squalling into the light of day. Our second birth places us laughing and worshiping in the light of God. Like Isaac. Laughter.

Amen.

4

"Make Us Gods"

EXODUS 32:1
1 TIMOTHY 1:13–17

The Exodus story is a pivotal story, the foundational story that provides the grounding for our salvation existence, a salvation that is completed in Jesus the Christ. The story begins in Egypt. God's people are in a quagmire of slavery. They have been there for 430 years, and it is not getting any better. Here are people who were created in the image of God and pronounced good, and not just good but very good. Here are a people whose ancestor Abraham pioneered the great venture of living by faith, leaving what he knew and possessed for what he believed and expected in God. Here are a people whose ancestors roamed the desert, their life histories saturated with God. It was a struggling existence full of agonizing doubts and painful disciplines. It was also an invigorating existence, packed with meaning and taut with purpose. There was suffering and there was blessing, but most of all there was vitality. They were alive at every level. Out of the deepest dimensions of their beings, extraordinary expressions of humanity blossomed into acts of worship and acts of faith.

Then it all disappeared in a swamp of slavery. The immense Egyptian system of bureaucratic religion and politics swallowed them up. They were absorbed in the anthill society of Egypt, carrying bricks, building arrogantly pompous tombs, the pyramids. Instead of living a free life under the Palestinian stars, listening to the voice of God, worshiping and praising, they were toiling under the whips of slave masters, commanded by the curses of cruel rulers, dehumanized in the impersonal machinery of slavery.

The contrast between their beginnings as a free people in Canaan and their slavery in Egypt cannot be overdrawn. For the patriarchs—Abraham, Isaac, Jacob, and Joseph (their stories are told in Genesis)—God was the initiating, activating, providing, creative word. They lived in a universe that was God dominated. They lived, in other words, by faith. But their descendants in Egypt lived in a world dominated by work. When God dominated their lives, they lived free. When man dominated their lives, they lived enslaved.

I think it takes us by surprise to realize that this world of slavery was at the same time a world of religion. Egypt was religious through and through, one of the most religious cultures in the history of the world. All the art and architecture was religious, either as a temple or as a tomb that ensured a continuing afterlife. All the politics was religious. The intelligence and engineering, mathematics and literature were staggering. Their accomplishments remain intact and beautiful still after four thousand years. Archaeologists and tourists alike continue to be dazzled by them. And the religion? Impressive, to say the least. It was a religion designed to keep order and control, to make things happen. It guaranteed a happy immortality, controlled the rising and falling of the Nile so the land would be fertile, controlled the people's every move so there would be law and order. The Egyptians talked endlessly about gods, addressed prayers to gods, built temples for gods. But the religion in Egypt was always what *they* were doing or had done.

Egypt was a thoroughly religious society, and Egypt was a thoroughgoing slave society. If you want to control a person or family or society, there is no better way than through religion. And that is just as true today as it was in ancient Egypt.

That is the background for this story in Exodus 32—430 years of slavery in Egypt. Moses was selected by God to rescue the Israelites from their miserable lives. He was an unlikely leader. Born of Hebrew parents, he had escaped from Egypt years before, after murdering an Egyptian. His escape route took him across the river to the Midian desert, where he ended up herding sheep. In that desert he ran into his birth people, the Hebrews, became one of them, married Zipporah and began a family, and named his first child, a son, Gershom, meaning "sojourner" or "stranger." And then he was selected by God to lead the Israelites out of slavery into a salvation freedom. You know that story. While herding his sheep, he came across a bush that was on fire, burning but not being consumed. The voice of God spoke to Moses out of the bush, and he found himself chosen to be a leader.

The next thing we know, Moses is back in Egypt, where he was born and raised in the king's palace, and now he is demanding that the pharaoh (the king's title) set the Hebrews free from their slavery. It was an outrageous request considering the circumstances: a shepherd from the desert making demands on the most powerful ruler in the world.

Against all odds they were delivered. God raised up Moses to lead the Hebrews out of slavery into a free salvation life. Eight months of negotiations were, as you can imagine, lengthy and complex. Promises were made and then retracted. And then, with the repeatedly dashed hopes of the Hebrews apparently beyond revival, they were delivered. One day they were a demoralized and unarmed people crushed under the cruelty of an enslaving religion; the next they were victoriously free, singing the praises of a redeeming God. They left their slave life for good. They also left security, culture, beauty, and routine. In the desert wastes of the Sinai, they were absolutely dependent upon a God they could not see and with no granaries from which they could get their allotment of food. All they had was the fact of their freedom, prayers and songs, and a precarious diet of nondescript flatbread (manna, which means "What is it?") and quail.

Moses led them across the hot sands to Sinai, a gigantic volcanic mountain in the Arabian desert. Here they camped and began a life of learning what it means to be God's people instead of Pharaoh's. Here they would discover how to live as free people and not as slaves. Discover what it means to live by faith and not by works. Discover what it means to live under the provident blessing of God and not under the tyranny of Pharaoh. For four centuries they had been building grandiose pyramid tombs to hold a few mummified corpses. Now they would go to work building a living community of faith.

Moses climbed the mountain to receive God's revelation. He returned with the Ten Commandments, the constitution and bill of rights for a people who from now on were to live the free life of faith. There are people today who mistakenly look at those commandments as restrictive, not realizing that for those who first heard them—and for those who hear them still, in faith—they provide for and preserve the values of the free life. The reality and truth of God is protected from commercialization and manipulation. Human life is honored. The dignity of work is protected. Close personal relationships are preserved. Truth is respected. Each of the commands articulates a reality and a value that protect a free life.

The life of freedom and faith is not caprice or tyranny, not randomness or chance. But it was going to take them a while to realize they were no longer subject to the moods and will of the strongest person who claimed to be a god. Their days no longer were to be stuffed into the megalomaniac ambitions of a pharaoh. What they hadn't quite realized was that each person was now of eternal value, in himself, in herself.

At Sinai the charter of freedom was proclaimed. Sinai was their equivalent to our Philadelphia. Now these people would begin the lifelong task of living free, by faith. After an interlude of instruction about the tabernacle and its furnishings (Exodus 24–31), Moses climbed back up the mountain to receive instructions dealing with the day-to-day routines that would support and develop a life responsive to God's love and salvation, instructions regarding the routines of worship and relationship and community growth. He was gone a long time. The people became restless and bored. Nothing was happening. They weren't going anywhere. There was nothing to do, nothing to see. Only that one treeless mass of granite that was Sinai, on which Moses had disappeared.

They knew they had been set free; they had all shared that experience. It was incontestable. They were going to learn to live by faith, live in relation to the vast but invisible reality of God, learn to center their lives in voluntary worship, not in compulsory slave labor. And now Moses was gone. Day after day there was nothing but emptiness. All their lives they had never known anything but work, forced labor and no respite from it. What they had yet to realize was that emptiness was a prerequisite to getting filled. Impatiently the people began to make demands. They came before Aaron, Moses's brother, who had been left in charge, and said, "Come, make us a god who will go before us; as for this Moses, the man who brought us up from the land of Egypt, we do not know what has become of him" (Exodus 32:1, NASB). *We are tired of waiting. We will wait no longer. We are tired of nothing day after day. We want something. Make us gods.*

They did not want to live by faith but by sight. They did not want to live in response to a God they couldn't see. They wanted gods they could use to get what they wanted, like the gods they had in Egypt. Gods they could move around and force to make things happen. Gods they could use to guarantee good crops. True, in Egypt it hadn't worked to their benefit, but that was because they didn't own the gods. The Egyptians owned them. But now that they were free of Egypt, they wanted gods of their own, gods they could use to display their pride, fulfill their ambitions. Something they could *see,* for goodness' sake, that could give some texture to the barren landscape. And when you stop to think about it, so do we.

—

So Aaron made a god, a golden calf. At that moment Aaron quit being their pastor and became their accomplice. There are some people who are always looking for a religion that makes no demands and offers only rewards, a religion that dazzles and entertains, a religion in which there is no waiting and no emptiness. And they can usually find someone like Aaron who will help them make it up, some sort of golden calf religion.

The next thing must surely have taken them by surprise: a volcanic eruption of divine wrath. God exploded in anger.

In Scripture, God's anger is always evidence of God's concern, his involvement, his commitment to his people. God is not indifferent to us, not unconcerned. God is not impersonally, unemotionally cold to us. He created us, saved us, has plans for us. A vast, beautiful, and complex creation is provided, a world in which we can live to the glory of God. A painfully achieved, deeply experienced redemption is enacted so we can experience the love of God. And then in a moment of boredom, some of us turn our backs on all this and say to someone or other, "Make us gods . . . entertain us . . . pamper us . . . amuse us . . . give us some supernatural gewgaw that we can play with." We abandon the awesome silence of worship and fill the air with third-rate jingles. We get tired of participating in the strenuous but invigorating life of freedom and faith, and we regress to the old slave religion that reduces God to a decoration or amulet.

And God is angry. It matters to God when we forsake these great gifts of a living faith and embrace an infantile superstition. It matters to God when, in stupidity or sloth, we degrade and diminish our lives by worshiping something that is beneath us at the very moment he is providing the means of exalting and enhancing our lives by showing us how to live in holy love.

The anger gets our attention, but it does not destroy us. What it does is provoke and stimulate prayers of intercession. Moses pleads for the people. Moses prays for mercy. He cries out for compassion. Moses, who has been bringing God's word of salvation and revelation to the people, now brings the people's need for mercy to God. Moses, the preacher of God's Word, now becomes the intercessor for the people in their need. In Moses we see what is finally accomplished wholly and wondrously in Jesus Christ—that eternal act of atonement in which we are saved from the consequences of our sins and experience the marvels of mercy and grace.

This is the heart of the story of the golden calf. In the midst of the power and the glory of God, there is this shabby story of disobedience and rebellion. It is not an accidental straying; it is deliberate and representative. And the consequence of this rebellion is forgiveness. It continues to be God's story, more about God than about us. "Israel and the church have their existence because God picked up the pieces. There was no golden period of unblemished saintliness. Rather, the people of God are from the outset the forgiven and restored community."[10] The Christian story is the story of human resistance and rebellion that are taken up into mercy.

And, friends, this is the story of *our* lives. God provides us with everything: a dramatic salvation, a thunderous revelation. And then in a moment of restlessness, of anxiety, of inattention, of boredom, of rebelliousness, we blow it all. "Come, make us gods," some pretentious but ridiculous piece of junk—a golden calf!—that we impulsively but naively think is going to take care of everything we need, eliminate the pain of being human, banish all moments of emptiness and waiting. And then we are devastated. We know we deserve the worst and will certainly get it. We abandon hope.

But then there is a surprising turn to the story: great intercession, magnificent mercy. "Father, forgive them." Moses, anticipating Jesus, forgives them! Worship resumes. Pilgrimage begins. Judgment is experienced. Blessing is lavished. Our sin

10. Brevard S. Childs, *The Book of Exodus: A Critical, Theological Commentary* (Louisville, KY: John Knox Press, 2004), 580.

doesn't have the last word. Sin interrupts but does not destroy our life of faith. God's passionate mercy and Moses's compassionate prayer create gospel. The story continues.

This is the story each person of faith lives. There is a notable passage in Paul's first letter to Timothy that is a striking follow-up to the golden calf story. Paul experienced with a freshness and an intense honesty the entire history of salvation. The same freshness and intensity are accessible to each of us. I came across these lines of Paul almost by accident this week after having spent hours thinking and praying over this golden calf story. When I came across this Timothy passage this week, it seemed as if Paul had just finished reading the golden calf story and had said, "Yes, I know exactly how it happened. The same thing happened to me."

Here it is, Paul's letter to his friend Timothy:

> The only credentials I brought to it [this life] were invective and witch hunts and arrogance. But I was treated mercifully because I didn't know what I was doing—didn't know Who I was doing it against! Grace mixed with faith and love poured over me and into me. And all because of Jesus.
>
> Here's a word you can take to heart and depend on: Jesus Christ came into the world to save sinners. I'm proof—Public Sinner Number One—of someone who could never have made it apart from sheer mercy. And now he shows me off—evidence of his endless patience—to those who are right on the edge of trusting him forever.
>
> Deep honor and bright glory
> to the King of All Time—
> One God, Immortal, Invisible,
> ever and always. Oh yes! (1 Timothy 1:13–17, MSG)

Amen.

5

"Love Your Neighbor as Yourself"

LEVITICUS 19:18
1 JOHN 4:19–21

Have you ever made a resolution to read the Bible through in one year? Some of you have. I know because a number of you have told me that you have done just that. Sometimes it is part of three or four other New Year's resolutions. After you have failed repeated attempts over the course of several years, the guilt has built up enough energy within you to try again. Sometimes you ask for my help: "Pray for me, pastor. I really want to do this."

Weeks and months pass. And then one day I run into you at the shopping mall, remember our earlier conversation, and ask, "By the way, how has your project of reading the Bible through in a year turned out?" You stutter a bit and say, "Not so good. It only lasted six weeks. Sorry. I'm just not very good at this." And my reply is usually, "It was Leviticus, wasn't it? You couldn't wade through Leviticus." You are surprised that I guessed right.

Leviticus, I am sure, is responsible for more people giving up on a systematic, page-after-page reading of the Bible than anything else. My response to this is not to pray harder for you but to give you some advice: "Skip Leviticus. Go on to the next book, Numbers. You'll find yourself back in the story again. Well, don't skip it entirely. Find verse 18 in chapter 19. Just one verse and let that do for now in reading Leviticus."

Here's the sentence, a five-word sentence: "Love your neighbor as yourself." This is the first time the word *love* as a verb occurs in the Bible. Memorize that sentence. And remember where it came from—Leviticus of all places! And then in a year or two, after you finish reading through the Bible—no hurry—go back and read Leviticus. Eventually you will need to know why this book is in the Bible.

—

You were probably right in quitting your Bible reading when you came to Leviticus. Up to now you have been reading an engrossing story of salvation with people just like yourselves, a huge salvation story with a cast of Abraham and Sarah, Isaac and Rebekah, Jacob and Rachel, Joseph and Asenath, Moses and Zipporah, Aaron and his sister Miriam, Bezalel and Oholiab. And now this abrupt transition to page after page after tedious page of rules.

True, there is little adrenaline in the rules, but there is also a good reason for their being introduced here, and far better now than later. Moses and his new salvation congregation are on a forty-year pilgrimage through the desert, being prepared to enter the land of Canaan, a good land "flowing with milk and honey" (20:24) but also a land occupied by people who know nothing of the God of Israel and the proper worship of him. Israel needs time while undistracted in the desert to assimilate these rules ("do this . . . don't do this") before being dumped into the moral chaos of pagan Canaanite culture, a cesspool of vile customs and sexual promiscuity. The Hebrews needed guidelines on fundamental, everyday issues of diet and nutrition, hygiene and diseases, agriculture and animals, sex and other aspects of moral behavior. Maybe most of all they needed worship rituals that would keep them attentive to God's preservation and forgiveness in their everyday lives, a sacrificial system that would replace the abhorrent child-burning sacrifices to the god Molech.

Most, not all, of these listed instructions were very local, necessary to protect them from being taken over by the totally pagan and morally corrupt Canaanite culture. The overriding concern in Leviticus is that everything in this life of salvation has to do not only with the big issues of God's promises and acts of salvation but also with their daily life of food and health, moral behavior and worship, among a people who "did not know Joseph" (Exodus 1:8).

And can you imagine yourself in this congregation poring over these lists, hour after hour, while being schooled by your pastor or teacher, and suddenly reading "Love your neighbor as yourself" (*'ahavtah l're'ak camok*)—a fiery sentence, an ember of coal warming and illuminating all those tiresome and dull dos and don'ts.

Or maybe more like a multifaceted gemstone you can hold to the light and delight in the refracted colors casting beauty and joy over every "do this" and "don't do that."

—

And of course that is what happened. No single word in Leviticus has been quoted more often or in so many different contexts than this imperative verb in Leviticus 19:18: *love.* The word is threaded all through the rest of the Hebrew Scriptures and embedded on nearly every page of the New Testament. *Love* as a verb is personal, relational, comprehensive. *Love* is the primary verb in our Scriptures as a whole and in our language still.

Wendell Berry, an American prophet if there ever was one, makes sure we don't turn *love* into an idea or a sentiment or a valentine card: "Love is never abstract. It does not adhere to the universe or the planet or the nation or the institution or the profession, but to the singular sparrows of the street, the lilies of the field, 'the least of these my brethren.'"[11]

The first two canonical gospels establish the primacy of this verb by having Jesus quote Leviticus 19:18 (Matthew 5:43; 19:19; 22:39; Mark 12:31), thereby giving it a prominent position. Not a single New Testament writer following Matthew and Mark fails to use *love* as a verb, most of them many, many times. It is one of the indispensable verbs providing an accurate and all-encompassing revelation of the love with which God loves the world. But it is worth remembering that it first occurs where and when you might least expect it, in Leviticus.

The entire Scriptures, following the precedent in Leviticus 19, speak of love in profuse particularity as the dominant characteristic of the community of God's people. But this love is not an item in a catalog available for Christians to order. It is the way of life that permeates and sums up the thinking and behavior of followers of Jesus in the company of the Trinity.

—

But there is also this to be said. *Love* is one of the slipperiest words in the language. There is no other word in our society more messed up, misunderstood, perverted, and misused as the word *love.* Complicating things even further, it is

11. Wendell Berry, *What Are People For?* (Berkeley, CA: Counterpoint, 1990), 200.

a word terribly vulnerable to cliché, more often than not flattened into nonmeaning by chatter and gossip. The most relational word in our vocabulary ends up being all me directed, all self. The largeness of love is reduced to the mouse hole of the ego. It is often used by the same person and in the same conversation in self-contradicting ways—seriously and frivolously, soberly and sentimentally, thoughtfully and teasingly. It is used in the worship of a holy God and as a euphemism for loveless sex. It is used to reveal heart intimacies and commitments and as a cover for telling every sort and variety of lies. An incalculable amount of violence, both emotional and physical, occurs in relationships either begun in or under a pretense of love. In no other human experience do we fail so frequently, get hurt so badly, suffer so excruciatingly, and get deceived so cruelly as in love. Still, we continue to long for love, dream of it, attempt it. We are incorrigible. Walker Percy titled one of his novels *Love in the Ruins,* an epitaph that too many families, neighborhoods, and churches in our communities can claim for their own. So when men and women of the Christian community are given responsibility for telling one another that God loves them, that he commanded every one of us to love one another—"as yourself"!—and when we assume responsibility for giving guidance and instruction in the life of love, we know we have no easy task. In fact, it is difficult to imagine a more formidable, seemingly impossible task. Because of the enormous importance love has for the way we live, it is important to get it right. We need to listen attentively to every conversation, read discerningly every book, if we hope ever to discern the truth and implications of the *love* word.

—

But back to Leviticus and the morally chaotic Canaanite culture that was seething with promiscuous sex and bringing children to sacrifice as burnt offerings to the god Molech, a culture into which the Hebrew people were soon to establish their homes. There was a need to establish clear guidelines on how to live among a people who didn't share their values and morals and worship.

It is hard to believe any culture could be so debased. I, for one, don't think American culture is nearly as bad as that, although sometimes I look around me and wonder.

But I am not sure that listing sins and compiling statistics on sins that disguise themselves as variations on love make much difference.

And so I come back to Leviticus. Here we have the command to love introduced into our vocabulary in a context that is totally indifferent to any appeal to what we can get out of it. Just "love your neighbor as yourself." Period. Just do it whether you feel like it or not, whether you get anything out of it or not.

Scripturally, *love* as a verb is initially presented as briefly as possible as a simple imperative without context. No confusion over how it feels or what you might get out of it. Just do it. No reasons given. No rewards promised. Just do it. Love your neighbor as yourself.

For anyone carefully reading or listening to Scripture, Leviticus 19:18, this out-of-the-blue occurrence, comes without conditions or arguments. It stands bare and unadorned, stark and unexplained.

And I find it interesting that the Jewish community still uses Leviticus as the textbook to teach children to read. It is an audiovisual book (*A* is for *apple, B* is for *boy,* etc.). Leviticus is the *McGuffey's Reader* of Hebrew schools. A picture or object is introduced to teach the sacrificial system. The sentences are short; the vocabulary is elementary. This is where Hebrew children learn the basics. And hidden away in Leviticus 19:18, totally without context, there it is: "Love your neighbor as yourself." I don't think they are going to forget that.

Fast-forward to the first letter of John in our New Testaments. Leviticus 19:18 references to love language occur steadily through Psalms and the Prophets, the Gospels and the Letters. Near the end, in a quite glorious climax, Pastor John's first letter outdoes all the previous mentions of love. The single sentence in Leviticus turns out to be a seed that brings forth a hundredfold yield.

This letter was written to a congregation that John was responsible for near the end of the first Christian century. His congregation, as it turns out, was pretty much a mess. He describes them with words and phrases like *lie* (1:6), *hate* (2:11), and *children of the devil* (3:10). He points out their failure to love their fellow Christians (3:10), how they "deceive" themselves (1:8), and how they refuse to help people in need (3:17). He mentions the antichrist three times (2:18, 22; 4:3), a scary word if there ever was one. And John uses forms of the word *sin* more than twenty times in five short chapters.

Not an ideal congregation by a long shot. And yet not unusual. The love command is daunting but also unavoidable. If love could be imposed on a community, it would at least be manageable. But the love that is first commanded in Leviticus has to be unforced, personal, and freely given by the members of the community. Ours must be lifetimes of accumulated acts of love—likely flawed, imperfect, juvenile, sputtery—but still love despite ourselves, loyal love.

An all-too-common response to this relentless, unqualified insistence on love is to scramble for definitions. "What exactly do you mean by *love*? Define your terms, please." But we will find no relief in hairsplitting definitions.

Love is the most context-specific act in the entire spectrum of human behavior. There is no other single human act more dependent on and immersed in immediate context. A dictionary is worthless in understanding and practicing love. Acts of love cannot be canned and then used off the shelf. Every act of love requires creative and personal giving, responding, and serving appropriate to—context specific to—both the person doing the loving and the person being loved. Because of the totally personal, particular, and uniquely contextual community dimensions involved in even the simplest act of love—the circumstantial complexity and inescapably local conditions—there is a sense in which we cannot tell a person how to love, and so our Scriptures for the most part don't even try.

Instead of explanations or definitions or generalizations, John settles for a name and the story that goes with it: Jesus. "We know love by this, that he [Jesus] laid down his life for us—and we ought to lay down our lives for one another" (1 John 3:16, NRSV). Then he lets us find the particular but always personal and relational way to do it in the Jesus way: "We love because he first loved us" (4:19, NRSV).

—

Friends, we are immersed in great and marvelous realities. Creation! Salvation! Resurrection! But when we come up dripping out of the waters of baptism and look around, we observe to our surprise that the community of the baptized is made up of people just like us: unfinished, immature, neurotic, stumbling, singing out of tune much of the time, forgetful, and boorish. Is it credible that God would put all these matters of eternal significance into the hands of such as we? Many, having taken a good look at what they see, shake their heads and think not. But this is the perpetual difficulty of living a life of love in the community of the beloved. We had better get used to it.

The thing I find so impressive here is how unrelenting John is in his insistence on love, even though he knows how often we will fail at it. He knows as well as any of us that it is impossible to bring it off satisfactorily. But he still insists. He will not water it down: "The commandment we have from him is this: those who love God must love their brothers and sisters also" (4:21, NRSV).

Every sentence in this elaborate pastoral exposition of the five-word command in Leviticus comes out more or less the same: God loves you. Christ shows you how love works. Now you love. Love, love, love, love. Just do it.

Amen.

6

"You Have Done Nothing but Bless"

NUMBERS 23:11, 22–24
2 PETER 2:15–16; JUDE 1:11; REVELATION 2:14

Do you know the story of Balaam? In the church culture in which I grew up, Balaam was my favorite. The funniest story in the Bible. But I mentioned the name Balaam to a few of you last week as we were working together, painting our Sunday school rooms, and I got blank stares. As adolescents, my friends and I thought the story was hilariously funny, but we let it go at that. Now after several years of being a pastor, I have realized how useful the humor is for training us in discernment regarding a kind of popular religion that operates totally out of the context of the biblical revelation that came to Moses at Sinai and has nothing to do with the full revelation complete in Jesus Christ. I want you to have this story working in your imagination so you will have a way to detect some of the sillier attempts at making God available and useful to you.

Here's the setting for the Balaam story. It takes place as the Hebrew people near the conclusion of a forty-year pilgrimage from a life of cruel slavery in Egypt to a salvation life of freedom in Canaan. Forty years? Yes, forty years. Even given the difficulties of moving a large group of people from Egypt to Canaan, it should have taken a couple of weeks or a month at most. How did they manage to stretch a one-year journey into forty years?

Well, here's how. They were the congregation of the people of God in formation, but they were not yet formed. They spent far too much time quarreling and rebelling and complaining. It is very difficult to make a transition from having every detail of your life dictated and regulated by an enemy to living in a community of friends. Moses was given the task of leading the Hebrews into a free life, getting them accustomed to being trusted, to being loved, to worshiping God instead of fearing him. Old slave habits are hard to overcome. It wasn't easy and it took a long time. It wasn't easy for Moses either. He got angry, disgusted, impatient, fed up. They also had enemies who harassed them. But slowly, steadily, they approached their destination. The Hebrews had amassed a series of impressive victories along the way. Stories were circulating in the neighborhood of the improbable Hebrew luck in defeating anyone who opposed them. It was rumored that it was because their God was on their side. They won some of their battles without even drawing a sword. Nobody seemed to make any headway against them by using military force. All the intelligence reports indicated as much. The Hebrews were now almost at Jericho, their entry point into Canaan. They only had to make it through the country of Moab, and they would be home free.

The king of Moab, Balak, listening to the reports of the accumulating Hebrew defeats of their enemies, panicked. He put two and two together and came up with a logical four. He needed help from the gods. He needed prayer. He needed sacrifices. He needed someone skilled in sorcery. And he knew just where to get it. To the east of Balak's country of Moab was a vast expanse of mostly empty land stretching to the Euphrates River. It was a land well known for charismatic leaders who worked spells and knew the magic arts. One name stood out: Balaam. If the sword was ineffective in stopping the Hebrew advance, why not try some spiritual force? If Balak could get Balaam to pronounce a curse on the Hebrews, that would stop them in their tracks. Balaam's reputation was that good.

Balak called his nobles, put together a delegation, and sent them off with a huge amount of money to hire Balaam to curse Israel. The nobles gave him Balak's message: "I need your help. A people has come up out of Egypt. The place is crawling with them. Nobody can stop them. They're pressing hard on me. Come and curse them for me so I can defeat them. You have a reputation: Those you bless stay blessed; those you curse stay cursed."

But Balaam was shrewd. He needed to think this over. He told the men, "Stay for the night. I need to pray about this. In the morning I'll do what God tells me."

Pay attention to whom we are dealing with here, this Balaam. He presumably knew nothing about the God of Israel. He had to feel his way. He was a pagan steeped in magic and séances and charms and spells. It was a slippery world of deception and sleight of hand in which he was a master. But he needed to know whom and what he was dealing with.

During the night God appeared to him and asked, "So who are these men here with you?"

Balaam answered, "Balak king of Moab sent them. He is being threatened by a strange enemy just come out of Egypt. He wants me to come and curse them so he can defeat them."

God said, "Don't go with them. And don't curse the others—they are a blessed people." Now Balaam was getting cold feet for sure. Maybe there were forces out there he couldn't control. No god had ever spoken to him out of the blue without being summoned with his sorceries. So he backpedaled.

The next morning Balaam got up and told Balak's nobles, "Go back home; God refuses to give me permission to go with you."

So the Moabites left and returned to Balak. They reported, "Balaam wouldn't come with us."

But Balak refused to take no for an answer. Desperate, he sent another group of nobles with this message: "Balak says, 'Please, don't refuse to come to me. I will honor and reward you lavishly—anything you tell me to do, I'll do. I'll pay anything. Only come and curse this people.'"

Balaam, beginning to be intrigued, put on a pretence of being disinterested in the money. "Stay with me tonight, and I'll see what God will say to me this time."

Balaam was obviously playing for time. He certainly was interested in the money, but he hadn't yet figured out the game they were playing. In the world of gods and spirits he inhabited, he was a master. The deck must be stacked.

Then God came again to Balaam that night and said, "Since these men have come all this way to see you, go ahead and go with them. But make sure you do absolutely nothing other than what I tell you." So Balaam got up in the morning, saddled his donkey, and went off with the noblemen from Moab.[12]

At this point a very humorous story is inserted into the narrative. Balaam, on his way to meet Balak, was riding his donkey. An angel of the Lord brandishing a sword stood in the road and blocked his way. The donkey turned off the road into a ditch. Balaam beat the donkey to get her back into the road. Next they entered a vineyard with a fence on either side. The donkey again saw God's angel blocking the way and plowed into the fence, crushing Balaam's foot against it. Balaam beat her again.

A third time the angel blocked the way in a very narrow passage, with no getting through whether right or left. Seeing the angel, Balaam's donkey sat down. Balaam lost his temper and gave the donkey a furious blow with his stick. Then the donkey *talked*. She said to Balaam, "Why have you hit me these three times? What have I ever done to you to deserve this?"

Balaam was so angry he didn't even boggle at a talking donkey. He said, "If I had a sword, I'd kill you." The donkey answered, "Haven't I been a good donkey to you? Have I ever done this before?"

Balaam admitted that she hadn't.

And then Balaam saw what the donkey had seen all along: the angel of the Lord with a sword blocking the way. Balaam had been so full of his plans, his mind so full of the reward he had been promised for working for Balak, that he had been blind to the presence of God. The dumb donkey was more alert to God than the famous prophet. Balaam, for all his fame as a spiritual powerhouse, was dumber than his donkey, his heart so full of himself and his plans that he couldn't see the most obvious signs of God's presence.

By now greed had pushed Balaam past the point of no return. He completed the

12. This retelling of the story of Balaam and Balak contains quotations and paraphrases of verses in Numbers 22–24 of The Message.

journey to work with Balak. He was going to get Balak's money come hell or high water.

Balak and Balaam made their plans. They constructed an elaborate sacrificial ritual: seven altars on a high hill overlooking the camped Hebrews. A bull and a ram were sacrificed on each altar. Everyone stood in readiness to hear Balaam utter the curses that would turn the Hebrews back. Balaam opened his mouth, and to everyone's surprise, including Balaam's, what came out was a blessing, a poem promising victory to the Hebrews.

But Balak and Balaam wouldn't be stopped. They hunted for a more likely mountain where the curse might work. They again went through the elaborate business of building seven more altars and sacrificing a bull and ram on each. Again, out came a blessing, this one better than the last. Still, they didn't quit, *couldn't* quit. They were obsessed: "Get God working for us and stop the Hebrews." They found a third mountain, the famous Pisgah from which Moses would later preach his farewell sermon. That would surely produce results. Another failure. The curse turned into a blessing.

Can't you just see them, hustling from one hilltop to another, trying to find the right combination of mountain and curse to make it work? Using all Balaam's spiritual skill, all the hocus-pocus, all the devices for ritual and incantation they could muster to get God to do what would let them live without God's people in their midst? Frantic, inventive, desperate. And every time instead of a curse, a blessing came out of Balaam's mouth, the final blessing a prophecy of the Messiah, the Christ who would be born in another thousand years:

> I see him, but not right now,
>   I perceive him, but not right here;
> A star rises from Jacob
>   a scepter from Israel. (Numbers 24:17, MSG)

Well, that's the story. Humorous, dramatic, lively. It was told and retold by the Hebrews, clearly one of their favorite stories. There are eleven references to the Balaam story in five different books of the Old Testament and three books of the New Testament (2 Peter, Jude, and Revelation).

As both Hebrews and Christians reflect on this story, it looms large as a warning against religious eloquence, whether your own or another's. Balaam had a great reputation as a spiritual giant. He was suave and knowledgeable. But it was all external. His oratory was all in his mouth, not his heart. He had nothing inside. There was no substance to him, a hollow man. What he really wanted was to make a lot of money. Balaam said all the right things; he did all the wrong things. His life was all greed, ambition, and selfish gain. The final Balaam reference in our Scriptures is in the book of Revelation in a sermon to the church at Pergamum with a warning to those who "hold the teaching of Balaam" (2:14)—people who are all words and no action. But you folks don't have to travel to the Euphrates River to find your Balaam. Just turn on your television.

Yet in contrast with this solemn warning against smooth-talking spiritual experts, there is an unmistakable mood of celebration here because nothing can stop the redemptive work of God. God's people are on the march from slavery in Egypt to freedom in Canaan. The Hebrews were nobodies while Balaam held center stage in that part of the ancient world, celebrated for his prophetic and priestly exploits. And he ended up a laughingstock, made a fool of by his donkey. As this story has been told in Hebrew and Christian families, it is impossible not to imagine a lot of laughter. "Poor Balak! Poor Balaam! Who did they think they were that they could stop God's salvation work?" The comical episode with the donkey, coupled with the frantic running around trying to find a mountaintop where the curses would be effective, when told with the right tone and chuckle would have to have been very funny.

Hilarity is integral to Christian pilgrimage. There is no question that being a Christian involves us in many sorrows, many struggles, sober hours of repentance and meditation. But there isn't the slightest suggestion in Scripture that grim resignation is characteristic of Christian character. How could it be when God is victor? The gospel is like a nail: the harder you hit it, the deeper in it goes. The Balaam story is good protection against the doomsday people when they get too assertive. Laugh at the devil and he will flee from you.

And then, maybe best of all there is the realization, deeply embedded in this story, that God's main business is blessing, not cursing. The widespread grassroots ignorance of this is reflected in common speech: "God damn" is far more prevalent in everyday American speech than "God bless."

In our fallen state we somehow imagine God is a being that can be called into action to denounce, to put down, whatever displeases or inconveniences us. We are disappointed, frustrated, and blocked by the people God has put in our lives. And we stupidly think we can get God to deal with them in a way that lets us indulge ourselves and then selfishly go on our way without the inconvenience of accepting and loving them.

We are wrong. God's characteristic way is blessing. When he looks on a man or woman, he sees his child, rebellious perhaps, immature almost certainly, but still his child, a child of God.

Balak thought the easiest thing in the world would be to get God to curse the Hebrews to damnation, especially with an ally as powerful in the spiritual world as Balaam. But all Balak got for his pains was four beautiful, lyrical, memorable blessings. In exasperation Balak yelled at Balaam, "What have you done to me? I asked you to curse my enemies, and, behold, you have done nothing but bless them."

And we say, "Sure, Balak, what did you expect? Blessing is God's main business."

Amen.

7

"Your Eyes Have Seen"

DEUTERONOMY 11:1–17
JOHN 5:45–47

Deuteronomy occupies a strategic place in our understanding of what goes into being formed as a people of God. Deuteronomy is presented through the voice of Moses as he preaches his final sermon, his plains of Moab sermon on the meaning and formation of the holy community that includes us. Working off the foundational material of creation and salvation narrated in the first four books, Moses now turns his language sermonic. After long training (forty years!) the people are addressed by Moses as if they are capable of doing what they have been created and saved to do: live as the people of God in the Promised Land of God. Live holy lives. Live the creation-salvation revolution. It has taken them a long time to grow up. They are now poised at the threshold of maturity and called to love. Love is our most mature act as human beings. Both statistically and sermonically, the word *love* holds a prominent place in Deuteronomy. Does that surprise you?

—

I first became interested in Deuteronomy, I mean *really* interested, through a story that took place five hundred years after Moses preached this sermon. It's the story of the discovery of the Deuteronomy sermon in a pile of rubble in the Jerusalem temple. We don't know how long the scroll had been there. Three hundred years is an educated guess. (The story is recorded in 2 Kings 22–23 and 2 Chronicles 34–35.)

Here's the story. Josiah became king when he was eight years old. He became king at such a young age through an act of violence: his father, Amon, was murdered by a cabal of conspirators in a bloody palace coup. The assassins were immediately apprehended and killed (2 Kings 21:19–26; 2 Chronicles 33:21–25). Josiah was rescued and promptly crowned king, the youngest king ever to sit on Judah's throne. The year was about 640 BC. Josiah's reign would end thirty-one years later when he was killed by the Egyptian pharaoh in a battle at Megiddo in 609 BC (2 Kings 23:28–30; 2 Chronicles 35:20–24). Violence launched his kingship and violence ended it. But the thirty-one years of his reign were simply stunning, in no small part because of the discovery of the Deuteronomy scroll.

The boy-king Josiah inherited a huge moral and political mess. His grandfather, King Manasseh, may have been the absolutely worst king Judah had ever experienced, filling the country with every imaginable evil and even some unimaginable ones during his fifty-five-year reign. Assyria was the dominant world power at the time. It had bullied the world for three hundred years and had acquired the distinction of making high art out of evil—cruelty, torture, lasciviousness, black magic, spirit-mediums, witches, sorcerers, child sacrifice—you name it. Manasseh was a great admirer of all things Assyrian and imported its evil by the truckload into Judah and Jerusalem. He constructed Assyria-inspired sex-and-religion shrines all over the country, erected obscene phallic pillars to the sex goddess Asherah, filled Solomon's temple with foul images and relics, and even built rooms in the temple for the use of male prostitutes—a moral cesspool, a spiritual nightmare, creation polluted, salvation repudiated, the holy community in ruins. Amon, Josiah's father, continued Manasseh's course, but he was assassinated two years later. Such were the conditions faced by the eight-year-old Josiah when he was put on Judah's throne (2 Kings 21; 2 Chronicles 33).

We don't know who rescued Josiah from the assassins and then guided and advised him through his childhood until he was mature enough to govern in his own right. We are not told that story. All we know is the results: at age sixteen he was seeking "the God of his ancestor David" (2 Chronicles 34:3, NRSV). By the time he was twenty, he was acting as king on his own and began cleaning up the Manasseh mess, scrubbing the country clean of the sex-and-religion idolatries. He embraced David as his mentor in all matters royal: he "walked in the ways of his ancestor David; he did not turn aside to the right or to the left" (34:2, NRSV).

When Josiah was twenty-six years old, Hilkiah, the high priest, in the course of extensive repairs being carried out in Solomon's temple, the place of worship, found a scroll, the "book of the law of the LORD given through Moses" (34:14, NRSV). The book was Deuteronomy. It had long been obscured in rubble during Manasseh's misrule. When it was read to Josiah, he immediately embraced it as his text for completing the reform he had launched six years earlier. It was the defining moment of his kingship. He had his text. Without a moment's hesitation he set about the extensive rebuilding of his country as a community of the people of God.

Jeremiah received his call to be a prophet four years after Josiah launched his reform movement. He began preaching repentance, using language that has many affinities with words and phrases in the Deuteronomy scroll. The king and the prophet, it seems, were of one mind, and Deuteronomy provided the text that God used in the lives of both Josiah and Jeremiah to pull the people of God back from the brink of extinction.

Jeremiah and Josiah were roughly the same age. (An educated guess is that Jeremiah was two years older than Josiah.) Jeremiah grew up in a priest's home in the village of Anathoth, only two miles and less than an hour's walk from the Jerusalem royal palace where Josiah lived. Were they boyhood friends? It is tempting to imagine they were. The scroll was discovered in the temple by the high priest Hilkiah. Jeremiah's father was a priest with the name Hilkiah. Was the priest who was Jeremiah's father the same as the Hilkiah who discovered the Deuteronomy scroll? Maybe.

At any rate, with the discovery of the scroll, Josiah launched a vigorous reform movement throughout the country, using Deuteronomy as the text for reform. Within four years of the discovery of the scroll, Jeremiah received his call to be a prophet. There is no hard evidence that Josiah and Jeremiah were partners in the reform movement, but it sure looks like it. Jeremiah mentions Josiah's name four times (Jeremiah 3:6; 25:3; 36:1–2) and alludes to him another time (22:15–16). From the records we have of his preaching (that is, the book of Jeremiah), we see that much of the language reflects the language of Deuteronomy. After Josiah was killed in the battle at Megiddo in 609 BC, Jeremiah preached Josiah's funeral sermon (2 Chronicles 35:25).

For thirteen years Josiah and Jeremiah, the young king and the youthful prophet, were allies in leading a major reformation in Judah, restoring the ravished, decimated, corrupted people of God to a true worshiping community. Josiah tore down the sex-and-religion shrines and vile phallic pillars, and he smashed the furnaces used for child sacrifice—a top-to-bottom housecleaning. And Jeremiah preached his sermons of repentance and forgiveness, wept rivers of tears lamenting the depths of degradation to which the people had descended, exposed the venality and lies that passed for religion in the popular preaching of the day, challenged the superficial, trivializing messages from the priests, who assured the people everything was just fine, who "healed the wound of my people lightly" (Jeremiah 6:14).

In one sense the revolutionary reform didn't last long, thirteen years to be exact. Then Egypt and Babylon got rid of Assyria (a good thing) but also conquered Judah (not a good thing). Babylon soon hauled Judah off into exile. But in another sense the reform that Josiah led and Jeremiah preached formed a people of God that not only survived a massive political defeat, enslavement, and exile but actually flourished. The Josianic reform, using Deuteronomy as its text, formed (reformed) God's people.

I was in the early years of being a pastor when I learned this story of the discovery of Deuteronomy and the revolutionary reform led by Josiah and Jeremiah. I suddenly knew why preaching is important. It develops an imagination adequate to embrace revolution. I now had the text that formed my preaching.

—

When I was an adolescent, one of the visions that filled my head with flash and color and glory was the French Revolution. I actually knew very little about it. Some vague impressions, incidents, and names were mixed haphazardly in my mind to produce a drama of pure romance, excitement, and the triumph of righteousness, something spiritually blazing and extravagant and glorious.

I had this picture of idealistic, devoted men and women with ringing affirmations of liberty, equality, and fraternity on their lips, marching through a corrupt, sinful world and purging it with their righteous ideas and actions. Names like Marat, Robespierre, and Danton had a ringing and righteous sound in my ears. Evil dungeons in the Bastille were deep shadows against which the fires of liberation burned purely. Heroism and villainy were in apocalyptic conflict. The guillotine was an instrument of the Last Judgment, separating the sheep from the goats.

Thus my imagination, untroubled by facts, spun a wonderful fantasy of the glorious French Revolution. When I arrived at my university and looked through a catalog of courses, I was delighted to find a course on the French Revolution. I signed up for it.

The class was one of the significant disappointments of my university years. I brought to it the kind of great expectations that adolescents often do to adult enterprises, but nothing of what I expected took place.

The professor was a slight, elderly woman with thin, wispy gray hair. She dressed in dark, shapeless silks and spoke in a soft, timorous monotone. She was a wonderfully nice person and was academically well qualified in her field of European history. But as a teacher of the French Revolution, she was a disaster. She knew everything about the French but nothing about revolution.

I, meanwhile, knew practically nothing about the subject, and the few facts I had in my possession were nearly all wrong. What I possessed, in fact, was a vast ignorance about the whole business. But I was right about one thing: it was a revolution. Revolutions turn things inside out and upside down. Revolutions are titanic struggles between antagonistic wills. Revolutions excite a desire for a better life of freedom. Sometimes they make good on their promises and set people free. More often they don't, but after a revolution nothing is quite the same again.

But sitting in her classroom, no one would ever know that. Ill-fated Marat, murderous Charlotte Corday, the black Bastille, the bloody guillotine, venal and opportunistic Danton, giddy Marie-Antoinette, ox-like Louis XVI—all the players and props in that colorful and violent age were presented in the same platitudinous, tired, and pious voice. Everybody sounded the same in her lectures, all presented as neatly labeled specimens, butterflies on a mounting board on which a decade of dust had settled.

For a long time after that, the French Revolution seemed to me a very great bore. Say the words *French Revolution,* and I yawned.

Years later as a young pastor, I was astonished to find men and women in my congregation yawning. Scott Ericson went to sleep every Sunday. He always made it through the first hymn but ten minutes later was sound asleep. Red Belton, an angry teenager, sat on the back pew out of sight of his parents and read comic books. Karl Strothheim, a bass in the choir, passed notes supplemented by whispers on stock market tips to Luther Olsen. One woman gave me hope. She brought a stenographic notebook with her every Sunday and wrote down in shorthand everything I said. At least one person was paying attention. Then I learned she was getting ready to leave her husband and was using the hour of worship to practice her shorthand so she could get a self-supporting job.

These were, most of them, good people, nice people. They were familiar with the Christian faith, knew the Christian story, and showed up on time for worship each Sunday. But they yawned. How could anyone go to sleep ten minutes after singing "Blessing and Honor and Glory and Power"? How could anyone practice shorthand when the resurrected Christ was present in word and sacrament? How could anyone sustain interest in Batman when Saint Paul's Romans was being read? I had a congregation of saints and sinners who knew everything about the Christian life except that the gospel had redefined everything and everyone, set everything and everyone in a participating relation to a holy God, something like what the revolution was to the French in the eighteenth century—the *energy* that created a community of free men and women plunged into a new life. My congregation knew the word *Christian* pretty well, but *holy*? Something blazing? A community bonfire? A revolution?

I knew I had my work cut out for me. When I was ordained and then called to be the pastor of a congregation, I had supposed my task was to teach and preach the truth of the Scriptures so my congregation would enter into the work of Christ as he worked out their salvation. I had supposed my task was to pray for them, gathering them into the presence of a holy God who made heaven and earth and sent Jesus to die for their sins. Now I realized that more than accurate learning was at stake, more than moral behavior, more than getting them on their knees on a Sunday morning. *Life* was at stake: *their* lives, their *souls,* their *souls in community.* People can think correctly and behave rightly and worship politely but still live badly: live anemically, live individualistically self-enclosed lives, live bored and insipid and trivial lives.

—

That's when I came across the story of the discovery of Deuteronomy after decades of neglect and the work of Josiah and Jeremiah that revolutionized the dormant Hebrew people and brought them back to new life. I determined to join Josiah and Jeremiah in my pulpit each Sunday, developing an imagination adequate to participating in a revolution.

Deuteronomy is the longest sermon in the Bible and maybe the longest sermon ever. Deuteronomy presents Moses, standing on the plains of Moab with Israel assembled before him, preaching. It is his last sermon. When he completes it, he will leave his pulpit on the plain, climb a mountain, and die.

Moses had entered the story of salvation as a baby born in Egypt under a death threat. Now, 120 years later, eyesight sharp as ever and walking with a spring in his step, he preaches this immense sermon and dies, still brimming with words and life.

This sermon does what all sermons are intended to do: takes God's words, written and spoken in the past; takes the human experience, ancestral and personal, of the listening congregation; and then reproduces the words and experience as a single event right now, in this present moment. A sermon changes words *about* God into words *from* God. It takes what we have heard or read of God and God's ways and turns them into a personal proclamation of God's good news. A sermon changes water into wine. A sermon changes bread nouns and wine verbs into the body and blood of Christ. A sermon makes personal again what was once present and personal to Isaac and Rebekah, to Ruth and Boaz, to David and Abigail, to Mary and Elizabeth, to Peter and Paul, to Priscilla and Aquila. To you. To me. No word God has spoken is a mere literary artifact to be studied. No human experience is dead history merely to be regretted or admired. The continuous and insistent Mosaic repetitions of "today" and "this day" throughout the Deuteronomic sermon keep attention taut and responsive. The complete range of human experience is brought to life and salvation by the full revelation of God. That is what Moses is doing from his great pulpit on the plains of Moab: Live this! Now!

The plains of Moab are the last stop on the forty-year journey from Egyptian slavery to Promised Land freedom. The people of Israel have heard a lot from God: commandments, covenant conditions, sacrificial procedures. And now, poised at the River Jordan, ready to cross over and possess the new land, Moses, preaching his great plains of Moab sermon, makes sure they don't leave any of it behind, not so much as one detail of their experience of God's revelation. He puts their entire experience of salvation and providence into the present tense (chapters 1–11). He puts the entire revelation of commandment and covenant into the present tense (chapters 12–28). And then he wraps it all up in a charge and a blessing to launch them into *today's* obedience and believing (chapters 29–34).

"Let's go."

Amen.

Part 2

"ALL MY SPRINGS ARE IN YOU"

PREACHING IN THE COMPANY OF DAVID

Introduction

God always has the first word. We live in a world in which "[God] spoke, and it came to be" (Psalm 33:9). In the company of Moses, we enter into a world that comes into being and then is shaped into a story, a creation and salvation story. We begin by listening, listening for this word and the stories that are formed by it.

But after the listening comes praying. Prayer is first of all a means of listening. Prayer is an act of attention.

We are not used to this. We suppose we are in charge of prayer. We aren't. God has spoken. We are required to enter a world of listening to God.

It is a deep tradition in the lives of the people of God that we acquire our basic orientation, this attentiveness and listening, in Psalms, the prayer book of the Bible. We learn to listen reverently and attentively by praying the psalms.

Everyone prays, kind of. It is our most human action. At the deep center of our lives, we are connected somehow or other with God. But that deep center often gets buried under the everyday debris of routine and distraction and chatter while we shuffle about out of touch and unaware of our true selves. Then a sudden jolt opens a crevasse, exposing for a moment our bedrock self. Spontaneously we pray. We pray because it is our most human response. We're made by and for the voice of God. Listening to and answering that voice is our most characteristic act. We are most ourselves when we pray.

The jolt comes variously—a stab of pain, a rush of beauty, an encore of joy. We exclaim, "God!" The cry can be complaint or curse or praise. No matter, it's prayer. When that deep, deep center of our lives is exposed—our core humanity that biblical writers so vigorously designate as "heart"—we unthinkingly revert to our first language. We pray.

For some that's the end of it, brief and random exclamations scattered haphazardly across a lifetime. But others of us, not content to be our true selves only occasionally, hunt for a way to cultivate fluency. More often than not, the hunt turns up its quarry in Psalms.

David is the name most prominently associated with writing and praying the psalms. His life is the most extensively narrated that we have in our Scriptures. We know more about David than anyone else in our biblical records. We know about his growing up and dying, his friends and enemies, his sins and salvation, his triumphs and defeats. Nothing is held back or suppressed. The entire range of the human condition is laid out for us in the narration of David's life. Alongside the story we are given his prayers, the inside of the story. Everything that happened in David's life became prayer, became the occasion for listening to and answering God. Nothing in David's life was left lying around on the surface. He took everything "to heart," interiorized it, welcomed it in God's name for God's work.

There is also this to be said: the psalms are poetry, as distinguished from prose. Prose is a way of using language to describe or narrate or explain some thing or some person. Poetry is a way of using language that draws us into participation. Poetry is language used with personal intensity. It is not, as so many suppose, decorative speech. Poets tell us what our eyes, blurred with too much gawking, and our ears, dulled with too much chatter, miss around and within us. Poets use words to drag us into the depth of reality itself. They do it not by reporting on how life is but by pushing and pulling us into the middle of it. Poetry grabs for the visceral. Far from being cosmetic language, it is intestinal. Calvin G. Seerveld described Psalms as "the gut of the Bible."[13] Root language. Poetry doesn't so much tell us something we never knew but brings into recognition what is latent, forgotten, overlooked, or suppressed.

The text of Psalms is almost entirely this kind of language: poetry. Knowing this, we will not be looking here primarily for information, for ideas about God or for direction in moral conduct. We will expect, rather, to find the experience of being human before God, exposed and sharpened. Praying in the company of David, we develop a praying imagination.

13. Calvin G. Seerveld, *Biblical Studies and Wisdom for Living,* ed. John H. Kok (Sioux City, IA: Dordt College Press, 2014), 25.

This is hard to get used to. Our habit is to talk about God, not to him. We love discussing God. The psalms resist these discussions. They are not provided to teach us *about* God but to train us in responding *to* him. This is poetry that dives beneath the surface of prose and pretense straight into the depths. We are more comfortable with prose, the laid-back language of our arm's-length discourse. But prayer requires that we deal with God, this God who is determined about nothing less than the total renovation of our lives. We would rather have a religious bull session. But to acquire a disposition to *listen* and *submit* to a poem requires both practice and patience.

—

When we open up our Bibles and begin reading and or praying the psalms, we find they have been arranged in five sections, each section ending with what appears to be a conclusion. Psalm 41 concludes with "Blessed be the LORD, the God of Israel, from everlasting to everlasting! Amen and Amen." It reads like a conclusion, but it is not, because other psalms follow. The final line of Psalm 72 is "The prayers of David, the son of Jesse, are ended." But Psalms continues. We arrive at two more "conclusions" (Psalms 89:52 and 106:48) before Psalm 150 definitively closes the collected prayers. We count up the conclusions. There are five.

We realize our Hebrew ancestors wisely arranged this book of prayers to protect us from presumptuous prayer. Presumptuous prayer speaks to God without first listening to him. Presumptuous prayers obsessively, anxiously, or pretentiously multiply human words to God with, at best, a distracted, indifferent, or fitful interest in God's words to us. But God speaks to us before we speak to him. If we pray without first listening, we pray out of context.

Protection against presumption comes in the editorial arrangement of Psalms into five books, showing that prayer is a response to the Torah's five books. The narrative of our lives received its classic form in the five books of Moses: Genesis, Exodus, Leviticus, Numbers, and Deuteronomy. Life from its inception (Genesis) to its fulfillment (Deuteronomy) is the result of God's making, redeeming, providing, and blessing word. God's word is *authorizing,* an author at work. The world and our lives are given a narrative shape. Story is brought into existence, with salvation as its plot. So we need to pray not only out of an awareness of our personal stories (David's life gives us that) but in the context of the "old, old story," the salvation story. Our daily lives have a narrative shape, but the Bible as a whole (the large context in which we live) is also cast in the form of narrative.

Language, by its very nature, is not monologue but dialogue. God does not impose his plot of salvation on the people in his story. He speaks in order to be answered. The character of each person in the story (and we are all in it) is allowed to form from the inside, in the give-and-take of dialogue, each of us with our own rhythms, at our own pace. We are in a world of salvation in which God is speaking to us. How do we answer? We are not good at this. The psalms instruct, train, and immerse us in answering speech, which is our part in the exchange of words by which our being in the image of God and redemption by the blood of Christ is formed internally into maturity.

By means of the psalms, we find our voice in the dialogue. In prayer we do not merely speak our feelings. We speak our answers. If we truly answer God, there is nothing we may not say to him.

But note this as well: stock answers are not prescribed. There is no verse-by-verse correspondence between, say, Psalm 19 and Genesis 19. The editorial arrangement does not give us a phrase book of rote answers. What we have, rather, is an immersion in language adequate to the dialogue. We acquire facility in personal language that is accurately responsive out of our changing lives and growing levels of faith to what God speaks to us in Scripture and in Christ. We need a vocabulary and syntax sufficiently personal and adequately wide ranging to answer everything that God says.

This unobtrusive, five-book arrangement is quietly but insistently provided to protect us against the presumption, whether inadvertent or willful, to pray in any other way than by listening to and answering God's Word.

I

"From the Womb of the Morning"

PSALM 110
MATTHEW 22:41–46

If we lived in the first century and went to worship with other Christians, the sermon text we would most likely have heard is Psalm 110, probably sooner than later. But I venture to guess that, in all your years of churchgoing, you have never heard a sermon on Psalm 110.

The earliest Christians did not have the same Bible we have. Their Bible was the Hebrew Bible, what we name the Old Testament. After the death and resurrection of Jesus, for something like twenty-five years, until the first letters of Paul began to appear, nearly all of what the first Christians knew about Jesus came through listening to and repeating what they heard from the eyewitness of those who knew Jesus in the "days of his flesh" (Hebrews 5:7): the stories Jesus told, the memorable things he said, the people he spent time with, the outsiders he included, and, of course, his crucifixion and resurrection and ascension. It wasn't until the second century that the church had the four gospels as we have them now.

The Jews were a messianic people. *Messiah* (literally, "God-anointed") was a word they were familiar with. They had a long history of God-anointed leadership, leaders anointed with oil and set apart to be kings and priests. But the terms *king* and *priest* were thoroughly contaminated by the pagan cultures close by that associated the word *king* with dictators and their armies and the word *priest* with huge temples and men who impersonally controlled religious life. Within the Jewish community, for a long time the word *priest* had been corrupted by moral debauchery, greed, gluttony and ambition, arrogance and pretension.

Anticipation of the Messiah was in the air those days. The Jews lived in a Roman-occupied country and needed rescuing. And of course there were many messiahs to choose from—schemes of salvation, saviors, miracle makers—making the rounds.

At the time of Jesus, the messianic expectations of the man on the street were centered on either a king or a priest. The king would be, of course, a dictator with an army. This was the primary popular image for leadership in the time of Jesus. But if you were a Jew, such leaders were the enemy. There was excessive taxation and peacekeeping by violence. The usual way of enforcing Roman authority was capital punishment by crucifixion. In the first century many Jews were fed up and formed guerrilla bands in the hills, determined to rid themselves of the hated Roman rule by using violence of their own—daggers and swords—to counter the cruel Roman crosses. There was a name for the Jews who held to it: Zealots.

The messianic expectation of a priest would be of a powerful figure working out of the splendid Solomonic temple in Jerusalem, controlling the worship and religious practice of the people. But their experience of such a priesthood in the several centuries preceding the time of Jesus had been of priests who loved money far more than God, who lived in opulent mansions, and who used the temple as a place of business. Just as Zealots came into being to oppose Roman violence and taxation, another group revolted against the corruption and sacrilege of the temple priesthood. There was also a name for the Jews who would have nothing to with such a priesthood, namely, Essene. They are best remembered today as the highly disciplined and morally austere community who left the Dead Sea Scrolls at Qumran, discovered in the last century. They were a minority among the Jews but still highly respected and influential. They were committed to replacing the corrupt high priesthood in the Jerusalem temple with a disciplined and pure priesthood, at which time heavenly armies of angels would bring about the messianic age in a holy war.

The fiercely militant Zealots and the morally disciplined Essenes had different strategies, but they were agreed in believing that violence and coercion were messianic, either the violence of using two-edged swords (the Zealots) or the violence visited by apocalyptic destroying angels (the Qumran Essenes).

—

And then Jesus shows up. Peter is the first to identify Jesus as Messiah ("You are the Christ," Matthew 16:16). But there is a problem. This Jesus that Peter identifies as Messiah is totally at odds with the stereotypes: a king without an army, a king without a sword, a king who ends up being murdered without angel intervention. And also a priest without robes, a priest who mingles with the poor and outsiders, a priest who touches lepers and heals disreputable women, a priest who disregards Sabbath rules, a priest who associates with politically suspect people.

Jesus the Messiah: a king who doesn't look like a king. When Jesus goes on trial for his life before Pilate, this governor who represents the emperor and the vaunted Roman judicial system refuses to govern, to represent justice. And so he lets a mob sentence Jesus to death on a cross and without cause.

Jesus the Messiah: a priest who doesn't look like a priest. Jesus, who had "nowhere to lay his head" (Matthew 8:20), is put on trial before the high priest, Caiaphas, who lives in opulence in a palace and is on cozy terms with the rich and powerful.

Centuries of expecting kings to operate from a position of military strength and centuries of expecting priests to control and regulate moral and religious behavior were wiped out in Peter's confession: a king without palace or army, a priest without temple or ritual.

Three months or so after Peter's confession, Jesus was dead—a public death, death by crucifixion. And plenty of eyewitnesses.

—

And then—resurrection! How do we assimilate the impact of that event? It was hard for those first Christians. While they were still reeling from watching Jesus die in that excruciating crucifixion, he appeared before them alive. He did not appear for just a brief moment. He stayed around for forty days while they listened and talked with him, touched him and ate with him. Forty days to come to terms with the impossible. As they spent time with him, they gradually realized that Jesus's death on the cross was the death of sin and that his resurrection was the birthing of eternal life.

With this, a complete renovation of the imagination took place among Jesus's followers. It began with Psalm 110. The week before his crucifixion, Jesus had been subjected to hostile questioning by the Pharisees and Sadducees. Jesus put an end to their questioning by asking them a question about the identity of the Messiah, referring to Psalm 110. They couldn't answer him. They were silenced. Jesus silenced them by quoting Psalm 110. Matthew, Mark, and Luke preserve that incident.

When Jesus was killed just a few days later, his followers had to totally reconstruct their preconceptions of Messiah. Was there any way this very ordinary carpenter could fill the qualifications of Messiah, the Messiah who would rule with justice, the Messiah who would make men and women holy? Jesus was remarkable enough on his own terms, but did he qualify for something both cosmic and intimate? As it turned out, he did.

After Jesus was resurrected and spent time with them, his followers started reading their Bibles, their Hebrew Bibles, their Genesis-through-Malachi Bibles, with fresh eyes. They quite literally ransacked the Scriptures for hints and anticipations of the Messiah that they now believed had lived among them in Jesus: his birth, life, death, resurrection, and ascension.

As these first Christians were avidly reading their Bibles, everywhere they looked they came across anticipations and hints of the Messiah just as Jesus had revealed him. They delighted in coming across foreshadowings of the Messiah, reading between the lines, putting two and two together, filling in the blanks, discovering the background of the person they knew as Jesus. They found a fullness they had not expected as they fashioned and developed a narrative sense of Jesus the Christ. They now realized the depth and immensity that had been implicit throughout their Bibles for such a long time. Later, as the Holy Spirit prompted four of them—Matthew, Mark, Luke, and John—to write the story for the next generations, these phrases and fragments of scriptural text were woven into what they were writing. And Paul, the earliest writer of what later became incorporated in the New Testament, could hardly write a paragraph that didn't echo something from their Hebrew Bibles.

The story of Jesus didn't begin with Jesus. Salvation, which is the main business of Jesus, is an old business. Jesus was the coming together of themes and energies and movements that had been set in motion before the foundation of the world. The story of Jesus was now told in the context of the entire messianic tradition, what we refer to now as the Old Testament. Phrases and words and images were woven into their accounts to highlight him as king and priest, but not like any king or priest they had ever heard of or seen. But no less king and priest.

These early Christians were busily at work building a thoroughly biblical imagination that was all encompassing and that in their lifetimes had come to fulfillment and focus in Jesus—Jesus the Messiah, the Christ.

And now as we read what Matthew and Mark, Luke and John, Paul and others wrote, we can appreciate and admire how skillful they were in blending those centuries of anticipation into the narrative we ourselves are now living.

—

As they did this, it turned out that their favorite and most used reference was Psalm 110. Psalm 110 is either quoted or alluded to fifteen times: eight direct quotes and seven allusions. For Martin Luther, Psalm 110 was "the main one [psalm] to deal with our dear Lord Jesus Christ."[14] No other item in the messianic tradition comes close. The community of first-century Christians pondered, discussed, memorized, and meditated upon these messianic anticipations but none more frequently than Psalm 110. It is, was, and will always be an extremely important and strategic psalm, skillfully and vigorously composed, a foundational word of God for all who live by faith in Jesus Christ.

Psalm 110 employs the images of king and priest in such a way that the popular stereotypes were totally reversed. The early Christians who were following Jesus by this time knew that this king, Jesus, was killed and that this priest, Jesus, cleaning up the temple sacrificial system, became himself the sacrifice.

Two sentences in Psalm 110 are statements of direct address from Yahweh, "the LORD," and one of them is addressed to "my lord." The Christians now understood "my lord" as Jesus. Verse 1 opens the psalm with "The LORD [Yahweh] says to my

14. Quoted in James L. Mays, *Psalms,* Interpretation: A Bible Commentary for Teaching and Preaching (Louisville, KY: Westminster John Knox, 1994), 350.

lord [Jesus]: 'Sit at my right hand, till I make your enemies your footstool.'" And then, precisely halfway through the psalm, at verse 4, comes this: "The Lord [Yahweh] has sworn and will not change his mind, 'You [Jesus] are a priest for ever after the order of Melchizedek.'"

"Yahweh says . . ." "Yahweh has sworn . . ." And the person that Yahweh spoke to both times is the Lord, whom the early Christians now recognized as Messiah, namely, Jesus.

Those two sentences provide the structure of the psalm: God the Father speaking to God the Son. They are the reason for the prominence of Psalm 110 in the early Christian community. These people were interested above all in hearing what God had to say to Jesus. Their thirst for the good news was insatiable. Their appetite for the Word of God was bottomless.

What do you think? Do you think this focused attentiveness to what God says might also account for its twentieth-century neglect? Think about it. The voices that command the largest audiences in our American culture are spokesmen for the ego, sometimes the religious ego, but nevertheless the ego. Deep-rooted, me-first distortions of our humanity have been institutionalized in our economics and sanctioned by our psychologies. And now we have gotten ourselves a religion in the same style, a religion that will augment our human potential and a gospel that will make us feel good. We want prayers that bring us daily benefits in the form of a higher standard of living, with occasional miracles to relieve our boredom. We come to the Bible as consumers, rummaging through texts to find something at a bargain. We come to worship as gourmets of the emotional, thinking that the numinous might provide a nice addition to sunsets and symphonies. We read "You will not fear the terror of the night, nor the arrow that flies by day" (Psalm 91:5) and are tranquilized. We read "He does not deal with us according to our sins" (103:10) and decide we have probably been too hard on ourselves. Then we read "The Lord says . . . , The Lord has sworn . . ." and reach for the newspaper to find out how the stock market is doing.

We are probably no worse than the first century in such ways. They did it too. But the remarkable thing about the first century is that there was a group of people, not many really, who, out of the prevailing religious sensuousness and opportunism, actually developed a taste for hearing what *God* had to say, so much so that their favorite psalm became one that centered and clarified that word. Psalm 110 became a touchstone for bringing them to attention before God and focusing their meditations on what God said to Jesus. It is energizing to know that in our America there are still persons who maintain a similar preference. For those of us who choose to be part of that minority, Psalm 110 continues to be important, establishing the clear priority of God's Word for framing our lives.

The preference is definitive. No other psalm comes close. The community of first-century Christians pondered, discussed, memorized, and meditated on Psalm 110. It shaped their identity as a people of God who *listened* to the Word of God. It is an extremely important and strategic psalm, skillfully and vigorously composed, and sets down an essential, foundational word of God for all who live by faith in Jesus Christ.

Jesus is king. Jesus is priest. No question about that. But he is neither king nor priest in the way we are in the habit of defining them. We have to let Jesus be king and priest in his own way.

In the life, death, and resurrection of Jesus, all the scattered materials of truth and revelation were assembled into an organic whole, a stunning act of redemption. Messiah is put together out of the fragmented functions of king and priest, the work of ruling and the work of saving. The king represented God's power to rule, to shape and guide life. The priest represented God's power to renew, to forgive and invigorate life. The king, associated with the palace, operated in the external realm of politics; the priest, associated with the temple, operated in the inner world of the spirit. The king was in charge of horizontal, earthly relationships; the priest was in charge of vertical, heavenly relationships. The one gave structure to life; the other gave life to the structure.

In Messiah the two acts are parts of a whole: God rules and God saves. All the parts of the universe fall into place. All the longings of spirit find a single goal. The life without and the life within become a single life: the life of God in Jesus Christ, King and Priest, Lord and Savior.

Jesus Christ becomes the putting together and centering of all things. The old prayer "Unite my heart to fear thy name" (Psalm 86:11) is answered. Frantic attempts to please a hundred gods and avoid a thousand demons are over. Desperate quests to find answers and acquire the knowledge that will provide access to the inner circles of God are over. Obsessive moral attempts to get a ticket to heaven are finished. Moral sweat and superstitious illusions are out of date.

"The LORD says to my lord: 'Sit at my right hand, till I make your enemies your footstool.' . . . 'You are a priest for ever after the order of Melchizedek.'" And then, without transition, this king and this priest are fused by a surprising and unlikely metaphor: "From the womb of the morning like dew your youth will come to you" (verse 3). It is my favorite line in the prayer.

Some Christians recognize here an anticipation of the birth of Jesus from the womb of Mary. Ronald Knox reflects this in his translation: "Thou art my son, born like dew before the day-star rises" (verse 3, KNOX). The womb of the morning, Mary's womb, bringing forth the infant Jesus, born from "before the foundation of the world" (Ephesians 1:4). Early Christians through oral tradition would have known the story of the virgin womb of Mary and Jesus's birth from it. They caught something here that gave them, I'm sure, great pleasure. Mary's womb delivering Jesus "like dew." Dew: inconspicuous, uncontaminated, glistening in the dawn's early light, without pretension, easy not to notice, especially if you were looking for substantial rainfall to water the crops. *King* and *priest* are large, dominating metaphors. Mary's womb brings something quite different: unspoiled intimacy and tenderness. The splendor of a king and the holiness of a priest are now fused in the early morning birth of a child to be loved and cherished.

Jesus himself was fond of using small, easily overlooked, seemingly insignificant metaphors to stimulate our imaginations to look for the essential in the small: salt, seed, leaven. Here's another: dew. Like dew, your youth, Jesus, will come to you. Dew appears before daylight, and when we walk out into the garden or field, we wonder, *How did it get there?* It didn't rain, no thundershower. It's just there. A virgin birth.

It is easy to see how these combined metaphors—king, womb, priest, with the womb at the center—interact with one another. As such, this succinct poem-prayer entered the imaginations of the first Christians, radically reimaging Messiah in a fusion of kingly splendor, priestly holiness, and, from Mary's womb, dew. Jesus.

Amen.

2

"Land of the Living"

PSALM 116
2 CORINTHIANS 4:13–18

I have a text and a story for you. The text is Psalm 116, with a focus on the phrase "land of the living" (verse 9; see also 27:13; 52:5; 142:5). The story is about a little girl with the old-fashioned name Charity. I'll come back to the text in a moment, but first I want to tell you the story of Charity.

Charity at the time of this story is a plump, bold, cute, and highly verbal five-year-old. I know Charity through her grandparents. When I visit in their home, I sometimes meet Charity. Her grandmother, my friend Brenda, told me this story. Brenda had arrived at Charity's home for a visit. Her other grandmother had left the day before after an extended visit, returning to her home on the East Coast. I have never met the other grandmother, but I do know she is a devout Christian who takes her spiritual grandmothering duties very seriously.

The morning after Brenda's arrival, Charity came into her bedroom at 5:00 a.m., crawled into bed with her, cuddled up, and said, "Grandmother, let's not have any God-talk while you are here, okay? I believe that God is everywhere. Let's just get on with life."

I like Charity. I like her very much, and I think she is onto something. What she is onto is that life is at the center of what we are all about as Christians. And what she is also onto is that life leaks out of what we say when we use language impersonally, when we fail to be in relationship with the person with whom we are talking. It is especially noticeable when we are using words like *God, Jesus, prayer, believe.* We are left with nothing but god-talk—talk about God but with all the God left out.

This salvation life, this Christian life, is a life to be lived, not just talked or written about. If the life leaks out of our words, if the Holy Spirit is no longer praying in and through us as we speak, we will most certainly offend or betray Charity and her many long-suffering friends with the dreaded god-talk. Charity missed something in her first grandmother's conversation that she was hoping her second grandmother would supply: "Let's just get on with life."

Charity was asking for a relationship with her grandmother in which God is not depersonalized into god-talk but is a personal presence alive in their dailiness, a dailiness in which God and life are organically one in both speech and action.

The phrase "land of the living" is my choice for naming this world we live in. For the Christian life is life, life, and more life. Following Jesus is life, life, and more life. We serve a living Savior: Christ is risen. Jesus said as much: "I came that they may have life and have it abundantly" (John 10:10, ESV). Life, created and redeemed by Christ, is not just one item among others. It is an expansive country that we inhabit. Everywhere we look in the creation, everything we read in our Scriptures, everything we hear in the company of saints is about life.

There is nothing more obvious than this. And yet, as we all can give witness, there is nothing more at risk among us. Too often the living Word made flesh is desiccated into propositional corpses and then sorted into exegetical specimens in bottles of formaldehyde. We end up with god-talk. T. S. Eliot put it like this:

> Knowledge of speech, but not of silence;
> Knowledge of words, and ignorance of the Word. . . .
> Where is the Life we have lost in living?[15]

—

Our text is embedded in Psalm 116, a prayer, that is, language addressed to God: "I love the LORD, because he has heard my voice and my supplications" (verse 1). Prayer is speech at its most alive. The breath that is breathed into us by God we breathe back to God. When we pray, we are using language close to the source of

15. T. S. Eliot, *Collected Poems 1909–1962* (Orlando, FL: Harcourt Brace, 1991), 147.

language. In our baptismal identity we habituate ourselves to the language native to the country of salvation, the land of the living. This is the land we live in. A land has a language. If we choose to live in France, it is important that we learn French if we expect to live well and feel at home there, participating in all the details of that land. It is the same in this land of the living into which we are baptized in the name of the Trinity. The psalms are our richest access to this language. The psalms are the Berlitz school for acquiring the fundamentals of grammar and syntax, vocabulary and idiom, so that as we walk through the land of the living, we can recognize what is going on, where things are, and make our way around this land without getting totally lost.

The dominant feature of this language is that it is inherently and insistently personal. If we use this language in a way that depersonalizes God into an abstraction or an idea or a project, the life leaks out of our words. We are left with nothing but god-talk. It isn't long before the depersonalized, nonrelational language used with or about God affects the language we use with the people in our company and reduces them into impersonal causes or projects or problems. God-talk is human speech in which God is depersonalized into a language of information, manipulation, propaganda, and gossip.

Life and language do not originate in us but in God. And so life is never, never what we can take over as if we know what we were doing, take over and do with it as we like, run it as if we owned it. We are social beings, and the society that is most intimate to us is the Trinity. We are part of something before we are anything, and that of which we are a part primarily is Father, Son, and Holy Spirit. God and all that God is and does and speaks is previous to who we are, "who were born, not of blood or of the will of the flesh or of the will of man, but of God" (John 1:13, NRSV).

This Trinitarian God in whom "we live and move and have our being" (Acts 17:28) is a God who speaks, and in the speaking he reveals himself. Our God makes himself known. Most thoroughly in Jesus, throughout Scriptures and sacraments, and continuing in endless derivative and confirming ways. Prodded by Charity's "Let's just get on with living, okay?" we will certainly want to be spending considerable company with God as he reveals himself, receiving his revelation in the listening and silence, petitions and praises.

The Christian life is not, in the first place, something we *do*. It consists of the healthy and mature formation of our lives by the Spirit, the *Holy* Spirit. Christian living goes off the rails badly when it is conceived as a program or routine that we engage in or skills that we master. Once we understand this, two things become obvious.

One: every word, every phrase, every sentence, every silence must be received personally, relationally. God does not reveal himself impersonally. God does not give himself to us as a thing or an idea or a project but personally, with all the intimacies that are involved in being personal.

Two: our participation in the land and language "of the living" must always be responsive. It is not, to use one of our more dreadful neologisms, *proactive.* We commonly use words like *believing, receiving, obeying,* and *hoping* to characterize the responsive, submissive nature of this participation. But we don't commonly consider the patient, human not-doing in which such participation necessarily begins. We are impatient to get on with it. But there is a kind of initial willed passivity in which all truly Christian creative living begins, a silence and a waiting, attentiveness and adoration, a letting go and simply being here.

Psalm 116 is prayer with an hourglass structure. The top half of the psalm (verses 1–11) takes prayers and feelings evoked by death, death threats, death-laden anxieties, death fears, and disappointment, mingles them with experiences of God's graciousness, mercy, salvation, and bounty, and then funnels them through a narrow aperture. Desperate, strangulated prayers for help are tempered into a composite witness ("I kept my faith," verse 10) to the help that God gave. They then slip grain by grain through the neck of the glass to flow as thanksgiving and freedom into the expansive base of the hourglass (verses 12–19). In this prayer, life expands, spreads out, acquires breathing room. The snares of death and pangs of Sheol suddenly become a rich and open and bountiful life.

How does this happen? Not so long ago we were calling out, "O LORD, I beseech thee, save my life!" (verse 4), and now we are asking the question "What shall I render to the LORD for all his bounty to me?" (verse 12) and raising our glass in a toast: "I will lift up the cup of salvation and call on the name of the LORD" (verse 13).

The first half of the psalm does not portray a bad life. God is wonderfully active in every difficulty. But the second half is markedly different—freer, happier.

We now discern notes of extravagance, of reckless spontaneity. "The land of the living" that was signposted in verse 9 is now homesteaded in verses 12–19.

The transition (the narrow neck of the hourglass) is marked typographically by a blank space. How do we get from the constricted "I said in my consternation, 'Men are all a vain hope'" (verse 11) to the expansive "What shall I render to the LORD for all his bounty to me?" (verse 12). How do we get from verses 1–11, a life marked by remembered pain and deliverance, dark and light mingled together, a saved life, true, but also a rough life, to verses 12–19, marked by a rush of energy put to the uses of praise and vows, a coherent, put-together life? Why didn't the psalmist, who presumably knew how these things work, fill in that blank space (the aperture in the hourglass), give us a handle or a formula so we wouldn't have to wonder how to manage that transition?

The blank space, the unmarked, unexplained transition from the cry for help to the celebratory thanksgiving, is fairly common in Psalms. It turns out that a lot happens in that blank space. And we have a name for it: growing up in Christ. It is the wind you can't see that makes the leaves flutter, the clouds scud, and the sails billow. It is the Spirit of God moving over the "form and void" (Genesis 1:2) of our spirits. We would very much like to be in charge of this transition into Christian maturity, but we cannot be. The work and presence of the Wind, Holy Wind work, is in the blank space between the lines and is the main thing, but it is a mystery to which we can only submit. We cannot manipulate or control the Wind-Spirit that forms us and sets us free in the land of the living. Our only access to it is prayer.

So it is fitting that we pause at this blank space on the page and reflect on what goes on when we aren't doing anything. Prayer is not a way in which we order things; it is a way in which we become ordered. The primary action in prayer comes from God, and more often than not he does not act in ways we can duplicate or even recognize at the time. Whether we like it or not or expect it or not, we enter a mystery when we pray. Most of us never quite get used to this. Do we ever get used to mysteries? We want to know how it works so we can do it too, so we are able to take charge of things (or others) ourselves. God knows that if we knew what he knows, we would quickly depersonalize what we know into information or figure out a shortcut that bypassed intimacy.

—

Psalm 116, this "land of the living" prayer that ends up displaying so much Christian maturity and joy, such exuberance in living, has a very interesting grammatical detail that I find fascinating. We are, remember, getting acquainted with the language as it is used in this land of the living. This item of grammar is too good to pass up.

Here it is. It occurs in the sentence "I walk before the LORD in the land of the living" (verse 9). The verb *walk* is a frequent metaphor in our Scriptures, whether in Hebrew or Greek, for living what we know and believe. It is a most useful metaphor because it clearly coordinates our entire body and mind in living out the life of the gospel. But in Psalm 116 the basic verb *walk* is drawn out by adding a syllable and lengthening the word, thus slowing it down. It is as if the writer is saying, "Let's get the most out of this verb that we can." It becomes something more on the order of "I walk back and forth," "stroll meditatively," "wander about leisurely," "saunter." Instead of walking straight to a destination by the shortest route, it suggests a casual walking around, taking in the sights, absorbing the beauty, communing with one's soul, conversing with a friend—what one of my friends calls prayer walking.

This is a rhythmic way of life, in touch with the seasons and weather, our families, the people we encounter, birdsong and children's chatter, the whispers of the Holy Spirit, and the words of Scripture. Prayer, and the maturity it develops, cannot be done in a hurry. It cannot be forced into a schedule. Which is to say that it is the kind of walking, the kind of living, most congruent with the *land* of the living. It is not a determined march headed for an engagement, not a hundred-yard dash to set a new world record in holiness, but a leisurely, attentive, conversational ramble among the living. Walking before the Lord in the land of the living is loitering along a garden path or taking a river walk or going for a beach stroll.

This is the form the verb takes in Genesis that shows God out for an evening stroll in Eden, anticipating a conversation with Adam and Eve (*mithallek,* Genesis 3:8). He wasn't headed for a destination. He was entering into a place and time for relaxed conversation.

This is the form the verb takes a few pages into the story in Genesis when Enoch's life is summed up as a person who was practiced in keeping contemplative company with God (*vayyithallek,* 5:22, 24).

This is the form the verb takes in characterizing Noah's life as a lifelong, companionable, conversational friendship with God (*hithhallek,* Genesis 6:9).

In a somewhat different context, when God asked Satan what he had been up to recently, it is the form of the verb used in Satan's answer: "Going here and there, checking things out" (*mehithallek bah,* Job 1:7; 2:2, MSG).

And when another psalmist prays for protection from the evil generation he is immersed in, it is the form the verb takes to describe the wicked as always in your face, prowling, stalking, dogging your steps day and night (*yithhallekun,* Psalm 12:8).

But this kind of walking doesn't require a shady lane or a quiet park or a cloistered monastery. This way of walking and living can be done anywhere, whether crossing a busy street, moving through a classroom of noisy kids, or pushing a shopping cart through a grocery store with three preschool children in tow. It is the way of living that both enters into and results from praying in the land of the living.

We live in a culture that knows little or nothing of a life that listens and waits, a life that attends and adores. What makes things even more difficult, we live in a church that knows even less of this life that makes friends with silence, a life that leaves time and space for the Holy Spirit to breathe into our hourglass lives and form a mature Christ life. The consequences are alarming as our great Christian heritage becomes more superficial by the decade, shallow and trivialized, noisy and glitzy with god-talk.

Meanwhile, the voice of Charity is being heard in the land: "Grandma, let's not have any god-talk, okay?" I don't know how many of us there are these days, but I think it might be considerable: men and women looking around and seeing signs that the ground is receptive and the soil prepared for something like Psalm 116. As we become practiced and fluent in this Psalm 116 language, it will become music to our ears.

Amen.

3

"The Beauty of Holiness"

PSALM 29
REVELATION 4:1–8

My text is a phrase from Psalm 29: "Worship the LORD in the beauty of holiness" (verse 2, KJV). The same phrase also appears in Psalm 96:9 (KJV), and 2 Chronicles 20:21 says the king appointed singers to "praise the beauty of holiness" (KJV). The translation is disputed, which doesn't make for a promising beginning. But the phrase is also provocative, setting two nouns that do not ordinarily hang out together, *beauty* and *holiness,* in the company of the energetic and all-involving verb *worship.*

Beauty: splendor, grandeur, adornment. Life—core existence—spills over the containers of mere survival or utility. There is something more going on in this world than just getting across the street.

And holiness: an interior fire, a passion for living in and for God, a capacity for exuberance in the presence of God. There are springs deep within and around us from which we can drink and sing God.

Beauty is the outside and holiness the inside of what is essentially the same thing: life full and vibrant, life God created and God blessed, life here and now. When we catch glimpses of the intricate connections between everything we see and can't see, the usual biblical metaphor is "heaven and earth." When we sense the pulse and surge of life within and around us, our spontaneous response is to worship.

Worship is the most soul-involving, reality-assimilating act available to human beings. We are most ourselves, most our image-of-God creaturely selves, when we worship: "O worship the LORD in the beauty of holiness."

But both beauty and holiness are perpetually in short supply. Beauty is commonly trivialized in our culture, reduced to decoration, equated with the insipidities of *pretty* or *nice.* But beauty is not an add-on. It is not an extra. It is not what we attend to when we have a break from necessity. Beauty is fundamental. It is the evidence of and witness to the inherent wholeness and goodness of things. It is life in excess of what we can manage or make on our own. We are, notes professor James Mays, "subconsciously moved by the need for a kind of ecstasy . . . the disclosure of another who is what we are not, confrontation by another in the aura of whose power we find possibilities not ours."[16] Beauty. It arrives through a sustained and adorational attentiveness to what is there: a rock, a flower, a face, a rustle in the trees, a storm crashing through the mountains. When our senses dull and our attention wavers, writers and singers and artists grab us by the ears and say, "Look, listen, feel. Embrace and respond to Life within and around you!" That is what the praying poet of Psalm 29 is doing.

My wife, Jan, and I spent a few hours last June at a museum in North Carolina that was holding an exhibition of the work of Auguste Rodin. Once Rodin's sculptures invade your imagination, it is impossible to look at a man walking or a woman loving and shrug him or her off as trivial or insignificant. Whatever pose or action Rodin found people in, he saw a flare of what can only be called, I think, beauty, and the beauty gave witness to something ecstatic, something more, to sheer life itself. I learned from the program notes that Rodin would often instruct his students, "Don't look for a good-looking model, some perfectly proportioned specimen. Take anyone you come across; they are all beautiful."

If the fate of beauty in our culture is to be trivialized, the fate of holiness is to be reduced to blandness, the specialty of sectarian groups who reduce life to behaviors and clichés that can be certified as safe: goodness in a straitjacket, truth drained

16. James L. Mays, *Psalms,* Interpretation: A Bible Commentary for Teaching and Preaching (Louisville, KY: Westminster John Knox, 2011), 137.

of mystery, beauty emasculated into ceramic knickknacks. Whenever I run up against this, I think of Ellen Glasgow's wonderful line in her autobiography where she described her father, a Presbyterian elder full of rectitude and rigid with duty: "He was entirely unselfish, and in his long life . . . never committed a pleasure."[17]

But holiness is in wild and furious opposition to all such banality and blandness. We are introduced to it through the stories of the burning bush in Midian, the mountain on fire at Sinai, the smoke- and angel-filled temple in Jerusalem. We find ourselves in the presence of God alive, with life far in excess of anything we imagined. This God-life cannot be domesticated or used; it can only be entered into on its own terms. Moses and Isaiah walked out of those stories on fire themselves, energized for lifelong, life-giving vocations. Holiness did not make God smaller so they could use God in convenient and manageable projects. It made those men larger so God could give out life through them, extravagantly, spontaneously.

A number of years ago one of our best novelists, Frederick Buechner, took on the task of reimagining holiness for our generation, and what a magnificent work he has done for us. He put the fire and smoke and angels back into holiness and holy living. Beginning with the unlikely but finally irresistible Leo Bebb in *The Book of Bebb,* going on to *Godric* and *Brendan,* and then with a final flourish, Jacob in *The Son of Laughter,* Buechner immersed us in convincing, contagious stories of holiness that exude life, stories of life-giving, life-enhancing, life-deepening holiness.

Now here's the thing: life, which is characterized by its modifier *holiness* as God's life and God-derived life, lavish and exuberant, beyond domestication and inaccessible to control, is mediated to us in beauty. Beauty is our sensory access to holiness. God reveals himself, that is, in creation and in Christ, in ways we can see and hear and touch and taste, in place and person. *Beauty* is the term we apply to these hints of transcendence, these perceptions that there is more going on here than we can account for.

And that is how we come to identify as apostles of the gospel the men and women and, yes, children, who use words and images and sounds and textures to wake us up to the beauty latent and implicit all around us. I want to reaffirm our baptismal vocation as witnesses to the beauty of holiness inherent in all reality.

17. Ellen Glasgow, *The Woman Within: An Autobiography,* ed. Pamela R. Matthews (New York: Harcourt Brace, 1954), 15.

These men and women (we are included) are here to call attention to the words and images, sounds and textures, that pull us into detailed and adorational and believing participation in God's life-giving revelation.

For it is not possible to have a Christian gospel apart from place and person. The gospel is not an idea or a plan or a vision. It works exclusively in creation and incarnation, in things and people. Disincarnation is the work of the devil.

Saul Bellow wrote recently of "the gray net of abstraction covering the world in order to simplify and explain it" that must be countered by the work of writers and artists insisting on the particularity of detail and the immediacy of place, giving us access to life firsthand so that we are "not bossed by ideas."[18]

We need to rub our noses in the stuff of this world, inhale its fragrance, press our hands into the clay, listen to the songs and stories. God is out recruiting every writer, artist, musician, pastor, child, and parent he can find to help us do just that so we can worship the Lord in the beauty of holiness.

This is the way the poet of Psalm 29 does it. The phrase "worship the LORD in the beauty of holiness" is embedded in the experience of a wild, crashing thunderstorm. The storm is then turned into an extended metaphor in which the thunder is the voice of the Lord, *qol-Yahweh.* Seven great thunderclaps, seven times the voice of the Lord peals out:

> The voice of the LORD is over the waters;
> the God of glory thunders,
> the LORD, over many waters. (verse 3, ESV)

In the Hebrew imagination, the waters were chaos, the uncontrollable and uncontrolled, the home of Leviathan, anticreation. But when the voice of the Lord thunders over the waters, chaos becomes subject to creation: life, an allusion to Genesis 1, our first glimpse of the beauty of holiness.

Storms are splendid, beautiful, awesome. God is on display performing the beauty of holiness, and we have a ringside seat.

18. Saul Bellow, *Ravelstein* (New York: Penguin, 2001), 203.

The voice of the LORD breaks the cedars;
the LORD breaks the cedars of Lebanon.
He makes Lebanon to skip like a calf,
and Sirion like a young wild ox. (verses 5–6, ESV)

Now the imagination of this praying poet takes off: the voice of the Lord splits huge trees into kindling for bonfires and turns immense mountains into a carnival of dancing animals. Lebanon is a grand mountain range to the north of Israel, and Sirion, more often called Hermon, is its largest mountain, a nine-thousand-foot snow-covered peak. The cedars of Lebanon, like the sequoias of California, were renowned for their monumental majesty. We are in a world at play to the glory of God, in the beauty of holiness.

The voice of the LORD flashes forth flames of fire. (verse 7, ESV)

Bolts of lightning stab the darkness in a magnificent light show, each lightning strike illuminating another detail in the beauty of holiness.

The voice of the LORD shakes the wilderness;
the LORD shakes the wilderness of Kadesh. (verse 8, ESV)

An earthquake. The Lebanon mountains at play to the north are matched by the Kadesh wilderness in ecstasy in the south. Earthquakes are normally frightening, but in this context we imagine something more like children skipping or bouncing on a trampoline—the austere badlands released into childlike exuberance, participating in the beauty of holiness.

The voice of the LORD makes the oaks to shake[19]
and strips the forest bare,
and in his temple all cry, "Glory!" (verse 9, ESV)

Imagine oak trees whirling like partners in a fast-paced folk dance, the voice of

19. See the ESV footnote on verse 9 for this alternate wording.

the Lord calling out the moves, leaves swirling from the trees like skirts and scarves of dancers, the rhythms and movements and exchanges beautiful in holiness.

And then all of a sudden they are assembled in the temple: oceans roaring, mountains playing, lightning flashing, wilderness skipping and tumbling, oak forest dancing. Make it this church sanctuary. All this in your place of worship or backyard, right here and now. Every time God speaks, there is more life. The energy and exuberance in place and people accumulate, and then we hear them: "In his temple all cry, 'Glory!'" Here they are, and if we've been paying attention, we're here with them, at worship in the beauty of holiness.

Friends, this is going on all the time. Mostly all we need to do is look and listen, touch and taste. Not infrequently our senses dull; we get distracted and need apostolic help. If we are lucky, an artist or writer or singer or child or pastor shows up with the image or word or song that connects us with the life right before us. If we're very lucky, this apostle will be at home with both the outside and inside of life, the beauty *and* the holiness, and before we know it, we are again in on it, worshiping—worshiping the Lord in the beauty of holiness.

Ten years ago Jan and I decided we wanted to become bird watchers. So much grace and melody and color—beauty—was swirling around us, and we were oblivious to it. We decided to be oblivious no longer. Early in our new enthusiasm a young friend who was an accomplished bird watcher visited us for a few days. We made him pay for his supper by teaching us what we needed to know. One day we were driving south along Flathead Lake, driving a piece of road along a marshy area just south of Elmo. Elmo, Montana, is a very small town in a poor, depressed place. There is nothing in Elmo: a few flimsy houses, each with a rusted-out 1951 Ford disintegrating in the front yard and a doorless refrigerator on the porch. A few men and women are sitting around here and there. There are no gardens in Elmo, just a few cattails at the edge of the lake, two or three cottonwoods. There is a pavilion where the Native Americans come for a powwow in July. That's pretty lively, and we often attend, enjoying the dances and crafts, but it only lasts a week. That's it.

After we had passed through this quarter-mile stretch, our friend David asked, "So how many different birds did you see?"

We hadn't seen any.

"I counted nine species," he said.

Nine species? In Elmo? We were astonished.

He was a patient teacher. He kept reminding us of what to look for: flight patterns, silhouettes, habitat. Gradually through the years, we see more. We're not experts by any means, but we do see birds where we never did before. The change has come about because we were taught to look, notice, be attentive. And when we don't see any birds, we know better than to complain that we live in a part of the country that is deficient in birds. Rather, our eyes have become lazy, our attention spans atrophied. Our self-preoccupation had reduced us to tunnel vision.

I get asked occasionally, as you do, "What's going on in your life? Anything exciting?"

And I say, "No, nothing much. Had lunch with that bore Jack Carson. Got stopped in the street by Millie Mitchell and had to listen to fifteen minutes of gossip monologue. That's about it."

An Elmo day, driving back and forth through Elmo where there are no gardens and no jobs and the powwow happens just once a year.

When a conversation like that occurs, not many minutes go by before I'm nailed by David's question of ten years ago: "So, Eugene, how many birds did you see?"

—

The Holy Spirit has descended on this old world of ours, and there's a Psalm 29 powwow in Elmo every day of the year: a grace-revealing gesture, a fresh snowfall, a friend's forgiveness, the first migrating yellow warbler, a miracle conversion, a truth-telling poem, a pasqueflower in bloom, the good death of a parent, resurrection—Father, Son, and Holy Spirit—all the endless permutations of life. The beauty of holiness. And we have ringside seats. Henry James once said that a writer is a person on whom nothing is ever lost. That sounds like a focused Christian identity to me: the men and women on whom nothing, at least nothing that has to do with life—and virtually everything does—is lost. "Worship the LORD in the beauty of holiness" (verse 2, KJV).

Amen.

4

"I Will Awake the Dawn"

PSALM 108
MARK 1:32–35

I memorized this psalm, this prayer, thirty years ago. It was the job that did it, a summer job working for the city of Kalispell, Montana, the town in which I had grown up and was now getting ready to leave. High school graduation was behind me and university ahead. In three months I would board the Great Northern Railway and head out for Seattle, five hundred miles to the west.

A single phrase got me started: "I will awake the dawn!" (Psalm 108:2). My job for the town that summer was working in the department of street maintenance. As US Highway 93 entered the town limits, Main Street in Kalispell was divided by a wide grassy boulevard. After four city blocks, the boulevard expanded into a park in the middle of which was the county courthouse. There the street split and curved around the park and then was joined together again. But it was still divided by the boulevard for another four blocks, at which point asphalt and concrete took over the center strip of green grass, and the Norway maples gave way to Wheeler's Jewelry and the Conrad Bank, the Woolworth five and dime and Montgomery Ward, the Jordan Café and the Stockman's Saloon.

It made for a welcoming entrance to our town, and I was always proud of it. Unlike many western towns that give the appearance of being as unplanned as a teenage pregnancy, our wide streets, ample boulevards, and generous planting of trees showed every sign of being the result of a thoughtful and affectionate courtship between the land and its first settlers.

My job that summer was watering those grassy and tree-studded boulevards. My workday began at eleven o'clock at night. I started early so the bulk of my work would be done while there was a minimum of traffic. With the help of an alarm clock, I would get out of bed late at night and be out on the street watering the grass and trees by midnight. After four hours of working in the dark, I would begin anticipating the arrival of daylight. Some nights seemed to last forever. Would the sun never come up? Come on, you old lazybones sun. Get up!

And then I found my text: "I will awake the dawn." My job expanded exponentially. After beginning with the modest responsibility of keeping the grass a welcoming green through a mostly rainless summer, I now found myself in charge of praying the sun up and over the mountains.

—

And then as so often happens with these wonderful scriptures we have been given, a word or phrase we are merely toying around with works its way into our lives. Instead of using it for our amusement or edification or whatever, it begins using us.

I was being playful with the phrase "I will awake the dawn." But soon I noticed two other wake-up phrases:

> Awake, my soul!
> Awake, O harp and lyre! (verses 1–2)

Was I awake? Truly awake? I was out of bed. I had my eyes open. I was going through the motions of my work. But was I awake, *God*-awake? Was my soul awake?

If I was awake, surely I'd be thanking and praising and singing. That is what awakened men and women do after all:

> I will give thanks to thee, O LORD, among the peoples,
> I will sing praises to thee among the nations.
> For thy steadfast love is great above the heavens,
> thy faithfulness reaches to the clouds. (verses 3–4)

I felt I had those summer nights all to myself. It was my first extended immersion in silence and solitude. The whole town asleep and I alone awake, alive, and alert to the movements of the summer constellations with the words *steadfast love* and *faithfulness* resonating through the phases of the moon, rising on the incense of the fragrant night air. There is something about getting up and going out late at night that seems to give you an edge on the rest of the world. The monks know what they are doing when they get up at two in the morning to pray Lauds, the first office of the day. All summer long I kept vigil, present to hear the first birdsong, catch the first hint of light coming up from behind the Swan Range of the Rocky Mountains. It was the closest I ever came to becoming a monk.

Wakefulness is the first thing—awareness. All our spiritual masters tell us that. *Awake, my soul!*

—

But that kind of thing is just a little too good to last. It never lasted long in the monasteries. Neither did it last on the late-night streets of Kalispell.

I watered my boulevards with a fire hose. I had fifty yards of fire hose wrapped around a reel and attached to a huge wooden cart. I would connect one end of the hose to a fire hydrant, unreel it to its full length, and then play the sprinkling nozzle back and forth across the grass. Whenever I was watering the median strip or the boulevard on the opposite side of the street from the hydrant, my hose would be exposed in the street. I had a little sandwich-board sign that I propped in the middle of the road fifty yards or so in either direction from where I was working, warning vehicles to slow down. When they read my sign and heeded it, I had plenty of time to get my hose out of the road and let them go through. But not everyone honored my sign. Mostly it was truckers who ignored it. They would roar into my silence and solitude, and I would dive to the curbside for safety, leaving my hose behind. And they would hit it—these huge steel juggernauts, logging trucks, and eighteen-wheelers—and the hose would spring leaks in three or four places. It was an old hose, donated to the maintenance department by the fire department when it was no longer fit for the serious work of firefighting, and it couldn't take much abuse. I would run to the fire hydrant, turn off the water, and spend the next hour or so repairing the leaks.

It didn't happen every night. Several nights would pass without incident. And then it would happen again. I would be meditating, relaxed in the stillness, at ease in the rhythms of my work, awake to God, praying:

> Be exalted, O God, above the heavens!
> Let thy glory be over all the earth! (verse 5)

And then without warning one of these diesel-fueled apocalyptic machines would be upon me, and my prayer would shift gears to

> That thy beloved may be delivered,
> give help by thy right hand, and answer me! (verse 6)

I never got used to the intrusions. The night always seemed so large with God. My work always felt so fitting, so appropriate, so congenial, for it wasn't long into the summer before I was feeling quite proprietary about these streets and grassy boulevards. My mother had been born in this town only fifteen years after it had been established. My immigrant grandfather, who died before I was born, had laid out the first concrete sidewalks. The homes of my several aunts and uncles were safe houses through the years of my growing up. There was hardly a street corner or alley that was not marked by the memory of a fistfight or an infatuation or an adventure. This was *my* town, and I had this wonderful summer of nights to touch it and smell it and care for it. The appreciation was heightened by the sense of my approaching departure for university.

—

As the summer unfolded, Psalm 108 continued to guide me in praying my experience. One night about halfway through the summer, in early July, I noticed that halfway through the psalm, the subject changed from me to God. "*My* heart is steadfast, O God, *my* heart is steadfast! . . . Awake, *my* soul! . . . *I* will awake the dawn! . . . Answer *me*!" *I, me,* and *my* eight times. I loved that. I was given a grammar in which I could express myself with a vocabulary tailor-made to my experience. Maybe that's why I liked it so much. I was a seventeen-year-old adolescent, full of myself and my town. I loved saying *I* and *me.* I still do, as a matter of fact.

Then abruptly it is God who is speaking:

God has promised in his sanctuary:
"With exultation I will divide up Shechem,
and portion out the Vale of Succoth.
Gilead is mine; Manasseh is mine;
Ephraim is my helmet;
Judah my scepter.
Moab is my washbasin;
upon Edom I cast my shoe;
over Philistia I shout in triumph." (verses 7–9)

This is Promised Land language: "I will divide up . . . and portion out." When Israel entered the land promised to them by their God, the tribes assembled at Shechem, the geographical center, and each tribe was assigned its portion, its God-promised place.

The lived Christian life always occurs in a place. It is never an abstraction, never a generality, never a technique. Place: Shechem, Sinai, Galilee, Bethany, Kalispell. Geography is every bit as essential to the Christian life as theology.

In the midst of relishing my place, I realized it wasn't my place at all. It was God's place, God's exuberant provision of a place where I could experience salvation and sanctity. "With *exultation* I will divide up Shechem."

Poets commonly love place-names, the punchy actuality of a named place, and the poet of Psalm 108 obviously did: Shechem, Succoth, Gilead, Manasseh, Ephraim, Judah, Moab, Edom, Philistia. Place-names are some of the very best words we have for evoking feelings, inciting emotions of desire or dread. It is impossible to reduce a place-name to an etymology or point on a map, to confine it to a location. A name is a verbal magnet that pulls facts and memories into its orbit and makes us feel at home or, and this happens too, makes aliens of us.

One of the delights of coming to a new place is hearing and learning and saying its names. An early pleasure when I arrived for my university years in Seattle was getting to say all the new place-names: Yesler, Ballard, Magnolia, Tacoma, Issaquah, Puyallup, Snoqualmie. Later I moved to New York and acquired the wonderful names of Manhattan, Bronx, Brooklyn, Harlem, Secaucus, Mamaroneck, Chappaqua, Tappen Zee.

When I would return home, to the country I grew up in, I realized that the old names had not lost their evocative power: Kila, Elmo, Hungry Horse, Creston, Coram, Jocko, Lolo, Kootenai, Salish . . .

But whoever had laid out my town was not a poet. All the streets and avenues were numbered: 1, 2, 3, 4 . . . The only street in the core town that had a name was Main Street, and there was precious little poetry in that.

And so I took it upon myself to christen the streets with names worthy of their significance in my life. I didn't go so far as to cross out the numbered street signs and spray-paint them with proper names, but I *said* them night after night: Shechem, Succoth, Gilead, Manasseh, Ephraim, Judah—interleaving the geographies. These were the streets in which I had first followed Jesus. At East Seventh and First Avenue, my little sister died, and I heard my first stories about heaven. At the corner of West Fourth and Second Avenue, I was baptized. This was sacred landscape, and I was not about to let a secular surveyor, who had done his best to reduce it to real estate, have the last word on it. So night after night I substituted names for the numbers: Shechem, Succoth, Gilead, Manasseh, Ephraim, Judah, Shiloh, Beersheba, Shunem, Cana, Chorazin, Gaza, Jezreel, Ziklag, Gezer. I had learned to walk and talk, play and go to school, make friends and work, sin and repent, read and pray and love on holy ground. God had provided this land not primarily for farming and mining and logging but for salvation. A holy land requires the proper names to evoke its character. Numbers don't do it.

There are nine place-names listed in Psalm 108, but I didn't find much use for the last three: Moab, Edom, and Philistia. These were enemy nations, and I didn't have a very strong sense of enemy in those days.

Except for those trucks, those bully trucks hurtling out of the darkness and puncturing my fire hose. I would yell after them, "Moabite! Edomite! Philistine!" They never heard me, of course, but there was considerable satisfaction in having access to some biblically sanctioned invective.

Of the three names, Edom (with support from Psalm 137 and Obadiah, which uses the form Esau) eventually rose to the top as my invective of choice. If someone crossed me, irritated me, or made life difficult for me, he or she was labeled an

Edomite. I would mutter under my breath, "Stupid Edomite! Good-for-nothing Edomite! Edomite scum!"

It was twenty years before I got the final movement of this prayer into my praying life. I had been a pastor for fourteen or fifteen years when one day I noticed I had quite missed the point of how Psalm 108 pulled the name Edom into the prayer. When I was young, I was so delighted I had a word I could use to curse people I didn't like or who didn't like me that I failed to pay attention to how the psalmist used the word. By now I had acquired extensive experience with Edomites. Edomites continued to take me by surprise, just like those truckers did, rudely invading my practice of the presence of God, my work in the name of God, my relished rhythms as I participated in the glory of God in my congregation. It is always a surprise to Christians, isn't it (and that includes pastors), when we realize how many people there are who do not want us to do our work, who have no idea what we are doing, who think nothing of interrupting us with their noisy agendas. Edomites?

The noticing took place gradually, but eventually it forced me to remove *Edom* from my vocabulary of invective and install it in my vocabulary of petition.

Here is how Edom ends up in the prayer:

Who will bring me to the fortified city?
    Who will lead me to Edom?
Hast thou not rejected us, O God?
    Thou dost not go forth, O God, with our armies.
O grant us help against the foe,
    for vain is the help of man!
With God we shall do valiantly;
    it is he who will tread down our foes. (verses 10–13)

I have a long way to go before I assimilate this final movement of the prayer and live it from the core of my being. But at least I now see the lay of the land: Edom is not the enemy that I curse or shake my fist at or avoid or dismiss. Edom is the enemy whom I, with God's grace and help, visit and embrace.

Edom starts out as a negative. Edom is not the town I grew up in that is filled with memories of salvation, of relationship, of community. Edom is not a name I say with affection as I revel in the expansive, God-revealing night skies. Edom is beyond my understanding in the purposes of God, beyond my affection, beyond my abilities to deal with.

But Edom doesn't stay a negative. For years now I've been learning to pray for, instead of against, Edom. Not very well many times. The sense of outrage and invective continues to linger, and all I can come up with many times is that God will "tread down [my] foes." But I keep at it, praying to the God who in Jesus is teaching me to love my enemies, my dear Edomites, praying that God will "lead me to Edom." When I started praying this prayer thirty years ago, I didn't know this is where I would end up. Prayer often involves us in what sociologists call unintended consequences.

So what do I do with Edom? I ask God to bring me to Edom—the place, the person fortified against God:

> Who will bring me to the fortified city?
>   Who will lead me to Edom?

God will. And God does. Over and over and over again. The person, the task, the threat, the frustration, the institution, the circumstance that my first impulse is to curse—you stupid Edomite!—becomes, through the wonderful praying of Psalm 108, the occasion for going beyond my strength or understanding or inclination to search out the purposes of God where God is working them out, not where I am cozily domesticating them. For it is God, not me, who treads down, that is, takes care of, our foes.

Amen.

5

"The Mountains Skipped like Rams"

PSALM 114
ROMANS 8:18–25

An ongoing concern I have as your pastor is the unfortunate separation of Scripture from prayer, or of prayer from Scripture, that is all too common in the Christian way.

The tradition of which we are a part doesn't separate them. Scripture is the Word of God understood, comprehended, honored. Prayer is the Word of God assimilated, absorbed, lived. Scripture without prayer has no soul; prayer without Scripture has no substance. What I hope to develop in our congregation is a fusion of the two: Scripture-prayer or prayer-Scripture. What is the use of knowing Scripture if you aren't living it? What is the use of praying if you don't know to whom you are praying?

Worship is a fusion of Scripture and prayer. Our purpose in gathering each Lord's Day is to prepare us to live what we hear, to get what we hear with our ears into our feet as we follow Jesus. You have heard this from this pulpit often enough, whether implicitly or explicitly. But the psalm that is my sermon text for today provides an excellent occasion to sharpen our participation in what I think of as answering God. Not just listening to God, but answering God.

—

When Israel went forth from Egypt,
the house of Jacob from a people of strange language,
Judah became his sanctuary,
Israel his dominion.

The sea looked and fled,
  Jordan turned back.
The mountains skipped like rams,
  the hills like lambs.

What ails you, O sea, that you flee?
  O Jordan, that you turn back?
O mountains, that you skip like rams?
  O hills, like lambs?

Tremble, O earth, at the presence of the Lord,
  at the presence of the God of Jacob,
who turns the rock into a pool of water,
  the flint into a spring of water. (Psalm 114:1–8)

What grabs our attention is the way the psalmist remembers what took place when the Hebrew people were saved from Egyptian slavery. The event is remembered but not as a date in history. It is remembered by creating an unforgettable poem that requires imaginative participation so we can engage with it personally.

The striking thing about Psalm 114 is its imagery: the sea fleeing, the Jordan running away, the mountains skipping like rams and lambs, the rock and flint gushing streams of water. This is prayer that is immersed in an awareness of the creation, at home on this earth, sensitive to the life of the nonhuman aspects of the environment.

But a second look at the psalm gives us a sharper focus. It is not about nature as such but about history. An event—the exodus from Egypt—is being prayed.

There are psalms in which our experience with and knowledge of sky and sea, animals and birds are used in the vocabulary of prayer, but this is something about God, not nature, that is being prayed. Psalmists praise God's act of creation (Psalm 33); express awe at his incredible condescension including humans in a responsible position (Psalm 8); juxtapose the twin glories of sky and Scripture in revealing God's design (Psalm 19); marvel at the intricate interrelations of light, wind, clouds, oceans, springs, birds, fish, storks, badgers, people at work, and people at praise (Psalm 104). But these psalms are never about nature; always they are about God.

When we look at what is going on here, we realize the biblical poets did not go in for nature appreciation. In fact, they were in vehement opposition to it. The opposition was quite deliberate, for the Hebrews lived in a world where their neighbors prayed to nature. The most prominent aspects of nature are fecundity and destruction: the hidden processes of birth in earth and womb on the one hand and, on the other, the terrible forces of volcano, earthquake, and storm that are quite beyond our control. The Canaanites were in awe of and prayed to these impersonal divinities.

The created world around us is wondrous. Any moment we attend to it, feelings and thoughts are roused that take us out of ourselves, feelings and thoughts that seem very much like prayer. These are so spontaneous and uncontrived, so authentic and unpretentious that there is little doubt we are in some deep communion with a reality beyond us, with gods—or God.

But the Hebrews never did that. Nature religion operates on the principle that there is something divine in mountains and rivers, in moon, in sun and stars, in seasons and weather. In "getting into" nature, one gets into the divine, participates in the fertility, enlists on the victorious side, experiences immortal ecstasies. There are divine forces in creation that can be offended or appeased. By engaging in the proper rituals and with a little bit of luck, we can manipulate nature for selfish benefit.

Nature is the origin of the antiprayer activity called magic. Prayer is willingness practiced before God; magic is willfulness exercised on nature. Magic is the skilled use of natural means to manipulate the supernatural (whether God or devil) in order to bend the natural to respond to our will. The magician is expert in using the concoctions of potions, the movements of planets, the incantation of sounds in order to impose his or her will on nature. In the days of the psalmist, this religion was Baalism.

The comic account in 1 Kings 18, in which the priests of Baal gashed themselves with stones so their blood flowed in an attempt to influence the skies to pour rain, is the most famous biblical story of this. If these priests could only make the vital, life-carrying liquid from their bodies flow in sufficient quantity, surely the life-carrying liquid from the sky-god Baal would also flow. Elijah by contrast does not "do" anything. In prayer we do not act. God does. In prayer we do not develop a technology that sets the gears and pulleys of miracle in motion. We participate in *God's* action. "Not my will but yours."

Modern technologists are in some ways the successors to pagan magicians. The means have changed, but the spirit is the same. Metal machines and psychological methods have replaced magic potions, but the intent is still to work our will on the environment whether it involves people or place. God is not in on it, or he is in on it only insofar as he can be *used* in ways that accommodate the lordly self.

Psalm 114 meanwhile holds the focus on prayer, not magic. It deals with the way God is acting but with nature as his accomplice. Nothing here suggests there is something we can do to shape history to our convenience. The earth is not here for us to use. The earth is the scene of God's action. In pride we approach nature to use it; in prayer the psalmist directs us to join it in praise and celebration of God's salvation.

When Israel went forth from Egypt,
  the house of Jacob from a people of strange language,
Judah became his sanctuary,
  Israel his dominion.

The most unobtrusive words in these lines, the pronouns, are the very ones that turn out to be most important: *his* sanctuary and *his* dominion, that is, *God's* sanctuary and *God's* dominion.

The formative experience for Israel's identity, the Exodus, is not arrogantly held up as a nationalist banner behind which they can march, boasting of their superiority. What is expressed instead is unpretentious submission to God's gracious rule. Geography (Judah) becomes liturgy (sanctuary). A piece of land in the ancient Middle East becomes an arena in which the divine action is played out.

It helps us to see that the two ways we commonly use to locate ourselves in reality (where we are and what we see) are subsumed into things both larger and more intimate: God's presence and God's action. History and geography are gathered into worship, into prayer.

The second stanza of this prayer ignites our imagination in a kind of playful exuberance:

> The sea looked and fled,
>   Jordan turned back.
> The mountains skipped like rams,
>   the hills like lambs.

At one level this is simply a colorful account of the Exodus. When Moses struck the sea, it divided, leaving a dry roadbed for the escaping Hebrews, and then when they had crossed, the sea "fled" back to its original seabed, burying the pursuing Egyptians. "Jordan turned back" remembers Israel's being blocked by the Jordan River. Then the priests, carrying the ark of the covenant, stood in the edge of the water, the river parted, and the people marched though and began their conquest of the land (Joshua 3:14–17). "The mountains skipped like rams, the hills like lambs" refers to the people's long wait at the base of Sinai in awe before the volcanic-rumbling and earthquake-shaken mountain while Moses was on the heights receiving the Law.

Why not say it plainly? For one thing, God's action and presence among us are so beyond our comprehension that sober description and accurate definition are no longer functional. The levels of reality here are so beyond us that they invite extravagance of language. But the language, though extravagant, is not exaggerated. The picture of the Red Sea as a fleeing jackal, the Jordan as a cowardly sentinel forsaking his post, the transformation of Sinai to frolicking rams and lambs—these are not journalistic accounts of what happened, but neither are they the fabrications of an unhinged imagination. It is people at prayer and witnessing salvation. The somersaulting of what everyone had assumed to be the limitations of reality (Red Sea and Jordan River) and the unexpected outpouring of energy in the revelation of God's Word (the Ten Commandments) from a huge, dead, granite pulpit in the desert (Sinai) called for new uses of old words.

In prayer we see far more than discrete *things.* We perceive everything in dynamic tension and in relationship with everything else. The raw stuff of the world is not matter but energy. Just as the language of ecology demonstrates the interconnectedness of all *things* (air, water, soil, persons, birds, etc.), so the language of prayer realizes the interconnectedness of all the words of Scripture.

Meanings interconnect. Nothing can be understood in isolation, pinned down under a microscope. No *word* can be understood by merely locating it in a dictionary. From the first moment we speak, we are drawn into the total web of language that God speaks in creation and that Jesus speaks in salvation. And so the imaginative statement "the mountains skipped like rams" is not mere illustration to portray the exuberance of the Sinai revelation. It is a penetrating realization that the earth itself responds to and participates in the revelation.

Paul uses a different, though just as striking, image for the action that prayer-Scripture draws us into: "We know that the whole creation has been groaning in travail together until now; and not only the creation, but we ourselves" (Romans 8:22–23). This is language that draws us away from being outsiders into being insiders, involved with all reality spoken into being by God's words.

The personal that is at the heart of the natural is expressed in the final stanza.

Tremble, O earth, at the presence of the Lord,
at the presence of the God of Jacob,
who turns the rock into a pool of water,
the flint into a spring of water.

"Earth" is comprehensive here: Egypt, Israel, Judah, sea, Jordan, mountains, hills. At the deepest level we are not divided into animal, vegetable, mineral. Together we are in the presence of God. God's presence is not Sinai's thunder, not Jordan's billows, not Egypt's chariots. It is that before which we are in awe.

"Tremble" here reaches for the transcendental: awed respect, reverent humility. Promethean man trembles before neither earth nor altar; he takes charge. Technological woman trembles before neither forest nor angel host; she operates her slide rule with steady hands. People at prayer tremble, along with the whole creation that "waits with eager longing" (Romans 8:19) and in hopeful adoration before the mystery of creation and salvation that "in everything God works for good" (Romans 8:28).

Trembling is not, as some outsiders suppose, being scared in the presence of God. It is something more like a holy playfulness, like faith frolicking. Nature is commonly viewed as a vast mathematical structure of cause and effect, the skies and oceans governed by rod-of-iron rules. Anyone who dares defy them is broken "in pieces like a potter's vessel" (Psalm 2:9). The iron rod of gravity shatters my leg as I fall out of a tree.

Prayer is not defiant or dismissive of these necessities, but it also knows there is more than necessity in the environment; there is also freedom. The moment we understand that, playfulness is born. Prayer that enters into relationship with earth and sky, sea and mountain plays. It skips and dances. We do not live in an ironclad universe of cause and effect. In the presence of the God of Jacob, there is life that is beyond prediction. There is freedom to change, to become more than we were in the presence of the God who "turns the rock into a pool of water, the flint into a spring of water."

Amen.

6

"Surely Goodness and Mercy"

PSALM 23
JOHN 10:11–16

It is possible and not at all improbable that any one of us, at least those who have lived in an urban or suburban place, could be born, live, and die without ever seeing a sheep or a shepherd. Both are still popular in nursery rhymes and fairy stories, but they have pretty much gotten squeezed out of our everyday lives. And to make matters worse, shepherds are nearly an extinct breed. I remember seeing a few in Montana where I grew up, but they never looked like shepherds ought to look. The one I remember best drove into town every Saturday, a rifle slung across the back window of his pickup truck and a big dog in the bed. He smoked roll-your-own cigarettes and was rumored, at least among the children I played with, to have murdered a man in a drunken brawl. If we spotted him on Main Street coming out of a saloon, we crossed the street, terrified. He was not a shepherd we would trust our lives to.

Yet, surprisingly, this experience never dulled or spoiled my appreciation for the Twenty-Third Psalm. And I would guess it wouldn't yours either. It was the first psalm I memorized and the one I expect you know best. It is *the* psalm of Psalms. For those of us who were reared in a Christian culture, Psalm 23 is deeply etched into our imaginations, and it's the psalm most likely to be remembered by the aged and dying.

And yet familiarity has its dangers. The sharp edges blur. Familiarity carries with it the danger of becoming a cliché. My intent this morning is to give this psalm some fresh meaning.

I want you to think about this: if our experience of sheep and shepherds is so remote from the world of Psalm 23, which comes out of a lived intimacy with sheep and shepherds, what accounts for the deeply embedded images and phrases so cherished by so many of us who have no firsthand experience with either sheep or shepherds?

There is something in this psalm that transcends the Palestinian countryside and the work of the ancient Hebrew shepherd-poet. I would like to search out the poetry and rhythms to see if we can realize in a fresh way how this prayer retains its beauty and truth in our world of concrete roads, fast cars, domesticated pets, and shopping malls.

The objective center of the psalm is the Shepherd, who is identified as an image of God. In a single sentence we are transported from a Palestinian countryside half a world away and three thousand years ago into our own neighborhoods and workplaces, where God is present. The Shepherd-Lord figure dominates the prayer-poem. God is good and present. Life is a miracle and brims with beauty and love.

But at the exact center (verse 4), a great shadow of all that is wrong in the world is introduced and threatens to blot out the good and merciful presence of the Shepherd: "Even though I walk through the valley of the shadow of death, I will fear no evil, for you are with me" (ESV). The shadow is death—death valley—or perhaps the darkest shadows are harbingers of death: cancer, Alzheimer's, depression, divorce, domestic violence, grinding poverty, homelessness.

Our lives are lived in the company of both the Shepherd and the shadow.

The first half of the psalm (verses 1–4) pictures God as a Shepherd with a flock of sheep, and we are the sheep.

Sheep are notorious for their stupidity. Left to themselves they wander aimlessly into danger. They need a shepherd. The psalmist, knowing himself as a sheep "prone to wander," knows God as his Shepherd. Many a time God's "rod" and "staff" have guided him around a deep chasm that gaped in black contrast to the glare of the desert sun, and by its sudden darkness, the chasm has blinded men and sheep that entered it to the beasts of prey—the lions and hyenas and jackals—that have their lairs in its recesses. And so with God's guidance, the sheep would find himself led to little hollows where water and grass made life possible and safe.

Life in the desert for both Shepherd and sheep is no soft, sun-drenched idyll on a south sea island. It is menaced by the dark shadows of the beast-infested valley. The threats to life are all around, but the presence of the Shepherd guides and leads, dispersing the threats.

The second half of the psalm (verses 5–6) exchanges the image of sheep for that of a fugitive: "You prepare a table before me in the presence of my enemies" (ESV).

In the ancient desert culture, if a man committed a serious crime, usually murder, and was in danger of his life, he fled to the uninhabited desert. The law of the desert was inexorable against that man. It was the law of blood revenge that would seek him out unremittingly. A murderer would be hunted down until found out. And if he was not discovered, the threat would be transferred to his son and wreaked on *him*. The desert was the home of the fugitive, but it was a horrible home, a home of fear, danger, and certain death.

But there was one huge exception to the unfriendliness of the desert for this man cursed by a past of sin and hunted down by the law of blood revenge, and that was the custom of open hospitality. One writer called it the "golden piety of the wilderness."[20] Every wanderer in the desert, whatever his character or his past, was received into a shepherd's tent as a "guest of God" (the Arabic term), furnished with food, and kept inviolate. The shepherd host took responsibility for his safety. This custom still prevails today in Bedouin cultures.

"You prepare a table before me in the presence of my enemies; you anoint my head with oil; my cup overflows." This is the fugitive speaking. A man threatened by his past, a man menaced by the curse of blood revenge, is welcomed into the Shepherd's tent, and there, "in the presence of my enemies," he is served a meal. In the Shepherd's tent he is safe.

---

20. George Adam Smith, *Expositor's Bible: The Book of the Twelve Prophets,* vol. 1, ch. 7, "Atrocities and Atrocities," Christian Classics Ethereal Library, www.ccel.org/ccel/smith_ga/expositorprophets1.v.iii.html.

—

The literal truth represented by the prayer of the psalmist is the truth of God. God in our everyday thinking is often relegated to beginnings and endings. We think of God as the force or power previous to all things. And when everything is finished, God will show up again. Somebody or something had to get things started, so God is permitted the honor. Baptism acknowledges this fact in the birth of human life. God is previous to us in love and creativity; in baptism we witness to his life and love. At the beginning of great enterprises—political terms of office, academic years, business enterprises, cornerstone ceremonies, etc.—prayers are often offered, acknowledging God's part in them. He is prominent in beginnings. And in endings God is present. At death the funeral service is a service of worship to God, remembering God's work in giving life and taking it, and witnessing that the end of our lives is not a diminishment of his action and presence. Likewise, at the conclusion of business careers, academic commencements, anniversaries, and birthdays, God is frequently acknowledged as being present and real.

But how about the in between, the large living interim between birth and death, the involved stretch between the start and the end? God is the first and the last, but how about what happens in the middle? It is this period we tend to belittle with our small faith. We think of God as our Father at the beginning, and we think of God as judge at the end. But God as our Shepherd guiding us through perils and sustaining us through fugitive years? Here we commonly fall short.

Psalm 23 is a convincing witness that God is our Shepherd, that God is the Shepherd who preserves us, accompanies us, and rules us. He doesn't just create us and turn us loose to make the best we can of it. He doesn't just let us fend for ourselves until we die and are hauled before the judgment seat for an accounting of our conduct. He is the Shepherd who guides us in our wanderings and sustains us in our fugitive lives.

Karl Barth, the towering pastor and theologian, who has taught me so much, puts it this way: "We need not expect turns and events which have nothing to do with His lordship and are not directly in some sense acts of His lordship. This Lord is never absent, passive, non-responsible or impotent, but always present, active, responsible and omnipotent. He is never dead, but always living; never sleeping, but always awake; never uninterested, but always concerned; never merely waiting in any respect, but even where He seems to wait, even where He permits, always holding the initiative. In this consists His co-existence with the creature."[21]

For the sheep in danger of the deep shadows in the valley, the Shepherd is a guide; for the fugitive pursued by the shadow of death, the Shepherd is a protective host. The Shepherd's rod and staff signal his leadership and a shared life of love and companionship; the Shepherd's table and cup anticipate his protection and sacrificial life of grace. For not only do we need guidance in life to protect us from daily peril, but we also need grace to free us from past sins, to deliver us from the tangle of bad decisions and faithless acts.

And how particular all this is, nothing abstract, nothing in general, but vividly specific: "green pastures," "still waters," "paths of righteousness" (meaning "straight roads"), "valley," "rod," "staff," "table," "oil," "cup," "house." The entire desert and range of experience of sheep and fugitive is brought into intimate and dependable connection with the Shepherd, a relationship of personal presence. To both sheep and fugitive, the Shepherd provides life and the conditions for living it. A personal God is protection and guidance on the one hand, and grace and refuge on the other.

—

The last word on Psalm 23 (as with so many of the psalms) was spoken by Jesus. They were often on his lips, and his life was a dramatic exposition of the best in them. "I am," he said, "the good shepherd" (John 10:11). He both spoke and lived Psalm 23.

There were, of course, both good and bad shepherds in Palestine. The final test of a shepherd was how far he would go in risking his life to protect sheep or fugitives. Would he lay down his life for them? Sheep can get themselves into dangerous and awkward positions. The decision to go into a deep and dangerous canyon for a single sheep at the expense of one's own life would not be an easy decision to make. And fugitives. Despite the nobility of the desert code of hospitality and the tradition of the "guest of God," neither fugitives nor the enemies hunting them down were harmless characters. A shepherd would think twice before welcoming a fugitive into his tent and seating him at his table, anointing his head and filling his cup

21. Karl Barth, *Church Dogmatics 3.3, The Doctrine of Creation* (New York: T&T Clark, 2000), 13.

in the presence of this man's enemies, who were out to kill him. A shepherd lived a dangerous life.

When Jesus announced to his followers that he was "the good shepherd" (John 10:14), I don't think they understood him to mean that he was a gentle, kind shepherd who would be nice to the sheep. They lived in shepherd country and knew something of the realities of a shepherd's life. Being a good shepherd meant taking the risk of life against beasts, robbers, and murderers (and they knew it).

And we know Jesus did just that. We know he entered Jerusalem when it was filled with shadows of hate and murder, and he faced on behalf of all the wandering sheep and fleeing fugitives of the world the combined accusations and assaults of religion and government. We know he blessed Judas Iscariot with a meal on the very night Judas betrayed him.

Jesus fills out in marvelous detail Psalm 23 in its entirety. Our Shepherd continues to work specifically and historically in the lives of men and women, guiding them, saving them—guiding *us,* saving *us.*

The prayer is filled with shadows, but the Shepherd is never absent: guidance and grace. Guidance for a wandering sheep and grace for a guilty fugitive. Guidance and grace triumph. The last words summarize what over a lifetime we can expect to experience: "Surely goodness and mercy shall follow me all the days of my life, and I shall dwell in the house of the LORD for ever."

But none of the ransomed ever knew
How deep were the waters crossed;
Nor how dark was the night that the Lord passed through
Ere He found His sheep that was lost.[22]

Amen.

---

22. Elizabeth C. Clephane, "The Ninety and Nine," 1868, public domain, www.cyberhymnal.org/htm/n/i/90_and_9.htm.

7

"Blessed"

PSALM 1
MATTHEW 5:1–10

The Scottish pastor Alexander Whyte, though he was long dead when I was born, became the faithful pastor and preacher who has influenced me most through these years in which I have been a pastor and preacher. Addressing a group of theological students, he said, "Ah! I envy you young men with your ministry before you, and especially that you have ahead a lifetime of explaining the Psalms to your people!" The delight and satisfaction in providing an exposition of Psalms, which Whyte felt so keenly, begin at the very outset. Psalm 1 stands before the whole Psalter as a kind of prologue. It was likely written last. In the editorial work that resulted in the 150 psalms in our Bibles, it is the finishing touch, defining the contents and fixing the atmosphere in which all of Scripture is prayed and lived.

Blessed is the man
    who walks not in the counsel of the wicked,
nor stands in the way of sinners,
    nor sits in the seat of scoffers. (verse 1)

The first word of the first psalm announces a sense of well-being, of wholeness, of happiness. It speaks of the person for whom "God's in His heaven—All's right with the world!"[23]

A number of years ago a middle-aged woman came to church here, her first time. I had just preached a sermon on David. As she left, she said to me, "I never heard that story before. Where have I been? I feel so lucky." She kept coming and frequently repeated her first response: "I feel so lucky." I thought at the time that *lucky* for her, the way she said it, expressed what *blessed* must have meant for David. I still hear echoes of her *lucky* every time I say or read *blessed.* A sense of surprise, unanticipated good fortune, a gift in a place you least expected it.

Later we got to know each other. I learned she had grown up in a family that was kind and good, but she had never been to church and knew nothing of the Bible. This was a new world to her. And through her, *lucky* became a biblical word for me. But I still prefer *blessed.* I have decades of association with it, which are not easily replaced.

Blessed took on a more extensive meaning for his followers when Jesus used it to anchor his first sermon, the Sermon on the Mount, by laying out eight ways of being blessed that they probably hadn't thought of before. Here, as in so many instances, "Christ captured the Psalms."

The psalm elaborates this blessed way of life by first describing the person "who walks not in the counsel of the wicked." As we travel this road of faith, this way, we are surrounded by others who counsel, advise, urge us in ways that guarantee our happiness. They support their counsel with statistics and document it by citing the latest sociological and psychological studies. But you and I, hopefully, are learning to not be impressed. We are learning to listen to a different drummer.

Neither do we stand "in the way of sinners." A more colloquial way of saying this is that we don't stand around or hang out with those who aren't going anywhere. They are "in the way," on the road, but each one "stands," making small talk. They make plans, dream up projects, are great conversationalists, but if we listen long enough, we realize it is mostly hot air.

And it stands to reason that we do not sit "in the seat of scoffers." A seat is a place to deliberate, to make judgments, to render decisions. And scoffers look down

23. Robert Browning, *Pippa Passes* (North Charleston, SC: CreateSpace, 2015), 17.

on those who haven't the sense to take a position. They sit in the company of know-it-alls. A place of cynicism, gossip, and superficial witticisms. They hold nothing in authority but their own cleverness. No judge sits over them; no counsel informs them. They are intoxicated with verbal wine and drunkenly survey the world, blearily reading into it their own confusion and malaise. C. H. Spurgeon, the famous British preacher, called them "Doctors of Damnation."[24]

The three rejected ways of living descend from "walk," "stand," and finally "sit"—from activity to passivity, from the dynamic to the sedentary, sluggish immobility, internal imprisonment. Dante's lowest denizens of hell were encased in a sheet of ice, frozen in their sins. The movement from "wicked" to "sinners" to "scoffers" is from the bad actor to the habitual wrongdoer to the person who is fixed in his ways and looks down on everyone else.

—

The blessed way of life is then elaborated in two phrases:

> But his delight is in the law of the Lord,
> and on his law he meditates day and night. (verse 2)

Here we are brought into the world of revelation, the Scriptures and Jesus, the Word made flesh. It is a world not of guesswork, superstition, and dogmatic opinions but a personal world of relationship between a God who is involved in our salvation as revealed in the Sinai Law of Moses, the preaching of the apostles and prophets, and the good news most comprehensively revealed in Jesus.

The way we take delight in this revelation of God, this Scripture and Jesus, is meditation. That is, we don't just read it on the run, don't just memorize a verse or two, but *meditate.* I wish we had a better word for it in English. *Meditate* gives the impression that it is something monks and nuns do in their monasteries or what you might do in contemplating a beautiful sunset on a beach. Something you do when you are really serious about God.

But here is a surprise. In the language of the psalmist, this word *meditate* has to do with slow eating, literally to slowly chew or masticate or suck on a lollipop.

24. Charles Spurgeon, "Psalm 1," in *The Treasury of David,* www.spurgeon.org/treasury/ps001.php.

My understanding of *meditate* in Psalm 1 took on a whole different meaning when I came across the same Hebrew word in Isaiah in the sentence "As a lion or a young lion growls over its prey" (31:4, NRSV). And I thought of a dog I once owned. When we were on summer vacations in Montana, he loved to explore the foothills where we stayed. He often came across the carcass of a white-tailed deer brought down by coyotes. Later he would show up on our lakeside patio dragging a shank or a rib. He was a small dog, and the bone was often nearly as large as he was. Anyone who has owned a dog knows the routine: he would prance and gambol playfully before us with his prize, wagging his tail, proud of his find, courting our approval. And of course we approved: we lavished praise, telling him what a good dog he was. But after a while, sated with our applause, he would drag the bone twenty yards or so to a more private place, usually in the shade of a moss-covered boulder, and go to work on the bone. The social aspects of the bone were behind; now the pleasure became solitary. He gnawed the bone, turned it over, licked it, worried it. Sometimes we would hear a low rumble or growl. He was obviously enjoying himself and was in no hurry. For a leisurely couple of hours, he would enjoy the bone, then bury it, and return the next day to take it up again. An average bone lasted about a week.

I always took delight in my dog's delight, his playful seriousness, totally absorbed in the "one thing . . . needful" (Luke 10:42).

Hagah is a word our Hebrew ancestors used for reading the kind of writing that deals with our souls. But *meditate* is far too tame a word for what is being signified. *Meditate* seems more suited to what I do in a quiet chapel on my knees, with a candle on the altar. Or to what my wife does while sitting in a rose garden with a Bible on her lap. But when Isaiah's lion and my dog meditated, they chewed and swallowed, using teeth and tongue, stomach and intestines. Isaiah's lion meditated his prey. My dog meditated his bone. You and I meditate the revelation in Scripture and Jesus.

And then this. The meditating person is

> . . . like a tree
>
> planted by streams of water,
>
> that yields its fruit in its season,

and its leaf does not wither.
In all that he does, he prospers. (verse 3)

Why a tree? Jeremiah, Ezekiel, and Jesus use the same image. In the semiarid Middle East, it was a conspicuous example of robust life: strength, beauty, long lived, great variety. A good image.

And I love this detail: "planted by streams of water." Which is to say that it is a domestic tree, not a wild species growing by chance. The "streams of water" are literally Babylonian canals cut into the desert to provide moisture and make agriculture possible in dust and sand. The Hebrews were in Babylonian exile when this psalm was written. They were the tree that had been the object of special care and cultivation, the knowledge and skill of the horticulturist God. Brains and purpose had been brought to bear on this tree.

The planning and planting are successful. The tree bears fruit and is perpetually green. Creation and redemption are effective and no illusion.

—

The wicked are not so,
but are like chaff which the wind drives away.
Therefore the wicked will not stand in the judgment,
nor sinners in the congregation of the righteous. (verses 4–5)

The wicked/sinners/scoffers with which the prayer opens have persisted in their diabolical conversation. They have persisted in their lack of seriousness and stubbornly maintained their course on roads that lead nowhere. Their ultimate end, *chaff,* is now contrasted with *tree.*

Chaff driven by the wind is the closest description of nothing that is available to the imagination. No weight, meaning, or use. Without meaning and responsibility, the wicked have no existence to speak of at all. Does chaff exist? It is the dried-up husk of something that once bloomed, bore fruit, and brightened the landscape. These *wicked* are far from what they had been created to be. They are now at the mercy of breezes and winds. No roots and no life. There is nothing to them, defined now only by what they are not.

The men and women we started out with, who made such a display of walking, standing, and sitting, are now, when it matters, unable to do any of that, totally without substance and strength. T. S. Eliot, changing the image slightly, provides a similar conclusion to this kind of nonlife in his poem "The Hollow Men," describing them as

> Shape without form, shade without colour,
> Paralysed force, gesture without motion.[25]

The terrifying conclusion to the life of the wicked/sinner/scoffer is the complete inability to *be* anything.

> For the LORD knows the way of the righteous,
> but the way of the wicked will perish. (verse 6)

The final two lines punch out the end result of these two ways of life, the life of the tree and the nonlife of chaff. The lead-off verb of the couplet, *knows,* is pregnant with gospel, almost literally, for it is the biblical word referring to the intimate sexual act, as with Adam and Eve: "And Adam knew Eve his wife; and she conceived" (Genesis 4:1, KJV).

Know in common usage among us mostly has to do with information. But in the Christian way, it is firsthand relationship, personal knowledge, historical, and existential. In Jesus Christ, God *knows* us, and then, because the initiative has been Spirit-given to us, we know God. But the knowledge is not speculative or literary. It is personal and experienced. In this knowledge we are in on the foundational reality of existence.

We are not finished with finding ourselves personally in Psalm 1 until we pay meditative attention to Jesus's comprehensive definition of himself in his last conversation with his disciples: "I am the way, the truth, and the life" (John 14:6, KJV). Jesus gives his life as an exposition, an incarnation, a *presence* of how this way works

25. T. S. Eliot, *Collected Poems 1909–1962* (New York: Harcourt Brace, 1991), 79.

itself out in our lives. We aren't left to ourselves to figure this out in working out the details of following Jesus. The way is not only the road we take to a destination. It is also the way we live on this road.

Psalm 1 gets our feet on the way of Jesus, reading and meditating on the Scriptures in a companionship in which we acquire a feel for the Jesus *way* of blessing.

Amen.

Part 3

"PREPARE THE WAY OF THE LORD"

PREACHING IN THE COMPANY OF ISAIAH

Introduction

Over a period of several hundred years, the Hebrew people gave birth to an extraordinary number of prophets, men and women distinguished by the power and skill with which they presented the reality of God. They delivered God's commands and promises and living presence to communities and nations who had been living on god-fantasies and god-lies.

Everyone more or less believes in God or gods. But most of us do our best to keep God on the margins of our lives, or, failing that, we refashion God to suit our convenience. Prophets insist that God is the sovereign center, not off in the wings awaiting our beck and call. And prophets insist that we deal with God as God reveals himself, not as we imagine him to be.

These men and women woke people up to the sovereign presence of God in their lives. They yelled; they wept; they rebuked; they soothed; they challenged; they comforted. They used words with power and imagination, whether blunt or subtle.

Sixteen of these prophets wrote what they spoke. We call them the writing prophets. They comprise the section from Isaiah to Malachi in our Bibles. These sixteen Hebrew prophets provide the help we so badly need if we are going to stay alert and knowledgeable regarding the conditions in which we cultivate faithful and obedient lives before God. For the ways of the world—its assumptions, its values, its methods of going about its work—are never on the side of God. Or, at least, rarely.

The prophets purge our imaginations of this world's assumptions on how life is lived and what counts in life. Over and over again, God the Holy Spirit uses these prophets to separate his people from the cultures in which they live and to put them back on the path of simple faith and obedience and worship in defiance of all that the world admires and rewards. Prophets train us in discerning the difference between the ways of the world and the ways of the gospel, keeping us present to the presence of God.

We don't read many pages into the Prophets before realizing there was nothing easygoing about them. Prophets were not popular figures. They never achieved celebrity status. They were decidedly uncongenial to the temperaments and dispositions of the people with whom they lived. And the centuries have not mellowed them. It's understandable that we should have a difficult time coming to terms with them. They aren't particularly sensitive to our feelings. They have very modest, as we would say, "relational skills." We like leaders, especially religious leaders, who understand our problems ("come alongside us" is one idiom for it), leaders with a touch of glamour, leaders who look good on posters and television.

The unrelenting reality is that prophets don't fit into our way of life. For a people who are accustomed to fitting God into our lives or, as we like to say, "making room for God," the prophets are hard to take and easy to dismiss. The God of whom the prophets speak is far too large to fit into our lives. If we want anything to do with God, *we* have to fit into *God*.

The prophets are not reasonable, accommodating themselves to what makes sense to us. They are not diplomatic, tactfully negotiating an agreement that allows us a say in the outcome. What they do is haul us unceremoniously into a reality far too large to be accounted for by our explanations and expectations. They plunge us into mystery, immense and staggering.

Their words and visions penetrate the illusions with which we cocoon ourselves from reality. We humans have an enormous capacity for denial and self-deceit. We incapacitate ourselves from dealing with the consequences of sin, from facing judgment, from embracing truth. Then the prophets step in and help us first to recognize and then to enter the new life God has for us, the life that opens up hope in God.

The prophets don't explain God. They shake us out of old conventional habits of small-mindedness and trivializing god-gossip. They set us on our feet in wonder and obedience and worship. If we insist on understanding them before we live into them, we will *never* get it.

Basically, the prophets did two things. First, they worked to get people to accept the worst not as a religious catastrophe or a political disaster but as God's judgment, and that not as punishment but as a way of setting things right. It can only be embraced, not denied or avoided, for God is good and intends our salvation. So judgment, because it is God's judgment, while certainly not what we human beings anticipate in our planned future, can never be the worst that can happen. We can see it as part of God's way of setting things right again, for it is the work of God to set the world—and us—right.

The second major work of the prophets was to get people who were beaten down to open themselves up to hope in God's future, to get them on their feet again. In the wreckage of exile and death and humiliation and sin, the prophet ignited the hope of opening their lives to the new work of salvation that God is working toward at all times and everywhere.

One of the bad habits we pick up early in our lives is separating things and people into secular and sacred. We assume the secular is what we are more or less in charge of: our jobs, our time, our entertainment, our government, our social relations. The sacred is what God is in charge of: worship and the Bible, heaven and hell, church and prayers. We then contrive to set aside a sacred place for God, designed, we say, to honor God but really intended to keep God in his place, leaving us free to have the final say about everything else that goes on.

Prophets will have none of this. They contend that everything, absolutely everything, takes place on sacred ground. God has something to say about every aspect of our lives: the way we feel and act in the so-called privacy of our hearts and homes, the way we make our money and the way we spend it, the politics we embrace, the wars we fight, the catastrophes we endure, the people we hurt, and the people we help. Nothing is hidden from the scrutiny of God. Nothing is exempt from the rule of God. Nothing escapes the purposes of God. Holy, holy, holy.

Preaching in the company of Isaiah we develop a comprehensive imagination. A new term, *globalization,* has been coined to account for the interconnection of everything and everyone. We are now required "to realize that who 'we' are is nothing less than everyone."[26] I prefer the more explicit term of Jesus—"kingdom of God"—an imagination that includes *all* under the rule of God, all nations and peoples and times in this together. In fresh ways we are learning to enter into the

---

26. Nicholas Lash, quoted in Donna Orsuto, "Walter Silvester Memorial Lecture," Melbourne, Australia, October 18, 2010, www.cam.org.au/News-and-Events/News-and-Events/Melbourne-News/Article/8948/donna-orsuto-walter-silvester-memorial-lecture#.WJ4gx2_yv4Y.

interconnectedness of everything and not just as disparate *things* but into the primacy of *relations*. Preaching in the company of Isaiah puts us in *good* company. Prophets expand our imaginations beyond our sectarian identities. Wendell Berry, one of our better contemporary prophets, continues to insist how important it is to have a sense of including and binding together all beings: the living and the nonliving, the plants and animals, the water and air, the stones and humans. All ultimately are of a kind, belonging together, interdependently, in this God-created, God-ruled world. Prophets make it impossible to evade God or make detours around God. Prophets insist on receiving God in every nook and cranny of life. For a prophet, God is more real than the next-door neighbor.

From the sixteen writing prophets I have selected Isaiah for these representative sermons. Isaiah is our most comprehensive prophet, our renaissance prophet, if you will, fluent in the language of revelation that delineates an embodied life of obedient faithfulness to the Word of God. When the ways and means by which God works interpenetrate the ways and means by which we work, we have a name for it: holy. The characteristic name for God in Isaiah is "the Holy."

1

—

"Holy, Holy, Holy"

ISAIAH 6:1–13
REVELATION 4:1–10

Isaiah is one of the looming giants in the human race. His life shaped the spiritual condition of an entire nation and has entered the Christian consciousness in a decisive way. You all know his name, know that he wrote one of the great books of the Bible.

I have no interest in putting one more name before you so you are more biblically literate than when you came here this morning. But I want you to be familiar with Isaiah so you will have some firsthand evidence of the way he lived and perhaps be nudged along into being that kind of person yourself.

Actually, we don't have a lot of information about Isaiah, not enough for even a sketchy biography. We have a vast treasure of sermons he preached and two or three incidents that define who he was and how he lived. The most comprehensive of the incidents is something that happened while he was at worship one day in Jerusalem.

Every Sunday I look across this congregation and wonder, prayerfully, what is going on. I know most of you pretty well. But there is a lot I don't know. I am here every week with the conviction that this place of worship is the most important place you can be right now, that the scriptures, hymns, prayers, and sermon can enter into your souls, your lives, bringing you into a deeper participation in eternal life. Not always, maybe even not often, but a lot goes on in this place that is formative even when you are not aware of it.

I have had enough feedback from you through the years we have been together to know that this hour of worship is an hour of potential miracle. Many of us will leave worship today the way we came, but even then, maybe we are not the same deep inside.

I mention this because the most comprehensive story we have of Isaiah describes a day in which he was in the temple in Jerusalem worshiping much as we together are doing right now. And the single word that sums up what happened is the word *holy*. It was the defining moment in his prophetic vocation.

—

But before the story of Isaiah and the Holy is told, a warning is posted in bold letters with a name: Uzziah. Everyone in Isaiah's world knew what that name meant: "Caution. Danger ahead. Watch your step."

Uzziah was king for fifty-two years in Jerusalem. (His story is told in 2 Chronicles 26.) He was a good king by all accounts. He subdued the enemy Philistines, built up a strong defense system and an impressive and well-equipped military, developed the country economically, and learned the fear of the Lord from his pastor, Zechariah: "And his fame spread far, for he was marvelously helped until he became strong" (2 Chronicles 26:15, NRSV).

Then he did a terrible thing: he desecrated the holy temple. His success at being a powerful king and the consequent popularity went to his head, and one day he arrogantly walked into the temple and took it over for his own purposes. He decided to take charge of his own soul and put God to his own uses. He went to the holy altar of incense (the same altar from which one of the seraphim would later take a coal to hallow Isaiah's lips) and proceeded to run things according to his own tastes and desires. The priest Azariah, accompanied by eighty other priests, came after him in alarm to prevent the sacrilege (only priests were permitted to offer sacrifices). Uzziah already had the censer in his hand and was about to make the holy offering. He lost his temper and angrily told Azariah and his priests to get lost. He joined the ranks of those who "close their hearts to pity; with their mouths they speak arrogantly . . . whose portion in life is in *this world*" (Psalm 17:10, 14, NRSV). He was king, after all, a very successful king with a long string of accomplishments, and he would deal with God how and when he wanted to deal with him as one sovereign to another.

The desecration had immediate repercussions: Uzziah turned leprous. The dread disease that in the Hebrew mind symbolized sin gave public visibility to the inward profanity.

What in Uzziah's mind was royal prerogative was in fact inexcusable sacrilege. It would be like one of us entering this church with a can of black paint and spraying graffiti on the pulpit and communion table, baptismal font and cross: "Under new management. From now on, I'm in charge here!"

Uzziah spent the rest of his life in isolation, banned by his leprous condition not only from the holy temple but from all contact with the community of holy people. He was still king but no longer in touch with either temple or people—the government of Judah in the hands of a man who defiled God's holy temple; the entire society and culture of Judah living under the shadow of unholiness, of desecration; Judah ruled by a leper king.

Uzziah posts a most necessary warning: hanging around the Holy is risky business. Holy ground is dangerous ground. The Holy is never, never something that we can take as if we owned it and use for our own purposes.

The contrast between what happened in the place of worship to Uzziah and Isaiah could not be more pronounced: Uzziah banished and Isaiah blessed.

Isaiah's experience in worship that day begins with a vision: "I saw the Lord sitting upon a throne, high and lifted up" (6:1). He describes the vision: a throne and royal robes trailing through the temple, blazing angel-seraphim hovering over the throne, each with six wings—two wings to cover their feet, two wings to cover their faces, and two wings to fly with. And then, as they hovered over the throne, they began to sing back and forth to one another.

> Holy, holy, holy is the LORD of hosts;
> the whole earth is full of his glory. (verse 3)

Then Isaiah felt the shaking of the foundations as smoke filled the place.

The hymn put into words what was experienced: *holy, holy, holy.* God is *other* than we are. *Holy* is a word that sets something apart. That which is holy is not derived from something we are or have. It cannot be related to something we know. It is "other than." It comes from outside. God is not a projection of our imaginations, not wish fulfillment, not a childish fantasy. God *is* holy.

At the same time "the whole earth is full of his glory." If *holy* describes God as way beyond anything we can imagine or approach, *glory* describes that which is here, close, evidential. I can see glory, touch it, weigh it. *Glory* in Hebrew literally means "weighty," something that has substance to it.

What I want to do right now is identify this place of worship, this sanctuary, this Christ Our King sanctuary, as our equivalent of the Jerusalem temple in which Isaiah was worshiping. This sanctuary is a set-apart place for worship, just as Isaiah's temple was. When you enter and take your place with other worshipers, you don't see God, but you see reminders of God, evidence of God—the cross, the pulpit, the communion table, the banners—all signposts to the glory. Each one, with its stories and history, carries with it a sense of the holy, expressive of a presence, God's presence, the holy God who is other than us and surrounds us with glory, his generous gifting of salvation.

This is where we are this morning. Before we do anything, we know this. There is nothing ecstatic about this. It just is. We need to get used to this. The place of worship is a channel, a channel in which God comes to us and we come to God. The place of worship provides a protected space for transactions to take place, our presence in God's presence. *Holy* and *glory* are two words that name what is going on: *holy* for the unseen, *glory* for the seen.

—

Isaiah's initial response to the vision is "Woe is me! For I am lost; for I am a man of unclean lips, and I dwell in the midst of a people of unclean lips; for my eyes have seen the King, the LORD of hosts!" (verse 5). In the presence of God, Isaiah is conscious of his sin, and he feels wretched.

There is no question that many people stay away from a place of worship because they don't want to be reminded of their sin. It is possible to do that, but you have to pick your associates carefully. You can usually find someone who is worse than you, more wicked, more selfish. In comparison with that person you don't look too bad.

But if you are playing that kind of game, stay out of church, stay away from the sanctuary that is full of reminders of the being of God. Consciousness of sin, of inadequacy, of unworthiness is a regular part of worship. We aren't what we should be. We fail miserably. In the words of one of the old confessions of the church, "We are miserable offenders."[27] Isaiah felt the full impact of that. His first reaction was despair. He thought he was going to die. But he was wrong. Consciousness of sin is a regular part of worship; despair isn't. Isaiah's anticipation was thwarted immediately. One of the angel-seraphim, using tongs, took a burning coal from the altar and touched Isaiah's lips, saying, "Behold, this has touched your lips; your guilt is taken away, and your sin forgiven" (verse 7). In this place of worship, sin is matched and then wiped out by forgiveness, the assurance of pardon. We don't confess our sins so we can wallow in despair but so we can hear the joyful words of forgiveness: "Friends, hear the good news of the gospel. In Jesus Christ we are forgiven."

Worship now opens a new dimension: *listening* to the word of God. God speaks to us. "I heard the voice of the Lord saying, 'Whom shall I send, and who will go for us?'" (verse 8).

God speaks to us. The word of God is at the center of our worship. God speaks to us in Scripture, in sermon, and in sacrament. It is the same word each time. The summary message is always, whether explicitly or implicitly, a question: Will we be God's people and do his bidding? Will we embrace his gifts and participate in his saving work? "Whom shall I send, and who will go for us?"

And so we come to this place of worship in Maryland just as Isaiah went to his place of worship in Jerusalem. We place ourselves in the presence of the Holy and in a world of Glory. We explore Scripture in detail; we try to understand its meaning in the language and culture of our time. It is not an easy task, and we repeat the task week by week. It is not as if we start over each time, but because we are a changing people in circumstances that are always in flux, we need fresh insight in order to stay alert and obedient to Christ's life for us.

Scripture and Sermon and Sacrament combine to develop a relationship

27. *The Book of Common Prayer* (New York: Penguin, n.d.), as part of the general confession in "The Order for Morning Prayer," 68.

between God's voice and our ears. We believe that God has something important to say to us, not just to inform us about the nature of the world, but to elicit our response. Questions and blessings and commands are the characteristic modes of address that get a response from us. God has plans that include us. Our lives are whole only when they are lived in dialogue with our Lord. The sermon is a weekly witness to that necessity to be open to the word of God and to be responsive to it.

—

And then the response: Isaiah says, "Here am I! Send me" (verse 8). Isaiah is immersed in a context of receptivity, ready and present, listening and obedient.

God is at work in the world beyond this place of worship. Worship is not just a private relationship with God. It is not just personal salvation. The world is included. Isaiah is called to participate in what God is doing. Isaiah responds and we respond. We pray. We name names: nations, presidents, friends, the sick, the anxious, the bereaved. We bring our offerings as a kind of down payment on our participation in God's work. For us it is usually money. In earlier times it was more likely to be animals or food. Someone would bring a goat and tie it to a leg of the communion table. Another would bring a bunch of carrots. A man would place a shovel beside the table, a sign that he was ready to dig a ditch. Today our economy is primarily a money economy, but the money is stored-up energy that can now be put to work in other lives. We declare our readiness, our obedience: "Here am I! Send me."

—

God has the last word: "Go, and say" (verse 9). God says, in effect, "Isaiah, you have been in this place of worship long enough. Now walk out those doors and live for others what you have experienced here. Give voice to *my* voice among the people in Jerusalem, your neighbors and the strangers on your streets."

This is the channel cut by the ecstatic vision of Isaiah, a channel cut deep into the Christian life by means of our worshiping habits. The ecstasy doesn't last, but it cuts a channel for something lasting. Occasionally one of us is visited by a vision that confirms Isaiah's vision, but mostly not. We learn not to be expecting such things. What we are regularly aware of is the shaping influence that worship has for life lived beyond the sanctuary, in our homes and places of work, among our neighbors—the reality of God as holy and this earth as a place of glory, the awareness of our failures and of God's reconciliation, the command that when obeyed enlists us as participants in God's holiness and the glories in which we are immersed daily.

There is a sense in which the hour of worship never ends. It is merely adjourned until the next appointed time for meeting. We are sent out with our hearts made right and our minds informed with God's plans for the world and our wills charged with response.

That's the pattern we repeat every time we gather in worship. It doesn't matter if we are bored with the repetition. It is cutting a channel for something lasting. Worship is the action that centers our lives in the holy life of God and sets us firmly in the glories of creation and salvation. Faithful and intelligent and reverent worship keeps us in touch with what is real.

Amen.

2

"A Garland Instead of Ashes"

ISAIAH 61:1–4
REVELATION 21:1–5

A single word can make a lot of difference. In today's text the word *instead* is repeated three times. Its repetition makes the difference between a life of gloom and a life of joy.

Instead is a word of exchange. Rather than one thing, there is another. In place of what we have or expect to have, there is something else. *Instead* usually represents a radical difference. It doesn't just add a little something to what is already here, nor does it take away a little of what is there. It contrasts and exchanges.

Look at what the three instances of *instead* exchange. First, "a garland *instead* of ashes" (Isaiah 61:3). In ancient cultures ashes were placed on the head when there was disaster. Burned-out debris placed on the head symbolized the desolation of the mind. The world burns out and hope fails. There is nothing of beauty or desire left. The ashes provide visibility for the inner experience of charred ruin. A garland, on the other hand, is placed on the head to represent jubilant victory. Fashioned out of laurel leaves or meadow flowers, it is woven in the shape of a crown and put on the head of a person who has won an athletic contest or is celebrating a birthday. The fresh, green leaves and colorful blossoms give visibility to the inner experience of exuberance and beauty.

And then second, "the oil of gladness *instead* of mourning" (verse 3). Mourning dries up the face. Tears streaming from the eyes and down the face leave, finally, a parched, dry skin. Through the days of lamentation, the face becomes a desert, baked and cracked by the sun. Oil, on the other hand, plentiful from the olive groves, restores softness and moisture to the face, loosens up the facial muscles, and softens the skin, and as the sun touches us, it brings out a glistening youthfulness.

The third *instead,* "the mantle of praise *instead* of a faint spirit" (verse 3), introduces the final exchange. A faint spirit is weak and lifeless. The person is inert, can't go anywhere, has no interest in getting out into the world, no strength to engage in work or recreation. He or she languishes in bed behind drawn blinds, not even getting dressed. No one to see. Nothing to do. The mantle, on the other hand, is the garment you put on when you go out into the world to do something or see someone. It is a piece of clothing that readies you for vigorous participation in the world. When you leave the house and throw a mantle across your shoulders, you are ready to work or play with confidence and zest.

The triple *instead* declares emphatically that an exchange is possible. A hundred and fifty years ago, trading posts were scattered all over the West. Trappers would spend months in the wilderness accumulating the skins of otters, minks, bobcats, beavers. But they didn't really want to keep those skins. They wanted something else. So periodically they would take their skins to the trading post and exchange them for food, for tools, for money. It still happens today in department stores. People bring in articles they received as gifts but don't really want. They don't sit around and feel sorry for themselves, wishing they had gotten something else. Instead, they take them back to the store from which they were purchased and exchange them for something they *do* want. Many of you have done it. Exchanges are possible. *Instead* is a gospel word.

Let me give you some documentation. The three *instead*s I just quoted to you were first preached by a prophet in Israel to a congregation that was very unhappy. The Jews had been in exile in Babylon for seventy years. And then the exile ended. While in exile, they lived for little else but restoration to their homeland. They had prayed. They had waited. They had remembered. The life of an exile is mostly a matter of fantasies and longings, and the Jews were exiles. They remembered the green fields, the fertile vineyards, the magnificent temple and city they had left. They remembered their homes and villages and the beauties of their festivals. But the first reports from their homeland were not encouraging. The holy city, Jerusalem, was rubble. The Solomon temple was a pile of rocks. The fields were overrun with brambles and weeds. Wild animals foraged in the vineyards. Nothing was like what they remembered. What was the glory in coming back from exile when it was to this they had to come? The entire nation experienced "ashes . . . mourning . . . a faint spirit."

And then this great prophet began to preach:

> The Spirit of the Lord GOD is upon me,
> because the LORD has anointed me
> to bring good tidings to the afflicted;
> he has sent me to bind up the brokenhearted,
> to proclaim liberty to the captives,
> and the opening of the prison to those who are bound;
> to proclaim the year of the LORD's favor . . .
> to comfort all who mourn . . .
> to give them a garland instead of ashes,
> the oil of gladness instead of mourning,
> the mantle of praise instead of a faint spirit. (61:1–3)

You are tired of exile? Take heart. There will soon be garlands, oil, and a mantle of praise.

The exchange did take place. This faint-spirited, mourning, ash-covered people came alive. They exchanged their faint spirits for mantles of praise, and they went to work rebuilding the city, refashioning the temple, reconstructing city walls. They planted fields and gardens. They restored the towns. Songs of praise began to sound in the streets and temple and synagogues. Some of the happiest songs ever written came out of this period and are collected now in Psalms.

Israel became a resurrection community. Their worship and study and service to God shaped a national identity and spirit. Eventually one person appeared in which the entire promise was summed up and exhibited: Jesus of Nazareth, who is the Christ. Five hundred years after the prophet first preached these words to the Hebrew people, Jesus, the Messiah himself, stood in a Nazareth synagogue and read from the Isaiah scroll: "The Spirit of the Lord is upon me, because he has anointed me to bring good news to the poor" (Luke 4:18, NRSV). After he read the passage, he said simply, "Today this scripture has been fulfilled in your hearing" (verse 21). And who today can doubt that it was? As Jesus lived out the prophetic role defined in Isaiah, all the great *instead*s became believable and operational in him.

The words and acts of Jesus became a trading post for exchanges. Look at some of them. A Samaritan woman spoke with Jesus at a well. She was a five-time failure at marriage. She was a member of a religious group that had failed. Her life was one failure after another, among a people who had a racial sense of inferiority. A life of ashes. Jesus spoke to her gently, firmly, and lovingly. He offered her the water of life. He gave himself to her as the Savior. Her life blossomed. She found joy as Jesus placed a garland on her head (John 4:1–42).

A Jewish ruler named Jairus had a twelve-year-old daughter who was seriously ill. She was on her deathbed. The house was filled with despair. Every heart there was a desert as the young life withered before their eyes. Jesus entered the home and raised the girl to health, new life. It was an anointing with oil. The faces once drawn and pinched in sorrow now glistened with joy (Luke 8:40–56).

A son left home with his inheritance and squandered it in reckless, immoral, irresponsible rebellion. A prodigal. He lost his pride, his purpose, his will to live—a broken and demoralized man. A faint spirit if there ever was one. He decided to return to his father and home. He was welcomed with a celebrative feast. His father's forgiving generosity restored him to the family: the best robe in the house was placed on him, a mantle of praise for certain (Luke 15:11–32).

The promise is clear: God invites us to make exchanges. The documentation is persuasive. Exchanges took place repeatedly with Israel and with Jesus. The expectation is reinforced in the final book of Scripture, Revelation, which entered the Christian church during a time of great suffering, with Isaian phrases that have kept the comfort current: "They shall hunger no more, neither thirst any more;

the sun shall not strike them, nor any scorching heat. . . . And God will wipe away every tear from their eyes. . . . Neither shall there be mourning nor crying nor pain any more" (Revelation 7:16–17; 21:4).

The possibilities for these transactions are embedded deep in the nature of the life that God creates in Jesus Christ: the ashes of disappointment traded in for the garland of hope, the mourning over sin traded in for the oil of a glad salvation, the faint spirit of depression traded in for the praise mantle of the God who makes all things new. Jesus continues to post his willingness to make the trades. Millions have done it. They continue to do it in this congregation. Jesus Christ is a most welcome trading post.

But I have a pastoral admonition to offer you when death or accident or betrayal occurs in your family or among your friends: don't use clichés; don't gloss over suffering with greeting-card sentiments. Be *with* the one who suffers, the one who grieves, the one rejected. Say little but be there as a silent, patient witness to God's *insteads*.

—

Outsiders to the gospel (and some insiders) stumble over what is sometimes named the problem of evil: How can an all-powerful God permit bad things to happen to good people? But I can't think of a better place than a congregation, *this* congregation, to live out circumstances of pain or difficulty. Jesus has the last word on what Isaiah first preached, in his second beatitude:

> Blessed are those who mourn, for they shall be comforted. (Matthew 5:4)

Amen.

3

"The Root of Jesse"

ISAIAH 11:1, 10
ROMANS 15:12

A prophet is a person who sees what God is doing and then tells us so we can get in on it. The most common misconception of prophets is that they are fortune-tellers with a crystal ball in which they see what will happen next year. We think it might be nice to have someone around to assist us in buying and selling the right stocks and bonds, choosing the proper political candidate, and betting on the right football team.

We could hardly be more mistaken. That is not what prophets are good for. Biblical prophets and contemporary biblically formed prophets are immersed in the present, what is going on in the present truly but maybe not obviously. If you are curious about the future, you will have to take your chances with your horoscope or Jeane Dixon, one of the best-known American self-proclaimed psychics and astrologers of the twentieth century, or one of a dozen or so radio or TV preachers readily available. But if you are interested in seeing what God is doing right now in our culture and contemporary history, a prophet is just the person to have at your side.

In Isaiah, chapter 11, we have a vision of something that is going on right now, as up to date as this evening's news.

> There shall come forth a shoot from the stump of Jesse,
> and a branch shall grow out of his roots. . . .

> In that day the root of Jesse shall stand as an ensign to the peoples; him shall the nations seek, and his dwellings shall be glorious. (verses 1, 10)

"The stump of Jesse . . . his roots."

But who is Jesse? Do you remember the biblical Jesse? That's right, the father of David, who was the ancestor of Jesus.

The sermon Isaiah is preaching to his congregation introduces the name of Jesse, who had been dead at least five hundred years at the time. And Isaiah is telling his people that a branch growing from a stump will become a tree, an "ensign." We would probably say "a large banner, a huge billowing flag."

Shoot and *branch* are vivid metaphors for life that is presently hidden in the stump but that will eventually become visible everywhere. But the word in the text that interests me right now is the word *seek.* "Him [that is, Jesus] shall the nations seek." *Seek* is a very important word for all persons who live by faith. Let's see how Isaiah's vision comes to feature this word.

A couple of months ago many of you took a day or part of a day and drove out to western Maryland or down the Skyline Drive in Virginia to enjoy the panorama of autumn color in the great forests of the Appalachian Mountains. These are splendid and beautiful forests that we are neighbors to. The forms and colors are magnificent, dazzling. When we look at them and walk in them, we are drawn into ancient orders of strength and serenity. Most of you have experienced these forests. You have seen them, appreciated them, enjoyed them.

Now imagine that one day you get into your car and say, "Let's drive to Hagerstown, spend a few hours hiking the Appalachian Trail, and enjoy the forest." When you arrive, you find that a gigantic logging operation has been underway and every tree is a stump. As far as the eye can see, there is not a single tree standing, only a cemetery of stumps. How would you feel? Angry? Depressed? Empty? Would you weep? Would you lose all interest in the world of nature and retreat into a kind of depressed paralysis? Or would you run around in a rage, bloodying your fists on the stumps? Whatever you did, it wouldn't do any good. The forest is gone. Nothing can bring it back. The trees are destroyed. All that is left is a wasteland.

That wasteland is Israel at the time of Isaiah's sermon. The Assyrian army had invaded the land and totally laid waste to it.

And then, while you are surveying the desolation, you notice one sprout of green. From one stump there is a shoot coming up. One stump has roots that under the earth are still alive and are pushing up, making a new tree. Your attention is diverted from the vast destruction to this surprising marvel of new life. Hope begins to build within you. There is something, perhaps, to be done. And not just perhaps. It *is* being done; you are looking at it. Things are bad, but they are not hopeless. Simply by observing that green sprout, you notice your feelings begin to change and your actions acquire purpose.

What you need to know about this picture is that I did not get it out of the newspaper columns but lifted it directly from Isaiah. I made only one change: I substituted the Appalachian range with its oaks and hickories and beeches for the Lebanon Mountains, famous for giant cedars. Otherwise it is just what Isaiah saw.

> See, the Lord Yahweh Sabaoth [God of Hosts]
> hews down the boughs with a crash.
> The topmost heights are cut off,
> the proudest are brought down.
> The forest thickets fall beneath the axe.
> Lebanon and its splendours collapse. (Isaiah 10:33–34, JB)

And then:

> A shoot springs from the stock of Jesse,
> a scion thrusts from his roots. (Isaiah 11:1, JB)

Isaiah's vision is charged with a hope and goodness that he received while standing in a field of stumps. He faced destruction with a congregation that experienced destruction and judgment. He knew thoroughly what was wrong with the world. He describes in other passages the painful details of human sin and human suffering and Assyrian brutality. I don't think there is anything you are facing or will face that Isaiah didn't face. But he was not stuck there. He was not reduced to the conditions he experienced. Within the emptiness and across the wasteland, he saw what God was already doing and would complete. He went on to describe it in such a way that we see it too.

In the midst of the Assyrian devastation, something new was being born—a shoot from the stump of Jesse. It would grow, blossom, and develop because "the Spirit of the LORD shall rest upon him" (Isaiah 11:2). Notice that the stump is now a person: from the stump of Jesse, *Jesus.*

> The spirit of wisdom and understanding,
> the spirit of counsel and might,
> the spirit of knowledge and the fear of the LORD. (verse 2)

Under the anointing of the Spirit, the sprout changes into a person, the Anointed One, that is, the Messiah, Jesus Christ, anointed to lead us into salvation.

Isaiah adds details. A new government: "With righteousness he shall judge the poor, and decide with equity for the meek of the earth" (verse 4). Even the animal kingdom will be transformed: "The wolf shall dwell with the lamb" (verse 6). And a thoroughly peaceable kingdom: "For the earth shall be full of the knowledge of the LORD as the waters cover the sea" (verse 9). This is not a superficial salvation slapped onto the surface of things but a deep transformation working itself out of the very heart of creation.

In another five hundred years, Paul will add more to this vision as he brings the first-century Romans into the picture by contemporizing Isaiah's text for his congregation with this: "May the God of hope fill you with all joy and peace in believing, so that by the power of the Holy Spirit you may abound in hope" (Romans 15:13).

And now, twenty-five hundred years after Isaiah, I am contemporizing it yet again, for you: first a sprig from a stump, then a righteous king ruling a peaceable kingdom, and finally the whole picture as it develops out of the life of God incarnate in Jesus:

> In that day the root of Jesse shall stand as an ensign to the peoples; him shall the nations seek, and his dwellings shall be glorious. (Isaiah 11:10)

Eternity is revealed in time, meaning becomes explicit, and hope is fulfilled. Everyone sees it. Everyone responds to it. "Him shall the nations seek."

About a month ago I was reading the newspaper at the breakfast table and learned that Elie Wiesel would lecture that evening at Goucher College. I determined to hear him, rearranged my evening commitments, and made the trip into Baltimore to find out more about this person who had for several years now interested and intrigued me.

I read my first novel by Elie Wiesel about five years ago. It was a powerful, moving story of an adolescent boy who was taken, with his family and all the other Jews who lived in his small Romanian village, to the Nazi concentration camp at Auschwitz. Later, after a transfer to Buchenwald, the boy saw his parents and his younger sister, along with most of the people he had grown up with, walk into the gas chambers, never to come out again. He wrote:

> Never shall I forget that night, the first night in camp, that turned my life into one long night seven times sealed.
>
> Never shall I forget that smoke.
>
> Never shall I forget the small faces of the children whose bodies I saw transformed into smoke under a silent sky.
>
> Never shall I forget those flames that consumed my faith forever.
>
> Never shall I forget the nocturnal silence that deprived me for all eternity of the desire to live.
>
> Never shall I forget those moments that murdered my God and my soul and turned my dreams to ashes.
>
> Never shall I forget those things. . . .
>
> Never.[28]

---

28. Elie Wiesel, *Night* (New York: Hill and Wang, 1985), 34.

I learned later that the novel was mostly autobiography. Wiesel grew up full of the stories and beliefs of Judaism. But his adolescent years in Auschwitz and Buchenwald left him with a heart full of ashes. The stories had been torn from his heart, the faith exterminated from his spirit.

He wrote the story over and over, each time disguised as a different novel. He changed the settings and the characters and rearranged the plot. But the story remained the same: the Jews, those people who are so strangely and insistently connected with the idea of God, were slaughtered on the most civilized continent in the world, the orders for their execution given by persons who listened to Mozart in the evening, who had been educated in the great philosophical traditions of Immanuel Kant, and who sang Luther's hymns in church on Sundays. Each novel has a similar conclusion: "My eyes had opened and I was alone, terribly alone in a world without God, without man. Without love or mercy. I was nothing but ashes."[29]

I read these stories and was deeply moved by them. Two years ago I found another book by the man and read it. But this one was different. *Souls on Fire* is a retelling of the old stories, Hasidic legends, that he had grown up on in his small-town Romanian synagogue. These were remarkable stories of the spiritual leaders in Judaism who emerged in eastern Europe in the eighteenth century and flourished for a hundred years in the villages and ghettos. It struck me as odd that a person who didn't believe in God should suddenly begin telling stories about persons who were passionate for God. This summer I read his *Messengers of God* and found Wiesel telling Bible stories, the narratives of Abraham and Moses, Joseph and Job.

That is why I was determined to see and hear Wiesel. My curiosity was aroused. What had happened to him? How is it that this tragic, Lazarus-like figure who had moved the world with his stories of the death of the Jews and the death of God was now telling stories about persons who lived by faith in God?

When he appeared on the lecture platform, with neither explanation nor apology, he began by reading Genesis 15, the story of Abraham, and spent the next hour leading us, an obviously secular audience of seven or eight hundred people, in what was essentially a Bible study. He said, "Nothing is worthwhile compared to this—searching Scripture, asking questions of the text, seeking the truth of God's

29. Wiesel, *Night,* xx.

Word." He was passionate. He was intense. He made frequent references to prayer. He was full of faith in a living God.

He didn't tell us how it happened, but he was evidence that it does happen: that a person can go through the worst, lose every vestige of hope, have every shred of faith pulled away from the soul, leaving it bare and shivering in a world where all the evidence says God is dead, live through that, and become a person of faith again, become convinced that nothing else is worth anything compared to discovering the truth and reality of God. Several times during the lecture Wiesel used the word *midrash.* "If we are realistic persons, honest persons, alert persons," he said, "then *midrash* will enter our lives." The word *midrash* is a Hebrew word that means "seek out."

You will recall that twenty minutes or so ago I quoted from the text for today: "In that day the root of Jesse shall stand as an ensign to the peoples; him shall the nations seek." I told you the word that had grabbed my attention was the word *seek,* the exact same word *midrash* that Wiesel gave such fresh aliveness to in his lecture, the root word in Isaiah's vision and Wiesel's lecture.

—

Out of that vast field of stumps, a shoot sprouts, and the sprout becomes a person anointed by God to save us. Christians have learned to identify him as Jesus Christ, raised high against the heavens as a banner, marking our destination, making it quite clear that God is our goal: "him shall the nations seek."

The opposite of *seek* is *dawdle.* To live aimlessly and listlessly. We either dawdle, or we live furiously, redoubling our energy when we lose our direction.

It is true that not everyone sees the sign and that not everyone who sees it seeks it. Which is why we need Isaiah's vision and the witness of persons like Wiesel and your faithful and attentive worship in this place where we set the Word of God over our lives so we can see what is true and be encouraged and helped to seek it. "To seek God means, in every part of Scripture, to cast all our hopes upon him."[30]

Amen.

---

30. John Calvin, *Commentary on Isaiah,* vol. 1, "Isaiah Chapter 11:1–16," Christian Classics Ethereal Library, www.ccel.org/ccel/calvin/calcom13.xviii.i.html.

4

"For to Us a Child Is Born"

ISAIAH 9:1–7
LUKE 1:28, 31–33

Once a year, on Christmas, my uncle Ernie came to church with us. The rest of the year he was a noisy unbeliever, argumentative and protesting. G. K. Chesterton once remarked that Aldous Huxley was always talking about the God he didn't believe in. That fits Uncle Ernie. So from an early age I knew he was not with us. But I liked him all the same. Of my six uncles, he was easily my favorite, full of jokes and fun. One Christmas when I was five or six years old, I was sitting beside him in church. The offering plates were passed, and I put in my nickel. He leaned over and whispered, "How much did you get?" At the same time he showed me, half hidden in his hand, a twenty-dollar bill.

He ruined my Christmas. I was ashamed to tell my parents or anyone else. Not only did my uncle not believe in God; he stole from the God he did not believe in. I kept hearing his words "How much did you get?" and seeing the edge of that twenty-dollar bill. It was several years before I realized it was a joke. And now that years have passed, it doesn't seem so much a joke as a parable. "How much did you get?" It is a pregnant Christmas question. It is a *gospel* question.

How much did you get? We are in the presence of what is *given.* Worship in this sanctuary is an act of anticipation and reception, realizing how much has been and is yet to be given by God for us. Saint John put it memorably for all of us when he wrote, "For God so loved the world that he *gave* . . ." (John 3:16). But Jesus was anticipated eight hundred years earlier by Isaiah's pungent sentence "For to us a child is born, to us a son is given" (9:6).

—

In the dark days of Isaiah's prophetic ministry, rumors were flying through Jerusalem of an impending military attack by the Assyrians. A glance over the walls of Jerusalem took in the sight of the enemy on every hillside. In the general panic, everyone was terrorized. "We've got to do something. We've got to get organized. What do we do? We've got to get our act together. Where do we start?"

Instead of offering a strategy, Isaiah preached a sermon. First, you need to know what has already been done. Are you aware of what God has done? Are you alert to what God is doing? Do you have any idea at all of what has been going on since God made heaven and earth and all the centuries since? If you devise a plan of action that doesn't take into account God's activity, you are going to do the wrong thing.

The basic, life-changing, mind-transforming, spirit-redeeming reality is not what we do but what God does. And he has done it. It is given. And the giving continues. It isn't something we invent or slap together hastily in our spare time. It is the massive, eternal, enduring gift of God. The world is given to us. We don't go out and buy it. We don't hire someone to find it for us. We don't acquire an education and training to make it happen. It is right here. Salvation is given to us. We don't earn it. We don't become educated for it. We are not trained into it. An expert does not package it for us. It is given.

So what do we do? How will we recognize it? Do we look in the newspapers for the breaking news? Do we put ourselves into the care of psychiatrists? Contemplate the sunset? Isaiah says it simply: "To us a child is born, to us a son is given."

—

God starts out where we start out: a child is born. He submerges himself in our biology, our psychology, our history. He becomes one of us so we can become what he is. He doesn't terrorize us with doomsday signs. He doesn't crush us with superior knowledge. He doesn't tease us with mysterious clues. He is here with us, in Jesus. God's way of revealing himself to us and giving himself to us is Jesus.

That saves us a lot of time and trouble. We don't have to look for God's presence in the skies, nor the schools, nor the churches, but in a child born among us.

God does not come as a mighty heavenly warrior, brandishing a sword and hurling thunderbolts. God does not come as a wise sage, calling a few superintelligent persons to a seminar at which he imparts the secret knowledge of salvation. God does not hide himself in the babbling brooks and whispering trees for us to piece together like some gigantic puzzle. No. God gave us a story: "To us a child is born, to us a son is given."

—

We ask, "Really? Can that make any difference? What can a child do?" Isaiah, we must remember, preached in desperate times. He was involved in an international crisis. He walked the streets of Jerusalem with persons stretched to the breaking point with anxiety, with pain, with fear, their hearts heavy with the burdens of sin, their arms aching from carrying the baggage of guilt. They were people like us—they needed help, they needed deliverance, they needed relief, and they needed hope. They needed all the things that persons who have been faithless and have lost their sense of integrity need, persons who have rebelled and lost a sense of security, persons who have trivialized the sacred and found themselves separated from meaning and reduced to boredom and banality. They needed a gospel adequate for their needs, and their needs were extreme and desperate. To such people Isaiah said, "To us a child is born, to us a son is given."

One would think that a thunderbolt would be more effective. Or something massive and worldwide like Noah's flood. Something attention getting like the fire and brimstone of Sodom and Gomorrah. Something spectacular like the battle of Armageddon. What they got was a child. What *we* get is a child.

—

And then Isaiah fills in the details. There is more to this child than meets the eye, just as there is more to you than meets the eye. Listen to this:

> The government will be upon his shoulder. . . .
> Of the increase of his government and of peace
> there will be no end. (verses 6–7)

If the way God reveals himself to us is to become one of us, the way he completes his work in us is to raise us to where he is: the government is on his shoulders—he takes responsibility for us. He bears the burden of us. His rule is not imposed so we are oppressed. It is a means of supporting and assisting and freeing us.

C. S. Lewis has a marvelous elaboration of this detail in Isaiah's vision.

> In the Christian story God descends to reascend. He comes down; down from the heights of absolute being into time and space, down into humanity; down further still, if embryologists are right, to recapitulate in the womb ancient and pre-human phases of life; down to the very roots and seabed of the Nature He has created. But He goes down to come up again and bring the whole ruined world up with Him. One has a picture of a strong man stooping lower and lower to get himself underneath some great complicated burden. He must stoop in order to lift, he must almost disappear under the load before he incredibly straightens his back and marches off with the whole mass swaying on his shoulders.[31]

Four names describe what God, via the child, becomes for us. The first name is Wonderful Counselor. He is not a dictator but a counselor. He listens more than he talks. He comprehends our needs and helps us find ways to meet them. He pays attention to us. When we are in his presence, we know we are significant, important, unique. And the result is that we find a will and the means to live with zest.

The second name is Mighty God. He is able to do what he sets out to do. And what he sets out to do is conquer sin, defeat the evil that would maim and cripple our aspirations to goodness. There is nothing passive about our Savior. He incarnates an aggressive assault on what is wrong with the world that will finally result in a new heaven and a new earth.

The third name is Everlasting Father. God is the origin of our existence and continues into eternity. He is no absent Father. There is continuity in God, and as we live in him, our lives have continuity. We escape the jumble of impressions and

31. C. S. Lewis, *Miracles,* in *The Complete C. S. Lewis Signature Classics* (New York: HarperOne, 2002), 401.

the chaos of experience. We don't have to start each day looking for something new to keep us going, to be happy or entertained. We have histories that accumulate in meaning and significance and worth, for we have both a past and a future in God.

The fourth name is Prince of Peace. As the prince rules, peace develops. He is thorough and complete in what he does. Peace is the harmony that comes from putting everything together so it fits. I try to get peace by getting rid of what irritates me; God gets peace by restoring everything to health. I try to get peace by getting rid of what I don't like; God gets peace by loving the unruly and unlovely into a life-changing salvation. I try to get peace by saying, "Shut up. I don't want to hear it anymore"; God gets peace by saying, "Be still, and know that I am God" (Psalm 46:10).

I want to pay attention to the fact that Isaiah's vision is not a sentimental picture of cherubic babies in whom everything is pure and innocent. The child does not remain a baby.

The four names are a frontal attack on all that keeps us from God, an all-out assault on what is wrong with the world.

Persons who don't yet see this are described by Isaiah as those who "[walk] in darkness." Those who do see it are described as men and women who "[see] a great light" (Isaiah 9:2). Many of us, maybe most of us, stumble around in darkness for years, oblivious to the light. And then we see. It is already given. It was only a matter of time before Isaiah's vision became fulfilled history in Jesus, who was born in a Bethlehem manger and walked in Galilee, touching, feeding, and speaking to all who came to him. At Calvary he conquered sin and the grave. He is now present among us, mighty to save.

—

Twice in the course of Isaiah's vision in chapter 9, the word *increase* is used. Near the beginning we read, "Thou hast *increased* its joy; they rejoice before thee as with joy at the harvest" (verse 3). And near the end of the vision there is this: "Of the *increase* of his government and of peace there will be no end" (verse 7). There is plenty given. It is given in a way you can receive it. What is given will do what needs to be done in you. It doesn't run out. It is inexhaustible. What is given increases week by week, year by year. What you got last week or last month is not subtracted from what you still have coming to you. "Of the *increase* . . . there will be no end."

Much as I liked and enjoyed my uncle Ernie, I must say that if he were in this congregation, I wouldn't trust him to supervise even the cribbery in our church school. All the same I have to admit that when he was in church, he asked the right question: "How much did you get?" For everybody gets something. A plate full of money is passed in front of you, the Word of God is opened before you, the praises of God are sung around you, prayers to God direct and bless you. With all of that given, surely you got something, didn't you? But how much?

The moment we ask the question that way, everything changes dramatically. The very reason we come together for worship changes. We are not here to find what is lost or perform a duty. We are here to receive what is given. How much did *you* get?

Amen.

5

"Speak Tenderly to Jerusalem"

ISAIAH 40:1–5
2 CORINTHIANS 1:3–7

As your pastor and a preacher of the gospel, I stand under the threat of some very solemn warnings that I'm not to say anything that will make you feel better at the cost of cheapening your lives, diverting you from the best God has for you.

God spoke through the prophet Jeremiah to the preachers of his day and accused them of healing the wounds of his people lightly by saying, " 'Peace, Peace,' when there is no peace" (Jeremiah 6:14). A peaceful, comfortable message may be an irresponsible message.

At another time Jeremiah fulminated against the prophets who were his contemporaries: "They say continually to those who despise the word of the LORD, 'It shall be well with you'; and to every one who stubbornly follows his own heart, they say, 'No evil shall come upon you' " (23:17).

A prophet and preacher can try to make things easy for people by baptizing the status quo, sanctioning whatever is going on, and making people comfortable in a selfish and irresponsible life by failing to challenge or expose them.

A few years ago Pierre Berton, a Canadian journalist, wrote a book with the title *The Comfortable Pew,* in which he renewed Jeremiah's calls to pastoral responsibility. People go to church, said Berton, to escape from painful grappling with the suffering of their times and their neighbors. Preachers have accommodated them by putting cushions on the pews, stained glass in the windows, and honeyed words in their ears.[32] (It is not without significance, by the way, that in this sanctuary there are no cushions on the pews or stained glass in the windows. This is not a place in which we cut ourselves off from reality. It is a place where we face the world as we find it, with courage and the whole armor of God.)

So I am keenly aware that when I say to you things like "God loves you; God will bind up your wounds and give you comfort," there may be people who, hearing it, will say, "Great, then I am well cared for. Thank you. I gladly accept that love and comfort." Words like *providence, love,* and *the compassion of God,* especially when the words come from a pulpit, can be used as an excuse for drifting and apathy, for not caring and not loving, for winking at the seriousness of life. "Woe to those," thundered the prophet Amos, "who are at ease in Zion, and to those who feel secure on the mountain of Samaria" (Amos 6:1, ESV).

When I hear words like these from Jeremiah and Amos, I want to put a label on the Isaiah text I am about to expound to you, a label like those on some bottles of medicine: "Dangerous. Take only under doctor's orders."

Are you well warned? Take care how you listen to Isaiah's words today. Will you agree not to use them as a sedative or narcotic? If you don't take the whole message as it is given in Scripture, it can be destructive, like putting on Band-Aids when our lives require radical surgery.

—

So. Are you ready? God says to Isaiah, "Comfort, comfort my people. . . . Speak tenderly to Jerusalem" (Isaiah 40:1–2). It is echoed unforgettably by Jesus when he says, "Come to me, all who labor and are heavy laden, and I will give you rest" (Matthew 11:28), to which Paul adds his voice: "Blessed be the God and Father of our Lord Jesus Christ, the Father of mercies and God of all comfort, who comforts us in all our affliction" (2 Corinthians 1:3–4). Isaiah's words continue to reverberate in the hauntingly beautiful tenor solo in Handel's *Messiah.*

Who needs such a message? Obviously, hurt and suffering people. There are many kinds of hurt and suffering. Israel in Babylonian exile certainly qualified. At the time of this sermon, Israel's exile was a couple of generations old. She was far

32. Pierre Berton, *The Comfortable Pew* (Toronto: McClelland and Stewart, 1965).

from her home country of Palestine and radically separated from the holy places of Jerusalem. Families had been broken up, the culture shattered, religious practices confused.

All the evidence indicates that economically and politically Israel fared quite well in exile. They were not mistreated by imprisonment or torture or even by consistent discrimination. But they were homeless. They longed for the holy places. One of their sung prayers was "By the waters of Babylon, there we sat down and wept, when we remembered Zion" (Psalm 137:1).

There was a great emptiness within, individually and socially. Their religion was mocked. Their worship of God was pilloried. Their memories of God's acts of salvation became nostalgic and remote. On a national scale they experienced homelessness. They had been wrenched from their homeland in a violent way. The change was sudden. Nothing was assured or certain. Most of them never got used to things in Babylon, the country of their exile.

But there was a deeper dimension to their exile than homesickness. They were in exile because of covenantal disobedience. They had made a choice as a nation to refuse repentance and spurn righteousness. The prophets had given them a hundred years of warnings, but they had persistently broken God's covenant. The threat of exile had hung over their heads for long decades before it became a reality. There was no confusion in anyone's mind about why they were in Babylon. This was the judgment of God.

So they were not only feeling uprooted from their land but uprooted from their God. There was not only the feeling of being a stranger outwardly but a sense of being a stranger inwardly, in their souls, their hearts. They experienced exile deeply and pervasively.

—

Looked at from one angle, we have no common experience with Israel at all. We are not exiled; we are not denied access to our holy places; our families have not been split up nor our culture destroyed. We might not be in the same town in which we were born and reared, but we are at least in the same country and speak the same language we learned from our parents.

But looked at from another angle, our experience is nearly identical with Israel's. One of the profound things about our Scripture is its accuracy in describing the human situation in such terms that persons in widely different times and places find themselves identifying in a personal way with what went on both then and now, there and right here.

Take uprootedness. It is one of the characteristic maladies of our lives. We suffer a loss of "at homeness." The world we live in is no longer the world we were born into. It has expanded through powerful weapons and machines, through space exploration, through information accumulation. It is an immense world where we haven't yet had time to find a sense of being at home. The world has been extended through the Internet, through rapid travel, through fantastically expanded mobility. We have been pulled two ways at once, outwardly and inwardly. We have been pulled up by the roots. We don't recognize a sense of identity with anyone. We feel like immigrants, like exiles.

And there is a new fragmented inner dimension to identity. No longer is God an accepted dimension of who we are. The world has been almost totally secularized. Guilt and anxiety are characteristic. If we could pin down how we feel, it would be not so much that God has left us alone but that we have wandered off and left *God,* and we feel both lonely and guilty. We have gotten far from home. There is a vast distance between us and our experience of God's presence.

Some of this is cultural, some circumstantial, some due to historical change. But there is some of it in all of us that is hauntingly inward; we are restless and anxious and homesick because we are away from God.

Erik Erikson is one of the better analysts of the human condition in these times. He says that our "discomfort over being all too rootless is rather well expressed in the joke about the man who boasted that he had paid five thousand dollars for his new electric automobile. In view of the smallness of the car, his friends wondered about the price. 'Oh,' he said, 'the car itself only cost a thousand dollars, but the extension cord cost four thousand.' "[33]

A sick person needs comfort because of being separated from health and vitality in his or her own body. The bereaved needs comfort because of being psychologically separated from a spouse or child or friend. The exile needs comfort because of

33. Erik Erikson, *Insight and Responsibility* (New York: W. W. Norton, 1994), 106.

separation from country and culture. All of us need comfort because we are separated from our origins in God and our future in Christ.

How does God comfort this person who is me, who is you? How does he close the gap that our sin has created? How does he get rid of that four-thousand-dollar extension cord we pathetically use to keep a connection with life and meaning? Isaiah has the relevant words.

> Comfort, comfort my people. . . .
> Speak tenderly to Jerusalem, . . .
> that her warfare is ended,
>   that her iniquity is pardoned,
> that she has received from the LORD's hand
>   double for all her sins. (Isaiah 40:1–2)

Israel was in exile as a consequence of breaking God's covenant with them. They had been well warned by Isaiah and other prophets that if they didn't repent, there would be consequences. And they did not repent.

Everyone knew that. Isaiah knew it. The people knew it. Nothing would ring true if that basic history was obscured or denied. But, and this is the important thing, that past was neither condemned nor condoned. It was accepted.

God did not say to them and does not say to us, "Quit your whining and sniveling. You only got what was coming to you. You were warned, and you didn't heed the warning. Now you are paying for it. Act like a mature person and get on with your work."

That response would have been true to the facts, but it wouldn't be the gospel. That would have meant they were still treated as persons who had failed and who couldn't walk a straight, righteous line. That would have meant the future would continue to be very much like the past, because they as a people could never maintain a national righteousness. That would not have been speaking tenderly. And comfort begins by speaking tenderly.

The people's unfaithfulness was not overlooked or whitewashed, but the people themselves were completely accepted. They were received by God as a forgiven people. They were treated sympathetically as a judged people.

We can learn from this. We can resist the prideful, superior "I told you so" when we come to assist someone who is suffering. Why is it so difficult to accept with grace and forgiveness the past that produced the suffering? We have a hard time realizing that the sufferer has already received not only what is due but double what is due. And because we have difficulty treating others in this new way, we have a hard time accepting God's treatment of us in this new way.

We suffer when we have been separated from what is vital to our wholeness—our bodies, our homes, our loved ones, our God. All these separations, though different in seriousness and ultimacy, feel the same. And they all have some personal guilt in them, for we all have some responsibility in the separation. That guilt needs to be acknowledged, forgiven, and accepted. If we deny it in either ourselves or others, we will never find out anything worthwhile about our past that can give us comfort and strength for the present and future. And worse, we will not recognize God's first words—note this—his *first* words that bring us comfort: "Speak tenderly to Jerusalem, . . . that her warfare is ended" (verse 2).

And then there is this: "In the wilderness prepare the way of the Lord, make straight in the desert a highway for our God" (verse 3).

When we're left to our own devices, one of our commonest ploys in comforting the suffering is to talk about the future even though we know nothing about it. We say, "Don't feel so bad. It will be better by and by." God's word about the future is quite different. It is not delayed; it is rooted in the present. God says, "In the wilderness prepare the way of the Lord." *Prepare*—present tense. "Don't build castles in the air. Don't construct an elaborate fantasy life about God's future for you." "In the wilderness prepare . . ." Right here where you feel comfortless. Here where the going is roughest. Here in Babylon. Here in Maryland. Comfort is not stored up in some remote future. Comfort focuses on the present. It is a particular, local present: "in the wilderness prepare." This dry, colorless, featureless, Babylonian desert that has seeped into the inner life of the sufferer—this is where the highway of the Lord is to be built. Don't try for some magic-carpet escape. Prepare for God's coming here, now.

He comes and changes things. The landscape is radically altered. Valleys are no longer dark, treacherous hideouts for bandits and bears. Mountains are no longer perilous, made miserable by icy winds and rocky paths. The valleys will be filled in and the mountains leveled. What has been a threat to our comfort and very existence will become the level highway of our God. It is here, precisely here, that "the glory of the LORD shall be revealed, and all flesh shall see it together, for the mouth of the LORD has spoken" (verse 5).

Friends, this is so important. Comfort is not something extra, like a soft pillow to moderate the discomfort of a lumpy mattress. It is God's word now, personally. A strong, challenging, energetic word that builds new strength and energy in you. That is what God's comfort does. Let Isaiah's words reshape your imaginations into the present tense. Let *my* words reshape your imagination into the present tense.

Hear this word of God and be comforted. Not in a future of fantasy, not in nostalgic longings for the past, but right now in your home, your workplace, your family, your heart. Build the Lord's highway right here. All the conditions have been met, your "warfare is ended," your "iniquity is pardoned" (verse 2).

And now that you have been spoken to tenderly, *you* can speak tenderly. Your tenderness will be able to tell others what God has told you, that *their* warfare is ended, *their* iniquity pardoned. This is what happens when God comes to his people. Christ was born for this.

Amen.

6

"Behold My Servant"

ISAIAH 42:1–4
MATTHEW 12:18–21

Behold is a favorite Isaiah word. All through the Isaian prophetic writings *behold* occurs frequently. It is a call to pay attention: "Listen to this!" It is most often used in relation to God, with an exclamation mark. It is the prophet's primary task simply to get us to pay attention to God. God first and foremost. Don't miss this!

God comes to us, but we are distracted, busy, preoccupied. The prophet's primary task is to pay attention to the presence of God in our world and in our lives. Before he can tell us about God, he has to get our attention that God *is* present, here.

Most of us have a sense of God, but more often than not the sense is vague, blurred, random—small gods privately formed out of our wants, needs, or wishes. But these trivial self-made gods scatter before the thundering prophetic exclamation "Behold!" We recognize that we need to "Stop! Look! Listen!" God is strong, loving, creative, wise. He is proclaimed to a people who are weak, hated, nonplussed, confused.

The central thrust of this attention-getting exclamation "Behold your God" is that God is mightier by far than our imaginations conceive him to be and that it is his will that we participate in this large God-life.

But there is a corresponding word that is equally essential and equally important: *servant.* "Behold my servant" anchors the text for today. *Servant* is the form in which God deals with his creation.

Servant is a word with low, even humble, connotations. It usually includes loss of freedom, economic restriction, a demeaned status. No one wants to be a servant. But in this passage of the prophet, *servant* becomes a major term. It is the key word in a series of four passages that focus on the way God works in this world as he deals with men and women in a redemptive way. It is one of the most prized and celebrated words for God in the Bible, but it is also difficult to assimilate in its entirety. Not that we have any difficulty understanding the dictionary meaning of the word. That is simple enough. But to get it into our imaginations, our prayers, our understanding of God that this is the chosen method of God to effect his will in the world? That is hard.

A servant is one who does things for other people. He or she is a slave in some cultures, in others the lowest person on the economic ladder. When we think of God, we instinctively think of the highest—power and might and glory. *Super*-natural. Often when things go wrong we say, "Why doesn't God *do* something? Why doesn't he intervene? Why doesn't he do something in keeping with his position as God of the universe?"

Well, a central concept in the Christian concept of God has always been that God *is* doing something. He is never inactive or silent. But he does not receive his directions from us. He doesn't conform his actions to our desires. But if we change our question to "What *is* God doing and where?" we get the prophet's answer: "Behold my servant." The God who in his majesty, strength, and wisdom is beyond our imaginations has chosen to work primarily as a servant who is almost beneath our imaginations, so far beneath we don't even notice him.

There are four servant songs in this part of Isaiah. This is the first:

> Behold my servant, whom I uphold,
>   my chosen, in whom my soul delights;
> I have put my Spirit upon him,
>   he will bring forth justice to the nations.
> He will not cry or lift up his voice,

or make it heard in the street;
a bruised reed he will not break,
and a dimly burning wick he will not quench;
he will faithfully bring forth justice.
He will not fail or be discouraged
till he has established justice in the earth;
and the coastlands wait for his law. (42:1–4)

The essential thing conveyed here is that *servant* is the word used to describe this person. There can be no doubt, no question, that God is totally at work in this servant. The servant *is* God: at work, the divine choice, the object of divine delight, animated by the divine Spirit, doing the divine will with universal justice. We must get this concept clearly in focus. No matter how or in what form this servant is among us, this is what he is here for: the sole agent of God's justice. I can't overemphasize this: complete endorsement, absolute authentication, credentials issued from God's ultimate authority.

The picture is of a true servant. He goes to work quietly and deferentially. He walks down the street and speaks in soft, conversational tones. There is no hard sell and no loud argument with anyone who chooses to deny or ignore him. In great gentleness he goes about his work. He will not break a "bruised reed"; a person who has little resistance will not be taken advantage of. A person who might seem like a pushover, "a dimly burning wick," he will not coerce. There is no element of necessity or force in his approach. His servitude is total. There are no humans alive, no matter how weak or useless, before whom he does not stand as a servant.

But this complete acceptance of the servant's role does not threaten the success of his mission. Quite the contrary, for this account concludes with the confident assertion that "he will not fail or be discouraged till he has established justice in the earth."

This is the way God works among us. We see the servant first of all working through the nation of Israel. Abraham was told "in you all the families of the earth will be blessed" (Genesis 12:3, NASB). Often weak and battered by political and military forces of the times, Israel nevertheless unleashed principles of justice that are the central roots in our world still. The Ten Commandments and the calls to morality and justice by the Hebrew prophets serve as the foundations of civilization. We have received our politics, our science, our philosophy, our economics from other nations, but the religion of Israel has infiltrated the world and is the root of the true and the good. She did it not by conquering but by being conquered. She did it not by shouting but by silently bearing witness, an unobtrusive servant.

But the servanthood established by Israel as a nation was not lived out completely. For the final and conclusive fulfillment of the servant, we go to Jesus Christ. The Christian faith is firm in its conviction that the form of a servant is fully and conclusively disclosed to our experience and understanding in Jesus Christ. Insofar as human experience can assimilate and insofar as human understanding can grasp, God is presented in his fullness as a servant in Jesus Christ. Do you want to see God as a servant in action? Look at Jesus, because Jesus said, "I and my Father are one" (John 10:30, KJV).

It is important, I think, to keep in mind that the God we are talking about and who is disclosed in Jesus Christ is the God of Isaiah 40: the God who sits above the earth in power and might, who holds the nations in the palm of his hand, and to whom the peoples of the earth are a drop in a bucket. With that in mind, what do we see when we see Jesus? We see God in action in the world. And we see him in action as a servant.

Though there were many auspicious signs that preceded and accompanied Jesus's birth that might have prepared us for something kingly and special, the birth of Jesus was of the humblest peasant parentage in an unimportant town and in the lowest conceivable of buildings, a stable. After his birth he moved from there to a despised portion of the country, Galilee, to an unsavory town, Nazareth. As he grew up, he took a blue-collar job as a carpenter. He achieved a measure of notice as an adult when he was a rabbi with several men and women following him, but even then he went out of his way to reject marks of status by touching lepers, washing the feet of his followers, befriending little children, letting women become prominent in his entourage, and finally being crucified under the most humiliating circumstances.

Everything about Jesus spoke of servitude. He said things that led some to proclaim him the Son of God, and he performed healings that were consistent with those words, but the *form* he took was that of a servant. There was nothing flashy or overwhelming about the life of Jesus. He was unobtrusive and quiet. He did not break any bruised reeds or quench any dimly burning wicks. In Saint Paul's words, "Though he was in the form of God, [he] did not count equality with God a thing to be grasped, but emptied himself, taking the form of a servant, being born in the likeness of men. And being found in human form he humbled himself and became obedient unto death, even death on a cross" (Philippians 2:6–8).

Jesus interpreted the life he was living with the story of the mustard seed, the smallest seed on the farm, which grows to be the greatest of shrubs. And the way of life he pursued was like yeast in bread: almost unseen when placed in a loaf but spreading throughout the dough and becoming a staple of life. The smallness becomes large and nutritious. This is the regular way in which God works his will in the world (Matthew 13:31–33).

—

Stories like these are important so we learn to recognize God in the unimportant and easily missed details but also so we might learn to recognize the same things in our own lives. He has called us to embrace his methods and be servants ourselves. The way of the world is to use power and coercion to get things done; the way of the Christian is to use love, gentleness, and service to redeem the race. The world uses the authority of kings and generals to compel justice; the Christian becomes a servant and provides justice.

Jesus said, "If I then, your Lord and Teacher, have washed your feet, you also ought to wash one another's feet. For I have given you an example, that you also should do as I have done to you. Truly, truly, I say to you, a servant is not greater than his master; nor is he who is sent greater than he who sent him. If you know these things, blessed are you if you do them" (John 13:14–17).

—

As we let this attention-getting "Behold my servant" penetrate our imaginations, we find ourselves becoming accustomed to recognizing the presence and work of God in ways that, for some of us at least, will be quite new and refreshing. God's way, this servant God, always descends in order to ascend. We take our place with him at the foot of the table so that by God's grace we might be raised to a place of honor, becoming small in order to become great.

Behold my servant, whom I uphold.

Amen.

7

"Strengthen the Weak Heart"

ISAIAH 35:3
HEBREWS 12:1–4

Have you ever been interrupted by Isaiah 35? If you haven't, you have missed one of God's great surprises.

I was reading a novel recently, and in the middle of a page, I began to get angry with the author. The main character was a thoroughly unlovely person, although nearly everyone around her thought she was charming. She interfered in other people's lives in the most intolerable and insensitive ways, making a thorough mess of emotions and relationships. "She can't do that!" I found myself saying to the author (although she had been dead for 150 years). "You can't let her get by with that!" And then I noticed I was only on page 103 with 276 pages to go. I recalled that in other novels by this author, things always get sorted out in the end, leaving me with a feeling of rightness. I was tempted to turn to the last couple of chapters and get to the end of the story, but I resisted, remembering that much of the satisfaction of the conclusion comes from giving my imagination to the contradictions and ambiguities of the plot. I am not absolutely sure the novel is going to turn out satisfactorily, but since I have read four other books by this writer and in each one she has managed to put it all together for me, I have fairly good expectations. Right now, though, I am thoroughly fed up with Jane Austen's *Emma.*

Just as I get thoroughly fed up at times with God's *Eugene.* God created me and inserted me as a character in the story of salvation. Sometimes I don't like the position I have in the plot. I don't like what I do and say. I don't like what other people do and say to me. I don't like the way things are going at all, and I get angry with the author. "If you are writing a story of salvation, surely you can make it more satisfactory than this!"

And then I get interrupted by Isaiah 35. The interruption forces me to observe that the story is not yet finished. When you yourself are in the story, you never know how near you are to the end. There may be a surprise ending on the next page, or it may go on for a thousand pages. But for as long as you are conscious of being in a story at all, it is not finished.

The interruption makes me aware, too, that I am not the only character created by the Divine Mind. There are many other persons created and led by my Lord. In the reading of Scripture, I find a magnificent salvation story, a glorious beginning and a magnificent ending holding together an intricate plot of God's love and of human sin, with all of it coming to focus and climax in the revelation—life, crucifixion, and resurrection—of Jesus Christ.

The interruption gives me a chance to catch my breath. I calm down and see that the contradictions, the inconsistencies, the impossibilities, the unresolved tensions, the lack of balance between reward and punishment, disappointment and blessing—all of these are materials in the process of being used by a master artist whose plot, I have many good reasons for believing, includes my personal salvation and the rest of the world's salvation.

—

I don't know exactly where *you* are in the Christian story this morning. We read and live at different speeds. Some of us zip along with great ease; others of us are plodders having to stop frequently to look up words in the dictionary. The chances are that none of us is on the same page this morning. But we have all had the feelings of dissatisfaction with the way our lives are going, and we have all raised questions with God: "Why am I plagued with this anxiety? Why do others seem to get all the breaks while I get one dose of bad luck after another? Why did this person whom I love so much die? Why doesn't my life seem to have any direction? How do these other people fit into God's will? Can I ever recover from this mistake I have just made? Can anything possibly be salvaged from it?"

Wherever you are right now in the story, I am going to interrupt you with Isaiah 35.

The wilderness and the dry land shall be glad,
the desert shall rejoice and blossom;
like the crocus it shall blossom abundantly,
and rejoice with joy and singing. (verses 1–2)

There is nothing wrong with a desert that a little rain can't fix. Dry land is not inherently barren; the dirt itself is not evil. We are after all "formed . . . of dust from the ground" (Genesis 2:7). And no one's life is apart from that basic ground from which God can bring his purposes to blossom. There are stretches of time when nothing is growing, but all the while nutrients are in the soil and seeds embedded just beneath the surface. A moment will come when the necessary moisture will bring faith to flower.

Strengthen the weak hands,
and make firm the feeble knees.
Say to those who are of a fearful heart,
"Be strong, fear not!
Behold, your God
will come with vengeance,
with the recompense of God.
He will come and save you." (verses 3–4)

You think that you have all you can take? That you can't lift another burden? That you can't manage another challenge? Well, "Be strong . . . ! Behold, your God." God comes. He comes in "vengeance." He will take care, decisively and completely, of all that is wrong with the story. He comes with "recompense." He will provide everything to make you whole and mature. The word *recompense* has a root meaning of "weaning from the mother's breast." A happy time, for it means you are making a transition from being a weak and dependent infant, but it's a terrifying time too, for it means you are no longer treated indulgently as an innocent. "He will come and save you." Everything God does is woven into the plot for your salvation—the judgments on your sin, the weaning from your innocence, the gifts of maturity. At the end of the story, for you who choose to be his people, you will have a put-together life, a life vibrant with health, a life whole and solid in love.

> Then the eyes of the blind shall be opened,
> and the ears of the deaf unstopped;
> then shall the lame man leap like a hart,
> and the tongue of the dumb sing for joy. (verses 5–6)

Every tragedy we experience will, finally, become a triumph. Every deficiency in our ability to see or hear or walk or speak will be healed by grace. Everything in our bodies that does not work will, finally, be made workable to the glory of God. Everything in our souls that does not respond to the will of God will become, through the power of forgiveness and the ministrations of mercy, an instrument of peace. The wholeness will be achieved on every level: material, physical, spiritual, personal, social.

But—now listen to me carefully—Jesus, by healing the blind and deaf and dumb and lame, makes sure we do not misinterpret Isaiah 35 by spiritualizing it, making poetic figures of it, symbolizing defects in our character. But Jesus also, by *not* healing all the blind and deaf and dumb and lame, makes sure we will not misinterpret Isaiah 35 by secularizing it, short-cutting God's purposes by trying to fix in our own strength all that ails the world and us. The wholeness will be the wholeness of the entire new creation brought to a redeemed finish. Every hour of every day we live is a word or sentence or paragraph of the story that will finally come to these conclusions. Which is why we sing, as we sang in last Sunday's worship, "Praise with elation, praise every morning, God's re-creation of the new day!"[34]

> And a highway shall be there,
> and it shall be called the Holy Way; . . .
> And the ransomed of the LORD shall return,
> and come to Zion with singing;

34. Eleanor Farjeon, "Morning Has Broken," 1931, www.namethathymn.com/christian-hymns/morning-has-broken-lyrics.html.

everlasting joy shall be upon their heads;
they shall obtain joy and gladness,
and sorrow and sighing shall flee away. (verses 8, 10)

One of our greatest and most knowledgeable pastors and preachers of Isaiah, John Calvin, commented on this passage to his congregation with these words:

> God not only begins, but conducts to the end, the work of our salvation, that his grace in us may not be useless and unprofitable. As he opens up the way, so he paves it, and removes obstacles of every description, and is himself the leader during the whole journey. In short, he continues his grace towards us in such a manner that he at length brings it to perfection.[35]

This "way" that Calvin speaks of is the way of faith in Jesus Christ, on which we are traveling (Acts 9:2; 19:23; 24:22). My paraphrase to you this morning is "You who put your faith in Jesus Christ are, even now, on this way. For did not our Lord say, 'I am the way'?" (John 14:6).

Some novelists in writing their books use a technique called a flashback. Instead of taking us day by day, year by year through the story, the writer begins in midstream and then every once in a while interrupts the flow by inserting an episode from the past. At an appropriate time you get the background and history you need to understand what is going on right now in the story. But no more than you need. What you don't need to know is omitted. We trust the writer. That way our attention stays in the present with only occasional and brief digressions into the past to keep a sense of coherence and depth. Biblical writers also do that, but sometimes they also flash-forward, a brief glance ahead. Just enough to inform us that there really *is* a future and that it makes sense and that we are included in it. The Bible is not *about* the future. "It is unwise," one of our wise guides in reading the Bible tells us, "for Christians to claim any knowledge of either the furniture of heaven or the temperature

35. John Calvin, *Commentary on Isaiah,* vol. 3, "Isaiah 35:1–10," Christian Classics Ethereal Library, www.ccel.org/ccel/calvin/calcom15.iv.i.html.

of hell."[36] The Bible is the revelation of God, personally told in such a way as to enlist our present participation in the all-inclusive story of salvation. But inserted from time to time through the story, there are confidently etched anticipations of the coming conclusion. Isaiah 35 is one of these.

If you were to sit down and read the book of Isaiah from the beginning, if you are at all like me, by chapter 34 you would be ready to quit. Everything has fallen apart, nothing is working, and the debris of failed morality and the wreckage of defective faith litter the landscape. And then, just in time to prevent you from closing the book in despair or disgust, is chapter 35. It is not the only instance of this kind of thing in the Bible. If fact, those who live by faith find themselves interrupted this way with fair frequency. It is the kind of thing William Cowper describes in his hymn: "Sometime a light surprises the child of God who sings; it is the Lord who rises with healing in his wings; when comforts are declining, he grants the soul again a season of clear shining to cheer it after rain."[37]

For you who have lost interest in your own story because it doesn't seem to be going anywhere, for you who are displeased with your story because it doesn't seem to be working out fairly, for you who are tired of your story because it has gone on too long without your getting anything out of it, put yourself into the Isaiah 35 story, God's personal gift.

> Be strong, fear not!
> Behold, your God . . .
> He will come and save you. (verse 4)

Amen.

---

36. Reinhold Niebuhr, *The Nature and Destiny of Man: A Christian Interpretation,* 2 vols. (New York: Scribner's, 1964), 2:294.
37. William Cowper, "Sometimes a Light Surprises," 1779, www.hymnary.org/text/sometimes_a_light_surprises.

Part 4

"ON EARTH AS IT IS IN HEAVEN"

PREACHING IN THE COMPANY OF SOLOMON

Introduction

Many people think what is written in the Bible mostly has to do with getting people into heaven, getting them right with God, saving their eternal souls. It does have to do with that, of course, but not *mostly.* It is equally concerned with living on this earth—living well, living in robust sanity. In our Scriptures heaven is not the primary concern to which earth is a tag-along afterthought. "On *earth* as it is in heaven" is Jesus's prayer (Matthew 6:10).

There is a distinctive strain of writing in the Bible that more or less specializes in dealing with human experience just as it is. *Wisdom* is the biblical term for this on-earth-as-it-is-in-heaven living. *This* is what is involved in being human, and don't you forget it. In the Hebrew tradition, the name of King Solomon was especially honored as a source of wisdom (1 Kings 10:1–10) and is reinforced by Jesus referring to "the wisdom of Solomon" (Luke 11:31). And so the wisdom books have traditionally been grouped under Solomon's name, even though it is likely he did not write all of them.

The word *wisdom* in this context refers more to a kind of seasoned, thoughtful attitude or distinctive stance than to any particular ideas or doctrines or counsel. As such, wisdom is wide ranging, collecting under its umbrella diverse and unlikely fellow travelers. What keeps the feet of these fellow travelers on common ground is wisdom's unrelenting insistence that nothing in human experience can be omitted or slighted if we decide to take God seriously and respond to him believingly. As we preach in the company of Solomon, we develop a quotidian imagination, an imagination soaked in the ordinary, the everyday. Kathleen Norris, with her remarkable book *The Quotidian Mysteries,* has done for us what Brother Lawrence, a lay brother with the Discalced Carmelites, did for his contemporaries in the seventeenth century with *The Practice of the Presence of God.*

It is somewhat common among people who get interested in religion or God to get proportionately *dis*interested in their jobs and families, their communities and their colleagues. The more of God, the less of the human. But that is not the way God intends it. Wisdom counters this tendency by giving witness to the precious nature of human experience in all its forms, whether or not it feels or appears "spiritual."

Proverbs and Ecclesiastes, Song of Solomon and Job, and Psalms serve as our primary witnesses to biblical wisdom. It is not as if wisdom is confined to these books, for its influence is pervasive throughout Scripture. But in these books human experience as the arena in which God is present and working is placed front and center. The comprehensiveness of these five witnesses becomes evident when we set Psalms at the center and then crisscross that center with the other four books arranged as two sets of polarities: Song of Solomon and Job, then Proverbs and Ecclesiastes.

Psalms is the magnetic center, pulling every scrap and dimension of human experience into a prayerful response to God. The psalms are quite indiscriminate in their subject matter: complaints and thanks, doubt and anger, outcries of pain and outbursts of joy, quiet reflection and boisterous worship. If it's *human,* it qualifies. Any human experience or thought can be prayed. Eventually it all *must* be prayed if it is to retain—or recover—its essential humanity. The totality of God's concern with the totality of our humanity is then elaborated by means of the two polarities.

The psalms have been explored already in part 2 as "Preaching in the Company of David." "Preaching in the Company of Solomon" deals with the two polarities. The Song of Solomon-Job polarity sets the ecstatic experience of love in tension with the extreme suffering of loss and devastation. The Song sings the exuberance and joy of two lovers finding their lives joined in intimacy. Job rages in pain and protest in the company of self-righteous "friends" who put all the blame on him. We find ourselves in the company of someone who discovered that the worst that can happen to us has already been staked out as *God's* territory as he hears God speak "out of the whirlwind" (Job 38:1).

The life of faith has to do with the best that comes our way; the life of faith has to do with the worst that comes our way. Neither cancels out the other; neither takes precedence over the other.

And the Proverbs-Ecclesiastes polarity? Pithy Proverbs sharpens our observations and insights regarding all that is going on around us so we realize that unobtrusive, undramatic dailiness is sacred: work and family, money and sex, the use of language and the expression of emotions. We are reminded in detail that there is meaning in the ordinary, in the everyday, in being responsible for and alert to what we have been given to do in this life of faith. In contrast, Ecclesiastes (or "The Preacher") has to do with doggedly putting one foot in front of the other as we fix flat tires, wash dirty dishes, and pull weeds from gardens.

The life of faith has to do with the satisfactions of living a responsible life and also with the boredom of dealing with the same old routines, wondering what the point of it all is. Neither cancels out the other; neither takes precedence over the other.

In such ways, these wisdom writers keep us honest with and attentive to the entire range of human experience that God the Spirit uses to fashion a life of holy salvation in each one of us. God and God's ways provide the comprehensive plot and sovereign action in the Holy Scriptures, but human beings—every last man and woman of us, as well as every detail involved in our daily living—are invited and honored participants in all of it. There are no spectator seats provided for the drama of salvation. There is no "bench" for incompetent players.

I

—

"Many Waters Cannot Quench Love"

SONG OF SOLOMON 8:6–7
1 CORINTHIANS 13:4–8

She came to see me at the recommendation of a friend. She had been troubled for years, seeing psychiatrists one after another and not getting any better. The consultation had been arranged on the telephone so that when she walked into my study, it was a first meeting. Her opening statement was "Well, I guess you want to know all about my sex life. That's what they all want to know." I answered, "If that is what you want to talk about, I'll listen. What I would *really* be interested in learning about is your prayer life."

She didn't think I was serious, but I was. I was interested in the details of her prayer life for the same reason her psychiatrists had been interested in the details of her sex life—to find out how she handled intimate relationships. I had to settle for the details of her sex life at that time. Sex was the only language she knew for describing relationships of intimacy. At a later time, when she came to understand herself in relation to a personal God, she also learned to use the language of prayer.

I tell you this story because it juxtaposes two things that crisscross constantly in living the Christian life: sexuality and prayer. And it juxtaposes them in such a way as to show that they are both aspects of a single, created thing: a capacity for relational intimacy.

—

One more thing that I think might surprise you. I want you to know that the Song of Solomon was at one time the most read, most popular, and most preached-from book in the Bible. Yet I have been preaching for ten years and have never preached a sermon from any part of it. Nevertheless, there was a time in the church when its lyrical love songs were familiar to every Christian and Jew. Bernard of Clairvaux, one of the best preachers of the Middle Ages, preached eighty-six sermons from the Song and didn't get much past the second chapter. Origen, an early church father who has the reputation of being by far the best biblical scholar ever, wrote a twelve-volume commentary on the Song. Rabbi Akiba, one of the most respected rabbis among the Hebrews, famously said, "For the whole world is not as worthy as the day on which the Song of Songs was given to Israel; for all the writings are holy but the Song of Songs is the Holy of Holies."[38]

For as far back as we have any evidence, both Jews and Christians have read the book as a description of a life of meditation and prayer.

My pastoral concern is not that you make this your new prayer book. I'm not sure that would work in this American culture, where sex is treated by far too many as recreational and not as a matter of love and intimacy. But I do think we all need to at least know that, deep in our Scriptures and traditions, there is an enormous dignity given to the body and its beauty and holiness. God created us with bodies, after all, and they are the means by which we love one another and God, and not just in a marginal way but perhaps most of all. When God chose to reveal himself to us completely, he didn't do it in words or ideas. He became flesh and lived in the neighborhood with us. Which means that our bodies are capable of receiving God and participating in God, not just with our minds or our emotions or our "hearts" as we sometimes say, but with these actual flesh-and-blood, skin-and-muscle *bodies.*

—

The full title of this book is "Song of Songs, which is Solomon's." That is a way of saying that this is the best song of any that has ever been sung. Solomon gave the inspiration for it. He stood for what is expressed in this book.

38. Rabbi Akiba, quoted in *Seder Tohoroth: Yadayim,* http://halakhah.com/pdf/taharoth/Yadayim.pdf, 6.

My intent with you this morning is not to tell you all you need to know to appreciate this book but just enough to realize the huge significance our Scriptures, and our ancestors, give to our bodies as we go about this Christian life.

But first let me give you a sample of the diction and rhythms of the poem so you will have a feel for what attracted so many of our ancestors.

There is no introduction. The poem begins boldly and bluntly, a passionate cry:

> O that you would kiss me with the kisses of your mouth!
> For your love is better than wine,
>   your anointing oils are fragrant,
> your name is oil poured out;
>   therefore the maidens love you. (1:2–3)

A young woman is in love with a young man. Her strong desire for him bursts forth in this lyric as poetic song. She wants to be with him and hold him. She wants him to kiss her. But hardly has she declared her burning passion before she is overwhelmed with unworthiness. She describes herself with something like embarrassed shame.

> I am very dark, but comely . . .
> like the tents of Kedar. . . .
> Do not gaze at me because I am swarthy,
>   because the sun has scorched me.
> My mother's sons were angry with me,
>   they made me keeper of the vineyards;
>   but, my own vineyard I have not kept! (verses 5–6)

But this self-deprecation is not confirmed by the young man. He responds by singing,

> Behold, you are beautiful, my love;
>   behold, you are beautiful;
>   your eyes are like doves. (verse 15)

And then there's this revealing interchange between them. She says,

> I am a rose of Sharon,
> a lily of the valleys. (2:1)

This is a self-deprecating remark. She says, in effect, that she is only a blossom of the plain, a mere lily of the dale, not really worthy of much notice. But the young man, while accepting what she says about herself, cleverly turns it into a compliment and says, "If you say so, yes, but . . .

> As a lily among brambles,
> so is my love among maidens. (2:2)

That gives you a feel for what the book is about. But what is a book like this, a book that doesn't once mention the term *God,* doing in the Bible? And it says nothing about worship, morals, sin, or forgiveness. The theme is love and holiness and the human body. It is developed in a series of love lyrics as the young man and young woman describe and desire each other in language that is predominantly physical, sensual, and emotional. There is no interpretation or explanation. The entire book is written in conversational exchange and is the only book in the Bible like this.

It is understandable that this kind of love poetry would be written, but how does it come to be Holy Scripture? What is the meaning of the church's belief that this is the Word of God?

In C. S. Lewis's novel *The Voyage of the Dawn Treader,* there is a conversational exchange between the children Eustace and Lucy, who have just landed on a remote island, and Ramandu, a dazzling personage of wisdom. Lucy has just asked Ramandu about himself.

> "I am a star at rest, my daughter," answered Ramandu. . . .
> "In our world," said Eustace, "a star is a huge ball of flaming gas."

> "Even in your world, my son, that is not what a star is but only what it is made of."[39]

Likewise the Song. It is made up of fragments of poems and songs of the culture, recounting a rustic drama of a youth with a country maiden. But that is not what it is—only what it is made of. What it is, is an introduction to the beauty of holiness in the love between two persons.

No book of the Bible has been served so badly by its modern interpreters (unless it is Revelation). They have made their way through the text like flat-footed Philistines. They have taken it apart and flattened it out in explanations that are about as interesting as a sex education chart in an eighth-grade hygiene class.

What having the Song in the Bible does is demonstrate and convince us that we have been created physically, emotionally, and mentally to live in love. The Creation story in Genesis—"So God created humankind in his image, in the image of God he created them; male and female he created them" (1:27, NRSV)—is replicated in the poetry of the Song.

It is very easy to lose sight of this because we have so much trouble with the intimacy and faithfulness that love requires. We are much more apt to concentrate on the problems of love, or to get mixed up trying to define love, or to become depressed and confused by our terrible failures in love. Maybe we mortals are created to love, but our experience is so unhappy and we do such a poor job of it that we remove it from the agenda. Why talk about it anymore? It reminds us of too many failures. We can talk instead about our careers, our work, our future, and our past, and we can leave the discussions on love to the dreams of poets and the confusion of adolescents.

There is no doubt regarding the facts of people who fall in love: they *are* very often, or soon become, unhappy. Sin infects all human relations with its disintegrating force. And we see this suffering most poignantly at the center where people come together in love. Because we have so much negative experience with love, we become by turns cynical, manipulative, and commercial in our attitudes toward it. At the same time, we deny and distort the love we are talking about.

---

39. C. S. Lewis, *The Voyage of the Dawn Treader* (New York: HarperCollins, 1994), 226.

Karl Barth probes these matters deeply but also hopefully. He wonders how the authors (he refers to them in the plural) of the Song are able to ignore the "well-known disturbance and corruption" in human love relationships. He wonders how they did not "see what almost hopeless problems" love brings into our lives: "Ought they not to have been afraid that by concentrating on this relationship they would merely add fresh fuel to a fire which is destructive enough without it? Who, then, is innocent enough to write these innocent passages? And who has eyes so innocent as to read them as innocent passages?"[40]

The person who reads Genesis and knows this is the created pattern of joy and mutuality can then read the Song of Solomon and see the goal and ideal to which we all press in fulfillment. Despite our sordid failures in love, we see here what we are created for. What God intends for us is the beautiful ecstasy and fulfillment that is celebrated in the lyricism of the Song of Solomon.

There is one other thing about the Song that I find fascinating. It was used by our Hebrew ancestors as a way of assimilating and appreciating everything that had to do with salvation.

Salvation is a huge word in the Christian vocabulary. The Hebrew name of Jesus, *Yeshua,* literally means "God saves."

The personal relationships for which we were created and in which we are confused because of our sins are re-created or redeemed by salvation. Salvation is the act of God in which we are rescued from the consequences of our sin (bondage, fragmentation) and put in a position to live in free, open, loving relationships with God and our neighbors. The double command "Love God . . . Love your neighbor . . ." assumes salvation as the foundational background for living in love.

The most pondered act of salvation in Israel was the Exodus, the freeing of the Jews from four hundred years of slavery in Egypt. It was *the* great act in which Israel experienced God as Savior and herself as saved. This reality was remembered in the Feast of the Passover, repeated every year. The annual repetition of the Passover Feast kept the memory fresh. The deliverance from Egyptian slavery and

40. Karl Barth, *Church Dogmatics 3.1, The Doctrine of Creation,* ed. G. W. Bromiley and T. F. Torrance, trans. G. W. Bromiley et al. (New York: T&T Clark, 1958), 308.

inauguration into new life as a free people of God was relived, understood, and sung within the domestic environs of the family in the ritual meal, storytelling, and psalm singing.

The people were *saved*—defined, shaped, and centered—not by military, political, or environmental forces but by the act of God. Salvation was God acting decisively in history so that all people, both individually and corporately, were free to live in faith. Salvation: God doing for us what we cannot do for ourselves.

Salvation means to be whole again, to be delivered in the midst of peril. The Passover is the concentrated, annual attention that Israel gave to God's definitive act of saving love.

But the repetition of the celebration carries with it a danger, the danger that salvation will become ritualized and institutionalized. The Passover ritual, designed to represent the great impossibilities and indescribable realities of grace, is very visible. It is acted out by the wise and the foolish, the bright and the dull, the pious and the impious, year after year, whether these persons feel like it or not. That which was charged with creative power in the beginning is in danger, through the years and with each repetition of the ritual, of becoming a shell, a husk of reality. If that continued, there would come a time when the entire nation would experience only the ritual and not the reality, knowing only the institution and not the salvation.

In order to protect against this danger, a person of genius (no one knows who it was) assigned the Song to be read after the eating of the ritual meal. This assignment, reading the Song as the concluding act of the Passover Feast, is a witness to and participation in the message that the once-for-all historical event of salvation is at the same time workable in the everyday settings of intimacy between persons. It bridges the transition from the Exodus event in Egypt to daily activities in kitchen and bedroom so there is no loss of wonder, intensity, or joy. The Song is the most inward, the most intimate and personal, of all the biblical books (except perhaps Psalms). No lyrics, ancient or modern, communicate the intimacies and the exuberances of being whole and good in relation to another person—that is, of being saved—more convincingly than the Song.

When we first encounter God's saving love, it may well overwhelm us. But over a period of years, it becomes a familiar part of the landscape, one religious item among many others. The vocabulary of salvation becomes hackneyed, reduced to the level of valentine-card verse. Whenever we are associated with greatness over a long period of time, there is a tendency in us to become stale. We lose, in the language of Revelation, our "first love" (2:4, KJV). We preserve its importance by assigning the event a date on the calendar. The form is honored, but the intimacy is lost. Praying, the most personal aspect of life, becomes riddled with clichés, a sure indication that it has ceased being personal. There are no clichés in the Song.

—

The associations formed by placing the Song in the context of Passover develop further insights in relation to the Lord's Supper, the Christian act of worship that owes so much to Passover.

The Lord's Supper, the act of worship that remembers the decisive act of salvation, also remembers the meal that demonstrates a continuing faith involvement in God's action. It is at the Lord's Table that the connection is maintained between the irreducible core of historical data (Christ crucified and risen), a faith in the presence of a living Lord, and the inner responses of personal prayer.

As you come to the Table today, remember the great act of salvation and your own personal participation in your ordinary life this week. And when you get home today, open up your Bibles and read the Song.

Amen.

2

"Out of the Whirlwind"

JOB 38:1–7
MARK 15:33–39

Job suffered. His name is synonymous with suffering. He asks, "Why?" He asks, "Why me?" He puts his questions to God persistently, passionately, and eloquently. He refuses to take silence for an answer. He refuses to take clichés for an answer. Job provides a precedent for Jesus, who cried out his hard question from the cross: "My God, my God, why hast thou forsaken me?" (Matthew 27:46).

Job does not take his sufferings quietly or piously. He disdains going to outside physicians or philosophers for a second opinion. Job takes his stance before God and in the presence of three "friends," who come to comfort him when he protests his suffering, protests mightily.

—

What you need to know is that the book of Job is the story of a person who has lived a good life, become accustomed to a life of blessings, and then, without warning, is plunged into a dark pit of loss. Disaster has wiped out his livestock, his children have been killed, and to top it off, he is afflicted with a painful case of boils. Three friends come to visit him and, in a blundering attempt to comfort him, lay down a thick fog of trite and hackneyed religion. Eventually the voice of God, silent through all this, brings it to a thundering, eloquent, and satisfying climax "out of the whirlwind" (38:1).

The heart of the book consists of a dialogue between Job and three friends; God speaking "out of the whirlwind" concludes it. This ancient story deals with suffering as well as or better than anything we have. It also is written in exquisite poetry. I once heard Job described as on a par with Shakespeare.[41]

The three friends, seeing that his suffering is so very great, sit in silence with Job for seven days and nights. Finally Job can take it no longer and makes the first move in the dialogue by cursing the day of his birth: "Let the day perish wherein I was born, and the night which said, 'A man-child is conceived.' . . . Why did I not die at birth, come forth from the womb and expire? . . . Why is light given to a man whose way is hid, whom God has hedged in?" (3:3, 11, 23).

That ignites the dialogue as Eliphaz, Bildad, and Zophar respond to Job's suffering. There are three exchanges, as each friend in turn attempts to comfort Job, and Job, uncomforted, responds to each.

First, I am going to give you a kind of mosaic of Job's responses to his three so-called friends as he insists to them that God has no reason to punish him and that he is innocent of any wrongdoing. He complains that it is impossible to get an audience with God in order to prove his innocence. Sure of his innocence, he is stymied: "For he is not a man, as I am, that I might answer him, that we should come to trial together. There is no umpire between us, who might lay his hand upon us both" (9:32–33).

When his friends try to advise him, they only make matters worse. Job calls them "worthless physicians" and "miserable comforters" (13:4; 16:2). He doesn't want their clichéd advice. He wants to deal with God firsthand. He complains that everyone is against him: wife, close friends, guests, servants, brothers, little children. They have all taken what they presume to be God's side against him while he himself lives on the thin edge of existence: "I have escaped by the skin of my teeth" (19:20).

But even in the face of such total rejection—and this is a surprise—he comes up with this: "I know that my Redeemer lives, and at last he will stand upon the earth; and after my skin has been thus destroyed, then from my flesh I shall see God, whom I shall see on my side, and my eyes shall behold, and not another" (19:25–27).

41. Samuel Terrien, *Job: Poet of Existence* (Eugene, OR: Wipf and Stock, 1957), 68.

Job sees signs of God in the world around him, in the natural creation and in the religious traditions, but he wants something more: "These are but the outskirts of his ways; and how small a whisper do we hear of him! But the thunder of his power who can understand?" (26:14).

Job concludes his complaint and the defense of his integrity by reviewing his past life. He calls his days of wealth and health his "autumn days" (29:4). There were children playing around him, all the young men admired and respected him, and he was honored by the old men. He was active in social justice: "I was eyes to the blind, and feet to the lame. I was a father to the poor" (29:15–16). But now that is all gone. He is mocked by young men whose fathers he would not even have hired as shepherds. And in addition to bearing the mocking, spitting rabble, he is in severe pain from his boils: "The night racks my bones, and the pain that gnaws me takes no rest" (30:17).

Job wraps it up by affirming his innocence from sin. Whatever is wrong with the world, it is not because of him; he is "righteous in his own eyes" (32:1). Job is at the God-crisis. If he ceased to believe in God at this point, his spiritual torture would vanish. He would still have physical and moral problems, but the anguish of his soul would cease. If he accepted the counsel of his friends, he would be relieved of his turmoil, but he refuses to be satisfied by their answers. Job will settle for nothing less than God himself.

If you had a friend in such a God-crisis, what would you say? What *do* you say? Job's friends are at least useful in this: they tell us what *not* to say. They expose three still-common ways of "comfort" that leave a person struggling with life itself and the meaning of God more than ever.

Eliphaz is the first friend. He begins his speech with a ghost story: "A spirit glided past my face; the hair of my flesh stood up" (4:15). Out of this came a message, supposedly with the authority of the supernatural behind it. Eliphaz finds that the source of Job's trouble is obviously sin. His reasoning goes like this: sin causes suffering, Job is suffering, therefore Job is a sinner. Job's protest that he is innocent only proves that Job is not only a sinner but a liar on top of it. "Man is born to trouble as the sparks fly upward" (5:7), says Eliphaz. He proceeds to compile an agenda of sins, accusing Job of a variety of misdeeds, and seeks to bring him to his knees in confession and abasement.

Eliphaz is a fundamentalist who uses other people's misfortune to document the truth of his black-and-white dogma. Job's suffering is evidence of his sin. Nothing could be plainer. No ambiguities here.

Bildad, the second friend, tells Job that whatever else takes place, he must remember that God is the most important part of existence and that Job must be careful not to blaspheme or deny him. Bildad's argument goes something like this: The reason we cannot understand many things is that God is so great and we are so insignificant. How can we hope to understand such a vast purpose and intelligence operating in the complexities of the universe? "Even the moon is not bright and the stars are not clean in his sight; how much less man, who is a maggot, and the son of man, who is a worm!" (25:5–6). Do you have any idea how busy God must be and how much he has to do? You are pretty insignificant in the great scheme of things. How can you expect to have answers to everything that is going on in the counsels of God?

Thomas Hardy, in one of his poems, tells about a messenger sent one day to remind God of the human race, and God cannot remember, cannot remember a thing.[42] That is the kind of God that Bildad is exalting. Bildad is an intellectual who has a head full of philosophical truths and ideas, but he has no ability to make any connection with the personal details of human life. He is all ideas and can talk about them endlessly, but he can never remember his wedding anniversary.

In magnifying God, Bildad minimizes humanity. Bildad the intellectual has bigger things to contemplate than a poor wretch in despair and suffering.

Zophar, the third friend, turns out to be a moralist. He advises Job, "If you set your heart aright, . . . your life will be brighter than the noonday" (11:13, 17). Zophar is not only straight; he is narrow. He is a zealot for the justice of God. His mission is to hustle people on the road to good works. Job must do good deeds, and his problem will be solved. Zophar has the universe well ordered in his mind, and Job is a disorderly spot in it. Zophar must do his part to put right what is wrong,

42. Thomas Hardy, "God-Forgotten," in Hardy, *Poems of the Past and the Present* (New York: Harper & Brothers, 1902), 329–32.

like a meticulous housewife straightens a crooked picture or removes a smudge. Zophar is impatient with Job. He insults and accuses him. Zophar is on God's side and wants to clean up the world. He never really hears Job's story or becomes sensitive to his plight. He is eager to jump in and sort things out into clearly defined lists of good and bad. "Keep the rules." It's that simple.

So much for Job's friends—Eliphaz with his fundamentalist altar call, Bildad the intellectual with his big ideas, and Zophar the moralist with his condescending self-righteousness.

"Miserable comforters" indeed.

There is one more named person, Elihu. Where did he come from? He has been sitting there all this time, taking it all in. Maybe he was too young to be considered worthy of inclusion in the conversation. When the three friends finished with Job, Elihu spoke up: "I am young in years, and you are aged; therefore I was timid and afraid to declare my opinion to you. . . . Behold, my heart is like wine that has no vent; like new wineskins, it is ready to burst. I must speak" (32:6, 19–20). He gives a far longer speech than any of the "comforters." He is young and was being politely deferent to his elders in their conversation. But finally he can take it no longer. He says that he has been listening carefully to both the advice of the "friends" and Job's responses and found them all to be quite weak. But when he has said all he has to say, he has said nothing new. Job and his friends ignore him.

Finally God "answered Job out of the whirlwind: 'Who is this that darkens counsel by words without knowledge? Gird up your loins like a man, I will question you, and you shall declare to me' " (38:1–3).

"I will question you." God takes the initiative not with answers but with questions that give a new perspective to everything: "Where were you when I laid the foundation of the earth?" (verse 4).

I counted sixty-one questions that God asks in the 123 verses of his response to Job. Midway through the whirlwind address, Job answers, "Behold, I am of small account; what shall I answer thee? I lay my hand on my mouth. I have spoken once, and I will not answer; twice, but I will proceed no further" (40:4–5).

And again, at the end of the whirlwind, Job releases a rumbling torrent of words: "I have uttered what I did not understand, things too wonderful for me, which I did not know. . . . I had heard of thee by the hearing of the ear, but now my eye sees thee" (42:3, 5).

G. K. Chesterton in his great hymn "O God of Earth and Altar" prays for deliverance from "all the easy speeches that comfort cruel men."[43] The easy answers of Job's friends are a cruel substitute for God himself. We live in an age abounding with such talk, such answers. Sometimes we talk them; sometimes we record them, putting faith in education, technology, counsel, moral programs, and spiritual techniques.

When all is said and done, Job declares the solution is not in another answer, another book, another counselor, another sermon, another speech, another scientific breakthrough, but in God, in listening to God's questions, each of which draws attention to something indisputably before us, something we can neither control nor manipulate. Answers are good in their place, but when the chips are down, when trouble comes, when doubt gnaws at our innards, when anxiety threatens, then only God himself will do. Job, of course, couldn't answer the questions, and neither can we, but they draw attention to so much around us and in us that is beautifully alive, that is life giving, that is beyond our understanding but not beyond our receiving and enjoying.

These God-questions (these sixty-one for a start) come to us and penetrate layer after layer of complacency, rationalization, suffering, and ignorance, and they wake us up to his world of creation and redemption all around and in us, making it possible for us to say with Job, "I had heard of thee by the hearing of the ear, but now my eye sees thee."

Amen.

43. G. K. Chesterton, "O God of Earth and Altar," 1906, www.chesterton.org/a-hymn-o-god-of-earth-and-altar/.

3

"Wisdom Cries Aloud"

PROVERBS 1:20–33
JAMES 1:5–8

I had an experience recently that I want you to get in on: my discovery of the book of Proverbs. I mean discovering it personally as the Word of God. I knew about it, of course. I had read it without enthusiasm here and there, but this was new, a new experience with Scripture. Proverbs, along with Ecclesiastes, I had long ignored. When I did occasionally read them, I was mostly bored. If I had purchased a new Bible from which Proverbs had been omitted, it would have been months, maybe even years, before I would have noticed the omission.

The omission, the lack of interest, was not exactly accidental. I had reasons to support my lack of interest and subsequent neglect. If you had asked me why I had this low opinion, I think I would have said two things.

First, my feeling that Proverbs, in contrast to the rest of Scripture, is secular rather than theological. The great energy that Scripture develops in us comes from the revelation of God and of salvation. We hear and see things in a radically different way than ever before. The world is described and defined from a demanding and revolutionary perspective—from the point of view of grace. We read Scripture and realize that God is the reality beneath and beyond all else.

Without Scripture it would be easy to suppose that natural law or blind chance or human decisions or some demonic ghost would be the power to reckon with in understanding the world. But Scripture tells us clearly, convincingly, that it is God who acts in history and in our lives. So we have these great narratives filled with passion and grace: the call of Abraham and his excruciating decisions and acts of faith; the leadership of Moses and that historic rescue operation out of Egypt; the years of desert survival and guerrilla infiltration of Canaan; the kingship of David, where everything in the human experience, the good and the bad, becomes redeemed into a life of holiness; and finally the event of Jesus with all its fresh, charming, joy-producing, life-changing effects in everyday life among ordinary people. All through this narrative God has been the major reality. If any of it had been written by a secular historian who didn't believe in or care about God, the story would have been written radically differently. And it would have been practically meaningless as far as we are concerned. For neither the Hebrew people nor Jesus Christ could be significant in secular terms.

But when I read the book of Proverbs, in contrast to the rest of Scripture, I didn't find the same kind of language or atmosphere. The name of God could be eliminated from Proverbs completely, and the material would not be greatly altered. The deepest conditions of our being—faith, sin, salvation, guilt, forgiveness, reconciliation, resurrection—are absent. They are not in the picture at all. It didn't seem to me that Proverbs was interested in the activities and reality of God the way the rest of Scripture is. And so I was not overly interested in Proverbs.

The second reason I would have given for my low esteem of Proverbs is its impersonal intellectualism, which is in contrast to the dominant note in Scripture of a personal, living quality. There is hardly a word about faith. There are no names or stories.

Nothing like the story of Abraham, for instance. Abraham taking Isaac to Mount Moriah, tying him up, placing him on an altar, and going through the agonizing, horrible preparations for killing him as a sacrifice to God—a chilling and awful story. We feel the enormous fear, the crushing anxiety, the incredible obedience in the face of all odds in that intense focus on Abraham and Isaac.

Or when Scripture tells us how salvation is accomplished. With an abstract theory of God and humanity about how the universe somehow produced salvation by means of some mathematical formula? No. We have a story, the story of Jesus Christ hanging on a cross, nailed to rough wood and left suspended to die. The story is written with detail and insight. You can almost hear the nails go through hands and feet, hear the ripping of flesh, and listen to the last words of abandonment: "My

God, my God, why have you forsaken me?" (Mark 15:34, NRSV). No theological abstractions, but a story and a bloody story at that. Friedrich Nietzsche wrote, "All truth is bloody truth to me."[44] They certainly were for Jesus. That is, every truth has to be lived in detail, not just talked about. There has to be flesh and blood, passion and feeling. It is just this quality, so completely characteristic of Scripture, that makes it such a moving, readable, God-revealing, but at the same time *human*-affirming, document.

But I missed this in Proverbs. No names. No events. No plot. Just this endless piling up of sayings. It seemed like the kind of thing an old man put together in a rocking chair on his front porch. It might be true enough as observed wisdom, but there wasn't any *life* in it. Nothing of the personal and God-revealing vitality that I was used to in Scripture.

I think I could sum up my feeling about Proverbs by saying there was not enough God in Proverbs and not enough human life—no names and no stories.

But obviously I have changed my mind. As in so many instances of wrongheaded prejudice, my position was not so much the result of wrong information as it was of inadequate information. The things I observed about Proverbs were true enough, but there are some other things to be reckoned into the picture too. And once they were in the picture, everything had a new look.

To begin with, I learned there was a huge tradition of wisdom in the civilizations bordering the Hebrews: Babylonia to the east and Egypt to the west. The Hebrews were familiar with and appreciative of these wisdom traditions. Many of these wise sayings were incorporated in their own Proverbs, some word for word. Even their own Solomon became named among the wise.

Until this time I assumed that priests and prophets dominated the worship and prayer life of Israel. *Priest* and *prophet* became working companions for me as I lived out my vocation as pastor. The prophets were the preachers declaring God's Word. They spoke the word of God in a challenging way to the people. They were very public movers and shapers of events by their words. I did that every Sunday

44. Scott R. Burson and Jerry L. Walls, *C. S. Lewis and Francis Schaeffer: Lessons for a New Century from the Most Influential Apologists of Our Time* (Downers Grove, IL: InterVarsity, 1998), 145.

from my pulpit. The priests led their congregation in worship and prayer. I did that every Sunday in our sanctuary. But the wise didn't have a job, a function. They didn't have a place or a title. They had reputations respected by the people they lived among, reputations for understanding the human condition. But I had no reputation; I was far too young. So I began looking around for wise men and women.

It didn't take me long to find them. The first I came upon was Dr. James Wall. I was new as a pastor, an associate pastor. The first summer of my work while the senior pastor was on vacation, I led worship and preached. Dr. Wall, the lead psychiatrist at the local mental hospital, sat with his wife in the front pew each Sunday. He was a large man, hard to miss. And, of course, I was intimidated. He always sat with his eyes closed. I assumed he was sleeping. But in the middle of my sermon in the third week, he opened one eye and smiled with approval at something I said. I was no longer intimidated; he was on my side. All that summer of preaching, when I encountered something I didn't understand and didn't know how to handle, I called Dr. Wall and he led me through it. I knew that he was one of the wise and that I could count on him for counsel. He told me once that he was a pastor to people without a church. Through the years I have gradually realized that the wise are all around me, and I have let myself by guided by them, often through their books.

I quit sorting books and magazines and journals into Christian and secular, with a preference for Christian. I read the secular, of course, but not with the same attention as the Christian. I had made a pretty sharp division between reading the Bible scholars and theologians and reading the newspaper, supplemented with detective novels and literary fiction. Eventually the division lines disappeared. It all took place in God's world and kingdom. The Holy Spirit used anything and anyone. And if the Holy Spirit could do it, so could I.

Wedged in between the tasks of prophet and priest, I found myself in the conversational company of wise men and women. Whether I read Proverbs or listened to a widow in a nursing home, the results were astonishingly similar.

Not everything I did or said took place behind the pulpit or in the sanctuary. Not everything I was learning about grace and holiness was coming out of the Bible. I was also being tutored by a woman recovering from a heart attack, by a family struggling in poverty, by young people finding words to express their newfound faith honestly and unpretentiously, or, in the words of our text, by hearing wisdom crying aloud in the street (Proverbs 1:20).

Preaching in the company of Solomon moved me into an immersion of the human situation where God is graciously at work in the everyday workplaces, hospital rooms, playgrounds, and family rooms—"the street."

The end result was simple and obvious, and it shouldn't have taken all that traveling to arrive there. I hope you grasped it sooner than I did. You probably already have.

It is simply this: even our so-called secular lives are permeated by grace. Even the nonreligious aspects of our lives are included in the Word of God. The Word of God to us is not only the radical invasion of our lives by Christ, not only that tremendous life-changing reconciliation that puts us in relationship with an eternal being, but also a detailed concern with every aspect of our humanity. The gospel is not only good news about the big issues and the deep realities. It is also about the time of day and the feeling you have when you get up in the morning.

Proverbs is the biblical statement that everything—ants, spouses, overeating, compliments, curiosity (see Proverbs 27:20), every detail of life—is of infinite, eternal importance. The factory is as high on the agenda as the church pew. Family life is discussed with the same seriousness as the life of the Godhead. The words of men are ranged along with the words of God for examination and contemplation. Nothing from life is excluded; everything is included.

Proverbs puts into Scripture, and therefore into our lives, all those details we might suppose are of no importance to God and therefore unaffected by grace: the way we speak to a friend, the disruptions of a family relationship, the loss of meaning and purpose in our jobs and confused goals in our professions, our feelings of inadequacy or depression, our personal doubts and struggles. We might label the list "Et Cetera."

In Proverbs, "Wisdom cries aloud in the street." She is not hidden away in a prestigious university, not reserved for a few gray-bearded men or the lucky possession of some highly endowed brains, not confined to words authorized by a Sunday pulpit. She cries aloud in the streets, the same streets you drive on going to school and work. Jesus expressed the dominant theme of Proverbs and fulfilled it when he said, "I have come that you might have life and have it more abundantly" (John 10:10, author's paraphrase).

In order to help us live life well, he gathers all its daily frustrations and commonplaces, incorporates them in his abundant life, and shares grace with us so that we live in hope and joy and love. This wisdom will give us skill in living abundantly. All we need to do is ask for it. The brother of our Lord, Saint James, made the promise: "If any of you lacks wisdom, let him ask God, who gives to all men generously and without reproaching, and it will be given to him" (James 1:5).

Amen.

4

"Train Up a Child"

PROVERBS 22:6
EPHESIANS 4:20–32

I got a surprise when I took a careful look at this proverb. It's the phrase "train up" that got my attention. It is the only time in the entire Old Testament that it is used just this way. Literally, the word means "to rub the gums of a newborn child with oil before it begins to suck its mother's breast," a practice used by midwives in the ancient East to train the infant to get nourishment, the infant's equivalent to table manners while using a knife and fork. It was a tender welcoming into the harsh and sometimes painful land of the living.

The word broadened out from there and was used to describe what you do for infants and children to get them started right in life. The word was later used for dedication rites for houses and temples. One of the most enduring and well known is the Feast of the Dedication, using *channuka,* the same word used to introduce infants into this marvelous life.

In that context the word sounds different, more human, more intimate. "Train up" in the church circles in which I grew up was used in the same sense in which you train animals to obey commands, and it was often used by the parents of my friends in conjunction with another proverb about one "who spares the rod" (13:24) to authorize physical punishments for wrongdoing, including disciplines of spankings, time-outs, or household chores.

But "train up" in the original language of Scripture carries overtones of warmth and celebration.

—

A critical question every Christian has to deal with is "How can I best assist others to a full, mature growth in the Christian way?" Parents ask the question regarding their children. Husbands and wives ask the question regarding each other. Individuals ask the question in regard to associates in the workplace and playground.

This Christian congregation, the kind we represent in our gathered worship this morning, has this question as part of the background in practically everything we do. We look around at one another and know, as we listen to God's Word, that we have a responsible relation to one another in assisting each other to "learn Christ" (Ephesians 4:20), to use Saint Paul's phrase.

And what I want to insist on here is that this "train up" is not limited to what takes place in our homes and churches. When we walk out of our homes and into our neighborhoods and workplaces, when we walk out of church on Sundays and enter a week of work and community life, we are being watched, listened to, assessed, and critiqued. The Christian is a public figure whether we quote scripture to the people we meet on the street or not. Our actions speak. Our attitudes convey relationship.

Some of us are without children, some of us are without spouses, some of us are without work, but none of us is without the proverbial imperative "train up . . ." The entire community of faith is engaged in responding to it. For the most part you are not going to be conscious of what you are doing as you are doing it. It will come out of a habit of relational intimacy.

When we activate the verb *train up,* it is essentially an act of personal intimacy. The midwife who rubs the gums of the infant to prepare him or her for the breast is acting in a warm, caring way, the purpose of which is to initiate the infant into a life of receptivity and love.

I do not exclude discipline from this training; I don't exclude information. Though if they are included, it must be with the intent of training into living well in intimacy. What emerges front and center are behavior and words in ways that initiate another person through skill and care into living trustingly in intimacy.

—

In Herman Melville's novel *Redburn,* there is an episode that underlines the proverb. Redburn is a young man who is making his first voyage across the Atlantic. His father died and left him without any prospects of inheritance, so he slips aboard a vessel as a cabin boy. His father had traveled across the Atlantic numerous times and had often talked of it. Redburn was full of these old stories as he began his trip. He took with him a green morocco–bound guidebook to Liverpool, his destination. It was a guidebook his father had owned and used fifty years before. All during the trip across the ocean, the boy would lie in his bunk and search through the guidebook. He mastered the columns of statistics, grounded himself thoroughly in the history and antiquities of the town. He was determined to make the entire subject his own and not be content with a mere smattering of it. There were seventeen engraved plates in the book. He scrutinized them and then examined the descriptions that went with them to see if they corroborated each other. He burned the impressions of every column and cornice into his mind so he had no doubt of recognizing the originals the moment he got off the ship. He thought he was building up within himself an unerring knowledge of Liverpool. He had so familiarized himself with the map that he would be able to turn sharp corners with marvelous confidence. He became so familiar with it that he began to think he had been born in Liverpool. All its features seemed familiar.

And then he arrived in Liverpool and began to search out the pattern of the city before him with the fifty-year-old guidebook in his hand. His first stop was an old castle fort. He searched the street where it was to be located but could only find a tavern bulging with sailors getting their glasses filled. How could a tavern be mistaken for a castle? But Redburn generously forgave it. For one small discrepancy he wasn't going to condemn this old family servant that had so faithfully served his father. The next day he went looking for Riddough's Hotel, where his father had always stayed when in Liverpool. He found the place in the guidebook, marked with his father's pen. He walked along the street, thrilled to be walking in his father's footsteps and then—nothing but a statue standing in the middle of a square. Inquiries revealed that the hotel had been knocked down thirty years before.

He sat down on a shop step to think. The guidebook he had relied on so devoutly was half a century behind the age. This book in its morocco cover, full of fine, old family associations, with the seventeen plates executed in the highest style of art—this book was next to useless. The thing that had guided the father could not guide the son.

Any of us who think we can train up another into the Christian faith by drawing some maps, compiling some statistics, and writing out some out-of-context road signs is going to end up with a similar disappointment. The world changes, fashions change, culture changes, and social structures change. The one thing that doesn't change is the living God and his way of loving and saving us. The one thing that doesn't change is the word *train* in the act of training an infant to live in safe and affectionate intimacy with the source of life in this place where he or she has just been delivered from a nine-month voyage to Liverpool or Baltimore or whatever is stamped on the birth certificate. Every person that knows anything of this from his own experience—and that, by definition, means every Christian—can, by giving witness to his experience and skills, *train* another, whether by words or example. But it is essentially a living act, an invitation to a certain kind of life, a living that centers responsively on Jesus Christ, who is the same and the only one who is the same "yesterday and today and for ever" (Hebrews 13:8).

I was in a conversation this week with a couple of First Nation people who had been raised by nuns in schools on the reservation. The woman told me that her mother had raised her with her fists. She didn't find out there was another way to train or be trained until she was, in her midtwenties, introduced to a Christian community.

The worst thing we can do with this proverb is to depersonalize it, make it a specialty occupation, or put a label on a box marked "train up a child" to be opened for direction when needed. What is required is that *train* takes place in a way that love and affection are absorbed, as they say, "with the mother's milk." Fists have no part in it. It must be an attitude absorbed into our entire life as oil is rubbed into our gums.

Some people have a box labeled "Sunday school," where training takes place for an hour every week. There is another box labeled for parents that is consulted occasionally when there is misbehavior. One of the most visible boxes these days is child psychology, which is fairly expensive, but at least you know the person working out of that box knows a lot more than you do, which relieves you of some of the responsibility.

All these boxes are useful from time to time, but they have little to do with what is involved in the biblical proverb. The proverb doesn't come from a box but out of a life lived. It has little to do with advice giving, counseling, or analyzing. Rather it is initiated through personal example and caring. It means that every time you engage in an act of faith in Christ, you are training another person. Every time you love another in obedience to Christ's command, you are educating someone else. Every time you forgive someone because Christ forgave you, you are assisting materially in the Christian growth of that person. Every time you hope because Christ has promised his help, you are opening up new possibilities of growth in another person.

Obedience to this command, "Train up a child," is both easier and harder than I used to think. It is easier because I don't have to be a certified educator or a skilled psychologist or a wise theologian. I don't have to know all the answers or understand all the intricacies of family dynamics or know much, if anything, about conflict management in the workplace. All I have to do is learn Christ myself and let the act of learning rub off on others. All I have to do is believe in the gospel and trust that others will notice.

And it is harder because I cannot delegate it. I can't leave it up to the church or Sunday school or a best-selling book or a lecture. I can't do it by passing on some moral information that was passed on to me twenty years ago.

I mentioned Paul's phrase "learn Christ" from his letter to the Ephesians. He was meticulously passionate that we, every person, "come to . . . maturity, to the measure of the full stature of Christ . . . [to] grow up in every way into him who is the head, into Christ" (Ephesians 4:13–15, NRSV).

First birth and then growth. Neither metaphor stands alone. Birth presupposes growth, but growth proceeds from birth. Is it an exaggeration to say that birth has received far more attention in the American culture than growth? And the results are not pleasant to observe. We are a nation of adolescents.

The most significant growing up that any of us does is growing as a Christian. All other growing up is preparation for this growing up. Biological and social, mental and emotional growing are all ultimately absorbed into growing up in Christ. Or not. The human task is to become mature, not only in our bodies and emotions and minds, but also in our relationships with God and other persons. Neither can your family and friends do it on their own. We are in this growing-up business together, training and being trained to live maturely in Christ.

Do you hear me? *You can't do this on your own.* Growing up involves the work of the Holy Spirit forming our born-again spirits into the likeness of Christ. It is the work anticipated by Saint Luke's sentence on John the Baptist. After the story of John's birth we read, "The child grew and became strong in spirit, and he was in the wilderness until the day he appeared publicly" (Luke 1:80, NRSV). And then a page or two later is this sentence on Jesus after his birth: "Jesus increased in wisdom and in years, and in divine and human favor" (2:52, NRSV).

Do you get it? John grew up.

Jesus grew up.

Paul tells *us,* "Grow up."

I think it is important to say here that conversational language is the speech most used and appropriate for this training, not preaching from a pulpit, not lecturing in a classroom. Conversational language. Because it is spoken in a quieter voice, it is often not noticed or, if noticed, not taken as seriously as its sister languages. Preaching has pulpit and sanctuary to dignify its authority. Teaching has lectern and classroom to spatially define its task. But a conversation takes place informally, anytime and anywhere, with no one officially in charge. The settings for this kind of speech range from a pair of rocking chairs on a nursing-home porch, to a parent bent over a cradle, to two men bent over coffee in a diner, to a telephone conversation between mother and daughter across three state lines. It could take place in a letter or succession of letters dealing with matters of heart and soul or among three or four friends at a weekly meeting before going to work, reading and pondering together the ways in which Jesus's discourse in John 6 intersects with the hours they have before them that day.

There are enough people right now, believe me, and a lot more of them than you might think, doing this training-up work inconspicuously and wisely. Many of you are among them. I want you to leave our worship today by praising God for them and to continue praying that there will be an increase in the number of those who are learning Christ and getting others started in the learning by rubbing the gums of the newcomers among us with the oil of the Spirit so they will be ready to receive the pure milk of the Word (1 Peter 2:2).

Amen.

5

"I Was Beside Him"

PROVERBS 8:22–31
JOHN 16:1–15

Some people have the idea that the church and Scriptures are first of all a warning: don't do this; be careful about that; you are in danger of this; beware of that. They think religion is a series of red lights, stopping us just when we are getting up speed and about to arrive someplace. We live jerkily, alternately accelerating and braking.

I felt that way for twenty years, and I'm still not quite over thinking that the church is primarily interested in keeping me from making mistakes, from sinning, from going wrong. If that is what you think, I hope to change your mind. The primary concern of what we are doing together in this Christian life is to help one another get in on the whole thing, a full life, not leaving anything out, not settling for too little.

When Ralph Waldo Emerson was sixty-one, he wrote in his journal, "Within, I do not find wrinkles and used heart, but unspent youth."[45]

One of the tasks of Proverbs is to create within us an imagination that is affirmative, that grasps the life that is given to us and makes the most of it, not making the most money, not having the most fun, not making a big impression, but entering

45. Ralph Waldo Emerson, *Journals of Ralph Waldo Emerson,* ed. Waldo Emerson Forbes and Edward Waldo Emerson (1914; repr., Charleston, SC: BiblioLife, 2012), 42.

into the life on God's terms and living it well. *Wisdom* is the term that specializes in living well. Wisdom is the skilled living of truth in everyday reality. We are familiar with the way skills work in specialized areas: a skilled guitarist, a skilled dancer, a skilled football player, a skilled teacher, a skilled engineer. These are all functions that can be observed and admired. But Wisdom is more wide ranging. Wisdom expands our imagination to realize that the base of it all is that we become skilled *persons* on the way to becoming artists of everyday life.

The aspect of God that enables us to do this is the Holy Spirit. The Holy Spirit is God moving in us to live God's life. In Proverbs this Holy Spirit is given a name: "Lady Wisdom" (1:20, MSG). What that does is personalize this aspect of God so that Wisdom is not just items of information or direction, not just good advice or a brilliant idea. Wisdom is God's Spirit working within us to fashion our lives into wholeness in the actual environment in which we find ourselves: in *these* circumstances, in *this* neighborhood, in *this* family. The Holy Spirit is involved in everything we are at the present time. Not just the good things about us but the unfortunate things also. Not only our potential for goodness but our inclinations toward evil. Not only our achievements but our mistakes and failures. God accepts us where we are, and he works in and with us to make a whole life.

By personalizing Wisdom as a woman, "Lady Wisdom," we find ourselves listening to a person rather than following a handbook of instructions. Not Wisdom in a book but Wisdom in a person.

Here is how Lady Wisdom introduces herself to us: "The LORD created me at the beginning of his work, the first of his acts of old" (8:22). This is Wisdom speaking, the Holy Spirit self-described. The story of Creation follows this identification and lays out the richness and vastness of God's work, the actual environment in which we are living right now.

Do you see what Lady Wisdom is doing with us? Describing life in its most complete form so we will live completely—not a religious piece, not a work piece, not a social piece, but the whole thing. As we get a sense of this, it is what we learn to designate *faith*. Life becomes coherent, holds together. In short, life is marvelous. There is wonder at every turn, a miracle burning in every bush. No one has even begun to exhaust the possibilities.

You don't have to remind me there are great tragedies, heartbreaking defeats, crushing guilt, and empty deserts still ahead. The human experience includes evil as well as good, ugliness as well as beauty, not only what is possible but what has failed. Lady Wisdom is present not only to make it possible to pursue wholeness but also to deal with brokenness. It is no use shutting our eyes to it and saying it does not exist. It is no use wallowing in it and saying there is nothing we can do about it. It must be faced, and Lady Wisdom is here to face it with us and make it possible to deal with it so that it becomes the right stuff for realizing wholeness.

Still, the primary message shouted and sung in this passage by Lady Wisdom is that life is good. Don't settle for anything less than the whole thing. Don't end up with any "unspent youth." Don't permit anyone to rob you with a counterfeit substitute. Don't drop out of the race. Don't negligently daydream when you could be attentively experiencing.

—

After describing in detail all the work she has done in the Creation at the right hand of God, Lady Wisdom says, "I was beside him, like a master workman; and I was daily his delight, rejoicing before him always, rejoicing in his inhabited world and delighting in the sons of men" (8:30–31).

God creates, Christ redeems. Then what? We have this magnificent creation; we have this great salvation. But who is going to build them into the individual personal history that is you? That is Wisdom's task. Lady Wisdom is a personification of the Holy Spirit. God assigns himself to you to fashion in you an individual history, including all your days, all your environment, all your circumstances—a life lived to his glory in which you enjoy him forever—"the Master Workman."

This is one of the most important sentences in Proverbs. As you read Proverbs, you will most certainly get overwhelmed with detail; it is a collection of more than five hundred separate aphorisms polished into pungent sentences. Can you imagine what it is like to have five hundred proverbs dumped on you? Have you ever been doing a difficult job and had several people standing around offering helpful advice? All the advice is well intentioned, much is useful, but none helpful. There is too much of it, and besides, the timing is off. What a relief it would be to have all those "helpers" finally realize it was time for supper and hightail it home and just then have the Master Workman show up, who knows both what you are doing and knows you.

Lady Wisdom, friends, is this Master Workman, the Holy Spirit who both knows you and is personally present to you. The Holy Spirit, along with the two metaphors of Lady Wisdom and the Master Workman, are three different ways of understanding God as present and working with us individually so we can live a good and saved life.

Three weeks ago a hailstorm came through our county and did a lot of damage. Part of the damage was my roof. It shredded it. When I learned my insurance would pay for the damage, I purchased thirty squares of shingles and fifty pounds of nails. My son Leif was going to help me. But as we prepared to repair the roof, I realized I didn't know where to start, what to do first, second, and then third. Do you know what I did? Sure you do. You would have done the same thing. I called up a friend, a master carpenter. He came over and got us started. He was there only a short time, fifteen minutes or so, and that was enough. Leif and I were on our way.

That is the position we are in with these five hundred proverbs. We are on the brink of something new in our lives, or something has been bugging us a long time, or we're surveying some recent damage. People keep showing up and telling us what to do—plenty of advice. But most of them don't know us. We need to know where to start and then what to do next with these five hundred proverbs that have been dumped on us. Then Lady Wisdom shows up, the Master Workman. From the very beginning she has been in on all that God has done in creation and redemption. She is at God's side, and now she is at our side, the One who knows where to put each piece of obedience, where to fit each insight so we can find our way into a complete, beautiful, coherent life, not just live with a pile of disconnected days and years.

God doesn't only make a world for us to live in. God doesn't only provide for our salvation. In the guise of Lady Wisdom and the Master Workman, God enters into the actual living with us, guiding and instructing and accompanying us as we live by faith. She corrects our mistakes, guides our choices, forgives our lapses, encourages our efforts.

—

When the Greek translators came to this passage in their Hebrew Bibles, a couple of hundred years before the birth of Jesus, they translated the term *Master Workman* as *harmodzousas,* the "Harmonizer." We all know what harmony is. There is a piano in our house that no one plays very well. Sometimes a child in the house will sit before it and bang on the keys. But that is not music. That is noise, and after a while the child gets removed. Another person sits at the keyboard and, using exactly the same keys, provides everyone with delight. The same notes are struck, but they are played harmoniously. The Master Workman is the Harmonizer. Lady Wisdom is the Harmonizer. The Holy Spirit is the Harmonizer. The Harmonizer takes the notes we are playing so clumsily and ignorantly, takes our hands, and we become a lifetime apprentice in the life of faith so that gradually our lives become more like a symphony than a two-finger rendition of "Three Blind Mice." This sounds simple, and in one sense it is, but life is complex, and all of us are going to spend the rest of our lives in apprenticeship to the Master Workman in this land of the living.

All of us are presented with materials for living. We have bodies and minds and emotions. We have families and neighborhoods and society. We have ground beneath us and trees, flowers, birds, and animals around us, and we have a sky above us. We have a government and hospitals and trains. We have a creation and a covenant. We have a life of forgiveness to learn to negotiate. We live in the world framed by Christ's death and resurrection. Existence takes place between those two poles, wondrous and immense. How can we avoid being overwhelmed by this crucifixion death? How can we adequately respond to this resurrection wonder?

The same Holy Spirit who was in on Creation is the Master Workman shaping in us a life that fuses this death and resurrection into a life of salvation. This Lady Wisdom, this Master Workman, is the Holy Spirit that Jesus promised: "The Counselor, the Holy Spirit, whom the Father will send . . . , he will teach you all things, and bring to your remembrance all that I have said to you. . . . When the Spirit of truth comes, he will guide you into all the truth" (John 14:26; 16:13). The truth is not just told to us, not just written down for us. We need guidance so we can live it out of ourselves. This is what the Holy Spirit—Lady Wisdom, the Master Workman, the Harmonizer—does.

—

One more detail. Lady Wisdom identifies herself as "daily [the Lord's] delight, rejoicing before him always" (Proverbs 8:30). In other words, there is a playful abandon to this kind of life. Life is not at its root an agonizing problem but a playful venture. The intent of the gospel is not to burden us down with guilt and solemnity but to release us for living gracefully and joyously.

Don't misunderstand me, and don't misunderstand Lady Wisdom. It is not that from now on you will live without struggle or pain or bewilderment. There is plenty of that yet to come. There will be unexpected encounters with the dark side of existence. When they come, Lady Wisdom will not blame you but help you develop strength to endure. Christ did not come to tell us how terrible we are but how forgiven we are. The dominant note is not warning but promising.

Today is a special day in the lives of some of you here. There are youth who will be confirmed in their Christian faith; other young people are graduating from high school. Those of us who are older look at the youth and see one period of life coming to completion: the physical, emotional, and mental development complete or nearly complete. Now the task is to do something with it. There are many people for whom life is downhill after the great youth years. There are many others who go from strength to strength, finding in each year of life a new level of intensity, a new dimension of blessing, a fresh experience of love.

The great danger for all of us, youth and adults, is not that we will make mistakes. We most certainly will. Given our nature and the conditions in which we live, there is no getting around that. The great danger is that we will live unaware, unresponsive, unbelieving.

The human task is to live completely, to live out the unspent youth that is still in us. We are unfinished creatures when we are born. Growth is the task set before us, learning how to use our muscles and emotions and thoughts. Deep within us are instincts to have a complete and expansive life. As the biological phase is completed, there is a transition to something more inward. The skillful use of what is given to us is developed into relationships with God and our neighbors, relationships that are whole and complete. We are placed in an existence, ruled and loved by God, that includes other creatures and creations, persons and animals and things. Our calling is to live it. It is never finally achieved. It is a lifetime of engagement, always in process.

But know that while we are at it, the God who created and saved us—as the Master Workman, as Lady Wisdom, as the Harmonizer, as the Holy Spirit—is at our side so that we will live in delight.

Amen.

6

"Sacrifice of Fools"

ECCLESIASTES 5:1–2
MARK 1:1–8

Ecclesiastes is a John the Baptist kind of book. It functions not as a meal but as a bath. It is not nourishment. It is cleansing. It is repentance. It is purging. *Ecclesiastes* translated into English is simply "the Preacher." As persons of faith, we invite the Preacher into our lives to get our souls scrubbed clean from illusion and sentiment, from ideas that are idolatrous, and from feelings that cloy. It is an exposé of pretenses that prepares us to accurately hear the proclamation of reality in God's revelation of himself in Jesus.

There are editions of the New Testament that have Psalms included at the conclusion. A very appropriate conclusion, for the gospel of Jesus needs to be answered, responded to with prayers—the prayers of David for a start—for the gospel is not just information about God. It is the life of God for us to live ourselves.

I would like to suggest another kind of inclusion, but this one as a preface to reading the New Testament, namely the Preacher. We bring so many mistaken expectations to the gospel, so much silly sentiment, so many petulant demands that we have unknowingly picked up in our work or play and that get in the way of eating a nourishing and safe meal. The Preacher is soap and water to clean us up. We get clean of the dirt and grime of the cluttered piety we supposed was faith and the yelling and blasphemies we supposed were religion, and we wash them down the drain. The Preacher is a well-orchestrated *no!* that frees us from the distractions and deceits that distort or drown out the gospel message. It is not itself the message. There is no "message" in the Preacher. ("With him there can be no talk of a message which he had to deliver, since all that is left for him to do is to warn against illusions."[46])

I think of the Preacher in terms of parents who call their children to dinner. The children come in from their play with dirty hands and are instructed, "Go wash up. As filthy as you are, you can't sit down to this table until you are clean."

You don't feel dirty. You were having clean fun. But you eventually learn that what feels natural to you is not natural to the culture of the Lord's Table.

There is a clearing away of what is often mistaken for faith so we are free to hear the Word of God. We are free to discover in a fresh way the emptiness of anything dissociated from the living God, the vanity of everything, however fine and respected in our culture, severed from the living God.

At the time, while letting the Preacher do his work, we may feel empty. But it is an emptiness that will be filled with the Spirit of God, the full abundance that flows in and through us, making all things new.

—

The fact is that much of what we encounter in this world under the name of *God* or *goodness* is neither God nor good. Not everything that happens is going to turn out to be good simply because we put a happy face on it. This is as true in the church as in the world. There is an incredible amount of sheer bilge in religion. There are shoddy morals and slovenly thinking. There is deceit and there is damnation. An unctuous smile and a sincere tone do not make a gospel.

Some of the last words Jesus spoke to his disciples before departing sound very much like the Preacher: "And then if any one says to you, 'Look, here is the Christ!' or 'Look, there he is!' do not believe it. False Christs and false prophets will arise and show signs and wonders, to lead astray, if possible, the elect. But take heed; I have told you all things beforehand" (Mark 13:21–23).

The Preacher's responsibility is to keep us affirmative without being gullible. To keep us alert and prepared to say yes to every sign of God in every part of existence without, at the same time, being a patsy for every confidence game in town.

---

46. Gerhard von Rad, *Old Testament Theology,* vol. 1, trans. D. M. G. Stalker (Louisville, KY: Westminster John Knox, 1962), 456.

To train us in robust acceptance without letting us become a passive receptacle for all the garbage in the street.

One of the ways the church fulfills that responsibility is to guide us in a periodic reflection on the book of the Preacher. The first words catch our attention: "Vanity of vanities! All is vanity!" (Ecclesiastes 1:2). Various meanings glance off the surface of the words as the context shifts: visible but unsubstantial, futile, spurious, illusory, fraudulent. That theme is repeated over and over again. In the brief allotment of space assigned to the Preacher, he uses the word *vanity* more than three dozen times. In the rest of the Old Testament, it is used only thirty-three times. That is surprising at first, considering Ecclesiastes as a whole is so full of affirmations. It is puzzling to find it read with appreciation in a church that gathers and repeats and relishes so many yeses, amens.

I have always liked the definition of *dirt* as "matter in the wrong place." What is more lovely than miles upon miles of sand on an ocean beach, picking up the sun's rays and reflecting them back into your eyes and to your skin in healing warmth? Or what is more delightful than finding a spider's web in a bush, glistening with dew, with the early morning sun etching a marvelous filigree suspended miraculously? But a bucket of sand dumped on your carpet is not lovely. And a spiderweb in the dark corner of the closet sends you running for a dust mop. The sand and the spiderweb in the wrong place get eliminated with no questions asked.

Religion is like that. In its proper setting, functioning in its created order, it is a thing of beauty, useful and attractive. In the wrong place or in the wrong light, it is unattractive, unhealthy, and unwanted. When matter is in the wrong place we call it *dirt.* When religion is in the wrong place, we call it *hypocrisy* or *superstition* or *self-righteous.*

Today's text reads, "Guard your steps when you go to the house of God; to draw near to listen is better than to offer the sacrifice of fools; for they do not know that they are doing evil. Be not rash with your mouth, nor let your heart be hasty to utter a word before God, for God is in heaven, and you upon earth; therefore let your words be few" (5:1–2). The Preacher is telling us that it is dangerous to go to church. Be on your guard when you get near a church, for there are some terrible things that can happen to you there. It is like walking on a glacier. A dangerous crevasse can swallow you up without warning. Or like driving a car. The moment you are behind the wheel and move into a flow of traffic, you expose yourself to numerous dangers. That doesn't mean you shouldn't drive a car. It *does* mean you must be extremely careful.

We can only understand the danger by understanding the situation. When we enter the realm of the life of faith in God, we open ourselves to an existence characterized by God speaking to us, promising to order our lives in love and to redeem us in his mercy. We are set in dimensions of eternity. We are creatures of God, so we are taken with absolute seriousness by him. He knows our names. He bears our burdens. He gives his life for us so we might live.

The danger, though, is that, as we get together in the name of God, we will merely chatter with one another about our morals and gossip about our neighbors, drowning out the voice of God. The danger is that we will get so busy running a religious institution that we have no energy or attention left over for prayer. The danger is that we treat the whole business of religion as something we are in charge of, to administer and complete. This is what the Preacher calls the "sacrifice of fools" and what I am calling "religion in the wrong place."

Religion in the Preacher's time had become flat and platitudinous. The majestic mount of revelation, Sinai, had been eroded into a dull hillock. The thundering commands of God had been muted and recomposed into soothing background music. The soul-stirring encounters between sinful man and holy God had been sentimentalized into soap-opera melodramas. The tremendously austere desert, where a homeless people had found themselves miraculously guided and provisioned by a God of mercy and love, had been surveyed and marked out in quarter-acre lots and put on sale at a price every middle-class family could afford. And now, instead of having the penetrating, foundation-shaking wisdom of a man like Job, they had the bromides of a Norman Vincent Peale. Instead of the "artful thunder"[47] of a prophet like Isaiah, they had the oily showmanship of a Jimmy Swaggart.

There was plenty of religion around, but it was religion in the wrong place—bits and pieces of God's revelation taken out of their original and awesome setting

47. Ralph Waldo Emerson, "Merlin I," *The Complete Works of Ralph Waldo Emerson* (Cambridge: Riverside, 1903–4), 9:120–21.

and arranged like bric-a-brac in the culture. The environment was cluttered with it, and all authentic needs were stifled. It was the kind of thing that, in a Saul Bellow novel, Augie March objects to in his mother: "It was kitchen religion and had nothing to do with the giant God of the Creation who turned back the waters and exploded Gomorrah, but it was on the side of religion."[48]

Jesus in the course of his life came across a great deal of "religion in the wrong place," what the Preacher lampooned as "the sacrifice of fools." He entered our history to exhibit the reality of God, the power of creation, the miracle of forgiveness, the drama of mercy, the thrilling pulsations of wisdom lived out in daily discipleship. Many people heard him gladly, thronged around him eagerly and attentively. But there were others who were bored and distant. They were the religious professionals, known as Pharisees. Their only interest in Jesus was that of window-shoppers—casual, strolling, well dressed, with no pressing needs but not indifferent to a bargain if they should happen upon one. Matthew 23 is a description of Jesus's encounter with these people. Six times in this chapter he confronts them with a warning accusation, "Woe to you . . . hypocrites!"

When you go home today, get out your Bible and read Matthew 23 again, and you will see that he at no time criticizes what they taught. In fact he prefaces his accusation of the Pharisees by advising bystanders to "practice and observe whatever they tell you, but not what they do; for they preach, but do not practice" (verse 3). The verbal part of their religion was faultless, but the bodily part was worthless. They talked a lot; they taught a lot; they pontificated a lot. But they did not live the majesties. They did not experience the realities. They did not share the mercy. They did not move under the omnipotence.

Some find it useful to use the word *religion* for what I am calling "religion in the wrong place" and to use the new Christian word *gospel* for "religion in the right place." I like that terminology but am not always consistent in my own use of it. But the distinction is useful. When we take the truth of God and use it in superstitious

48. Saul Bellow, *The Adventures of Augie March* (New York: Penguin Books, 1996), 12.

or manipulative or prideful or selfish ways, that is *religion.* Its opposite is *gospel:* the truth of God heard in all its originality and power in the person of Jesus Christ, listened to in faith, responded to in faithful discipleship. People are always taking the gospel and trying to turn it into a religion. And God keeps calling us back, back into the wide-open country of gospel where, in the Preacher's words, "God is in heaven, and you upon earth; therefore let your words be few" (Ecclesiastes 5:2).

It is surprising how many people only seem to have encountered God in the wrong place. When they hear the word *religion,* they think of stuffy, self-righteous people. When they think of worship, they remember the smell of musty hymnbooks and the dirge of ponderous tunes. When they hear the term *evangelism,* they recall the rudeness of a religious huckster selling his brand of God.

The Preacher is one of the most effective voices in Scripture dealing with this problem. He is not the only one. It is surprising to those who are not familiar with Scripture how much antireligion there is in it. The Bible employs some of its most vigorous prose in putting down as bad what a lot of people assume must be good simply because it is "religious." You don't have to read very far in the Bible to find that it is intolerant of humbug that masquerades as pious rectitude. It is scathing in its rejection of the incredulous acceptance of almost anything just because it looks like it might be miraculous or supernatural. It is tireless in its exposure of the fraud of idolatry, the illusions of magic, and the silliness of superstition.

For as long as people try to make a religion without God and achieve wholeness without faith, the Preacher's work must be repeated. His is the primary biblical voice insisting that religion taken out of context is vanity. He will admit no pleasure, possession, or piety to an independent existence. He strips us of *religion* so we might be dressed for God.

Amen.

7

"Let Your Garments Be Always White"

ECCLESIASTES 9:1–10
PHILIPPIANS 1:3–11

When God spoke to Job "out of the whirlwind" (Job 38:1), he told him that when he, God, "laid the foundation of the earth," that is, created everything that exists, "the morning stars sang together, and all the sons of God shouted for joy" (verses 4, 7). Which is to say, if we throw our minds back into the past as far as we can imagine, what we find is joy: the stars of God and the sons of God singing and shouting joyfully.

Then go the other direction as far into the future as we can imagine, into heaven, and we find a similarly joyful pleasure. In John of Patmos's apocalyptic vision, all creation is gathered around God's throne, and songs of joy are lifted up by great multitudes in exuberant chorus. In the midst of the assembled joy, twenty-four elders, representing the twelve tribes of Israel and the twelve apostles of the church—venerable and dignified figures who represent symbolically the centuries of discipleship and faith in a grand finale—take off their crowns and throw them into the air, pitching them before God's throne (Revelation 4:1–11). The picture is one of hilarity, almost of frivolity—these ancient, bearded figures heaving crowns into the air before the throne. Think of West Pointers throwing their white hats into the air in the jubilation of graduation or of football players filling the air with their helmets in the triumph of victory. It is almost, if it were possible, as if they would like to take off their heads and fling them into the air to show their joy.

The story of our faith, our very existence, begins and ends in joy. And between the beginning and the conclusion there is joy: "a river whose streams make glad the city of God" (Psalm 46:4). Jesus said it plainly: "These things I have spoken to you, that my joy may be in you, and that your joy may be full" (John 15:11). And Paul, in our epistle reading, wrote to the Philippians how much he knew about and wanted others to share in what he called "joy in the faith" (1:25).

When we leave the pages of Scripture and immerse ourselves in the life of the church, we find the same joy. Christians for twenty centuries now have been exhibiting joy. True, there have been plenty of sad Christians, morose and gloomy followers of Jesus. But the ones that give us hope seem full of joy. In the days when the Roman Catholic Church was in the business of canonizing certain of our brothers and sisters in faith, giving them the honorary title *saint* and indicating thereby that they had lived an exemplary life of faith, one of the standard items for qualification was evidence of *hilaritas*—joy. The proposed saint had to be a hilarious woman or a hilarious man, capable of laughing, of praising, of enjoying.

Joy at the beginning, joy at the end, joy everywhere in between. Joy is God's creation and gift. No authentic biblical faith is conceivable that is not permeated with it.

How does it happen then that so many people get into trouble trying, as they would put it, to have a little fun? Why is it so many pursue pleasure with such unhappy results? For it is certainly true that a great deal of the misery we survey seems to have been initiated in the pursuit of pleasure, whether on the highs of drugs or the ecstasies of sex or the gluttonies of consumption. If pleasure is from God, why do we get into trouble when we try to get as much of it as we can?

Ecclesiastes, the Preacher, helps us with an answer. I often think of the Preacher as the garbage collector in the kingdom of God. He goes up and down our alleys and backyards, empties our wastebaskets and attics, and hauls off everything that has accumulated, under the supposition that we might need it someday but that it is, in fact, worthless. He gets rid of those things in life that may have been once good in themselves—we paid a lot for them on one whim or another—but actually divert us from a life of faith in God. Just as we clean our houses occasionally and get rid of what doesn't contribute to good living, so we read the Preacher occasionally to houseclean our lives of the illusions and sentimentalisms that clutter our days as we follow Christ in faith.

One conspicuous area in which we need the Preacher's help is the pursuit of pleasure, of joy. There is no way to experience God without also experiencing joy. Anyone who gets in touch with God gets in touch with joy. But what happens when we separate the joy from the God who gives the joy? Hold on to the joy but dismiss the God of joy to the sidelines? And then we wonder why the joy we were looking for has turned into something dull, boring, and meaningless! We need to be rescued from that tiresome fate. The Preacher is on hand to do it with us.

But first a clarification. The Preacher is not going to instruct us in right and wrong pleasures. That is not his style. He is not a moralist. We do live in a moral universe and need to learn to make moral decisions, to choose the right and refuse the wrong, to choose God and deny evil. But the Preacher has more to do with discriminating between the real and the illusory, the authentic and the false, the actual and the fantastic. It is in these matters that the Preacher is a guide. His question is not "What is right?" but "What is real?" His repeated conclusion regarding much of what we value and center our lives on is that it is vanity, "hot air." One Hebrew scholar I studied under translated it irreverently as "flatulence."

In that light we are not surprised that in the Preacher there are no lists of good pleasures and bad pleasures, of what is legitimate and illegitimate. His view is that all joy, every pleasure, is God's gift. Our task is to find out how to enjoy the joy. Joys are profuse and various. But the capacity to enjoy them is questionable. Actual enjoyment of joy is spare in our culture. Reaching for or holding on to joy does not automatically convey the ability to enjoy.

I've always been amused by the comment of the novelist Ellen Glasgow on her grandfather, a dour Presbyterian elder, who never once "committed" a joy.[49]

But that's not the Preacher. He believes ardently in joy. He knows that our deepest likings and impulses are raw material furnished by God to bring us into the presence of God. But he also knows they can be perverted and deflected into a way of life that is sheer boredom and cynicism. The intent of joy is to lead us to wholeness, but the ways we engage in it frequently lead to malaise.

---

49. Ellen Glasgow, *The Woman Within: An Autobiography*, ed. Pamela R. Matthews (Charlottesville, VA: University Press of Virginia, 1994), 15.

—

The Preacher makes his point by role-playing the figure of King Solomon. Solomon, who began as the wisest and ended as the most foolish of the Hebrew kings, was in Ecclesiastes's day a shadowy figure of antiquity. In a skillful bit of role-playing, the Preacher assumes the character of Solomon to demonstrate joy gone wrong.

"Solomon" speaks: "Come now, I will make a test of pleasure; enjoy yourself" (Ecclesiastes 2:1). I am now going to paraphrase the rest of this section:

> I am going to pursue pleasure. I am going to have more joy than anyone has ever had. The first thing I will do is organize the world around me to suit my taste. I will construct great houses so I will have everything absolutely at my convenience. I will make vineyards and gardens so what I want to look at and what I want to taste will be completely under my control. I will fashion parks and pools so all the land and water around me will be just the way I want them. I will take absolute control by arranging everything exactly the way I want it. The next thing I will do is turn everything into a commodity so I can use it my own way, and the most convenient way to do that is simply to multiply it. Each item will lose its individual quality and be under my control. I will multiply servants so each loses identity and becomes a mere robot doing my will; I will multiply flocks and herds so they lose individuality and become simply food and clothing; I will multiply silver so it is not a means for exchanging goods in personal relation with others but will put my power and importance on display; I will multiply concubines so each woman loses personality and becomes an object for my personal pleasure. The world will be at my beck and call. Nothing has character in itself. I will be in complete control of every pleasure and every thing. The environment will be shaped to my specifications, and things will be under my control. (see verses 4–8)

The Preacher brings his little role-play to a climax by having Solomon say, "Having arranged the world, I will indulge in it completely: whatever my eyes desired I did not keep from them; I kept my heart from no pleasure" (see verse 10).

—

That exposes the fraud of the whole enterprise. Note the impersonalism in the statement that his eyes *tell him what to do.* What he sought to control now controls him. He loses the capacity to say yes or no, to choose or discriminate. He is swept into an orgy of indulgence. The world of pleasure that he has depersonalized so he could control it now depersonalizes him. He began by arranging the world for his pleasure, and now he is part of the arrangement. He made pleasure into an idol he could use, and now the idol has a life of its own and is using him. He has come under the control of the stimuli he had supposed he could control. He is reduced to the level of Pavlov's dog, salivating at the sound of the bell of pleasure. He is a knee-jerk king, stupidly obedient to whatever his glands command. He is completely in the clutches of what I once heard described as gonadic determinism.

The Preacher has used the Solomon mask as a prop in a brief charade, showing the crudeness in supposing that getting things and arranging the world to our whims has anything to do with joy. No matter how great a reputation you have for wisdom, if all you can do with it is buy castles and bed whores, you are a fool all the same. The Preacher is not impressed by a big name, even if the name is Solomon. He looks behind the reputation and sees only alienation and vulgarization. Making and getting are dead-end streets to joy: "I considered all that my hands had done and the toil I had spent in doing it, and behold, all was vanity and a striving after wind, and there was nothing to be gained under the sun" (2:11).

The Solomon mistake in regard to God's gift of joy can be summarized in two statements: you must not pursue pleasure; you cannot purchase pleasure.

—

One: you must not pursue pleasure. Pleasures are gifts to be enjoyed, not goals to be pursued. No pleasure, however delightful, provides a reason for living or a goal for growing. The pursuit of pleasure leads into a swamp of boredom. The foundational human appetite is for God. God has filled the world with all manner of delight. To enjoy it we need the light touch of one who accepts a gift. We need protection from the sweaty, enslaving compulsions of taking a God-gift and immediately de-godding it into an idol. It is possible to accept all the gifts of life and enjoy them completely only if we refuse to make gods out of them. No one is more insistent than the Preacher that we enjoy life. At the same time no one is more careful in warning of the danger of investing these enjoyments with a life of their own. We will pray, then, for grace to live joyously and abundantly and for caution to live discerningly and carefully. We will be wary of sin and enthusiastic in grace, watchful of temptation but awake to the Spirit.

Two: you cannot purchase pleasure. If we can leave off the anxious work of plunder long enough, we will discover the occupation of joy. Joys are given by God; they can only be received by us. We can neither create nor earn them, neither hoard nor accumulate them. In our culture every commonplace novelty is breathlessly proclaimed as an original creation that we can acquire by purchase. But joys cannot be bought, only received. The one thing we can do to develop a capacity for enjoyment is to practice generosity. In the words of the Preacher, "Cast your bread upon the waters, for you will find it after many days" (11:1), a kind of reckless sharing that imitates the divine largesse. Or in a paraphrase of Jesus's words, "We cannot gain the world except we lose our own soul, but he who loses his own soul will find it" (see Matthew 16:26).

C. S. Lewis made a specialty of probing and understanding joy. All through his works there are references to it with wise counsel for those who would grow in it. In one of his wittiest books, *The Screwtape Letters,* a senior devil instructs a novice devil, Wormwood, who has been assigned the task of keeping a certain man from becoming a Christian. After Wormwood fails in that assignment, his task shifts to tempting this new follower of Christ. The novice tempter thinks he can ruin the young Christian by leading him in the path of pleasure. His boss, the senior devil Screwtape, reprimands him: "Never forget that when we are dealing with any pleasure in its healthy and normal and satisfying form, we are, in a sense, on the Enemy's [God's] ground. . . . It is His invention, not ours. He made the pleasures. . . . [God's] a hedonist at heart. . . . Everything has to be *twisted* before it's any use to us. . . . Nothing is naturally on our side."[50]

And, conversely, everything is by its nature on God's side. Every pleasure.

50. C. S. Lewis, *The Screwtape Letters,* in *The Complete C. S. Lewis Signature Classics* (New York: HarperCollins, 2002), 210, 249.

Every joy. Every delight. The Preacher opens our eyes to the distortions and corruptions of pleasure—our attempts to pursue it, our attempts to purchase it—and leaves us free to accept it as God's gift and to enjoy it as his will. One of the most joyful passages to come from his pen is

> Go, eat your bread with enjoyment, and drink your wine with a merry heart; for God has already approved what you do.
>
> Let your garments be always white. (Ecclesiastes 9:7–8)

Amen.

Part 5

“YES AND AMEN AND JESUS”

PREACHING IN THE COMPANY OF PETER

Introduction

Virtually all scholars agree that the gospel Mark wrote was the first one to be written. Matthew, Luke, and John embrace Mark's outline and then go on to develop their own respective accounts.

But what is quite clear is that the gospel Mark wrote was, in its actual formation and writing, the apostle Peter's gospel. Peter is the first one named in all the listings of the twelve apostles, the lead apostle. Following the crucifixion of Jesus, Peter ended up preaching in Rome with Mark as his companion and "secretary." Mark is described in an early church tradition as the "interpreter of Peter . . . [who] wrote down accurately whatsoever he remembered. It was not, however, in exact order."[51]

No one had written a Christian gospel before Mark took up his pen, although there were some Roman and Greek writings that could be viewed as rough precedents. It turned out to be a form of writing that quickly became both foundational and formative for receiving and living the Christian life. We are accustomed to believing that the Holy Spirit inspired the content of the Scriptures (2 Timothy 3:16), but it is just as true that the form is inspired, this new literary form we call *gospel.* There was nothing quite like it in existence, although Mark had good teachers in the Hebrew storytellers who gave us the books of Moses and Samuel. He also had successors in Matthew, Luke, and John, who expanded the basic story, each in his own way.

Matthew's version features Jesus's teaching. I've selected a sermon on the Beatitudes to represent Matthew's concern to provide continuity with the teachings of

---

51. Papias, "Fragments of Papias from the Exposition of the Oracles of the Lord," https://sites.google.com/site/christanitystudies/home/fragments-of-papias-from-the-exposition-of-the-oracles-of-the-lord.

Moses. Luke's version represents Jesus's concern for the "outsiders": Gentiles, tax collectors, women, and Samaritans, maybe especially Samaritans. I've chosen the Lukan parable "Manure," long a favorite of mine, to witness Luke's concern to include the outsiders, the left out, to represent Jesus's inclusion of these and other outsiders. John of Patmos retains the basic form established by Mark, but he is different enough to get a section all to himself (part 7: "Preaching in the Company of John of Patmos"), which includes his gospel account, three letters, and the Revelation.

The Bible as a whole comes to us in the form of narrative, and it is within this large, somewhat sprawling biblical narrative that we encounter the form of gospel, which I would render more precisely as "*incarnational* storytelling," God revealing himself in human form: "the Word became flesh and . . . we have beheld his glory, glory as of the only Son from the Father" (John 1:14). In this sense Mark's gospel is a unique genre that is further developed in Matthew, Luke, and John.

Wallace Stegner, one of our great contemporary storytellers, tells us, "If the forms are bad, we live badly."[52] Gospel is a true and good form by which we live well. Storytelling creates a world of presuppositions, assumptions, and relations into which we enter. Stories invite us into a world other than ourselves and, if they are good and true stories, a world larger than ourselves. Gospel invites us into a world of God's creation and salvation and blessing, God in human form in action on the very ground on which we also live. It is an incarnational *story,* that is, a flesh-and-blood-on-the-ground story, a story worked out in actual lives and places, not in abstract ideas or programs or inspirational, uplifting anecdotes, but a *story* in which we recognize the action of God in the everydayness of a local history in our stories.

This is important, for there is a widespread practice in our postbiblical church culture to take the story and then essentially eliminate it by depersonalizing it into propositions or "truths" or morals or ideas. The story is eviscerated of relationships and persons. Jesus, the center of the Christian faith, is thus depersonalized into an abstract truth, and men and women are depersonalized into "problems" to be fixed. Eventually there is no story left.

52. Wallace Stegner, quoted in Hans Boersma, *Sacramental Preaching: Sermons on the Hidden Presence of Christ* (Grand Rapids, MI: Baker Academic, 2016), foreword, https://books.google.com/books?id=Q3tSDAAAQBAJ.

We don't read very long in this text by Saint Mark (and his successors, Matthew, Luke, and John) before we realize it is about events that actually took place in a thin slice of ancient history in Palestine under Roman rule. Before we have finished, we realize it is about God working out our salvation personally in Jesus Christ, God "in the flesh" (*incarnate*) in our lives and in the places and times in which we now live.

The distinctiveness of the gospel form is that it brings the centuries of Hebrew storytelling—the Holy Spirit telling the story of creation and salvation and blessing—to fulfillment in the story of Jesus, the mature completion of all the stories, in a way that is clearly revelation (that is, God's self-disclosing), in a way that invites and even *insists* on our participation.

In some respects this is an odd kind of story, this Jesus creation-salvation-blessing story. It tells us very little of what ordinarily interests us in a story. We learn very little about what we are really interested in. There is no description of Jesus's appearance. Nothing about his friends or schooling and very little about his childhood. Very little reference to what he thought, how he felt, his emotions, his interior struggles. There is a surprising and disconcerting reticence in regard to Jesus. We don't figure Jesus out; we don't search for Jesus; we don't get Jesus on our terms. If we stay with the story long enough, we recognize that Jesus and the life he embodies are not consumer items.

There are others in the story, of course, many others: the sick and hungry, victims and outsiders, friends and enemies, and, by implication, all of *us*. When we join the company of Peter in our preaching, more often than not our sermons turn out to be an attentiveness and response to the God-revealing Jesus, gospel texts shaping our attention and responses. Line after line, page after page: Jesus, Jesus, Jesus. None of us provides the content for our own salvation; it is given to us. Jesus gives it to us. The text allows for no exceptions.

After Peter's death by crucifixion in Rome, Mark went to Alexandria in Egypt and became the church's first bishop. Now he had the time and protected leisure to reflect upon and write what he had experienced during those years in Rome in the company of Peter as he preached Jesus. Mark wrote the gospel of Jesus as Peter had preached it. The story of Jesus then became the first gospel of Jesus with Mark as Peter's "secretary." That, at least, is the fairly well authenticated tradition.

Somewhere along the way, Saint Mark acquired a nickname: *Colobodactylus,* "Stumpfinger." One suggestion accounting for the name is that Mark was a large man whose stubby fingers didn't quite fit his stature. The nickname was an affectionate one, the kind we give to friends we joke around with: Shorty, Slim, Blondie, Kitten—Colobodactylus, "Stumpfinger." Perhaps it originated in the circle of friends in Rome who saw Mark working away day by day in the company of Peter, listening to Peter, and writing what he heard Peter preach, with those short, thick fingers pushing his stylus pen back and forth across the parchment, those short, thick fingers contrasting with the swift-paced drama of the sentences laid down. The American novelist Reynolds Price imagines a different origin of the nickname, namely, the similarity of the inelegant fingers to what he observed as Mark's "pawky roughness of language."[53]

The apostle whom Mark had served, Simon, also had a nickname: Peter, Greek for "Rock." But unlike his master's, Mark's nickname did not stick. The tradition is that after Peter was martyred in Rome and Mark became bishop of Alexandria, "Stumpfinger" probably did not seem appropriate for a bishop, so Mark recovered his proper name.

An immersion in the company of Peter, the first of the apostles to recognize and confess Jesus as the incarnation of the Trinitarian Godhead, the Christ, is the best way I know for preachers to develop an incarnational imagination. The first followers, Peter and his fellow apostles, saw it take place in their company and before their eyes, saw that the "Word became flesh" (John 1:14) in the humanity of Jesus and actually lived among them. Peter was the first to name what they had seen and heard as God took human form and, over an extended period of time (three years), lived in their neighborhood.

Reynolds Price uses the term "narrative hunger" to call attention to our "need to hear and tell stories . . . second in necessity apparently after nourishment and before love and shelter. Millions survive without love or home, almost none in silence; the opposite of silence leads quickly to narrative, and the sound of story is the dominant sound of our lives."[54]

The American poet Christian Wiman, exploring his newly realized Christian

53. Reynolds Price, *Three Gospels* (New York: Touchstone, 1997), 37.
54. Reynolds Price, *A Palpable God: Thirty Stories Translated from the Bible with an Essay on the Origins and Life of Narrative* (San Francisco: North Point Press, 1985), 3.

identity, says it like this: "I begin to think that *anything* that abstracts us from the physical world is 'of the devil.' . . . Christ speaks in stories as a way of preparing his followers to stake their lives on a story, because existence is not a puzzle to be solved, but a narrative to be inherited and undergone and transformed person by person."[55]

We need an incarnational imagination, a Jesus-soaked imagination, so that every truth becomes a lived truth, lived in the homes and workplaces that our congregations face us with every time we preach a sermon.

55. Christian Wiman, *My Bright Abyss: Meditation of a Modern Believer* (New York: Farrar, Straus and Giroux, 2013), 117–18, 90.

I

"Who Do Men Say That I Am?"

PSALM 2
MARK 8:27–30

Every once in a while a person speaks a brief sentence, three or four words maybe, that dams up a sea of wisdom and insight, that keeps the words available for the use of all of us. In an instant we know they are true, and we spend the rest of our lives pondering and living into them.

Socrates summed up a life of acquiring wisdom with two words: "Know thyself." That is, "Don't spend your days ransacking libraries and consulting experts. Get acquainted with who *you* are. There is no one quite like you. Start here."

In the early church, when the community of the gospel was threatened by overwhelming attacks and the Christian churches seemed about to be overwhelmed by heresy and assault, a young pastor named Athanasius came successfully to its defense. Someone described it as *Athanasius contra mundum:* "Athanasius against the world."

More recently Martin Luther King Jr.'s magnificent "I Have a Dream" speech has been a catalyst for the civil rights reforms that are taking shape in this decade of the sixties and after.

But for us Christians, four words continue to give definitive focus to the way we live our lives. The words came two thousand years ago from the lips of a fisherman who was walking on a country road in Palestine, with his friends, in the company of Jesus. The fisherman's name was Peter. The four words were "You are the Christ," spoken in answer to Jesus's question "Who do *you* say that I am?" (Mark 8:29).

—

When Jesus began his public ministry in Palestine, he chose twelve men to be his companions. Peter was the first, along with his brother, Andrew. Eventually there were twelve. Every time they are listed, Peter is the first one named. He was clearly the leader.

The Twelve spent the next three years with Jesus, walking—always walking—along the shores of Lake Galilee, in the hills, and through the villages. When you are walking, especially with others, you tend not to be in a hurry. Conversations are relaxed. There is time to meet strangers. You have the leisure to do nothing. So in their time with Jesus those three years, there was plenty of time for the Twelve to observe him, ask questions, discuss what was going on in the world and their neighborhood, observe him in all moods and weather. It would never have crossed their minds that he was not human, just like them.

Everything Jesus said and did was done in a place, just as everything we do is done in a place. All living is local: this land, this neighborhood, these trees and streets and houses, this workplace, these people. One of the seductions that interferes with mature Christian living is the construction of utopias, ideal places where we can live the good life totally without inconvenience. The imagining and then attempted construction of such utopias is an old habit of our kind. But it always turns out that we can't actually do it. *Utopia* is literally "no place." We can only live our lives in an actual place, not in an imagined or fantasized place.

Jesus lived almost his entire adult life in the hills and villages and on the lakeshore of Galilee, all parts of which can be reached in a single day on foot. And when Jesus began his public ministry at the age of thirty, he spent the first three years right there in Galilee, a kind of backwater cousin to Israel. The only exceptions were occasional three-day walking pilgrimages to Jerusalem to celebrate Passover.

But once, suddenly and uncharacteristically, he led his twelve followers straight north of Galilee for about two days of travel on foot to the town of Caesarea Philippi. This is the only time this place is mentioned in the narrative, and understandably so, for most if not all of the people who lived there were Gentiles, Greeks and Romans mostly. Roman soldiers were garrisoned there. It was well known for its pagan shrines. And it was stunningly beautiful, having a temple of white marble dedicated to Caesar. A spring of water provided an attractive center for bathing and relaxation. The largest mountain in Palestine, Mount Hermon, loomed magnificently over the whole area and stayed snow covered all year. Four rivers came together to create the River Jordan, form the Lake of Galilee, and water all the land to the south, emptying finally into the Dead Sea.

So why at this point did Jesus leave the familiar world of the Galilee hills and villages and take his twelve disciples into the foreign territory of Caesarea Philippi, where Latin and Greek were spoken and pagan religions practiced?

—

Here is a plausible conjecture. For Jesus, after three years in the public eye, two things were developing. First, increasing hostility from the Jewish high priests, the Pharisees, and the Sadducees. Jesus's popularity had roused the suspicions of the professional religious elite. This "nobody" from "nowhere" was being talked about by so many. Their authority was threatened.

And second, crowds were flocking to him. Jesus, for the people on the street, had become a guru. People wanted to see him in action, hear him speak, observe the ways in which he was taking the common people seriously.

For one segment of the people, he was fast becoming the enemy; for another segment, the latest celebrity. Jesus had become famous, whether as a rival or as the latest in fashions.

So Jesus needed a neutral place where he was not well known in order to clarify with his twelve disciples just exactly who he was and what he was about. It was time to clarify his core identity to his twelve followers and assimilate them to it.

So he took them to Caesarea Philippi on what I think of as a kind of contemplative retreat to a protected, quiet place where the events and conversations would come together and bring to recognition what had been slowly germinating: that this Jesus they had been following was both more and other than they supposed. I'm sure they had some sense there was something more to Jesus than they could articulate. Jesus now prompted them to give a name to it in an environment uncontaminated by accusations that he was the enemy and by larger-than-life fantasies that obscured who he really was.

Jesus cut to the chase.

"Who do people say that I am?"

"Some say John the Baptist, others Elijah, still others one of the prophets."

"How about you? Who do you say that I am?"

Peter answered, "You are the Christ." (Mark 8:27–29, author's paraphrase).

Peter was the first to say it: "You are the Christ." But the words were not spoken out of the blue. There were three years of relaxed, intimate conversation, eating together, getting to know one another's stories. One thing they knew for sure was that he was human. But was that all?

In Caesarea Philippi, Jesus was away from those who didn't trust him and from those who admired him for all the wrong reasons. Jesus was the enemy for some, a larger-than-life guru for others. Was there any other possibility? The unfamiliarity of pagan Caesarea Philippi provided an uncluttered environment for something not yet on their radar. Like, maybe, Christ?

The Greek word *Christ* (in Hebrew, *Messiah*) is a word they knew well. Growing up as good Jews, the Twelve knew it meant something special. Translated into English, it means "anointed." It marks the custom among the Hebrews of pouring oil over the head of a priest or king or judge. It symbolizes the presence of God's Holy Spirit filling or shaping a person in the role of a representative of God. The word *Christ* had a long history of use in their culture, with which they would have been very familiar. They had hundreds of years of handed-down memories of anointing stories. In some ways it was the most extravagant attribution that could be made. When Peter named Jesus as "the Christ," he was saying that Jesus was set apart for something special.

In the everyday speech around us, the term *Christ* occurs more often as profanity than as naming an actual person, an expletive without content. In Peter's ears it would have been a witness to the presence of God's Spirit-filling, shaping a person in a new role as priest or king. It had a long history of use in the Hebrew culture and Scriptures. In the Scriptures it meant that something special was going on here, that this person was set apart to represent God's presence among them.

So when Peter said, "You are the Christ," he was saying, "You represent God among us." Or maybe even "You *are* God among us." In some ways it was the most extravagant attribution that could be made. It would have had both political and religious connotations.

—

This was the critical insight and recognition that the three years of association with Jesus finally produced. But what now follows is a total revision of what the Twelve must have understood the identity of Jesus to be. The concept of *Christ* brought with it an understanding and image that were quite glorious: God among them in Jesus, God coming down to their level, to their everyday, ordinary lives consisting of family, work, eating meals, and going to the market.

Jesus's response to the confession was a stern command that they were to keep this totally quiet. It was as if he said, "If you talk about this, you will only be misunderstood. If people hear you use this word *Christ,* they will certainly jump to the wrong conclusions. So, *shut up!* Don't say anything to anybody. Not one word."

—

But why would Jesus want this to be kept a secret? Isn't this what had been going on all this time—preparing their imaginations to recognize God in Jesus?

It had taken three years to make sure that the disciples accepted and participated with Jesus as a human being, totally human. Now they were faced with recognizing him as Christ, the anointed of God, God among them. Jesus knew he had his work cut out for him in providing a way for them to understand that God was being God for and with them in a way they would never have come up with on their own: in a flesh-and-blood human being, just like them.

With Peter's identification of Jesus as Christ, God-anointed, Jesus had to totally revise their idea of what it meant to have God among them. Jesus lost no time, saying he "must undergo great suffering, and be rejected by the elders, the chief priests, and the scribes, and be killed, and after three days rise again" (Mark 8:31, NRSV).

Jesus "said this simply and clearly so they couldn't miss it" (verse 32, MSG).

Peter, who had just realized the true, underlying identity of Jesus, couldn't believe his ears and told Jesus he didn't know what he was talking about. Peter rebuked him and told him he was talking crazy. And Jesus just as emphatically told Peter to shut up and for emphasis called him "Satan": "Get behind me, Satan! Right now you are the devil talking. You have no idea how God is working in me among you" (verse 33, author's paraphrase).

Jesus then elaborated on what he had just said. "Anyone who intends to come with me has to let me lead. You're not in the driver's seat; I am. Don't run from suffering; embrace it. Follow me and I'll show you how. Self-help is no help at all. Self-sacrifice is the way, my way, to saving yourself, your true self. What good would it do to get everything you want and lose you, the real you? What could you ever trade your soul for?" (verses 34–37, MSG).

Annie Dillard, one of my favorite theologians, echoes Jesus with her pithy "A life without sacrifice is an abomination."[56]

It had taken three years to saturate the apostles' imaginations and for them to assimilate the fact that Jesus was indisputably *human*. We are at the midpoint of the story of Jesus as Peter preached it. It is now going to take three months, the second half of this gospel story, for his followers to realize that at the same time Jesus was also indisputably *God* among them, embracing the sacrificial death that became our eternal salvation.

Jesus, the presence of God among us, was human, just like us. God in human form. A human form that I can verify simply by touching my nose, my elbow. A historical person who walked the paths and roads on the ground in Palestine in the first century, just as I walk the trails of Maryland and Montana in twenty-first-century America. Jesus spent nine months in the womb just as I did. We know not only his name but the name of his mother. There was a family. There are named friends. This takes a great deal of the guesswork out of knowing God. Do you want to know what God is like, the form in which God reveals himself? Look in the mirror; look at your friends; look at your spouse. Start here: a human being with eyes

56. Annie Dillard, *Holy the Firm* (New York: Harper and Row, 1977), 72.

and ears, hands and feet, eating meals with friends. Walking to the store for a bottle of milk, hiking in the hills and picking wildflowers, catching fish and cooking them on a beach for a breakfast with friends. There was work to do—carpentry and masonry and fishing. Prayers were prayed. He walked in and out of houses and synagogues and the temple, just as we walk in and out of houses and schools, Walmarts and churches. He died and was buried just as we will be.

What this means, and by and large Christians have insisted on it, is that Jesus is not a principle or a truth, nothing abstract, nothing in general, nothing grandiose. When God revealed himself to us, he did it in a human body, an incarnation.

There is, of course, more to it than this. Jesus is not *just* human; he is also divine. Not only very human but very God. But what we have to face first of all, and what the gospel writers do face, is that the divinity does not overpower, does not diminish by so much as a fingernail, does not dilute by so much as a teardrop, the humanity. First of all—our four gospel writers are emphatic in their witness—we are told in no uncertain terms that God became flesh, the human flesh of Jesus, and lived among us. We start with the human. This is the way God makes himself known to us. They are also emphatic in their witness to his crucifixion and resurrection—our salvation. Our human life is personal in Jesus; our eternal life is personal in Jesus.

Can you think of any other way that God could have made it easier for us to know him? To meet him? To follow in his ways? *Jesus.*

But for many, maybe most, it is far easier to believe in an invisible God than in a visible God. Jesus is the form in which the invisible God can be seen.

—

You would think this would be enthusiastically embraced as good news, unqualified good news. But when it comes right down to it, I would rather be like God than have God be like me. It turns out that a lot of us, more times than we like to admit, aren't all that excited that a very human Jesus is revealing God to us. We have our own ideas of what we want God to be like. We keep looking around for a kind of religion or style of spirituality that gives us some promise that *we* can be godlike, be in control of our lives and the lives of others, exercise godlike authority or at least be authorities on God.

When the know-it-all Serpent promised our first parents that they could be "like God" (Genesis 3:5), you can be sure they were not thinking of anything human with all the limitations of being human that we know today. They were thinking of something far grander: knowing everything there is to know and getting an edge on the rest of the creation. When they heard those words, "like God," from the Serpent, we can easily imagine what went on in their heads: power, control, being in charge of everything, knowing everything, getting their own way, indulging every whim, able to do anything they desired without restriction.

The usual way we try to become like God is first to eliminate the God who reveals himself in human form and then to reimagine God as the god I want to be, invest this reimagined god with my own god-fantasies, and then take charge of the god business.

The old term for this reimagined, replacement god is *idolatry*. It is without question the most popular religion in town, any town, and it always has been. In previous generations these idolatry-gods were made of wood and stone, of gold and silver. More often these days they are made of words and ideas, abstractions and principles. But the common elements that define them as idols is that they are nonhuman, nonpersonal, nonrelational.

But idolatry always backfires. In the attempt to become more than human, to be godlike, we become less human, nonhuman: "Those who make [idols] and all who trust them shall become like them" (Psalm 135:18, NRSV). You'd think we would learn.

As we cultivate a relationship with God, we need to be wary of god-fantasies so we don't end up less human, less personal, less relational, less than who we were created to be. I want to grow up fully human. I want to be as human as Jesus was human. I want to live the Jesus Way, robustly human. And I want to do it with you.

Amen.

2

"With the Wild Beasts"

ISAIAH 40:1–5
MARK 1:1–13

The first significant word in Mark's gospel is lifted from the first significant word in Genesis, *beginning:* "In the *beginning* God created . . ." Mark's gospel opens with the identical word: "The *beginning* of the good news . . ." (NRSV).

Mark's first readers would be his fellow Jews. *Beginning* would certainly catch the attention of the people he grew up with and was writing to. The *beginning* of God's creation and the *beginning* of the story of the Son of God, Jesus, in parallel. The authorial intent is explicit: the story of Jesus is not a new story but a continuation of the first story.

Mark continues to locate the new in the old by quoting Isaiah, in which the terms *way* and *path* are prominent. *Way* and its synonyms were familiar to every Jew, especially because of their frequency in Psalms, where *way* is not only the path we walk on but the way we walk on the path. *Way* is not only a route we take but the way we go on the way, whether by foot or bike or automobile. The way we talk, the way we use our influence, the way we treat one another, the way we raise our children, the way we read, the way we worship, the way we vote, the way we garden, the way we ski, the way we feel, the way we eat . . . and on and on, endlessly, the various and accumulated *ways* that characterize our lives.

Later, Jesus will explicitly identify himself as "the way": "I am the way, the truth, and the life" (John 14:6, KJV). Later still, it was used by Paul on trial before Felix to designate the Christians in community: "according to the Way, . . . I worship the God of our ancestors" (Acts 24:14, NRSV). As the story develops, we see Jesus as the way we come to God. Jesus is also the way God comes to us.

—

Mark is not yet done in locating Jesus in the story he is telling in parallel to Genesis. Jesus "in the wilderness forty days, tempted by Satan" (1:13) recalls Eve in the Garden of Eden tempted—"tricked" was her term (Genesis 3:13, NRSV)—by a serpent, described as "more crafty than any other wild animal" (verse 1, NRSV). We don't know how to visualize this serpent. Probably not as any snake we have ever seen. Certainly not repulsive, but an intelligent being posing as a friend. When confronted by God, Eve gave the excuse "The serpent tricked me" (verse 13, NRSV), suggesting the serpent had not yet been cursed to be a snake that slithers in the grass. It is interesting to me that Saint Paul wrote to Christians in Corinth warning that sometimes Satan comes disguised as "an angel of light" (2 Corinthians 11:14). Maybe this Genesis serpent was more like an impressive "angel of light" or something equivalent, certainly nothing that appeared threatening like a python or a cobra. More often than not, evil doesn't look like evil. At any rate, Jesus is not seduced, not, in Eve's word, "tricked."

—

Three things happen in rapid sequence. Jesus is baptized; he is tempted; he begins his saving work in the world. The baptism is the event that marks Jesus as God's "beloved Son" (Mark 1:11). Jesus's work is salvation for the world. Jesus, capable and compassionate, goes directly to the center of what needs to be done and then does it. The temptation is sandwiched between the baptism of Jesus and the work of Jesus. It is not an option; temptation binds the two, baptism and work, together.

The Holy Spirit is behind the temptation, which is to say that God is behind it. It is not an unfortunate interlude, not a freak interruption of an otherwise smoothly planned strategy. The same Holy Spirit who descends upon Jesus at his baptism and later empowers him to the work of preaching and healing, here drives him out into the wilderness. A strong word, "drove him" (verse 12). This is necessary. This is not a gentle nudge, not a "still small voice" (1 Kings 19:12) advising the conscience. It is a relentless push.

The Greek term translated "tempted" (Mark 1:13) carries a double meaning: "temptation" and "testing." So I am going to keep us alert to both meanings by hyphenating *temptation-testing* for the single word Mark used.

If there is going to be any enduring connection between Jesus's baptism and Jesus's work, there must be temptation-testing. If Jesus submits to baptism and is obedient to his work, he must undergo temptation-testing. If there is going to be a connection between *who* he is and *what* he does, there must be something like temptation-testing combining them.

—

The site of the temptation-testing is the wilderness. It was a place rich with spiritually charged associations. When the Hebrews passed through the Red Sea, a kind of baptism, they entered the waters as a slave people and emerged on the other side as free men and women conscious of their new life as God's own people. They then spent forty years in that wilderness. Tempted and tested, they learned how to live a life of freedom with God as opposed to life in Egyptian slavery. It was a time to learn how to be God's free people instead of Pharaoh's slaves. They learned how to depend upon God. They learned how he cared for them. They learned his laws. They learned to discriminate between the demands of the gods of other nations and the will of the God of the covenant. The wilderness was empty of most of what this world counts important. There were no cities, and there was precious little culture. But it was packed with the experience of God. In the absence of other things, God became *the* reality with which they had to deal. When this wide range of God-experience, this temptation-testing, had been assimilated, they left the wilderness and began a new life in Canaan, a life of salvation freedom. There was no way, it seems, for them to go directly from the Red Sea baptism to Canaan freedom.

And now Jesus, the Messiah for whom Israel had been waiting, shows up in the wilderness.

We are not, it is clear, to think of the wilderness as a bad place, an empty place, a desolate place. It was empty of vegetation and human artifacts but full of God.

—

In the wilderness Jesus "was with the wild beasts; and the angels ministered to him" (Mark 1:13). It is a world reminiscent of Eden. The wild animals are unspoiled by human domestic drudgery and distractions. We are in the context of God's creation, a creation full of life as typified by the wild beasts. We are also aware of the rarefied atmosphere in which God is present without competitive voices from his inattentive children. Angels are the servants of God, ministering to our needs. There is a return to that original, uninterrupted, unspoiled community of created beings. If the wild beasts represent the entire order of natural creation, seething with a kind of raw beauty and innocent energy, the angels keep us in touch with the infinitely complex and diversified intimacy the Holy Spirit provides. The desert empty? Not at all. There are wild beasts and angels.

Henry David Thoreau was after something like this when he retreated for more than two years to Walden Pond. *Walden* is an important and wise document, full of insight. But it only deals with the aspect of God's creation that is natural and visible. Where are the angels? The providence and blessing? Half of creation is omitted. Grateful as we are for what is there, we want more. We want everything that God created, visible *and* invisible, animals *and* angels. And in the wilderness we get it.

In the wilderness we are back to basics: creation and the God of creation. Very physical and very spiritual. It is a place where physical life is important and where spiritual life is important, neither one to the exclusion or diminution of the other. So as Jesus enters the desert, we are not to feel apprehensive. He is being plunged into the best possible place to find the meaning of his baptism and discover the strength for his work.

We know the ancient associations of *wilderness*. We know its atmosphere. But what happened there? The action is described as Jesus being "tempted by Satan" (verse 13). However glorious the word *wilderness* sounds, the word *Satan* sounds ominous. In the pure air of the wilderness, there is suddenly an intruder, one who would corrupt the place as Eve's serpent had poisoned the ground of Eden.

We have seen that the word translated as "tempted" has a double meaning. It means "test" and it means "seduce." It can mean either, or it can mean both at once.

Testing in everyday experience is necessary. We test airplanes to see if they are safe for passengers. We test fishing lines to see if they will hold big fish. We test medicines to determine if they will heal or harm. David going forth to meet

Goliath was loaded down with King Saul's magnificent armor. But David, who had never worn anything but a shepherd's cloak, took the armor off and said in essence, "I can't go with these weapons because I have not tested them. I have no experience with them. I wouldn't dare risk them in an important battle" (see 1 Samuel 17:39).

Testing is not something we want to omit from life, at least in the things that matter. If there is no testing, there will be no confidence.

But *tempt* also means "seduce" or "test with hostile intent," as in to put the pressure on in order to ruin. No one objects greatly to being tested, for even if the process is arduous, the results are useful. But we don't welcome temptation, for there we are being subjected to hostile, negative pressures. The person who tests us wants to make us better; the person who tempts us wants to make us worse. But the tempter may make us better, for he forces us to a decision. He awakens in us the power of choice, where we find we have the ability to transcend pressure, circumstance, and heredity and then embrace who and what we will be.

Jesus experienced both aspects. He was pushed into the wilderness by God in order to be tested. While he was there, he encountered Satan, who tempted him. The testing-tempting combination was an ordeal in which Jesus experienced all that is possible to endure in the struggle between God and Satan, good and evil, faith and doubt. Later the pastor who wrote the letter to the Hebrews made Jesus's experience relevant for us when he wrote, "For we have not a high priest who is unable to sympathize with our weaknesses, but one who in every respect has been tempted as we are, yet without sin. Let us then with confidence draw near to the throne of grace, that we may receive mercy and find grace to help in time of need" (Hebrews 4:15–16).

Jesus in the wilderness was tested to assure him that he was able to commit himself wholly to God, to *be* in his work what his baptism had proclaimed him to be as God's Son, that Jesus is to us what he is to the Father.

Jesus was in the wilderness forty days. The specific number forty emphasizes the purpose of the testing. Forty days, according to the physicians of Jesus's era, was the length of time it took an embryo to mature to the point where it made its first movements and took on discernible human form. Often in the Greek world, men had to be at least forty years old to take on professional jobs. Moses was on Mount

Sinai for forty days as he was instructed in the Law. That was followed by the people of Israel, who spent forty years in the wilderness to become mature as the people of God. The forty days for Jesus was a concentration of growth that resulted in maturity. Jesus moved from baptism, the Messiah in embryo, through the forty-day period of temptation, and came out the other side as the complete man—the Son of Man—equipped to be God's Messiah and to inaugurate the rule of God's kingdom.

Forty is a finite number; it does not stretch out interminably. When counting to forty, we know there is an end to the counting, and then something starts. However necessary the wilderness is, it is temporary, an in-between time, and a place not intended to characterize an entire life. Wilderness life is a strenuous life. It cannot be endured indefinitely. Some have tried to make a permanent home in it. Saint Anthony and other Desert Fathers were heroic, but their lives were aberrations. Desert life is not necessarily congenial to serious work. We cannot be always "preparing."

What we are focusing on here is a time of testing to find out what works for us and what work we will do. A time of intensified experience in which we find the meaning of what is conveyed in our baptism. It makes sure that no part of the gospel life, this kingdom life, will remain simply as data, information, or a mere idea.

So here we have Peter, with Mark faithfully writing out his message, introducing Jesus to us as the incarnation of God in a human life, a life just like ours. Take Jesus's humanity seriously as God's gift. Take *your* humanity seriously as God's gift, God's gift to you.

Amen.

3

"Jesus Went up the Mountain"

GENESIS 1:22, 28; 2:3
MATTHEW 5:1–11

I was recently with a friend who has spent his life in the foreign service of the State Department. He has lived for extended times in Japan, England, Belgium, and Cyprus and eventually was ambassador to Fiji, with shorter stays in several European nations. He remarked on how long it took him, even in cosmopolitan London, to get in tune with the unspoken assumptions, the mental and spiritual world, of the people. And how many mistakes he made in the process, how many misunderstandings he both experienced and caused.

We think we know exactly how a person thinks and feels just by looking at him or her. Of course others think and feel just the way we do! And if they don't, they are either irrational or undeveloped.

International diplomacy takes time and careful listening. Parenting takes time and careful listening. Friendship takes time and careful listening. And Scripture takes time and careful listening.

Scripture, the Word of God, is our basic grammar for becoming fluent in kingdom-of-God language, the meaning of the words and the way sentences are formed.

—

Our text today is the introductory preface to Jesus's most famous sermon, the first of his that is recorded, the Sermon on the Mount, with eight beatitudes as an introduction. When we get this introduction right, we will have acquired an accurate and comprehensive imagination with which to interpret virtually everything Jesus taught concerning kingdom-of-God language. It consists of eight sentences, each brief and pithy. Each sentence begins with the word *blessed*.

Jesus is a teacher. But he is not first of all a teacher. Matthew in his first four chapters makes it clear that Jesus is first of all "God with us" (1:23). God coming to us in the flesh, as a human—what we designate as Incarnation. Thoroughly God, God through and through. And at the same time human, human through and through—living through everything we live through, speaking our language, and understanding our language. We can never reduce Jesus to one dimension: Teacher. Nevertheless it is necessary to pay attention and understand as accurately as possible what he taught, this new kingdom-of-God language. So here it is, his first sermon, introduced by eight sentences.

> Blessed are the poor in spirit, for theirs is the kingdom of heaven.
> Blessed are those who mourn, for they will be comforted.
> Blessed are the meek, for they will inherit the earth.
> Blessed are those who hunger and thirst for righteousness, for they will be filled.
> Blessed are the merciful, for they will receive mercy.
> Blessed are the pure in heart, for they will see God.
> Blessed are the peacemakers, for they will be called children of God.
> Blessed are those who are persecuted for righteousness' sake, for theirs is the kingdom of heaven. (5:3–10, NRSV)

And then there is a transition, a ninth blessing. The first eight blessings are designated for people in general (*theirs, they, those*). But there is also a ninth, and the ninth is personal—"blessed are *you*"—and leads into an intensification from the general to the personal throughout the rest of the sermon that Jesus preached on the mount (Matthew 5:13–7:27).

—

For men and women like us, with short attention spans, the Beatitudes are ideally suited for memorization, which I hope you will do. It is the scriptural equivalent to the famous *McGuffey's Reader,* out of which our grandfathers and grandmothers, many of whom emigrated from Norway and Italy and Germany and Palestine, learned to read English along these Maryland rivers and across the Appalachian hills and mountains that we enjoy so much. Think of the Beatitudes as the *McGuffey's Reader* in the kingdom of God. By establishing them in your memory bank, you will be able to develop an imagination adequately comprehensive to take in the entire kingdom-of-God teaching that Jesus puts before us.

Framing everything Jesus said in his teaching with these eight beatitudes will make an enormous difference in the way we conduct our everyday lives. Quality of life is at issue here: whether we live well or badly, by truth or by falsehood, taking time to listen carefully to these beatitudes before we rush on to something else or assuming we know Jesus's teaching inside and out.

Jesus is instructing us in what it is like to live in the world where God rules, the kingdom of God. He is training us to live not in reaction to our sin and guilt, not in response to people stronger than we are, not in desperation by any means at hand, not to survive in a sea of cynicism and malice, and certainly not to live egocentrically with the self as center and master. He is training our minds and emotions to live in response to the realities inherent in the kingdom of God: to live by faith and love, two words so shopworn and hackneyed that they need to be recontextualized in the kingdom of God.

—

Jesus begins with the word *blessed.* He repeats it eight more times. It is nearly impossible, though, for us at this point in time to comprehend the revolutionary impact of that word. By a great effort of the imagination, we can put ourselves back into that first-century world and immerse ourselves in what we know of its culture, literature, economy, social structure, and daily life. When we do that, one of the most striking things is how strange the word *blessed* sounds.

Americans assume that happiness is everyone's right. Our national creed has "the pursuit of happiness" as doctrinal orthodoxy. We surround ourselves with happy faces. Advertisements have people smiling happily. Entertainers, no matter what else they do, smile. Politicians, regardless of how far to the right or left they go, smile. We learn early how to smile whether we feel like it or not. It is a mark of decency to be happy, even when we have to fake it.

The ancient world was not like that. Nobody expected to be happy. Only the gods were happy. Happiness was not the lot of mortals. People were exhorted to pursue virtue, courage, excellence, goodness. But not happiness. Life was full of suffering. Tragedy was the truth of existence. Tragedy was the most common dramatic form in the theater of that world. It was important to live well and bravely, to live with grace and beauty. But not happily.

If by some chance you were happy, you hid the fact. The gods might notice and spitefully rob you of your brief happiness because they resented your infringing on their turf.

Then an obscure tribe of people in a remote corner of civilization started expressing a sense of happiness. Their word for it was *blessing.* And they used it a lot. In their account of the creation of the world, they used it four times in critical places. They used it constantly in their prayers and hymns. They talked of being blessed by God and blessing one another. They perceived an essential rightness at the heart of things and an exuberant wholeness that flowed out of it into their lives. They became a source of blessing, of happiness for all nations, just as it was promised to their father Abraham. They sang great hymns of blessing. They pronounced blessings on one another.

It was all very odd and was largely ignored by the nations.

When Jesus came and began teaching his generation what is involved in a world ruled by God (not by a king or emperor or general), he picked up the great word *blessed:* "happy, fortunate." And then, for emphasis, he repeated it eight more times in his inaugural teaching sermon. As people learned to live in this kingdom-of-God world, they experienced this blessedness. Communities multiplied and spread through the surrounding villages, cities, and nations and across oceans onto seven continents. By now the message has been heard nearly everywhere. Many believe it. Some even live it.

We are now in a very curious position. A lot of people believe happiness is possible. We tell one another that we are happy. We exhort one another to happiness. But many are unhappy. There is discontent and resentment. Gnawing covetousness and misery are widespread. But we are ashamed of it. We don't dare go public with it. We put on happy faces. We use cosmetics to mask the misery. We deck ourselves in brightly colored clothes to distract from the discontent. We surround ourselves with pictures of smiling celebrities to divert attention from our self-pity.

The ancients were often afraid to display their happiness for fear the gods would punish them. We moderns are afraid to display our unhappiness for fear our neighbors will disapprove of us. The ancient world never expected to be happy and was sometimes surprised by little episodes of it. The modern world expects to be happy all the time and is full of resentment when it isn't.

And then Jesus appears and says, "Blessed are you." He repeated it. His disciples repeated it. Christians continue to repeat it, even if only as a kind of talismanic gesundheit. The repetitions accumulate, and the world changes. The world changes from a place where people expect, as a matter of course, to be unhappy to a world where people expect to be happy. The change pivots on Christ's word. I think that is an astounding accomplishment, a terrific victory, reversing that climate of expectation. Obviously it is not universal and complete, but something significant has happened.

—

But something else, maybe even more astounding, has also taken place. Much of the world has become convinced that happiness is possible for everyone. Yet this same world at the same time ignores the person who instructs us in the way it comes. That doesn't make much sense, does it? To take Christ's goal and ignore his instructions on how to get there? To accept as true the promises of Christ and then reject the process he lays out so they are fulfilled in our lives?

God wills our blessing. Nine times he leads off with the word. He never lets us lose touch with the basic goodness, this blessedness, that he wills for us.

And then he points out eight acts by which we enter that blessedness:

- **the poor in spirit:** We empty *ourselves* of pride so we can be filled with *God's* spirit.
- **those who mourn:** We *share* the sufferings of others rather than avoid them.
- **the meek:** We hone our passions to a skilled gentleness.

- **those who hunger and thirst for righteousness:** We reject the appetites of a consumer society and cultivate deep personal relationships with God and others.
- **the merciful:** We refuse to react to the wrongs and troubles in the world by condemning and blaming, but instead we involve *ourselves* in compassionate serving.
- **the pure in heart:** We don't allow ourselves to be distracted and dissipated in gossip and trivia, but we center ourselves in God.
- **the peacemakers:** We decide to look at others, whatever their position, whoever they are, not as rivals to beat out but as brothers and sisters to love into wholeness.
- **the persecuted:** We reject the comfortable conformism of fitting into whatever the majority is doing, and we take instead the nonconforming narrow way of living out the difficult truths requiring love and grace.

God wills our happiness. He blesses. There is no question about that. He also graciously describes the kind of life that is able to receive and live out the blessings that he wills. He does not say, "I want you to be happy, but how to be happy is your business to discover by trial and error the best you can. Good luck!"

Not at all. He gives a precise description.

Unfortunately, these eight conditions involved in blessings are commonly despised and rejected by men and women who think they will *interfere* with happiness. And so they continue unhappy—but puzzled. Why? Perhaps they need to take another look at the depth of joy in these eight invitations to happiness.

The Christian accepts and honors them and becomes, to the surprise of onlookers, cheerful and complete. Blessed are you!

Amen.

4

"Do for Us Whatever We Ask"

ZECHARIAH 8:1–8
MARK 10:17–22

The man asks Jesus the right question: "What must I do to inherit eternal life?" (Mark 10:17). He wants to live intensely, deeply, thoroughly—the kind of life that lasts, eternal life. There are overtones of exuberance in it. Not just living for a long time or living forever, but the kind of living that has staying power. I would contrast it to living trivially, living frivolously.

In ancient Israel, in the early church, and in our life together now as God's people at Christ Our King Church, God is the living center of this life, life now. God is not a distant deity that we will meet for the first time only after we die. Jesus taught us to pray "Your will be done, on earth" (Matthew 6:10, NRSV). He told us, "The kingdom of God is in your midst" (Luke 17:21, NASB). We are a here-and-now people. The present is always the point at which eternity enters our lives.

The man's question is the right question, and he is eager, in a hurry, running to get his question answered, running to Jesus. When we see him kneel before Jesus as he asks his question, we realize the urgency that impels him.

He asks the right question, and he asks the right person, Jesus. It is Mark's task, as Peter's spokesperson, to make it as clear as possible for us to recognize that when we are listening to and observing Jesus in conversation and action in first-century Palestine, we are dealing with God firsthand, God accurately and personally revealed in Jesus. Jesus lived out the God-life in the conditions in which we ourselves are living. He said it himself: "I am come that [you] might have life, and that [you] might have it more abundantly" (John 10:10, KJV). It is Peter, with Mark writing what Peter experienced with Jesus, bringing us into the loop so we understand that when we are dealing with Jesus, we are dealing with God. Quite literally, the words and presence of God—all that is life affirming and life restoring—as we ask questions and listen to the answers of Jesus.

Not only do the conversations and meetings of Jesus recorded in our Scriptures make this evident, but the testimony of millions of persons, from every walk of life, speaking in every known language, on every continent, corroborates it.

This man comes running up to Jesus with great enthusiasm; he kneels before him with expectant reverence; he asks the right question and asks the right person. Jesus listens to him, loves him, and answers him. Then, having had the experience of being listened to, loved, and answered, the man leaves sorrowfully with his face clouded over.

I want to run after that man and say, "You are making a huge mistake. You must not have understood what you heard. Do you not realize whom you have just been with? Come back and listen again. Let Jesus say it to you again. You are not happy in what you are doing. Otherwise, why did your face cloud over? You are not free in the way you are living. There is no joy in your future, no hope in the path you are traveling. Don't leave. Don't walk away from this love."

But he does leave. I wonder if there are people here this morning who are face to face with Jesus's love right now, who hear Jesus's words—and will walk away from them.

The conversation begins with an energetic, expectant meeting; it concludes with a disappointing departure. What's going on here?

This man has lived a good life. He has lived a moral life. He has made a good living. But something isn't working. Otherwise, why would he have come to Jesus? Somehow his excellent moral track record and the years of material prosperity are not producing what he expected, so he comes to Jesus for help. He has done everything he could think of doing to live well: kept the commandments, used his abilities well. "What have I missed?"

The man was, I think, genuinely puzzled over his sense of incompleteness in life, real life, eternal life. Doesn't moral excellence give a person a satisfied self-image? Aren't material blessings a sign of God's blessing? If you do the right things and get the good things, shouldn't you be content?

Jesus looks at him and loves him. And out of that love, God's love, Jesus tells him what he needs: "You lack one thing; go, sell what you have, and give to the poor, and you will have treasure in heaven; and come, follow me" (Mark 10:21).

What does he lack? He lacks the freedom to enjoy who he is and what he has. His morality practiced for its own sake has made him muscle-bound. He is capable only of not doing evil; he is not able to do good. His material possessions are piled up around him and crowd him into a tiny space in which there is no room to enjoy or use them.

So "Sell what you have, and give to the poor." *That* takes care of the millstone possessions hanging around his neck. "Come, follow me." *That* takes care of the obsessive-compulsive morality. Neither material goods nor moral habits are dismissed. Rather, both are made useful by setting them in a new relationship, a personal God relationship.

You understand, I hope, that Jesus has nothing against possessions. Christianity is the most material religion the people of this earth have ever seen. Everywhere in our Scriptures and our history, we are told that matter is good. God creates it; Christ redeems it. God comes to us in the human flesh of Jesus of Nazareth, and we behold his glory (John 1:14). In the story of God with us, there is touching, seeing, hearing, tasting, smelling. All five senses are used and developed to their highest potential in the life of faith. We become materially and sensorially alive when we live by faith. Every time someone says that the body is wicked, that flesh is an embarrassment, that matter is evil, that mere things are profane—every time someone tries to isolate the spiritual from the physical, the invisible from the visible, the thinkers and saints in the church have stopped them and brought them back to earth, poured the water of baptism on their heads, put the bread and wine of the Lord's Supper in their mouths, and thrust the memory of Christ on the cross before their eyes.

So when Jesus tells the man to sell his possessions and give to the poor, it is not because there is anything wrong with the possessions. If there is something wrong with owning things, it is as wrong for the poor to have them as for this man. No. Matter is good; things are good; possessions are good. But if they get in the way of relationships of love and block them instead of blessing them, if they clog the channels made for the flow of love, then they need to be put in their place. Sell them. Give them to the poor. Use them to express your life, *God's* life.

And Jesus has nothing against morality. Christianity is the most moral religion that people on this earth have ever seen. The revelation at Sinai proclaimed by Moses penetrates into the heart of every action and shows there is nothing we feel, nothing we think, nothing we do that is not moral at its very core. *Moral* means that everything can be used for someone's good or for someone's ill, to bring about life or to cause death, to help or to hurt. *Moral* means that nothing is neutral. *Moral* means that nothing exists apart from its purpose, apart from the will that participates in it. All actions, feelings, and thoughts become creative or destructive when combined with our intentions, shaped by our love or hatred. All power is moral; all conversation is moral; all work is moral. Everything either builds up or tears down.

Christ initiates us into the terrible and awesome dignity of words and acts, even the most random and everyday ones. He trains us in such ways that all words and deeds become life affirming and love expressing.

—

What must we do? Simple. Use our possessions as gifts. Use our morality as a means of love. Use the stuff of creation, this marvelous material world, and use the stuff of our personhood, our capacity to choose and express love. Use what we have in our hands and what we have in our hearts. Put it to use in our neighborhoods with our neighbors.

Do you know what the key sentence in this story is? This: "Jesus looked him hard in the eye—and loved him!" (Mark 10:21, MSG). Jesus loves you. It is the key sentence in every story that involves a meeting with Jesus. It's the key sentence in your life.

Love is the most comprehensive and intimate relational term in our language. That God *is* love is basic to understanding everything in this salvation-faith life. God is never impersonal, never instrumental. He is love to the core. Without this sentence, "Jesus looked him hard in the eye—and loved him," nothing that follows can be understood. It is Jesus loving him that sets the stage for what follows.

And do you know the key command that Jesus gives to the man who asks the question? Actually there are two commands. First, "Sell what you have, and give to the poor." The second is this: then (that is, after you have let go of this identity that is all wrapped up in being moral and making money), "Come, follow me." But I wonder if the man even heard the second command.

Jesus invites him to be his companion, to learn a new way of life, a life of receiving love, instead of keeping moral rules, and making something of his life. In effect, Jesus is saying, "Okay, I've told you what you can do. Now let me do something for you. I love you, so let me give you back your life; let me reveal to you the real you."

Here is what I want you to hear in this conversation. Everything Jesus says and does has this premise: Jesus loves us just as we are. And with that as the premise, he invites us to join him and let him be our companion—in other words, to follow him, to experience his love in our everyday lives, our work lives, our family lives, our joys, and our sorrows.

—

There is something about this story that seems to me to be very American. In my lifetime there has been a sea change in the religious church culture, from *following* Jesus to *getting something from* Jesus. The basic terms that get people into churches these days are almost entirely in consumer language: the gospel will put you in position to be in charge of your life, to be happy and successful. And under such a campaign, we suddenly have churches springing up all over the country with ten, twenty, thirty thousand members. People flock to these churches to *get* something. They are consumers to the hilt.

But Jesus does not always meet our expectations, does not always give what we ask for or what we think we need. When he doesn't, we feel let down, deflated, disappointed, or we surf to another channel on the TV, or we try out another church that will, hopefully, give us what we ask for.

But not every gospel story is a success story on our terms. Some of the people who come to Jesus do not get what they want, do not hear what they want to hear. The man in this story didn't.

A lot of people in our culture come to Jesus, to God, wanting him to help them put the finishing touches on what they have very industriously and capably begun. They want to pull God in as a part-time assistant, usually low paid, but they want to stay in charge. When Jesus does not do it, instead of letting his love and truth change them, they leave and go off to look for someone who will do what they want on their terms.

—

In his love for this man, Jesus saw what was going on. He saw that the man's riches were tentacles strangling his life. He saw that the man's moral obsessiveness had degenerated into self-righteousness and was turning his life into an impersonal wasteland. Jesus's command, "Follow me," was an invitation to learn how to receive God's love and let that be the centering focus of his life.

Jesus does that still. He sees deep into our lives and senses what we need in order to live a salvation life. He doesn't *say* the same thing to everyone, but he does *do* the same thing. He sets us free to follow him. In a story later told by Luke, a man asked Jesus the same question: "What must I do to inherit eternal life?" Jesus told him the story of the Samaritan with the message to "Love your neighbor" (Luke 10:25–37, NRSV).

In his love Jesus diagnoses what is unique in us. He understands the precise ways in which things have gone wrong and diagnoses the particular aberrations that have seeped into our lives, and then he commandingly and mercifully saves us from them. Jesus's love awakens the sleeping parts of our lives to the colors and delights of eternal life. This waking is not without pain or difficulty or struggle. Being awake requires more energy than sleeping. There is also the possibility of more pain. Sleeping people don't suffer.

—

Here's a picture I have found helpful. I learned it from a book by Norbert Wiener.[57] In the early stages of development, creatures with exoskeletons (that is, skeletons on the outside, like crabs and beetles) have all the advantages, as they are protected from disaster. But at a certain point, they lose the advantage. Survival is at a higher rate, but development stops. Even when they molt into a different form, there is no development because there is no memory. They don't carry their development with them. Creatures with endoskeletons (that is, with their skeletons on the inside, like kittens and humans) are much more disadvantaged at first, being highly vulnerable to outside danger. But if they survive through the tender care and protection of others, they can develop higher forms of consciousness.

57. Norbert Wiener, *The Human Use of Human Beings* (Jackson, TN: Da Capo, 1998).

The man who asked the question of Jesus had lived his life with an exoskeleton. His material goods and moral achievements were all on the outside like a crust, and they separated him from both his neighbor and his God. He needed a conversion, a change. God's love does that. Jesus loved him. Jesus loves you. As we respond to that love, we will become more alive than we have been in our entire lives. That love will equip us to use everything we own as a way to share joy and blessing. That love will release us to use everything within us to create relationships of beauty and peace.

One last word. Did you notice that when the man asked what he must do to inherit eternal life, the word that stands out in the context is *inherit*? *Inherit* is what comes to us in the future. But Jesus gives his answer in the present tense: "sell . . . give . . . come . . . follow," four verbs in the present tense. Eternal life is not just life in the future. It begins right now.

I have long been impressed by the words of Teresa of Avila, the Spanish saint: "The pay starts in this life."[58]

Will you do it? Follow him?

Amen.

58. Heard this quote in a lecture in a Carmelite monastery fifty years ago.

5

"Sir, Let It Alone"

HABAKKUK 3:17–19
LUKE 13:6–9

Jesus told stories. As it turned out, he was a very good storyteller. His stories, as good stories always do, penetrate our imaginations and take on lives of their own in us. We find ourselves, often without even being aware of it, inhabiting the world of the story. Now Jesus has us where he wants us, understanding life from *his* point of view, seeing ourselves, God, and one another from the inside, from inside the kingdom of God.

It is the devil's own work to take the stories Jesus told (and the many other stories that provide so much of the content of our Scriptures) and distill them down to a truth or a moral that we can then use without bothering with the *way* we use them—unconnected from the people whose names we know or the local conditions in which we have responsibilities, apart from what we know about Jesus, who tells the story. The devil is a great intellectual. He loves getting us to discuss *ideas* about God. He does some of his best work when he gets us so deeply involved with ideas about God that we are hardly aware that while we are reading or talking about God, God is actually *present* with us, and the people whom he has placed in our lives to love are right there in front of us.

All the gospel accounts present Jesus as a storyteller. The stories that Jesus told have a style all their own. We call them *parables.* "Without parables he did not speak to them" (Matthew 13:34, DRA). A parable is a way of saying something that requires the imaginative participation of the listener. They are brief stories that Jesus created more or less on the spot as he was talking with people on the road. The word *parable* literally means "something thrown down alongside of." Our first response is "What is *this* doing here, right in front of me?" We ask questions. We think. We imagine.

"Parables appear in quick, precise strokes. A parable is feeble; almost all the power is in the one who hears it."[59] We start seeing connections, relations. A parable is not used to tell us something new but to get us to notice something we have overlooked even though it has been right there before us for years. Or it is used to get us to take seriously something we have dismissed as unimportant because we have never seen the point of it. Before we know it, we are involved.

A parable keeps the message at a distance, in the shadows. It slows down comprehension, blocks automatic prejudicial reactions, dismantles stereotypes. A parable comes up on a listener obliquely, on a slant. We listen, unsuspecting. And then, without warning, without the word being used: God! John Dominic Crossan says that the parable is an earthquake opening up the ground at your feet.[60]

Most parables make no explicit reference to God or the kingdom of God. They are stories about farmers and judges and victims; coins and sheep and prodigal sons; attending wedding banquets, building barns and towers, and going to war; a friend who wakes you up at midnight to ask for a loaf of bread; the courtesies of hospitality; crooks and beggars; and manure.

Parables were Jesus's primary language of choice to converse with the people he met.

Most of us have a favorite Jesus parable. The parables of the good Samaritan and the prodigal son are the favorites of many of us. My favorite is the manure story.

Here it is.

> A man had a fig tree planted in his vineyard; and he came seeking fruit on it and found none. And he said to the vinedresser, "Lo, these three years I have come seeking fruit on this fig tree, and I find none. Cut it down; why should

59. Jean Sulivan, *Morning Light: The Spiritual Journal of Jean Sulivan*, trans. Joseph Cunneen and Patrick Gormally (Mahwah, NJ: Paulist Press, 1988), 64.
60. John Dominic Crossan, *The Dark Interval: Towards a Theology of Story* (Salem, OR: Polebridge Press, 1994), 57.

> it use up the ground?" And he answered him, "Let it alone, sir, this year also, till I dig about it and put on manure. And if it bears fruit next year, well and good; but if not, you can cut it down." (Luke 13:6–9)

Jesus tells this parable while they are on their way from their home country in Galilee to Jerusalem for the Passover Feast. The road they take passes through Samaria. Samaria is hostile territory for Jews. There had been seven hundred years of bad blood between Jews and Samaritans.

The first day after crossing the border into Samaria, Jesus and his disciples attempt to find a place to stay for the night. The Samaritans let them know in no uncertain terms that they are not welcome. The "thunder brothers," James and John, are outraged and want to kill them on the spot by calling down supernatural fire. For them it is a natural response. They have a solid biblical precedent. This is the same Samaritan territory in which Elijah several hundred years before had called down fire from heaven to incinerate King Ahaziah's minions (2 Kings 1:1–16). But Jesus was not Elijah. Jesus rebukes the brothers.

In Jesus's parable the violent impatience of the farmer's command to "cut it down" matches the outrage of James and John when confronted with the rude Samaritan inhospitality. And the gardener's response, "Master, don't touch it this year till I have had a chance to dig round it and give it a bit of manure," sounds very much like a response Jesus himself might make.

For some time Jesus had been preparing his followers not to have any illusions that people would receive either him or them with open arms. Twice before setting out on the journey through Samaria to Jerusalem, Jesus told his followers what they had to look forward to. In the days to come, he would be rejected and killed (Luke 9:22, 44). And, of course, as we know so well, the opposition and hostility that greeted Jesus when he arrived in Jerusalem for the Passover Feast did its work. Jesus was killed.

Jesus is not a word in a book to be read and studied. He is not a word to be discussed. Jesus is the Word made flesh (see John 1:14). He is the living Word, a live voice, God's Word that took on human form and lived in an actual country

(Palestine), in a real time (the first century), and ate meals of bread and fish and wine with named people (Mary and Martha, Peter and Andrew, James and John). In order to respond rightly to this voice, this Word-made-flesh voice, we must listen and answer in our actual neighborhoods while eating meals of tuna casserole and spinach salad in the company of people who know us and whose names we know: our spouses and children, friends and fellow workers, just for a start. Nothing in general. Nobody anonymous. No disembodied or unvoiced words.

The Christian community and its leaders know this well. We know that without vigilance we can easily erode into faithlessness, drift into unthinking betrayal, lose this responsive, obedient, person-to-person, voiced relationship with Jesus and with one another. And so we are encouraged to develop a language of participation, of following, of listening with the intent of obeying, of being on guard against depersonalizing god-talk.

Have you ever noticed how significant Jesus's parables are in keeping our language involved and participatory—not a language *about* but a language *with*—getting us in on and keeping us alert in acts of justice, loving-kindness, and walking humbly with our God (Micah 6:8)? The parables are basic verbal defenses against disengaged complacency. And parables are Jesus's favorite way of getting us in on who he is and what he is doing.

—

We are used to our spiritual leaders motivating and energizing us into action for God and God's kingdom. But this manure story is just the opposite. There are occasions when not-doing is commanded, times when restraint is called for. The manure story is all about being patient with God. God is not in a hurry.

The manure story stops us in our tracks. Instead of goading us into action, it takes us out of the action. We have just come across something that offends us, some person who is useless to us or the kingdom of God, just "[using] up valuable space," and like the farmer we lose patience and either physically or verbally get rid of him or her: "Chop him down . . . Chop her down . . . Chop it down." We solve kingdom problems by amputation.

The manure story interrupts our noisy, aggressive problem-solving mission. In a quiet voice, Jesus (the gardener?) basically says, "Hold on. Not so fast. Wait a minute. Give me some more time. Let me put some manure on this tree." But for his trouble, Jesus was killed.

So Luke ensures that we pay attention to the response Jesus makes to strategies of impatience like "Chop it down" by commanding "Let it alone."

—

Manure is not a quick fix. It has no immediate result. It is going to take a long time to see if it makes any difference. If it is results we are after, chopping down a tree is just the thing: clear the ground and make it ready for a fresh start. We love beginnings: birthing a baby, christening a ship, the first day on a new job, starting a war. But spreading manure carries no such exhilaration. It is neither dramatic nor glamorous. Manure is a slow solution. When it comes to doing something about what is wrong in the world, Jesus is best known for his fondness for the tiny, the invisible, the quiet, the slow: yeast, salt, seeds. And manure.

Manure does not rank high in the world's economies. It is refuse, garbage. We organize efficient systems to collect and haul it away, out of sight and smell. But the observant wise know that this apparently dead and despised waste is teeming with numerous microorganisms and the things needed for life: enzymes, minerals, nutrients, energy sources. It's the stuff of resurrection.

There are many things we must not do, *cannot* do, if we are to be faithful to Jesus. Like taking things into our own hands, getting rid of the offender along with the offense.

—

Manure. God is not in a hurry. We are told repeatedly to "wait for the Lord." But that is not counsel that is readily accepted by followers of Jesus who have been conditioned by American promises of instant gratification. Eugen Rosenstock-Huessy, one of our great modern Isaian prophets who had extensive experience with violence in two world wars, wrote, "The greatest temptation of our time is impatience, in its full original meaning: refusal to wait, undergo, suffer. We seem unwilling to pay the price of living with our fellows in creative and profound relationships."[61]

61. Eugen Rosenstock-Huessy, *The Christian Future: Or the Modern Mind Outrun* (Eugene, OR: Wipf and Stock, 2013), 19.

Manure. Silence. Manure means reentering the conditions of "Let it be done to me" (see Luke 1:38), submitting to the silent energies that change death into life, the energies of resurrection. Language consists of equal parts speaking and silence. The art of language requires skills in silence quite as much as skills in speaking. Much mischief and misunderstanding result from talking that is not embedded in much listening. I like Saul Bellow's comment: "Silence is enriching. The more you keep your mouth shut, the more fertile you become."[62] Silence is the manure of resurrection.

God is a God who acts. We are constantly called on to pay attention to "his wonderful works to the children of men" (Psalm 107:31, KJV). But he is also the God who waits: "The Lord is not slow about his promise, as some think of slowness, but is patient with you, not wanting any to perish, but all to come to repentance" (2 Peter 3:9, NRSV). All who follow Jesus must learn to put up with this slowness, "as some count slowness."

—

A few days after this manure story had entered into the imaginations of the company of men and women who were following Jesus, he entered Jerusalem. Before a week was out, he was hanging on the Golgotha cross.

Pilate and Caiaphas in an unholy alliance agreed that Jesus had to go. He was a threat to the precarious peace the Roman army was trying to preserve. He was a threat to the highly profitable business Caiaphas and his Sadducean henchmen were running from the Jerusalem temple. He was "[using] up the ground" (Luke 13:7) needed for their own purposes. And so they killed him. They eliminated both him and his kingdom from this earth. Or so they thought. Jesus responded to their hostile violence with a word out of the manure story, this parable he had told just a few days earlier on the road through Samaria. As Jesus was hanging from the cross, his first words were a prayer: "Father, forgive them" (Luke 23:34).

Our translations obscure the connection of this word that Jesus prayed from the cross with his earlier word in the manure story. The farmer's order, "Cut it down" (Luke 13:7), is echoed in the Holy Week "Crucify him" (Luke 23:21).

62. Saul Bellow, *It All Adds Up: From the Dim Past to the Uncertain Future* (New York: Penguin, 1995), 310.

Jesus's prayer to his Father, "Forgive them" (Luke 23:34), is a verbatim repetition of the gardener's intervening "Let it alone" (Luke 13:8). In some contexts the Greek word (*aphes*) means "Hands off . . . Cool it . . . Leave it alone." In contexts having to do with sin and guilt, it means "Forgive . . . Remit . . ." It is the same word used in the prayer Jesus taught us: "Forgive us our sins" (Luke 11:4). Here the contexts of parable and prayer converge.

The farmer's impatient "Cut it down" intended for the fig tree is deflected by the gardener's "Let it alone." The violence visited on Jesus is countered by "Father, forgive them."

—

For those of us who are up to our necks in manure, which is to say, up to our necks in forgiveness, it is perhaps important to note that the forgiveness Jesus prayed for us is not preceded by any confession or acknowledgment of wrongdoing by the crucifixion crowd—or by any of us since. Preemptive forgiveness. Jesus prays that we be forgiven before any of us have any idea we even need it, "for they know not what they do" (Luke 23:34). No preconditions. Amazing grace.

Amen.

6

"The Death of Death"

PSALM 22:1–3
MARK 15:6–41

Christ is the revelation of God in the person of Jesus: God in the flesh, God incarnate. We read and pray the Jesus story, letting our imaginations be shaped by his life, by his words and his behavior. Irenaeus, an early church father, famously wrote, "The glory of God is a person fully alive."[63] Which is certainly true. But there is more.

As Mark's gospel, as preached by Peter, approaches its conclusion, Jesus, on his way to Jerusalem for the Passover Feast, three times prepares his followers for what is coming: he is going to die (8:31; 9:31; 10:33–34). And then it took place—not only death but a slow, excruciating, violent death, death by crucifixion.

—

Death is the defining act, the "reason" of Jesus's life: In his words, "It is for this *reason* that I have come to this hour" (John 12:27, NRSV). The dying took three hours, from noon to three o'clock in the afternoon, on a Friday, just outside Jerusalem. As Jesus was dying, he prayed. He prayed seven one-sentence prayers. None of the four gospel writers gives us all seven. Mark gives us the first one: "My God, my God, why have you forsaken me?" (15:34, NRSV).

The community of the church has prayed these last words of our dying Savior,

63. Mons. Philippe Delhaye, "Pope John Paul on the Contemporary Importance of St. Irenaeus," www.ewtn.com/library/Theology/Irenaeus.htm.

a quote of Psalm 22:1, to practice the presence of Jesus. We sink our souls into this mystery, these "depths" (Psalm 130:1) in which our salvation is forged. We want our own deaths to be congruent with Jesus's death, congruent with his sacrificial life, a willed offering of all that we are, and a witness to the resurrection.

—

Jesus's death is a real death. His death is a historical fact. Nothing in Jesus's life is as meticulously documented as his dying and death. "Dead and buried," as our Apostles' Creed has it, a death every bit as physical as each of ours will be. His heart stopped; his brain stopped. There was a precipitous drop in body temperature. Dead. But there was more, far more than the cessation of vital signs. Salvation was accomplished. A divine event was enacted in the death of Jesus. His death, a willed and sacrificial death, was an offering for the death-dealing sins of the world, a death that conquered death. It was the death of death.

This is a great mystery, perhaps the greatest mystery in the cosmos, in heaven and earth, and, strictly speaking, unfathomable. Not that some of our best minds haven't tried. Their thinking and praying are not without use. They turn up insights and glimpses into the profound and eternal workings of the Trinity that prevent us from being complete outsiders to this salvation mystery in which our lives are radically and comprehensively re-created, "ransomed, healed, restored, forgiven," as we so robustly sing. But when all is said and done, we realize that we will never get much beyond what Job called "the outskirts of his ways" (26:14) in comprehending the inner workings of the Cross and our salvation. If you think you understand God, you have misunderstood him.

This mystery shapes the way Christians live and die, believe and love, forgive and are forgiven. It is a mystery we inhabit, not just stand before and ask questions of out of curiosity.

—

The death of Jesus on the cross can be understood and accounted for easily enough on a physical and historical level. But the salvation Jesus accomplished on the cross cannot be. And it is this accomplished salvation, not a coroner's autopsy of the death, that brings us back to the cross over and over again. Revisiting Jesus's death is different from visits we make to a cemetery, bringing flowers, keeping the memory of our beloved dead in focus. We are not at the cross to remember or do homage. We are here to probe the meaning of our daily dying in the company of Jesus's dying for us.

Saint Paul gives us the vocabulary for doing this: praying our own daily dying as participation in these eternal dimensions of Jesus's death. When Paul writes, "I have been crucified with Christ" (Galatians 2:19, NRSV), he probes the salvation dimensions of Jesus's death as he experienced them. When he writes, "I die every day!" (1 Corinthians 15:31), he is giving witness to the sacrificial offering of his life that he makes every day as he follows the way of Jesus to the cross. When he writes to his brother and sister Christians, "You have died, and your life is hidden with Christ in God" (Colossians 3:3, NRSV), he is drawing them into participation in the salvation workings of Jesus's death. When he writes from a prison cell in Rome, himself condemned to a Roman execution, that Jesus "became obedient to the point of death—even death on a cross," he urges his readers, "Let the same mind be in you that was in Christ Jesus" (Philippians 2:8; 2:5, NRSV).

—

We Christians die twice. The first death is when we set out to follow Jesus, deny ourselves, take up his cross, and choose to live obediently and believingly in his sacrificial company and not pridefully isolated in our own.

We pray in company with Jesus as he prays about his death. It is a way of prayer that brings us into an embrace and acceptance of the death we die as we are baptized into Christ and become witnesses to a resurrection when we, having died, are raised with Christ (Romans 6:5–11).

Death is a nonnegotiable element in being a human creature. It is also nonnegotiable in being a follower of Jesus.

But there is also this: meditating and praying with Jesus as he dies on the cross is not an invitation to morbidity. There have been times in the community of Christ that Christians have attempted to experience and appropriate the suffering of Jesus on the cross by indulging in practices of mortification: extremes of fasting, deliberate sleep deprivation, wearing hair shirts, and self-flagellation (the medieval forms of "discipline"). There is a story I like very much of a monk who imposed on himself the discipline of not smiling. How could he even think of smiling when Jesus is suffering? A sacrilege! A fellow monk in exasperation told him, "Go ahead, make yourself miserable. But do it on your own time. Don't make everyone around you miserable too."

We begin all our prayers, and most emphatically when repeating his prayer from the cross, at the empty tomb, the place of resurrection. We start from resurrection. Neither Jesus's death nor ours can be understood or participated in apart from resurrection. Cross and resurrection are the South and North Poles, true gospel polarities, of a single, undivided, salvation world. Remove either pole and you gut salvation. Morbidity (a neurotic obsession with suffering) and masochism (self-imposed suffering) have no place in prayer. Our basic approach to the cross is gratitude.

—

So, back to Jesus's first prayer from the cross, the three opening sentences of Psalm 22.

> My God, my God, why have you forsaken me?
> Why are you so far from helping me, from the words of my groaning?
> O my God, I cry by day, but you do not answer;
> and by night, but find no rest. (verses 1–2, NRSV)

Death cuts us off from our moorings. It is the final dismissal. It is also the ultimate incomprehensibility. I no longer belong. I no longer fit. And I am not given an explanation. These metaphorical minideaths as we follow Jesus on our way to the cross anticipate and prepare us for what many Christians make a habit of praying for: a good death. These minideaths (some of them not so mini)—dead ends, rejections, bewilderments, snubs, abandonments, unanswered questions, wrong turns—are each in turn a shadow of the final death. We die ten thousand deaths before we are buried.

One of the surprises that inevitably come to followers of Jesus in the way of salvation is the vast number of people who experience and cry out in despair at being abandoned, whether by God or spouse or child or friends, asking, "Why?" We hear Jesus's cry of dereliction repeated, echoing down the corridors of the centuries, ricocheting off the walls of our churches and homes.

But however long or attentively we listen, we never get an answer to the "Why?"

Does it help to find ourselves praying in the company of Jesus as he prays his "Why?" I think it does.

Does it help to find Jesus in our company as we pray our "Why?" I think it does.

Does it help to realize that as Jesus prays his sense of God-abandonment, he is praying a prayer that he recited as a child, these first lines of Psalm 22, a psalm that expresses excruciating isolation, emotional devastation, physical pain? I think it does.

Does it help to realize that the prayer, prayed to its finish, ends up in a congregation, "the great congregation" (22:25, NRSV) of men and women among whom we (David and Jesus and so many others) have been able to give witness that God "did not hide his face from me, but heard when I cried to him" (22:24, NRSV)? Does it help to know this prayer ends up quite differently than it begins? I think it does.

And does it help to observe that this first prayer from the cross is not the last? Jesus keeps praying. Six more single-sentence prayers, broken shards of prayer from broken lives.[64]

Jesus is not done praying. And neither are we.

Amen.

64. The other six are "Father, forgive them; for they know not what they do" (Luke 23:34); "Truly I tell you, today you will be with me in Paradise" (Luke 23:43, NRSV); "Father, into your hands I commend my spirit" (Luke 23:46, NRSV); "Woman, here is your son. . . . Here is your mother" (John 19:26–27, NRSV); "I thirst" (John 19:28); and "It is finished" (John 19:30).

7

"He Is Not Here"

PSALM 16
MARK 16:1–8

You may find this hard to believe, but the hardest sermon in the year for me to prepare is this Easter sermon. It has always been that way for me. I keep thinking I will get the hang of it and it will get easier, but it doesn't. Why isn't it easier? More people come to worship on this day than any other; the music is exuberant, with the choir in full voice and the hymns triumphant; the budding trees and blossoming plants and warming weather provide a terrific supporting cast. Every place I look, there are affirmations of Easter and of what I want to do in an Easter sermon. It should be easy. But it isn't.

My difficulties are compounded this year by the text I have before me: Saint Mark's gospel, chapter 16. Four gospel writers—Matthew, Mark, Luke, and John—tell the story of Jesus's arrival in our history to reveal in human form (the Incarnation) God's love and then our salvation. God himself taking on human flesh to make sure we would have an accurate and accessible means by which we could both understand and receive God. It is a fascinating story: a story of surprising compassion, of vivid teaching, of strenuous conflict. We hear this story told to us in turn by these four writers, and as we read this story for ourselves, we suddenly (or gradually) come to understand that this is not instruction in religion. This is an *announcement: God is here.* God present to us, God on our side. He wants us to know what is going on, and he wants us as healthy participants in what he is doing. All this is conveyed personally to us in Jesus.

One of the surprises in this story is that even though there are many wonderful things in it—that *God* is everywhere in it—the people are all very ordinary. There is not a single celebrity or hero. Everything takes place and is worked out among the kind of people and circumstances we are familiar with. There is not a single line here that couldn't be convincingly uttered in Maryland.

I walked out of my house on Saratoga Drive at six o'clock Wednesday morning, and as I walked to church, I smelled Galilee. Twice I have spent a week in the spring in Galilee, and it is identical to spring in Maryland. And the Christ who walked and talked there is identical to the Christ taught and preached here.

A great deal of care is taken by each of the four writers to make this plain: this has to do with *us.* No one is excluded; everyone is included. If you have any experience of being treated as unimportant or insignificant because you are a woman or a foreigner or a child or sick or handicapped or a newcomer or poor or a criminal or a failure or too young or too old, you don't have to read very far in these books before you find that you are in on the action. You are named, you are loved, you are called, you are saved—you are *in.* You are included in God's story as lived by Jesus.

The story ascends to a climax as one influential group of people, to whom Jesus made it plain that they are included in God's story, decide they don't want God in their stories. And so they arrest him, put him on trial, and kill him. This story of Jesus's passion—his suffering and crucifixion—is the most powerful piece of writing in the world. It has embedded itself in our imaginations so deeply, so thoroughly, that there is scarcely a story or play or poem written since then that isn't influenced by it in some way or another. Even people who don't know the story actually do know the story, for it is so powerfully and pulsatingly *there* and now *here:* in our experience, in our history, in our world. The four gospel writers surpass themselves in giving us this event: details etched, energies orchestrated, characters believable.

—

There is a lot of suffering that takes place in the world, a lot of evil. If we are going to have a religion that is worth anything to us, if we are going to believe in a God who makes any difference in our lives, we have to know the very worst that happens. This is the worst. And this worst is not a kind of embarrassed exception to everything else. It is the climax. This is that toward which everything has moved. The cross of Jesus is not an unfortunate episode that we should try to sweep under the rug, the skeleton in the closet of the gospel. This is the place of arrival, the goal. And none of us fails to be moved by it. If Jesus could enter this world and be unflinchingly courageous in this extreme adversity, be such a magnificent "failure," then I can also live with meaning and love in whatever comes my way.

But this end is not the end. There is resurrection. The Jesus who was killed by the people who didn't want God in their lives is raised by God to be their God, whether they want him or not. Christ is risen. We celebrate the resurrection on Easter. We go further, go on to celebrate it every Sunday: fifty-one mini-Easters every year.

All four gospel writers tell, each in his own way, this resurrection story. It is a happy ending to a terrible experience. Except for Mark, alone of the gospel writers, who doesn't tell it as a happy ending.

Matthew, Luke, and John in their resurrection conclusions narrate stories of the risen Jesus Christ confirming his presence to his disciples. The three evangelists walk us through the apostolic difficulties in believing this extraordinary event—the doubt and bewilderment—and then move through verifications and confirmations that cement their belief and rejoicing and obedience.

But not Mark. Mark does not show us Jesus alive. Mark does not show us the disciples believing. Mark has no one rejoicing. Mark has no one obeying.

Mark's resurrection story is the briefest of the four. Listen carefully to this:

> When the sabbath was over, Mary Magdalene, and Mary the mother of James, and Salome bought spices, so that they might go and anoint him. And very early on the first day of the week, when the sun had risen, they went to the tomb. They had been saying to one another, "Who will roll away the stone for us from the entrance to the tomb?" When they looked up, they saw that the stone, which was very large, had already been rolled back. As they entered the tomb, they saw a young man, dressed in a white robe, sitting on the right side; and they were alarmed. But he said to them, "Do not be alarmed; you are looking for Jesus of Nazareth, who was crucified. He has been raised; he is not here. Look, there is the place they laid him. But go, tell his disciples and Peter that he is going ahead of you to

> Galilee; there you will see him, just as he told you." So they went out and fled from the tomb, for terror and amazement had seized them; and they said nothing to anyone, for they were afraid. (16:1–8, NRSV)

Mark shows us three women coming to tend the corpse of Jesus. He shows us an empty tomb. There is a young man, probably an angel, telling the three women that Jesus is risen and commanding them to tell the others. And then we have the three women disobeying the angel's command by saying nothing to nobody (the Greeks love double negatives). And the last words of Saint Mark's gospel are, if you can believe this, "for they were afraid."

We know these women's names: Mary Magdalene, Mary the mother of James (Jesus's brother), and Salome. Mary Magdalene is mentioned first. The only thing we know about her is that she had lived a spectacularly wretched life and been rescued from it by Jesus, and in consequence she was a particularly grateful and appreciative disciple. All three were at the tomb because they owed Jesus respect and gratitude, and they were grieved at his death and loyal to his memory.

But loyal as they were and owing him, as it were, their very lives, their response to the announcement that Jesus lived was disobedience and unbelief. They were commanded to pass on the angel's message, and instead of obeying they refused. They had at least verbal supernatural evidence that Jesus was alive and keeping his promises, but instead of worshiping and singing, they were scared into silence. Why would anyone who was told the terrific news that God was alive in the person of Jesus refuse to believe it? Why would anyone commanded by an angel to tell friends the news disobey? But that is what the two Marys and Salome did.

Let us try to disregard what we know already from the Matthew, Luke, and John accounts of what turns out. We know that these women later on did become obedient and pass on the message. We know that they did worship and rejoice and believe. But for right now they do not. And Saint Mark takes great pains to let us know they do not. He leaves his gospel story dangling. Is this any way to end a Bible story? Is this the kind of thing you want from your pastor on Easter morning?

Here is what Mark is doing. He is telling us that now we are at the hard part, that this is not going to be easy. It wasn't easy for Mary Magdalene. It wasn't easy for Mary, the mother of James. It wasn't easy for Salome. And it isn't going to be easy for you.

Up to now, everything was easier than this: getting in on the healings, listening to the teachings, following Jesus to Jerusalem, experiencing the terrible sufferings, watching Jesus die, coming to the tomb to care for Jesus's dead body. Taking your children to Sunday school, attending church, deciding to live a Christ-attentive life, loving the neighbor you don't like. Not that any of that is a piece of cake, but it was easier than this.

The picture has suddenly changed radically. This is not simply a continuation of what they had experienced previously. This is different: God is alive and present in Jesus and in you. Nothing they did accounts for this. Nothing we do accounts for this. They are not in charge. We are not in charge. They are not in control. We are not in control. They are not customers getting from Jesus what they want. We are not customers getting from Jesus what we want. We are not tourists visiting holy places with Jesus as our tour guide.

Resurrection turns the tables. No longer am I doing something for God; God is doing something for me. No longer am I drawn by need or curiosity to God; God is drawn by compassion and love to me, whether I'm ready for him or not, whether I feel anything for him or not.

The Easter resurrection is the dividing point between a consumer religion and a gracious gospel. This is the event that separates us into two groups: the people who want God to give them something, and the people who find out what God wants to give to them. The people who want to get some meaning into their lives by running a few errands for God, in contrast to the people who are willing to let God work his salvation in them. The people who come to church to tell God what he must do to improve their living conditions, in contrast to the people who come to church to let God tell them how to live in love and faith and hope.

There is nothing wrong with wanting something from God or doing things for God or telling God what is on our minds. But there comes a point when we realize that God is for us, loose and alive in our lives and our world, and he is the One we must simply believe and obey and worship and adore. This is what I want to call the resurrection fulcrum, the tipping point from being occupied with yourself to paying attention to the God who is occupied with you. This is the point marked by Easter morning and all our subsequent Sundays. Now the preliminaries are over; the play begins. The race starts. Eternal life is launched. Are you ready for this? Is it going to be yes or no?

That is why it is hard to prepare an Easter sermon, for what can I say? I find it easy to teach you, to explain what Jesus said. I find it easy to tell you what you do wrong, to point out your sins. I find it easy to urge you to action, to give you advice and motivate you to good works. But on Easter none of that sounds very important. What is important is that Jesus is alive; God is alive.

And that means that neither I nor you are in charge, and God is. That means you aren't coming to God; God is coming to you. That means you are not needed anymore to take care of the dead Jesus; the alive Jesus is commanding a new life in you.

We didn't expect that. We never expect that. And we do well to be afraid, for it means the end of one way of life, in which we know where we stand, and the beginning of another, in which we don't know what will happen.

The moment Mary Magdalene, Mary the mother of James, and Salome realized Jesus was alive among them and the little religious jobs that gave them their identity weren't needed anymore, they were afraid. They were on the edge of the abyss of faith and grace, of hope and obedience. They were ready to *live.* And yet they were not ready.

How long did they fearfully hold back? Hesitate? Waver? A few minutes? A few hours? Mark doesn't tell us. But they didn't hold back forever. Before the day was over, the other gospel writers tell us they did believe. They did obey.

They were readier than they realized to live, Christ living in them. And you are too. Don't let the sun go down on this Easter Day without believing and obeying, ready to live, Christ living in you.

Amen.

Part 6

"CHRIST IN YOU THE HOPE OF GLORY"

PREACHING IN THE COMPANY OF PAUL

Introduction

Paul of Tarsus was the first theologian in the Christian church. For many of us he is still the most influential preacher for shaping our preaching theologically. In every generation men and women of God have emerged as theologians, pastors who have disciplined themselves to guard us from misunderstandings, from being distracted by moralistic bullying or sentimental trivialism. Preaching must be anchored in God, God's revelation to us in the Scriptures. In cultures that are teeming with lies about God and well-meaning superstitions about God, pastors need all the help we can get. The consensus of the church since its formation is "Begin with Paul." There have been great and competent theologians every century since, but Paul is the gold standard in the world of theology.

—

Four elements form Paul's theological imagination, elements that are basic for forming our imaginations as theological pastor-preachers.

The first is his submission to Scripture. I take it as a given that all gospel preaching comes out of familiarity with and submission to Scripture. *Submission* is the word here. We don't read Paul's letters very long before we realize that Paul is not an independent thinker figuring things out on his own. Nor is he a speculative thinker playing with "religious" ideas, searching for some novel ultimate truth. His thinking is subordinated to all that God has revealed of himself and his purposes in the Holy Scriptures. Scripture for Paul was the Hebrew Bible that we now designate the Old Testament. As he writes his letters, Paul's mind is entirely harnessed to Scripture.

Prideful condescension is a common product of superior minds. It is easy to assume that a person who writes excellent books ranks higher than a migrant worker, that a woman who manages the financial affairs of a large corporation is worth more than the woman who cleans the toilets in a public washroom. But Paul, who made his living as a tentmaker and had one of the most competent minds in history, shows no such arrogance. All his mental processes are subdued and submissive to what has been handed to him by revelation in Scripture. The words of the scriptural revelation are the means by which he thinks and prays. Paul's relation to Scripture was not as a student boning up for an exam, finding out what was there, but as a disciple of Jesus *living* the text. He spent the first part of his life as a Pharisee, using the Scriptures zealously but wrongly. He spent the second part of his life as a Christian, *living* these same Scriptures just as zealously but very differently. The difference was this: as an activist Pharisee he *used* the Scriptures to support an angry crusade against Christians; as a believing Christian he let the Spirit use the Scriptures to form Christ in him: he *submitted* to them. The Scriptures furnish his vocabulary, shape his imagination, form his life. They are vast presences, suggesting the immense horizons within which he writes.

In Romans alone, for instance, the first letter that we read, there are seventy quotations, cited from seventeen of the thirty-nine Old Testament books available to him. Isaiah (with twenty citations) and Psalms (with fifteen) are his favorites, but he ranges widely, covering most of the territory from Genesis to Malachi. And that is just a start. There are eleven more letters to come. It is not only that he quotes; he *inhabits* the story. He gives the impression of being on familiar terms with everything written by his prophet-poet ancestors, totally at ease in this richly expansive narrative of God's Word. The Scriptures have become for him "all autobiographical" (Alexander Whyte's phrase).

A second characteristic of Paul's theological imagination is his extravagant embrace of mystery. It is easy for preachers to think they have to explain everything. Paul is comfortable with mystery, delights in mystery, accepts mystery. Listen to his celebrated outburst in Romans 11:33–35 (NRSV):

> O the depth of the riches and wisdom and knowledge of God! How unsearchable are his judgments and how inscrutable his ways!
>
> "For who has known the mind of the Lord?
> Or who has been his counselor?"

"Or who has given a gift to him,
  to receive a gift in return?"

It is significant that this exuberant but still reverent stance before the God who cannot be figured out or diagrammed comes in the context of some of Paul's most vigorous reasoning. Mystery, for Paul, is not what is left over after we have done our best to reason things out. It is inherent in the very nature of God and his works.

As the Spirit forms the life of Christ in us, we necessarily encounter in God more than we can grasp, more than we are capable of explaining. But the more is not some secret kept hidden from us. It is not classified information from which common people are excluded. It is an open invitation to live in a world larger than our own sin-cramped selves.

There is a kind of mind, too common among us, that is impatient of mystery. We want to *know* what is going on. But such impatience short-circuits maturity. The ability of the human intellect to penetrate areas of ignorance and map reality is, of course, formidable. Aggressive intellectual activity produces results that stagger the imagination. It is understandable that the modern mind, accustomed to seeing the tangled undergrowth of mystery cleared out by the knowledge bulldozers, might retain little appreciation for the kind of mystery Paul is dealing with, a mystery that deepens even as our knowledge increases.

The mystery Paul embraces is not the mystery of darkness that must be dispelled but the mystery of light that may be entered. God and his operations cannot be reduced to what we are capable of explaining and then reproducing. It takes considerable humility to embrace mystery, for in the presence of mystery, we are not in a position to control anything, to manage or pose as authorities.

Another element conspicuous in forming Paul's theological imagination is his use of language. This comes as no surprise since language is primary in the making of a salvation gospel: "The word is near you, on your lips and in your heart" (Romans 10:8, quoted from Deuteronomy 30:14). And Jesus, of course, is *the* Word. Language, one of the defining characteristics of being human, is integral to the way God—the Word made flesh—reveals and works. It follows that the *way* we use language, not simply *that* we use it, is significant. The way Paul uses language in his writing is to load it with metaphor. There is hardly a paragraph he writes that lacks a metaphor.

This needs to be taken seriously, for metaphor is not a precise use of language but quite the opposite. Instead of pinning down meaning, metaphor lets it loose. Metaphor does not so much define or label; it expands, forcing the mind into participating action. When we use *rock* as a metaphor for God, as in "The LORD is my rock" (Psalm 18:2), *rock* does not define God. Taken literally, the statement is absurd. What it does is force the imagination into action to find meaning at another level, engaging the imagination to look for relationships and resonances that tell us more than anything literal. We cannot be passive before a metaphor; we imagine and enter into. Metaphor enlists us in a believing-obeying participation.

Do we like things tidy and neat, without loose ends and devoid of ambiguity? Ivory-tower intellectuals and rubber-hits-the-road pragmatists like things organized and orderly. That is not the kind of language we find in Paul. Paul uses words not to define but to evoke. He doesn't serve up God's truth depersonalized, like a specimen under a microscope. He doesn't take sentences apart, prying the truth out of them. He does not "murder to dissect."[65]

Paul's language is a living energy field. He doesn't develop a technical jargon for the sake of being precise about God. He takes the language of common discourse, redolent with metaphor—common things, common actions—and uses it freely, at ease with the ambiguities necessarily inherent in it. He uses language as a poet. A living faith requires this lively, participatory language.

And a fourth element in Paul's theological imagination is that it comes to us through letters written to men and women (many of them named) who worshiped in named towns that can still be located on maps. A letter, handwritten, is the most personal way to write words. Paul's theological imagination enabled him to keep the soaring truths and beauties of the gospel of Jesus Christ accessible and understandable to the very people that gather still in our congregations: the ordinary and extraordinary, the healthy and the sick, children and elderly, skeptics and believers.

Theological study in the academy is useful and important, but the actual practice takes place in congregations. Theology comes alive in conversations and prayers, in worship and community. Theology is not talking about God but living in

65. William Wordsworth, "The Tables Turned," Poetry Foundation, www.poetryfoundation.org/poems-and-poets/poems/detail/45557.

community with persons in relationships, who, like Paul, live in communities whose names they know.

For those of us who have learned theology in a classroom, we remember theology as primarily an attempt to understand the faith in the form of propositions, abstractions, and explanations. There is no story in it and no people. But not so with Paul. His theology is written in community with a host of people in the context of living out the faith. Paul brings people by name into his theology, making sure we will not conceive theology as something impersonal, something to think about and argue over without living it.

We are fortunate to have as our first and definitive Christian theologian a person who worked out the meanings and relationships of this salvation life on the ground with people like us, all of it, without exception, through the most personal of writing forms, namely, letters.

As we soak our minds and souls in the company of our theological master Paul, we note the absence of both large abstract truths, on the one hand, and chatty anecdotes, on the other. What we have is a working model of what continues to work in the formation of mature salvation lives: submission to Scripture, embrace of mystery, metaphorical language, and an insistence on a relational community—men and women with names.

I

"But Now the Righteousness of God"

PSALM 80
ROMANS 3:21–26

There is a long, morose, tedious play in the current avant-garde circles of the theater that has been seen by some in the church as an almost clinically accurate portrayal of the modern stance before God. It was written by Samuel Beckett under the title *Waiting for Godot.*

Two tramps are waiting, passing the time in desultory conversation, and waiting. The stage is bleak: a tree, a log for sitting, and a path along which someone might walk. The action is unrelieved by variation or change. It is one long, unbroken exposure to the two tramps and their conversation. They have nowhere to go. They suspect that life must hold something better for them, but they have no clue to what it might be. So they wait for Godot to come and break the monotony and senselessness of their lives. They are further troubled that when he does come, they won't recognize him. Their minds fumble at everything. They are all thumbs when they try to think and converse about what might come next. They are disturbed about the absence of Godot but no less disturbed about his anticipated presence, for they probably won't recognize him if he does come.

The play is a parable about our lives and the absence of God. We are tramps baffled by the absence of God and disturbed that, if he does come, we will miss him. We are unsettled by the gaping emptiness of God's absence. We are anxious and insecure about what might happen if he should appear. Whether he shows himself or not troubles us to the depths. The possibility that he *will* show himself further threatens us with anxiety and confusion. Both God's presence and absence present difficulties in the deepest parts of our lives.

But we are in Rome, or rather in Romans, not on Broadway. Conveniently for us, Paul is interested in identical matters as he speaks of his subject: God and our relation to him. We have the advantage of Paul's thinking and understanding. So we decide to follow the maxim "When in Rome, do as the Romans do." And so we think with Paul as he guides us on these matters concerning the things that matter most.

Paul has a gift for epigrammatic speech. He has the gift of being able to put a complex truth in a single sentence. Here is his sentence: "Now the righteousness of God has been manifested apart from the law, although the Law and the Prophets bear witness to it" (Romans 3:21, ESV).

Law in Paul's dictionary means "the Law of Moses" or "Torah," and when the Law is set alongside the Prophets, it refers to the entire Old Testament. And the word *manifested*? Jesus, of course. Jesus is the righteousness of God, no longer words in a book or in a story told around a campfire, but the Word made flesh. God in person, flesh and blood, on real ground and in real time.

The four gospel writers, beginning with Mark, did their level best to draw us into the realization of and participation with Jesus of Galilee, and as we do, we find that in Jesus we are dealing with God in person. Paul is simply expanding on that manifestation, that revealing, that disclosure, telling us that everything of God is available to us in the context of living our daily lives. Nothing abstract, no bloodless "truths." In other words, God is here, and *we* participate in his being here.

Our Scriptures have a word for what happens in this showing. The word is *doxa,* "glory," usually put into English as *doxology,* which is often sung when we worship. Some translate it as "splendor." A sense of brilliance, effulgence, spreading light, rare worth, dazzling purity is what needs to be conveyed.

What I am trying to do with you right now is to convey the force of the stream of tradition that Paul was standing in: a rushing stream from which men and women caught the flashes of light manifesting God's presence. These flashes were woven into everything Paul knew about God.

There is a spectacular instance of it in the early part of the Bible. Moses is on Mount Sinai for the second time, getting a new edition of the Ten Commandments.

Feeling insecure, Moses wonders if God is pleased with his recent leadership, so he asks God to show him his ways (Exodus 33:13). Moses is bold: "Now show me your glory." God agrees and tells him, "When my glory passes by, I will put you in a cleft in the rock" (Exodus 33:18, 22, NIV). And then, with Moses adequately protected, God shows himself, manifests his glory in a stunning and dazzling brilliance, a display of splendor.

Here is another confirmation: the testimony in Psalm 80. The psalm is a powerful prayer that calls out three times, with steadily increasing intensity, "Restore us, O God; let thy face shine, that we may be saved!" (see verses 3, 7, 19). The prayer is evidence that those who prayed it knew enough about God to know that it was part of God's way with us to manifest himself to us, to shine, to show his splendor and that the most realistic prayer when you feel in need of him is to simply and directly ask for evidence, a manifestation, of that glory.

As a Hebrew, Paul looked over his history, the history of Israel, and recognized God's revealing, or unveiling, acts all the way from Abraham to Ezra, deliverances and judgments on every side. History was conspicuous with the activity of God, activity that invariably served to show God at work—a manifestation, a revelation. "He plants his footsteps in the sea, and rides upon the storm."[66]

God is no hidden manager of the universe, no enigmatic universal force, no mysterious secret occult spirit. He is a God *known* among those who worship him. The evidence? He shows himself. Paul was heir to a tradition that was full of God's splendor. There were plenty of gods, far more than enough to go around. But they were not gods that showed themselves or announced their intents. The gods were, in fact, conspicuous for their absence, and the most eloquent religious monument in Paul's culture was the Athenian altar to the "unknown god" (Acts 17:23).

Like the two tramps talking about Godot, the ancient world talked about the gods, passed around rumors about them, engaged in endless theological gossip. But the gods neither acted nor talked plainly. It was an age, as is ours, of the absence of God.

Cicero, one of the really intelligent men of the ancient world, set himself to bring some order out of the chaos, to make some sense out of the world of the gods,

66. William Cowper, "God Moves in a Mysterious Way," 1774, www.hymnary.org/text/god_moves_in_a_mysterious_way.

and the result was a book titled *The Nature of the Gods.* In it he tells the story of someone named Simonides, who was asked by the tyrant Hiero what or who God was. The sage Simonides asked for a day to ponder. On the next day he asked for an extension of the time. He continued to double the time in which to think it over. Finally he gave his reply: "The longer I consider this, the more obscure it seems to me."[67] Which is to say, he took his place with Beckett's tramps on their log. Just waiting.

So when Paul says the righteousness of God is manifested, shown, we keep in mind the world to which he speaks: the dark world of rumor and omen and bewilderment, the world of the two tramps! Paul asks us to keep in mind the long record in Hebrew history of manifested glory: Moses in the cleft of the rock, and Psalm 80, with a kind of splendor that was called by our theologian John Calvin a "dazzling theater."[68]

—

So now we ask, "If God so clearly shows himself, why are there so many who do not see him?" For it is undeniable that there are many brilliant, intelligent, honest, and sensitive men and women who profess not to see him. Bertrand Russell, whose erudition no one can doubt, published a collection of essays, including one called "Why I Am Not a Christian." And Albert Camus, a rare combination of intelligence and sensitivity, said that the supreme act of cowardice was to believe and trust in God. How should we respond?

We come back to Paul for help. Paul says that "the righteousness of God has been manifested *apart from,*" that is, in addition to, this long history of what we have learned from Moses and the Prophets (Romans 3:21). His righteousness is manifested in Jesus, who was God-in-person with us in our own times. In other words, Paul is telling his congregation of Christians in Rome that seeing God is not first of all a matter of intelligence or sincerity or honesty or sensitivity but quite simply a matter of looking in the right place, namely, at Jesus Christ, who lived practically in their neighborhood, just fifteen hundred miles or so away as the crow flies. Paul asks his readers to realize that, for them, this is practically a current event.

67. Cicero, *The Nature of the Gods,* trans. P. G. Walsh (Oxford: Clarendon, 1997), bk. 1, para. 60.
68. John Calvin, *John Calvin: Selections from His Writings,* ed. John Dillenberger (New York: Anchor Books, 1971), 341.

Paul is saying, "Pay attention to Jesus, in whom God revealed himself so we can get in on what God is doing." The Christian church has held from its beginning that this is the central focus of a saved life.

To the non-Christian, the person who does not enter into this commitment—this relationship in Christ where God has definitively and conclusively showed himself—our attention on God appears to be monumental arrogance. But to the Christian, to the person who has actually fixed his attention on Christ and realized God's splendor there, it seems to be a commonsense truth arising out of ordinary logic. It would be a digression to try at this point to understand the reasons for the disbelief, on the one hand, and the belief, on the other. What is germane right now is to understand that Paul's belief in, expectation of, and experience of God showing and manifesting himself reached a conclusion, a climax, a final definition in the appearance of Jesus Christ. In Paul's words, "In him dwelleth all the fulness of the Godhead bodily" (Colossians 2:9, KJV).

Paul's phrase "the righteousness of God" speaks of exactly what is shown, manifested, made plain. *Righteousness* is not a word we use in everyday language, so some reflection here might be in order. We are more apt to talk specifically of the character of God, what God is like. But if we did, we would miss much of what Paul meant.

The term *righteousness* in the Scriptures has two sides to it. It means on one side "final, ultimate right." It is the absolute truth to which everything else is relative. It is like those weights and measures preserved in atmospheric immutability at the Bureau of Standards. It is the basic and unchangeable standard of the right and the true: complete righteousness.

But there is another side to it, for this absolute standard of righteousness is not an object, not a perfect yardstick, lifeless and passive. There is an activity connected with righteousness that seeks to make everyone and everything like itself, that is, to make everything right. There is an energetic personal dimension to rightness, a person with a name—Jesus—seeking to develop that righteousness deep into the lives of men and women. He is truth, but he is also love, seeking to save what was lost. Through Jesus the Christ we learn that God is absolute truth and that God seeks to share love. The first by itself would be icy and cold and remote; the second in isolation would be sentimentalism.

Friedrich Nietzsche may be an unlikely witness, but he catches our attention when he says, "All truth is bloody truth for me."[69] We must realize the righteousness of God in these terms. Not as an abstraction, not as a subject for a philosopher to figure out. Righteousness is *lived* in Jesus and also in us. It is the Creator and Sovereign of the universe expressing himself to us in love, seeking to draw us into participation in his righteousness. It is one of Nietzsche's bloody truths as Jesus on the cross quite literally shows.

This is the recurrent theme of Paul's letter to the Romans, the good news that God seeks to save us, with Jesus Christ as evidence. In Paul's words it is "the power of God for salvation to everyone who has faith. . . . For in it the righteousness of God is revealed through faith for faith" (1:16–17, NRSV).

—

Let's return to where we started, with Beckett's two tramps. You will recall that they shared a double problem. They were disturbed by the absence of God but were even further disturbed by the anxiety that they might not recognize him if he did show up. They were waiting, but there was no serenity, no hope, and no joy in their waiting. And the tramps are us.

Does God show himself? And if he does, will we recognize him? Paul says in effect, "Yes, he does show up, and we will recognize him in the person of Jesus. God does show himself, that is, he shows his splendor, his glory. And that splendor is righteousness." Paul names this "good news" *gospel.* And it certainly is.

This is the central message of Christian teaching and preaching about God. Paul's entire attention is given to getting *us* to pay attention, for it does require mature attention. J. B. Phillips once observed that there are a vast number of people who have never given Paul's thinking and writing the benefit of their mature attention.[70] They quit thinking about Christian claims when they gave up coloring pictures in Sunday school or when, intoxicated by sophomoric omniscience, they tossed all religion into a Freudian wastebasket. Francis Bacon wrote this sentence: "What is truth? said jesting Pilate, and would not stay for an answer."[71] The sentence arrests us, provokes our imagination. What if he had stayed and watched and

69. Scott R. Burson and Jerry L. Walls, *C. S. Lewis and Francis Schaeffer: Lessons for a New Century from the Most Influential Apologists of Our Time* (Downers Grove, IL: InterVarsity, 1998), 145.
70. J. B. Phillips, *New Testament Christianity* (Eugene, OR: Wipf and Stock, 1956), 6.
71. Francis Bacon, *The Essays of Francis Bacon* (Raleigh, NC: Lulu, 2014), n.p., essay titled "Of Truth."

listened? Might he not have learned truth? But Pilate was preoccupied with matters of state, of justice, of politics, of society. He had no time for the answer. He did not attend to the answer.

Neither *God* nor *truth* nor *love* can be defined by an entry in a dictionary nor dismissed by a politician's jest. But all of it has been and is being lived by men and women all over this planet Earth. You are probably sitting by one of them right now. And that is why we show up in this place of worship regularly, to exercise our attentiveness to this righteousness of God manifested . . . in Christ.

Amen.

2

"Jews Demand Signs and Greeks Seek Wisdom"

ISAIAH 53:7–9
1 CORINTHIANS 1:18–25

I have a profound distrust of slogans. Anything in the nature of a formula or a pat answer makes me uneasy. Those who promise to cure all disease by vegetarianism, or end all wars by passing out flowers, or banish all ignorance by teaching everyone to read, or guarantee freedom by killing all communists. The people that Eric Hoffer calls "true believers," who whittle away at reality until it fits into their schemes. The simplification is achieved by amputation.

For reality is, in fact, complex and diverse. The world is rich and intricate. Life is sundry and profuse. The formula that explains everything, the slogan that interprets everything, the answer that fits all questions—all leave out too much. In the years I have been a pastor, I have found myself doubly on my guard. The world of religion, maybe more than any other, seems to attract the "terrible simplifiers."

But there is one summary phrase I have come to have more and more respect for. It came out of the Holy Spirit genius of Saint Paul. In various letters to first-century congregations, he said or wrote it eight times, just two words: "Christ crucified." Not what you might think. Not "God is love." Not "Love your neighbor." Not "Keep the commandments." But "Christ crucified." The more you think about it, although brief, it is not a reduction but a concentration, not a blurring of reality but a focusing, not a watering down but a distillation.

The sharp-edged, mind-clearing phrase originated in a place of mass confusion.

Paul is writing to the Christians in the Greek city of Corinth, as clamoring, arguing, cantankerous a congregation as ever got together in the name of Christ. Each person, it seemed, had a different idea of how to interpret or express the Christian faith. It was Paul's task as their pastor to make sense out of it all, to shape their diversity into a unity, to turn their confused complexity into an organic harmony.

Some were big on education: "Let's turn this church into a lecture hall. After all, we are Greeks in the land of the great philosophers and moralists, and in Christ we have all the wisdom of God. Let's use these philosophical resources and show how they are completed in the wisdom of God. Just take Heraclitus and Plato and Aristotle and show how Jesus completed them."

Others were high on the supernatural. "Look," they said, "we are in a city seething with religion. People making extravagant promises: Egyptian mysteries, Greek myths, Persian secret societies. Places that feature healing, groups that promise visions, rituals that take you into experiences of ecstasy. And we Christians have the greatest miracle religion ever. We worship the God who split the Red Sea, stopped the sun over Gibeon, fed a people on bread and quail for forty years in a wilderness, healed the leper Naaman, and raised Jesus from the dead. All we have to do is demonstrate a bigger and better miracle, and we will have the whole city standing on tiptoe, breathless with excitement."

They discussed it and argued over it. Paul heard all about it and wrote them a letter, telling them, "We preach Christ crucified" (1 Corinthians 1:23). They recognized the truth of what he said. "Of course, how could we have missed seeing that?" The two words became central in the church's preaching, the symbol for their worship, the explanation for their existence. And they still are.

Several years ago as this sanctuary was nearing completion, elder Robert Sharrock drove back to Ohio and salvaged some timbers of American black walnut from the family farm, lashed them to the roof of his car, and brought them back here. In his workshop he fashioned the cross in the chancel that brings everything in our sanctuary into focus. As you enter this place of worship, you can't miss it.

I am wearing a cross this morning that is a gift from this congregation. Many of you wear crosses. The cross is everywhere recognized as the defining symbol of the Christian faith.

—

I have two favorite congregations. One of them is right here, the Christ Our King congregation. I am in the middle of it day after day, week after week, year after year. I don't know if it is better or worse than other Christian congregations, but it is the one I am in, and it is full of life, diversity, and difficulty. There is enough here to keep me occupied and stretched and challenged. I have learned much here and experienced much.

Every time we come to worship together, I have a fresh, focused sense that God is doing something extraordinary with us, that we are being nudged out of ourselves into something large and gracious. Then we are dispersed through the week. Some of us barely making it as we wade through swamps of suffering, others of us wondering if this is all life amounts to as we work at a boring job or live in relationships that have gone flat, others of us hearing music in the air and whistling along with it—a wide range of living in different settings. None of us quite the same from weekday to weekday, changing, growing, regressing, faltering.

I like holding you before the Lord in prayer, seeking to be attentive of the blessing that God wills for each of you. I like studying the Scriptures and looking for ways in which I can say this word of God to you so it retains its accuracy in this present moment of our life together. I like being with you both casually and in crisis, in our shared humanity, to live into what it means for brothers and sisters to dwell in unity, to see Christ in one another. I like all of that. I like hearing your voices, being in your homes, seeing the look in your eyes.

Sometimes I get tired of it all. There is too much pain, too much suffering, too many questions I can't answer, too much sin, too much misunderstanding. I want out. I want to live with less intensity. I fantasize about life as a gossip columnist so I won't have to take anybody seriously or personally. I know enough of the seamy underside of people's lives that I could probably make a pretty good living retailing to the nation what I know.

But I think I would get bored pretty soon. Those fantasies don't last long. I sleep, I pray, I worship . . . and I am soon in the thick of things again, enjoying the life of grace with you.

—

The other congregation, the congregation that shares top billing with Christ Our King, is Corinth. There are seventeen Christian congregations in the first century that we know something about, some more than others, but at least something. Of all of them, the congregation in Corinth is my favorite. It is not the best. Philippi was probably that. It is not the most influential. Jerusalem was probably that. It was not the largest. Ephesus was probably that. It was not the most strategic. Antioch was probably that. But it was the earthiest.

There seemed to be more going on in Corinth than anyplace else, a mixture of sin and grace and emotion. Everything that can go wrong in a congregation went wrong there: arguments, factions, sexual improprieties, discrimination, outrageous rudeness, stupidity, snobbishness. But nearly everything that can go right in a congregation went right there too: forgiveness, a deeply felt life centered in acts of baptism and the Eucharist, passionate acts of reconciliation, reckless generosity in giving offerings, a determination to live the life of the Spirit in community.

I am not attempting to give an objective rating of the New Testament congregations, only telling you my personal preference. Part of this is no doubt that we know more details about Corinth than any other place. And it is the details that draw me to the place, the sense of specificity, always dealing with actual people in actual circumstances, which is what gives life in a congregation its richness and texture.

—

Corinth . . . Christ Our King; Christ our King . . . Corinth. I myself have lived deeply into each of these congregations. None of the cultural details, of course, matches up with what we are experiencing. First-century Corinth and twentieth-century Bel Air don't share much socially. But in a lot of other things that matter, the things that always matter and will never quit mattering, we are together. To begin with, we owe our origin, our root existence, to something that happened.

What happened? Christ was crucified.

Nobody wants to start here. And especially we who come to church. We want to start with a big idea: God is love; there is purpose to life. Or a grand vision or a terrific proposal: "Let's get America back to God." Or a rousing challenge: "Be all that you are meant to be." Or a shattering rebuke: "Repent or perish."

But "Christ crucified"? Who wants that?

Who wants that? Paul gives two alternatives: "Jews demand signs and Greeks seek wisdom" (1 Corinthians 1:22). Paul sorts people like us who come to church into two categories: Jews and Greeks. Jews would be the men and women who have some biblical background and orientation. They grew up on stories, miracle stories of their ancestors: God speaking to Moses out of a burning bush that didn't burn up. Salvation out of Egyptian slavery. Manna and quail in the wilderness for forty years. Walls falling down at the battle of Jericho. The Greeks would include everybody else, with their search for wisdom and answers. The Jews are those who expect miracles from God. The Greeks are those who expect answers from God.

But Paul returns us to the basic act that changes everything from the ground up: Christ crucified.

Our society is cheapened by expectations of miracles: God as a supernatural shortcut so we don't have to engage in the deeply dimensioned, endlessly difficult, soaringly glorious task of being a human living by faith. Or by expectations of answers to all the big questions: What does it all mean? Why did this happen to me? Is there life after death? What is the formula that will make me happy in love and successful in my work?

But that is not how God wants us grounded. Not with miracles and signs—power without relationship, spectacular entertainment without relationship.

And not with ideas and wisdom—knowledge without relationship, information without involvement.

We preach Christ crucified.

Something actually happened. Not an idea we can ponder and study, not a power we can manipulate and put to use, but a fact. A historical, time-and-place fact. A person fact: Christ crucified.

This is the anchor. Paul is writing to a mixed but intensely religious community, these Corinthians, who are clamoring for answers and curious about miracles. Not so different from us, really. He brings them back to what anchors their lives: Christ crucified.

The issue is this: that we give our full attention to what God has done among us. He came to us, revealed his love to us, demonstrated his commitment to save us and to restore us to himself. He offered himself as the sacrifice that would give us back our true selves. There is great mystery here: How can God become one of us? How does it happen that a sacrificial death one day in ancient Palestine effects a radical change in you two thousand years later and nine thousand miles away? But deep and impenetrable as the mystery is, there is nothing obscure about the fact.

Something happened. Jesus was crucified. A real life. A real death. And God in it showing his passionate love for us and working his salvation in us.

If we are going to ask questions, what we need to ask is "What has God done?" and "What is he doing?" Let's look at what he has done and what he is doing. I want to train your imagination from speculation to participation. God is doing something still. He was in action in my life yesterday. Help me to see it. He is in action in my life right now. Do I notice?

God does not act impersonally. He does not speak impersonally. So don't expect miracles and don't clamor for answers. Pay attention to God in the Word made flesh. Pay attention to Christ crucified, his sacrificial offering for you.

You did not come to worship this morning just to listen to a sermon. You also came to participate in the sermon as we celebrate the sacrament of Holy Communion. We celebrate and worship Christ crucified in this sacrament. In some ways this is so simple, so everyday, so matter-of-fact. Bread and wine. You and I sitting in this place. Speaking and listening to words passed down through generations of Christians.

We are not here because of a great idea or a set of answers that explain your life. We are here not to see some spectacular performance that will lift you out of a humdrum existence. We are here to receive Christ. We preach Christ crucified. God came among us in great love. We cannot live a full, whole, eternal human life without God. We try a lot of different ways to live well, to be complete. Nothing does it. We cannot achieve it on our own. God achieves that completion for us: Christ comes. Christ is crucified. It happens. Our lives are saved. Our sins are forgiven. We take what is offered and revealed: what God has done, what God does. It is done for us, offered to us.

Secularized salvation stories are just rescue stories. A person from outside arrives and pulls us out of the trouble we are in. But Christ crucified works from the inside, enters the troubled condition, receives it into himself, becomes the sacrifice that becomes the life of salvation. The cross of Christ is the sacrifice to sum up all sacrifices, the final sacrifice that has accomplished and continues to accomplish salvation.

Amen.

3

"For Freedom Christ Has Set Us Free"

GENESIS 15:1–6
GALATIANS 5:1–2, 13–15

The letter to the Galatians is Paul's angriest letter. Paul became a follower of Jesus and entered the community of Christians in the early stages of its formation. After Jesus's crucifixion and resurrection, Peter and the other apostles were preaching the good news in Jerusalem, and many people were becoming converted. The earliest converts were mostly Jews. The Jewish authorities tried to stop the apostles from preaching about Jesus, even imprisoned some of them, but were mostly unsuccessful. At one point there were three thousand converts in a single day in Jerusalem (Acts 2:14–41). But the anti-Christian violence continued. One day while Stephen, one of the local church's deacons, was preaching, the hard-line Pharisee Jews decided to stone him to death for questioning the validity of the Hebrew tradition, the same "criminal" charges that earlier had resulted in the crucifixion of Jesus. Saul, an ardent Pharisee at the time, was guarding the clothes of the murderers, who "laid their coats at the feet of a young man named Saul" (Acts 7:58, NRSV). And so it is that Stephen, our first Christian martyr, was stoned to death, while Saul (later to be renamed Paul) was an accomplice in the execution (Acts 6:8–7:60).

The stoning of Stephen marked an acceleration of the epidemic of violence against the Christians, but it didn't interrupt the conversion of many people, both Jews and Gentiles. Barnabas was commissioned along with Paul, who had recently been converted, to work among the Gentiles, evangelizing the Greeks and Romans, beginning in the Roman province of Galatia, part of modern Turkey.

Halfway through the Acts of the Apostles, our earliest history of the New Testament church, the leadership emphasis among Christians shifts from Peter and the apostles in the primarily Jewish territory of Jerusalem to Paul and Barnabas, and later Silas, in the Roman-Greek population in the Gentile world of the Roman provinces. Peter and his disciples were to work primarily in the Jewish world; Paul and his disciples were to work primarily in the Gentile world.

The emergence of Paul as the lead character in the formation of the Christian church is a surprise. Until his sudden and remarkable conversion on the Damascus Road while on his way to arrest Christians for heresies against the Jewish Law, the penalty for which was death by stoning, he was a card-carrying Pharisee.

One of Paul's early trips into the Gentile world was in the Roman province of Galatia. He mentions four towns: Pisidian Antioch, Iconium, Lystra, and Derbe (see Acts 13:13–14:7). Paul and Barnabas were given a warm welcome.

It becomes apparent that in Galatia there were Jews of the pharisaical stripe who had heard about the dynamic mission of Paul and Barnabas to convert members of their synagogues to the Jesus Way. Alarmed and angry, these Jews descended on the new converts to try to "save" them from what they considered a falsehood being spread by Paul and Barnabas. When Paul heard about it, he wrote an angry letter, the letter to the Galatians.

We can tell just how angry Paul was by the way he writes. All of Paul's other letters (he wrote seventeen that we know of to various churches and individuals) follow a stylized form. He typically begins with a greeting and then gives thanks for the church or persons to whom he is writing. First the greeting and then the gratitude. Primary in Paul's heart is gratefulness for his friends, gratitude for what God has done in them, and a sense of blessing in knowing them and sharing the life of Christ with them. Every letter he writes follows this pattern—with one exception. When he writes to the Galatians, he is so irate and upset that he forgets the thanksgiving. Then he unloads a double curse on certain persons who were preaching a "contrary" gospel (Galatians 1:6, AMP), that is, lying about God. These lies were ruining the Galatians' newly experienced free life in Christ, so Paul says of these persons, "Let him be accursed. . . . Let him be accursed" (verses 8–9). Strong language!

The truth about God came to Paul in the person of Jesus Christ while Paul was on the road to Damascus. Jesus showed him that he had it all wrong, that what he had followed was a contrary gospel. Paul was convinced that God is on our side. He was persuaded that sin is not God's excuse to get rid of us but the occasion for entering into our lives and setting us free.

Paul had a favorite word for this great, all-encompassing truth about God: *gospel.* Good news. He was not the first to use it, but he used it more than any other writer in the Bible. In the writings we have of his, he uses the word sixty-five times.

He learned the word from Isaiah, that greatest of all the preachers of Israel, who introduced the word as he addressed a people who had sunk into the deepest kind of gloom. The people had just survived a colossal disaster and were now a conquered people living in Babylonian exile. They were cut off from their traditions and were the laughingstock of the world community, humiliated and mocked.

Isaiah's sermon was the turning point for those people: "Comfort, comfort my people, says your God. . . . Get you up to a high mountain, O Zion, herald of good tidings [*gospel!*]; . . . lift [your voice] up, fear not; say to the cities of Judah, 'Behold your God!' " (40:1, 9).

Good tidings. Good news. Gospel. Isaiah's six-hundred-year-old sermon rushes into Paul's mind, and the word *gospel* is there to be used, to tell the people that God is not angry or indifferent or impersonal, but that God loves us, and salvation is at the center of absolutely everything, and from that center all of life is freely lived.

Every Christian story is a freedom story. Each story tells how a person has been set free from the confines of small ideas, from the chains of what others think, from the prisons of the self, sin-separated from God. We are free to change. The process of that change is always a good story but is never a neat formula.

Robert Penn Warren, one of America's finer novelists and poets, said in an interview, "Everybody wants a big solution to everything. For a long time I would stop people in the street and explain to them what made the world change!"[72] But as he matured, he came to distrust what I am calling the one-answer system. What he learned to do instead was to tell stories.

And that is Paul's way: stories. We know a lot about Paul's life from the stories that Luke tells, three stories written in Acts (9:1–30; 22:1–21; 26:1–23). Paul, in his own words, adds a fourth, the story he tells the Galatians about the change that took place in his life and that is behind everything he is writing. I'm breaking it into three parts.

—

In the first part of his story, he describes "my earlier life in Judaism" (Galatians 1:13, NRSV). Paul was reared in a Jewish home and educated under the famous Jerusalem rabbi Gamaliel. Great heritage, fine education. To that privileged birth and education, Paul brought extraordinary energy and ability. "I advanced in Judaism beyond many of my own age among my people" (verse 14). He was no rebel trying to find an alternate way, no prodigal son out to sow wild oats, no black sheep determined to defy the family expectations. He was excited by and worked within his heritage.

He describes what he did in these words: "I was violently persecuting the church of God and was trying to destroy it" (verse 13, NRSV). In the religious world he grew up in, he was taught that the church of Jesus was evil. He was consumed with ambition to make the world orderly and people good. If they wouldn't be good on their own, he would force them to be good. If they proved to be absolutely intractable, he would see that they were eliminated.

Religion, for Paul, was a matter of doing things and making things happen. But is that what religion is? "Religion has primarily to do with is-ness not oughtness."[73] Religion is an awareness of God. It is first of all a desire for what God gives us. It is a free and unforced reaching out for the mercy and love that God offers.

In T. H. White's final volume of his story of King Arthur, he refers to Guenever, now an old woman and abbess in a cloister of nuns. Guenever, he says, "never cared for God. She was a good theologian, but that was all."[74] That describes Paul in his

72. Robert Penn Warren, in *Talking with Robert Penn Warren,* ed. Floyd C. Watkins, John T. Hiers, and Mary Louise Weaks (Athens, GA: University of Georgia Press, 1990), 168.
73. Friedrich von Hügel, *Letters to a Niece* (Vancouver, BC: Regent College Publishing, 2001), 10.
74. T. H. White, *The Book of Merlyn* (Austin: University of Texas Press, 1977), 132.

"earlier life in Judaism": a good theologian but not personally interested in God. He was too busy using his education, too busy with his religious projects, too involved in imposing his rich cultural heritage and theological expertise on others. He didn't have time for God, at least for the God that Christians were talking about.

—

The second element in Paul's story is God's revelation: "when God . . . was pleased to reveal his Son to me, so that I might proclaim him among the Gentiles" (Galatians 1:15–16, NRSV). Until this time Paul was a privileged Hebrew with a rabbinic education and an aptitude for religion. Here is a complete reversal in Paul's life. Until this time he was confident, well born, successful. Suddenly everything is turned around. God is no longer at the periphery but at the center. Paul is no longer a person who does things for God; God does things for him. God is not background for the dramatic events in which Paul is the chief actor; God is the central mover and maker, and Paul is the one moved and made.

Paul realized that God's will for him was in action even before he was born. "He who had set me apart before I was born" (verse 15) is a phrase he remembers from God's address to the prophet Jeremiah (Jeremiah 1:5). He hears it now as God's personal word to him.

Those words can be applied to any of us. We are not a last-minute intrusion on God's attention. We are not incidental to God's will. We did not just happen along in the course of certain biological goings-on in the human race. We are, each of us, set apart. We are *pre*loved by God.

When God revealed himself to Paul in the person of Jesus, it was as if God said, "Listen, Paul, you have it all wrong. You have good ideas, your theology is intelligent enough, your sincerity is above reproach, but you have it all wrong. You think religion is a matter of knowing things and doing things. It is not. It is a matter of letting God do something for you: letting him love you, letting him save you, letting him bless you, letting him command you. Your part is to look and believe, to pray and obey. For a start I am going to show myself to you in Jesus. In him you will see that what concerns me is being with you, making you whole. In him you will see that I do not force my way, that I do not shout my will. In him you will see that the way I deal with evil is by offering myself as a sacrifice, embracing crucifixion, and in that act the power of evil was broken and salvation accomplished. As for the resurrection, examine the evidence, and you will see it is not a hysterical rumor but fact, as soberly and reliably reported as anything on this earth can be."

Maybe for the first time in his life, Paul is listening, not talking. He is looking, not demonstrating. He is worshiping God, not pushing people around. Until then he had supposed that his Jewish traditions and rabbinical education provided him with everything he needed to know about God and that all that remained was to go out and put it to work. Now he realized the central reality was not what he knew about God but what God knew about him and willed for him and showed him and commanded him. God was at the center, not Paul. Paul submitted himself to that will of God and agreed to let God work in him. At the same time he quit trying to subject other people to his own will, forcing them to fit into what he thought was best for them.

It is significant, I think, that Paul did not describe this Damascus moment by saying "When I decided to be a Christian" but rather by saying "When God . . . was pleased to reveal his Son to me" (Galatians 1:15–16, NRSV). Conversion is God's work. We cannot command the heavenly vision. We cannot manipulate the divine will. "It is not given to men to make God speak. It is only given to them to live and to think in such a way that, if God's thunder should come, they will not have stopped their ears."[75]

After that meeting with Jesus, Paul went into Arabia to assimilate it all. "I did not confer with flesh and blood, . . . but I went away into Arabia" (verses 16–17). He seemed to be in no hurry to get back to work. He didn't have to be in a hurry, for he knew that God was at work. God didn't need him. He needed God. Arabia was a desert place, empty and quiet, where he could realize what had happened to him.

The third element in the story takes place in Jerusalem: "Then after three years I went up to Jerusalem to visit Cephas [Peter], and remained with him fifteen days" (verse 18). "Visit" in Greek is *historeo,* the word behind *history.* It has a colloquial tone to it: "to sit down and swap stories." Paul didn't go to visit Peter to "check him

75. Peter Berger, quoted in "Peter L. Berger," Goodreads, www.goodreads.com/author/show/29173.Peter_L_Berger.

out" or to prove something to him, that his conversion was really authentic. He went to visit. The two men put their feet up in front of a few coals of fire and traded stories.

"How did God get hold of you, Peter?"

"Well, it was a day on the beach on Lake Galilee . . . And how about you, Paul? Tell me your story."

And Paul recalled his trauma and ecstasy on the Damascus Road.

Every Christian story needs sharing. We require a few other persons to whom we can tell our stories. Every story is different. But it is also the same, a kind of revelation, personal truth revealed. How are we to know that what we feel is legitimate and healthy? How are we to know that our story is not a fragment of abnormal psychology? Tell the story. In the telling we recognize the common plot of God's grace setting us apart, personally calling us and revealing his Son to us. We also recognize the great care with which he respects and uses every individual feature of our bodies and emotions and minds so that each story is totally fresh and original.

Paul doesn't exalt his story into a model to which others must conform. He shares it in a conversation with friends who also have stories to tell. In the Jerusalem visit, Peter and Paul become partners instead of rivals. Paul had become a Christian in a very different way from Peter. Peter had been a rough, profane, ungodly person; Paul a sophisticated, urbane, pious person. Peter had been converted from a life of sin; Paul from a life of religion. Peter had been converted in a process of long and intense personal association with Jesus, with whom he ate, talked, and worked. Paul never spent time with Jesus in person, having only a brief vision of him along the Damascus Road. Peter had immediate confirmation of the authenticity of his experience by being installed as the leader of the Christian community. Paul had to live for years with a reputation of being a sadistic killer of Christians.

There is no model conversion. There is no prescribed ritual, whether emotional or liturgical. We are all different. God is the same and has the same salvation to work in us, but he creates an original story every time. We acquire an appreciation for and delight in the features of our own stories and the stories of our friends as we tell our Jesus stories to one another in the community of faith.

Amen.

4

"Speaking the Truth in Love"

PSALM 68
EPHESIANS 4:1–16

What does it really mean to become a mature Christian, growing up, in Paul's words, to the "stature of Christ" (Ephesians 4:13, NRSV)? Paul's letter to the Ephesians provides the context to answer that question. A sentence from the pivotal center of the letter gives us our focus: "Speaking the truth in love, we are to grow up in every way into him who is the head, into Christ" (verse 15).

All of us are born. It is one thing we have in common with everyone around us. No exceptions. Birth brings us alive, kicking and crying, into a world that is vast, complex, damaged, demanding . . . and beautiful. In increments, day by day, we begin to get the hang of it. We drink from our mother's breast, go to sleep, and wake up. One day on waking, we stand upright and amaze everyone with our pedestrian acrobatics. It isn't long before we are old hands at the language, using nouns and verbs with the best of them. We are growing up.

Jesus used the birth event as a metaphor for another kind of birth: becoming alive to God. Alive to God-alive. Alive to God's holiness, God's will, God's kingdom, power, and glory. There is more to life after birth than mother's milk, sleeping and waking, walking and talking. There is God.

Jesus introduced the birth metaphor in a conversation with Rabbi Nicodemus one night in Jerusalem, telling him, "You must be born again" (John 3:7, ESV). Nicodemus didn't understand the metaphor, didn't get it. Literalists, maybe especially religious literalists, have a difficult time with metaphors. A metaphor is a word that makes an organic connection between what you can see and what you can't see. In any conversation involving God, whom we can't see, metaphors are invaluable for keeping language vivid and immediate. Without metaphors we are left with colorless abstractions and vague generalities.

Jesus liked metaphors and used them a lot. "Born again" is one of his most memorable. But Nicodemus didn't get it. "Can one enter a second time into the mother's womb and be born?" (John 3:4, NRSV). But as Jesus elaborated on his born-again metaphor (verses 5–21), we can be fairly certain Nicodemus eventually did get it. Despite the metaphor, or more likely because of it, Nicodemus was born again. And not only born but growing. His presence at Jesus's burial is evidence that ever since that conversation with Jesus, he had been growing, growing in understanding and participation, on his way to maturity in the world of God-alive.

So birth. Then growth. The most significant growing up any person does is to grow as a Christian. All other growing up is preparation for or ancillary to this growing up. Biological, social, mental, and emotional growing are all ultimately absorbed into growing up in Christ. Or not. The human task is to become mature, not only in our bodies and emotions and minds within ourselves, but also in our relationships with God and other persons.

The Scriptures frequently refer to growth and growing, almost always containing elements of fascination and delight that we are used to as we watch trees, flowers, and children grow. The concluding word on the growth of John the Baptist is this: "The child grew and became strong in spirit" (Luke 1:80). An almost identical observation is given of Jesus: "The child grew and became strong, filled with wisdom; and the favor of God was upon him" (Luke 2:40). Paul uses a similar vocabulary in describing the agenda he sets out for Christians in the Ephesian letter, using *grow* as a metaphor for maturity in Christ. We "come . . . to maturity, to the measure of the full stature of Christ. . . . We must *grow up in every way into him* who is the head, into Christ" (4:13, 15, NRSV).

About six years ago, the first spring after we moved here, a peach tree began to grow out of a compost heap we had started in our backyard. We didn't have any trees in our yard, so any addition was welcome. We transplanted it and watched it grow. It isn't a very pretty tree, neither the largest nor nicest of those we now have. We talked about cutting it down. But this summer we got some peaches from it. The tree is growing, and we are keeping it.

It is always fascinating to watch things grow. There is so much mystery to it, so much coming out of so little, so much beauty coming out of a hole that not long ago was a gallon of dirty dirt. And the process goes on quite independently of whatever else is going on at the time. The sheer doggedness of growth is daunting, intriguing, delightful to contemplate.

—

Paul here uses physical growth as a metaphor for what we can't see: "strong, filled with wisdom; and the favor of God was upon him" (Luke 2:40).

One of the conspicuous elements in Paul's use of language is his skill in the employment of metaphor. He learned it by reading his Bible. One of the most frequent biblical metaphors is *rock,* referring to God. "God is my rock" (Psalm 18:2, NIV). None of us on coming across an interesting rock while hiking in the mountains would think of putting it on a pedestal and worshiping it as God, although that has happened. And no one would think of sorting through some small stones from a river, picking out a favorite, putting it in a purse or pocket, rubbing it fondly, and praying to it, although I have heard of people doing that with a rabbit's foot.

What makes metaphor such a critical element in language for people of faith is that much, maybe most, of what we deal with is inaccessible to our senses. Most reality is invisible, inaudible. There is plenty to be seen and heard and touched and tasted and smelled: a rainbow of colors in flowers and sunsets; a symphony of tunes and melodies, rhythms and accents; textures smooth and rough; flavors sweet and sour; fragrance and stench. But life in the kingdom is an immersion in a much larger, more comprehensive reality. Most of what I see and hear, smell, touch, and taste, I soon discover is an opening, a window or door, to something invisible: beauty, truth, goodness, and most of all, God. But not those words as such, not abstractions, nothing quantifiable or measurable. The Incarnation ("the Word became flesh and dwelt among us," John 1:14) puts us in touch with what cannot be touched. More often than not, it is a *metaphor* that puts us in touch.

Here Paul fuses physical growth with spiritual growth: the whole person, inside and outside, body and soul. Growth is used as a metaphor of Jesus's description of how God is working in the world of his creation-salvation, the kingdom of God.

—

Is it possible to recapture some of the vivid rush of excitement that the words "grow up . . . into Christ" (Ephesians 4:15) ignited in the minds of those who first heard or read them?

Let's try.

If we are going to arrive at any satisfactory outcome in our growing up, we have to keep the accompanying words, "into Christ," constantly before us. "Into Christ" defines the growing up, but not as is usual in our language: to grow up to be an adult man or woman.

In the way our culture uses the phrase "grow up" to be a man, usually *man* is debased to selling suntan lotion, cologne, and Camel cigarettes. To grow up to be a real woman calls up stereotypical Miss America mannequins—all measured and categorized, with smiles stenciled on. And the word *adult* defines a movie produced for emotional adolescents.

So Paul doesn't trust us to know exactly what he means by "grow up." He makes sure he has "into Christ" in the sentence. Christ is what a mature adulthood looks like. Christ is what it means to grow up. If we don't keep that in our minds, we are going to end up with something like a star athlete or popular movie star—not all bad, but not exactly what we were hoping for.

Christ defines our growth to true adulthood. The person of Jesus Christ, who lived thirty-three years on our planet, trains our imaginations in the meaning of mature adulthood. So we immerse ourselves in the Jesus story and find the shape of our lives defined by Jesus.

—

And here's another thing about growing: the entire person is necessarily involved. There is no way for just part of us to grow up. Growing up is not a specialty task. You can't specialize in just arms or legs or ears and feet. If successful, you would be a freak, useful for nothing but employment in a circus or carnival.

To make sure we will not misunderstand, Paul qualifies what he means: "grow up in *every way*" (Ephesians 4:15). No part of you is an exception. "Every way" is absolutely inclusive.

There will be some people on the block who confine their growth to Sundays, others to an hour of meditation, others to their children. They often dismiss difficult people from consideration. Without even thinking, many of us ignore certain people or classes of people in sharing in or contributing to our growth. Or we eliminate our life with a spouse or our children or our boss. We can claim as many exceptions for not growing up in one area or another as we are able to squeeze out in our income-tax forms.

Paul will not have it: "grow up *in every way.*" We can't remain juvenile or immature or ignorant in *any* place.

It would be easy to overlook the obvious in all this, namely, that Paul is writing to adults about growing up. We often confine the term *growing* to children, both physically and emotionally. But adults are the primary targets of what Paul is talking about.

What I want to say is this: we don't respond to what Paul is writing about—growing up into Christ—by focusing on our children or someone else's children. It is I, it is you, that has to grow up. Peter said the same thing using different words: "Long for the pure, spiritual milk, so that by it you may grow into salvation" (1 Peter 2:2, NRSV).

Paul has a striking phrase to clarify what is involved in growing up: "speaking the truth in love" (Ephesians 4:15). This is the curriculum for the growth we are called to. Be the kind of person who expresses truth in your whole being, using love, not just words, to do it. Assert your integrity. Be yourself as yourself is defined by love.

The one thing it does not mean is to say true things or to make true statements. You don't grow up or help others grow up by giving them accurate advice or precise information. Your life tells the story, not just your words.

So the commitment we make to grow up into Christ has "speaking the truth in love" as its source and fuel, has consequences that feed into generation after generation. Our growth is of interest not only to God; it is also of interest and full of consequences for our children, our friends, our neighbors.

Some of Jesus's best stories are about growing up. One of my favorites is his manure story. It is about a man who had a fig tree and went looking for some fruit. There wasn't any. He told his farmer to cut it down, that there was no sense in this barren tree taking up valuable space. But the farmer argued for giving the tree another chance, a year in which he could give it special attention, digging around it to add manure, so it would bear figs in the future. "If it bears fruit next year, well and good; but if not, you can cut it down" (see Luke 13:6–9).

The farmer arguing for a reprieve for the fig tree is Jesus. Would a visitation to your life reveal any figs? Any growth? If the answer is no, it is not the last word. No cursory judgment is executed. That farmer is preaching the gospel to all of us—to you, to me. Jesus is preaching it. Jesus is actively digging manure into our lives, working with us to produce all that God intends for us until, in Paul's affirming words, "all of us come to the unity of the faith and of the knowledge of the Son of God, to *maturity,* to the measure of the *full stature* of Christ" (Ephesians 4:13, NRSV).

Amen.

5

"In Him Who Strengthens Me"

ISAIAH 26:1–9
PHILIPPIANS 4:2–20

I read a report in the *New York Times* this week of a British gentleman who had purchased his first Rolls-Royce. He could find nothing in the advertising material, the manual, or on the automobile itself that told him the horsepower of the engine. On making inquiries he learned it was not the policy of the Rolls-Royce corporation to talk about the horsepower of their automobiles. This man, though, was curious. And having paid the rather substantial purchase price, he thought he was entitled to know what the horsepower was. So he wrote the company and asked them to provide him with this piece of information. In a few days a telegram was delivered to his house with a single-word answer: *Adequate.*

Adequate. I find the same quiet confidence in our New Testament. There is no frenzied advertising. There is no shouting hucksterism. No high-pressure salesmanship. No boasting. No braggadocio. Rather, there is the sureness and ease of persons who through long experience are sure of where they are, in touch with what matters. When they talk about the new life of faith, a life in which they trust God and in which they experience God loving, forgiving, and guiding them, they convey a tone of adequacy. Hyperbole by understatement.

—

As Paul wraps up his letter to the congregation in Philippi, there are some sentences I want to set before you today that demonstrate this adequacy and invite our participation in it. Three words spaced through these sentences add up to *adequate.* The three words are *all, full,* and *every.* "I can do *all* things in him who strengthens me. . . . I have received *full* payment, and more. . . . My God will supply *every* need of yours according to his riches in glory in Christ Jesus" (Philippians 4:13, 18–19). *All. Full. Every.*

It is hardly possible to get an accurate understanding of these three words apart from their context. They are near the conclusion of this brief letter that Paul wrote, a letter crammed with the energies of joy and the vitalities of faith. The letter as a whole is the product of a vast, working, and magnificent reality that is called the life of faith, the gospel. These are not just words but words that issue from lived experience. It is also important to know that Paul is in a Roman prison as he writes this. Three times he mentions that he is in chains (1:7, 13, 14, NIV).

I say this because it is very easy to take simple and joyous words apart from the life out of which they have emerged and to dismiss them as puffery. To set them aside as the slogans of a propagandist. To dismiss them as the exclamations of an excited cheerleader. So I want to insist that you remember the man who wrote them is steady on his feet. He is a scarred veteran in the political and spiritual conflicts of the first century. Paul is far too honest to have been bribed to write something he didn't believe in. He is far too experienced to have any untested illusions about life. He is far too authentic a man to pass on to us anything he had not already incorporated into his own life. Paul is near the end of a life that was rife with persecution and oppression, doubt and fear, anxiety and evil. When we hear the simple, strong words *all, every, full,* it is impossible to dismiss them as hyperbole. We cannot disregard them as wishful thinking. We do well to take them seriously.

These are authentic, serious, tested words. Take them seriously. Test their authenticity. Experience their adequacy in this act of worship this morning with your friends in this congregation, in your private prayers as you live this life of faith this week.

All, the first of the three words, documents a solid maturity. "I have learned, in whatever state I am, to be content. I know how to be abased, and I know how to abound; in any and all circumstances I have learned the secret of facing plenty and hunger, abundance and want. I can do *all* things in him who strengthens me" (4:11–13).

In our vernacular, Paul has been around the block a few times. He has been up and he has been down. He is a veteran. He is solidly mature. There are surprises that neither adversity nor success could deal him. He has visited the extremes. And what he knows is that what God has done within him is far more important and lasting and real than anything that could be done to him from the outside by weather or government or persons.

Immaturity is that in-between stage between innocence and experience, when we think that by changing what we have or whom we are with or where we are, we can change ourselves. Maturity arrives in a way of life that has form and substance developed from our insides and that knows the significant acts are our responses. Christian maturity experiences that responsiveness when shaped and renewed by faith in Christ.

Mature Christians are able to do all things because they don't have to do everything. They acquire strength to live because they don't have to be anxious and constantly attentive to trivia, and they don't have to take responsibility for the whole world on their shoulders.

There are a great many things we can do little or nothing about. The weather is out of our hands. Other people's emotions are out of our hands. The economy is out of our hands. Mostly we have to live with what families or our bodies or our government hands to us. But there is one enormous difference that *is* in our hands: we can offer up the center of our lives to the great revealed action of God's love for us. We can discover that each of us is an absolutely unique individual. We can cultivate the vitality and centering of life that develops out of risking our lives in a relationship with God.

When we do that, we find Paul's statement neither extravagant nor fanciful: "I can do *all* things through Christ who strengthens me" (verse 13, NKJV).

—

Full is the second word. It advertises a satisfied customer: "I have received *full* payment, and more; I am filled, having received from Epaphroditus the gifts you sent, a fragrant offering, a sacrifice acceptable and pleasing to God" (verse 18).

If you examine this text carefully, you find that Paul had just gotten a purse of money from his friends. He had been in need of financial assistance, and the congregation in Philippi heard about it. They went around and took up an offering, and one of their number, Epaphroditus, offered to go to Rome and deliver it to Paul.

It is Bible passages like this that I prize above all the others. I'm not dismissing the more famous, glorious passages, like "God so loved the world" (John 3:16) and "God was in Christ reconciling the world to Himself" (2 Corinthians 5:19, NKJV) and "I am the resurrection and the life" (John 11:25). But all the same I have a special fondness for things like this: "I have received full payment, and more." He was paid. In actual money. This isn't a truth to believe. This isn't a sentiment to stir your hearts. This isn't a hymn to lift to heaven in a choir. Paul got his hands on some money he needed. And Epaphroditus took the trouble to bring it to him. A named friend. Someone willing to take a long trip on foot, roughly six hundred miles as a crow flies, to bring it to him.

I have heard people complain that they hear too much about money in church. I think I know what they mean, but the complaint is badly phrased, for that is one of the things I would like to hear less of outside the church and maybe a little more inside. Why? Because I want to be with people who take all of me seriously, not just my soul. I want to know that the nitty-gritty of my life is taken seriously by the gospel, not just the state of my soul. I don't want a religion that consists of soupy verses on Hallmark cards. I don't want a religion of neat little slogans about sunsets and heartthrobs. I want something practical that gets into the working parts of my life, into my wallet and pocketbook, and leaves evidence on my check stubs. And named persons who know my name. People I can serve and who will serve me when I am in need.

The gospel of Jesus Christ creates a community in which people take care of one another, respond to others' needs, take people into their homes, give them beds, feed them meals, collect money to meet their needs. "It was kind of you to share my trouble," said Paul (Philippians 4:14). How did they share it? They gave him some money. Christians don't separate body and soul, the material and the spiritual. The Philippian congregation didn't. And then one of their number, Epaphroditus, volunteered to take the money to Rome.

Every is the third word. It signals a shared generosity: "And my God will supply *every* need of yours according to his riches in glory in Christ Jesus" (verse 19).

Paul is not selfish or private or idiosyncratic. He is convinced that what has just happened to him in Christ can happen to anyone. What he has found in Epaphroditus's visit to that Roman prison, anyone can experience. What he has received, anyone can receive. Faith is not what comes to persons with just the right temperament or who go through a particular upbringing or who have certain predispositions or who get all the breaks. The act of faith deals with something that is foundational and basic in our personhood. At that level we are met and changed and satisfied by Christ: "My God will supply every need of yours." *Every.*

We don't all get the same feelings out of it. We don't all get the same ideas out of it. We don't all develop the same lifestyle out of it. We don't all arrive at the same standard of living. But we all get the same God who takes us seriously, forgives absolutely, and loves eternally, who supplies all our need.

I need someone like Paul around to tell me this. Thank you, Paul, for writing this letter! Many of the people I meet look at me and tell me in one way or another—mostly nonverbally, but the message gets through nevertheless—that I lack something fundamental. I am deficient in sensitivity. My mind can't grasp the whole truth. I am inadequate. And I usually recognize they are right. And then someone like Paul comes along and sees through and around these flaws or deficiencies in me, recognizes what is created and promised by Christ, and announces to me, "Every need."

The gospel doesn't impose a way of life on us from without and tell us that we have to live up to it. It creates a new life within and then encourages and directs us to the living out of it. It is not an ironclad, inflexible demand but a surging promise. This is what is offered to us and what becomes real and experienced in the act of faith. For a few moments we take our eyes off our unsolvable problems and are released from being obsessed with the dead-endedness of our lives. We discover a new way of looking at ourselves, a new way of feeling about ourselves. We see how God looks at us. We realize the way he feels about us. We hear someone say, "My God will supply every need of yours according to his riches in glory in Christ Jesus," and suddenly it doesn't sound like a fantasy fairy tale but the soberest and most everyday truth.

—

All documents a solid maturity: "I have learned, in whatever state I am, to be content. . . . I can do *all* things in him who strengthens me" (verses 11, 13).

Full advertises a satisfied customer: "I have received *full* payment, and more; I am filled" (verse 18).

Every signals a shared generosity: "And my God will supply *every* need of yours" (verse 19).

All, full, every—adequate.

Amen.

6

"Aspire to the Realm Above"

PSALM 110
COLOSSIANS 3:1–17

To get a glimpse, however faint, of the purpose of God for us in and even beyond creation is a welcome development. Christian doctrine accurately perceived carries with it a sense of spaciousness. But there often comes a time after we have become familiar with the ideas and beliefs of the Christian faith that we lose the cantering rhythms of poetry and settle into plodding workhorse prose, when the flashing world of the imagination gets submerged under the heavier, grayer world of conduct.

Christian thought is beautiful. Theology was once called the queen of the sciences. Dorothy Sayers once named the Christian gospel "the most exciting drama that ever staggered the imagination of man."[76] But when we move into the realm of conduct, the glamour fades. One man said the trouble with being a Christian is that "it is such a daily sort of thing." But if the Christian life means anything at all, it finally has to get into the world of what we do between waking and sleeping, into the realm of the routine, ordinary speech, habitual responses, casual reactions. We cannot sustain the adventure-on-the-high-seas emotional pitch too long. We cannot think big thoughts all day. We are not Hamlet, surrounded by intrigue and murder, plunged into profound soliloquies three or four times a day. We are much more like T. S. Eliot's J. Alfred Prufrock who says,

---

76. Dorothy Sayers, *Letters to a Diminished Church: Passionate Arguments for the Relevance of Christian Doctrine* (Nashville: W Publishing Group, 2004), 1.

No! I am not Prince Hamlet, nor was meant to be;
Am an attendant lord, one that will do
To swell a progress, start a scene or two,
Advise the prince; no doubt, an easy tool,
Deferential, glad to be of use,
Politic, cautious, and meticulous.[77]

So we have finally to talk about Christ in our conduct, in our ordinary "Prufrock" lives. If Jesus makes it into our daily behavior, observers will begin to think there might be something to this after all. And we ourselves are not going to be satisfied for long with just talking about ideas and truths that don't filter into the ordinariness of our living.

Paul, in his letter to the Christians at Colossae, doesn't begin by instructing us on our behavior, but before he is halfway through the letter, he gets to it.

Our text consists of three verses in the third chapter: "Were you not raised to life with Christ? Then aspire to the realm above, where Christ is, seated at the right hand of God. . . . Put to death those parts of you which belong to the earth. . . . Put on the garments that suit God's chosen people" (Colossians 3:1, 5, 12, NEB).

Paul marks this transition from getting the *story* right to getting our *lives* right with a rhetorical question followed by three imperatives. If we take these commands seriously and reflect on them prayerfully, we can be led a long way along the road of Christian conduct. But before we obey the commands, it is essential that we listen to the question.

The question "Were you not raised to life with Christ?" assumes a yes answer and puts us into a positive relation with what has gone before. We recall Christ in the Creation. We recall the tremendous history of God's redemption, the numberless instances of his love and grace, the whole world of salvation. And then we recall how we have found ourselves incorporated into the activity and made a working part of it, all summarized here in the phrase "raised to life with Christ." Before we

77. T. S. Eliot, "The Love Song of J. Alfred Prufrock," in *The Poems of T. S. Eliot, Volume 1: Collected and Uncollected Poems,* ed. Christopher Ricks and Jim McCue (London: Faber and Faber, 2015), 9.

start talking about our behavior, we need to rehearse Christ's behavior on our behalf.

If Paul is right, and he has a good reputation for that, then in any discussion of Christian truth, the first word has to be about God and his work in us. If we fail to maintain that priority, everything gets hopelessly muddled. Paul never fails to establish that priority. In the letter he wrote to the Romans, he gives eleven chapters to the activity of God before he writes four chapters on our conduct. In Galatians the first four chapters are oriented around God's plan, the last two toward our response. Ephesians is split exactly in half: the first three chapters on God's purposes, the final three on our part in it.

So it is not possible to begin a discussion on Christian living by talking about what we do. It would be like talking about the performance of a new sailing vessel before the ship was even in the blueprint stage. Or like talking about going to the moon before you were even sure there was a moon. Or like planning to write a novel in Chinese before you knew a single word of Chinese.

Paul's question, then, reminds us that we have been participants in a great saving event: we have been raised with Christ. All the redemptive activity of God has been focused on us. We are not ourselves by ourselves; we are men and women in Christ. Only as we realize that and reflect on it frequently is it safe to talk about our conduct.

—

We would be far off the mark if we saw this as only an invigorating call to a higher life, an idealistic challenge toward better things. The area of our conduct is defined as the realm "where Christ is, seated at the right hand of God" (3:1, NEB). It is the place where Christ is seated, where redemption is the central concern, where love is in operation, where grace is dispensed freely. In other words, our aspirations are not directed to a generalized upward direction but specifically to Christ as he rules our lives.

If we obey this command, it is bound to have a deep effect on our conduct, for in the ruling, Christ will become vigorous and alive in our goals and purposes, which will inevitably affect our conduct.

Imagine a young man starting off on a two-mile walk across town to see a girl. Seeing her and spending the evening with her is the purpose and goal of his walk. She is very much alive in his imagination. He can't keep her out of his mind.

Passing a delicatessen, he remembers her favorite candy and buys a box. Passing a flower shop, he is inspired with the thought of how lovely she would look with flowers on her shoulder, so he buys a corsage. Passing old acquaintances, he entirely misses even seeing them. Passing a church, he looks particularly long at it, for he once heard her remark that that was where she would like to be married. Nearing her home, he glances at his reflection in a store window, straightens his tie, and fixes his hat. By the time he arrives at her door, we will have been able to list at least a dozen specific actions in the course of the two-mile walk, all caused by the girl in his imagination. She was in his conduct.

The image put before us is the ruling Christ, that we should "aspire to the realm above, where Christ is" (NEB). If this ruling Christ is alive in our aspirations and dreams, we will do things we never dreamed of doing before. Christ will be in our imaginations, in our purposes, in our goals.

—

The second command is nearly macabre by contrast: "Put to death those parts of you which belong to the earth" (verse 5, NEB). The logic of the movement from the first command to this one is well marked by George MacDonald:

> We are and remain such creeping Christians, because we look at ourselves and not at Christ; because we gaze at the marks of our own soiled feet, and the trail of our own defiled garments. . . . Each, putting his foot in the footprint of the Master, and so defacing it, turns to examine how far his neighbour's footprint corresponds with that which he still calls the Master's, although it is but his own. Or, having committed a petty fault, I mean a fault such as only a petty creature could commit, we mourn over the defilement to ourselves, and the shame of it before our friends, children, or servants, instead of hastening to make the due confession and amends to our fellow, and then, forgetting our paltry self with its well-earned disgrace, lift up our eyes to the glory which alone will quicken the true man in us, and kill the peddling creature we so wrongly call our *self*.[78]

78. George MacDonald, *Unspoken Sermons*, Series 1, 2, 3, in *George MacDonald Christian Writings* (Oxford: Benediction Classics, 2013), 72, italics in the original.

"Lift up our eyes . . . and kill the peddling creature." There is not only that primary set of the soul, the fixing of the imagination on the rule of Christ. There is also this ruthless dealing with something that could sabotage the whole enterprise. There is this rooting out of that which could make our conduct a sham performance and a laughingstock charade.

Saint Anthony, an Egyptian desert hermit of the fourth century, is the most celebrated example in the history of the church of a person who took this command as literally as possible and "put to death those parts . . . which belong to the earth." As a young man, and an already fairly well-to-do farmer, he was sitting in church one day and heard the gospel lesson read as if personally to him: "Sell your possessions and give the money to the poor and come and follow me" (see Matthew 19:21). So he sold everything, gave the money to the poor, and went out into the desert where he stayed for the next eighty-five years, with only four brief returns to the city. His strenuous encounters with the devil and his demons, his vivid temptations, his extreme efforts to deny himself, and his single-minded pursuit of God have marked him as the greatest of all the Desert Fathers. As literally and as completely as he could, he put to death the things that belonged to the earth. His only companions were the jackals that roamed the desert and the scorpions that lived with him in crumbled tombs. In his own day he attracted many imitators so that when he finally died at the age of 105, the desert was swarming with hermits weaving mats and baskets and emulating Anthony's asceticism and devotion.

But many times among the Desert Fathers there was a tendency to publicity-oriented austerity, a kind of pride in denial, which almost certainly missed the Christian point completely. So we do better by taking Jesus Christ as our interpreter in understanding this command. In him we see no denial for its own sake, no conspicuous rejection of the world, no trace of asceticism. Rather we see the elimination of everything that would either distract or encumber his service of God. We see the disciplined rejection of any interest that might dissuade him from laying down his life for others. In other words, in Christ we see the putting to death of self, the killing of self-centeredness, the crucifixion of the ego. And this is what we are to put to death.

—

The third command: "Put on the garments that suit God's chosen people" (verse 12, NEB). It is a positive injunction to dress in clothing that openly demonstrates what we are within.

We live by symbols. We arrange all our relationships on the basis of signs. None of us can look inside another and discern the development of thought in someone's brain or the change and movements of emotions in anyone's heart. That doesn't mean we are consigned to ignorance. We have ways of finding out what is inside. Expressions on the face, words in the mouth, the manner of a walk, the choice of clothes, the gestures. A person shows in any number of ways what the internal realities are. We do it by "putting on garments," that is, by giving signs, outward evidences of what is inward.

Paul has already said that our life is "hidden with Christ in God" (Colossians 3:3, NEB). No one can see it. The man in Christ and the man not in Christ look exactly the same. A cardiograph will not discern any Christian difference in their heartbeats; an IQ test cannot separate Christian from non-Christian brains; a customs inspector examining passport photographs can't sort out the saints from the sinners. Our life truly is "hidden with Christ in God."

So what are the "garments that suit God's chosen people"? Paul suggests "compassion, kindness, humility, gentleness, patience" (verse 12, NEB). These are words, acts, attitudes that reveal Christ in us.

This is not an imitation of Christ for its own sake but an attempt to provide signs and symbols of his inward reality. Putting on these "garments" is a witness not of our own goodness—for so many times they do not reflect our feelings on the matter at all—but of that hidden reality of Christ within us.

Having been "raised to life with Christ," we are then commanded to do these three things: "aspire to the realm above, where Christ is," "put to death those parts . . . which belong to the earth," and "put on the garments that suit God's chosen people" (verses 1, 5, 12, NEB). These are the things that provide Christ areas of our activity that our neighbors can observe.

If I read Paul right, I see little or no interest here in Christian performance as such. He is not concerned that we make a good record. The Christ life is no cheap legalism, no grim custodian of the rules of God.

Thomas à Kempis, in what may be the most read book on what we are talking about, *The Imitation of Christ,* wrote this parting challenge for us: "So many people are kept back from spiritual growth, and from tackling their faults in earnest, by one single fault—running away from difficulties; we don't like a tussle."[79] "The devil does not sleep, nor is the flesh yet dead; therefore, you must never cease your preparation for battle."[80]

And then he prays this prayer: "O Lord! make that possible to me by grace, which I find impossible by nature."[81]

Amen.

79. Thomas à Kempis, *The Imitation of Christ,* trans. Ronald Knox (San Francisco: Ignatius Press, 2005), book 1, section 25, paragraph 3.
80. Thomas à Kempis, *The Imitation of Christ,* trans. Aloysius Croft and Harold Bolton, ed. Susan L. Rattiner (1940; repr., Mineola, NY: Dover, 2003), 38.
81. Thomas à Kempis, *The Imitation of Christ,* trans. John Payne (Glasgow: William Collins, 1836), 210.

7

"On Behalf of My Child, Onesimus"

ECCLESIASTES 11:1-6
PHILEMON 1:8-14

There are three persons named in the brief, personal letter we want to look at this morning. One name you know well. The other two may be unfamiliar. Paul's name is famous among us. He wrote letters to Christians of the first century that continue to be read by us. By all accounts he is one of the most creative, dazzling persons in human history, one of the giant figures in the history of civilization. He is the writer of this letter.

The second person in the story is Philemon, the one to whom the letter is addressed. You may recognize the name if you are one of that diminishing company of people who as youth memorized all the books of the Bible, because his name is on this letter. Paul wrote it to him. It is stretching things, though, to call it a book. It is a single page, a brief, personal letter Paul wrote from a Roman prison to his friend who lived in a town (Colossae) in what is now Turkey. Years earlier, when Paul was traveling through that country preaching and organizing congregations, he had met Philemon. Philemon became a convert and invited others to meet in his home. There they worshiped, prayed together, searched the Scriptures, celebrated the sacraments, and encouraged one another in the shared life of Christ, just as we ourselves do.

The third person, and this name will be obscure to many of you, is Onesimus, a slave in the household of Philemon. Since the Colossian church met in Philemon's home, Onesimus would have been acquainted with this group of early Christians. But for him these so-called Christians just meant more work: more cleaning to be done, more meals to be prepared, more errands to run. Onesimus didn't like being a slave, and more particularly—I'm imagining this—he didn't like being a slave to a bunch of Christians who were always talking about freedom. So one day he had had his fill of it. He had taken all he would take. His bitterness reached a critical point, and he left, stealing a sum of money from his master to finance his escape. Rome was a favorite destination for runaway slaves, a big city where they could easily be anonymous, so Onesimus headed for Rome. It was easy to be unseen among the large, shifting population of newcomers in Rome, easy to disappear into the underground.

In Rome, Onesimus met someone he never expected to meet. He met Paul, who was in a Roman prison. We know nothing about how the meeting occurred, only that as a result of the meeting, Onesimus became a Christian.

Onesimus then decided to return to his old master, Philemon, and give himself up. Paul wrote a cover letter for Onesimus to take with him, addressed to Philemon. It is one of the most remarkable letters ever written, maybe ranking with Martin Luther King Jr.'s "Letter from a Birmingham Jail."

—

After the customary opening remarks to Philemon and a couple of others in the congregation—a woman, Apphia (maybe Philemon's wife), and a man, Archippus (perhaps the son of Philemon and Apphia), described by Paul as "our fellow soldier"—Paul gets down to business, which is to reconcile Onesimus to his master Philemon.

He begins by assuring Philemon of his respect for him and the way he is living out his new Christian faith: "I thank my God always when I remember you in my prayers, because I hear of your love and of the faith which you have toward the Lord Jesus and all the saints, and I pray that the sharing of your faith may promote the knowledge of all the good that is ours in Christ. For I have derived much joy and comfort from your love, my brother, because the hearts of the saints have been refreshed through you" (Philemon 1:4–7).

It is obvious that Paul has the highest regard for Philemon. He had been in his home many times and observed there the working out of love and faith. Philemon was a man whose entire life had been transformed by the gospel. Reports kept coming in to Paul in his Roman prison cell as travelers would stop by, bringing news of what was happening among the scattered Christian congregations. In those reports, Philemon's name must have come up repeatedly. Philemon combined what often gets separated—faith in Christ and love for others. He had a solid and mature faith in Jesus Christ and a solid and mature love for the people around him. He shared what he had. What he experienced as good, others experienced as good through him. The lives of others were refreshed by him. When you were around Philemon, you didn't feel left out or put down or cheap or worthless. Philemon had that quality of bringing out the best in his friends and leaving them nourished.

Now Paul gets to the heart of what he is writing: "Accordingly, though I am bold enough in Christ to command you to do what is required, yet for love's sake I prefer to appeal to you—I, Paul, an ambassador and now a prisoner also for Christ Jesus—I appeal to you for my child, Onesimus, whose father I have become in my imprisonment" (verses 8–10).

Wouldn't we like to know how that came about? Onesimus was living out his precarious existence as part of the runaway slave population in Rome, in constant danger of exposure. The penalties, if captured, were severe: torture at the least, death at the worst. Most fugitive slaves found it very difficult to live on their own. They had been dependent for their entire lives on a slaveholding master and now found they didn't have the resources for living independently. And what good was their freedom if they had to spend the rest of their lives hiding, thieving, and begging?

The backstory that we will never know is how Onesimus discovered Paul in a prison cell. Onesimus, who had spent his entire life as a slave, was now free; Paul, who had lived his entire life as a free person, was imprisoned. But Onesimus wasn't enjoying his freedom, and Paul seemed unperturbed in his incarceration.

Conversations must have developed between Paul and Onesimus during Onesimus's prison visits. Onesimus became a Christian. Onesimus put his new life to use in serving Paul, voluntarily taking up the servant role from which he had so recently escaped. Affection developed between the two men, like that between a father and a son.

And then one day there was a decision. No doubt it had been preceded by long conversations and prayers. Onesimus decided to return to Philemon and give himself up. He had been a bad slave. He had stolen from his master and escaped. Now, as a Christian, he would return to the place that he had found intolerable and there live out the conditions of his salvation. Under Paul's spiritual guidance he had come to realize that the reason he was so unhappy in Philemon's house was not that he was a slave of another man but that he was a rebel against God, not because of his social condition but because of his spiritual condition.

So he made preparations to return to Colossae. In an earlier letter, written to the church in Philippi, Paul had written, "I want you to know, brethren, that what has happened to me has really served to advance the gospel, so that it has become known throughout the whole praetorian guard and to all the rest that my imprisonment is for Christ; and most of the brethren have been made confident in the Lord because of my imprisonment, and are much more bold to speak the word of God without fear" (Philippians 1:12–14).

Now he writes a personal letter to Philemon in Colossae, interceding for Onesimus. This letter to Philemon was entrusted to the same messenger as the epistle to the Colossians. We are not expressly told that Philemon belonged to the church in Colossae, but this is apparent from the mention of Onesimus in the Colossian letter as "one of yourselves" (4:9). Tychicus, one of the Christians with Paul in Rome, decided to accompany Onesimus on the journey (verses 7–9). The two friends, new companions in Christ, set out with the letter.

I can't help but imagine that on the way they talked over the contents of Paul's two letters, the earlier letter to the Colossian church and the letter to Philemon. I wonder if they chuckled over the joke that Paul made in the letter to Philemon: "Formerly he was useless to you, but now he is indeed useful to you and to me" (1:11). The name Onesimus means "useful." Paul playfully puns, "Here comes Useful—and you will remember that he was the most useless slave you had. But now he is useful to both you and me. Useless-Useless is now Useful-Useful, a double Useful, a *real* Onesimus!"

Onesimus and Tychicus set off. It was a long journey back to Philemon and the Colossian church, the first stage by foot, succeeded by a longer journey on a ship.

Finally the long sea voyage is completed. They disembark in the port city of Ephesus and walk the thirty or so miles to Colossae. Anticipation builds. The last time Onesimus walked this road, he was angry and frightened. Now he is light of heart, sure of himself, confident of his decision. Then he was alone, running for his life; now he is with a good friend, Tychicus, and looks forward to acquiring even more friends in the Colossian church community. And Philemon? How would Philemon receive him?

They knock on the door. Archippus runs to the entrance, sees who is there, and shouts back into the house, "It's Onesimus!" Apphia and Philemon, surprised, maybe a little apprehensive, come to the door. They never expected to see what is before them. The man they remembered as surly and recalcitrant is now self-assured, with a smile on his face. Onesimus hands Philemon Paul's letter. Philemon reads aloud, Apphia and Archippus listening: "I am sending him back to you, sending my very heart. I would have been glad to keep him with me, in order that he might serve me on your behalf during my imprisonment for the gospel; but I preferred to do nothing without your consent in order that your goodness might not be by compulsion but of your own free will" (Philemon 1:12–14).

What a wise faith-friend Paul is to Philemon. He knows that goodness cannot be forced. He knows that virtue cannot be squeezed out of a person. He knows that no amount of pressure, either mental or physical or emotional, can increase or stimulate or develop the life of faith in Christ. It is up to Philemon. Paul will not impose a solution on Philemon in regard to Onesimus. Paul will not define the way in which he must express his love. Philemon's response must be absolutely free: "that your goodness might not be by compulsion but of your own free will" (verse 14).

Paul's restraint is rare. When I know what is good for someone, I want to *make* the person do it. After all, it is for his or her own good. I want to develop a strategy that ensures it will take place. But that is always a mistake. Paul's way is the only way, "that your goodness might not be by compulsion but of your own free will."

Philemon continues to read the letter: "So if you consider me your partner, receive him as you would receive me. If he has wronged you at all, or owes you anything, charge that to my account. I, Paul, write this with my own hand, I will repay it—to say nothing of your owing me even your own self" (verses 17–19).

All the neighbors knew that the richest kind of hospitality was characteristic of that house. The home of Philemon and Apphia and Archippus was open and warm and cheerful. The church in their house flourished under their smiles and embraces. They delighted in nothing quite so much as being able to share their rich family life with others: their meals, their conversation, their songs and stories. Paul had often experienced it. But Onesimus, even though he had observed it, had always been an outsider to it. He was now an outsider no longer. He was a brother: "Receive him [Philemon] as you would receive me" (verse 17).

As far as the money was an issue, Paul took over the debt. The slate was clean. Onesimus had no honest way to get money together to make restitution for the theft. Paul would do that for him. When he got out of prison, he would make a few tents and have the money in no time.

And then this finishing touch. A masterful line: "Yes, brother, I want some benefit from you in the Lord. [Here is your benefit, your Onesimus.] Refresh my heart in Christ" (verse 20).

Amen.

Part 7

"IN THE BEGINNING WAS THE WORD"

PREACHING IN THE COMPANY OF JOHN OF PATMOS

Introduction

Pastoral preaching is rooted in language: God speaks. When God speaks, things happen. Holy Scripture opens with the Genesis words "God said . . ." ringing out eight times. After each sounding we see, piece by piece, one after another, elements of heaven and earth coming into being before our eyes and then climaxing in man and woman, formed in the image of God. Psalm 33 compresses Genesis 1 into a single sentence: "For he spoke, and it came to be" (verse 9). Genesis 1 sets the stage for everything that follows in our Bibles, this profuse outpouring of commands and promises, blessings and invitations, rebukes and judgments, directing and comforting that make up our Holy Scriptures.

In the quartet of gospel writers, John gets the final storytelling word. John writes his Jesus story in quite a different way from his canonical companions—Matthew, Mark, and Luke—who all follow the same basic outline. John's approach gives us the same story, but the shift in perspective and tone engages us differently. Novelist John Updike observes that if we view Matthew, Mark, and Luke as "progressively sedimentary," then John is "like a metamorphic rock in which these strata have been violently annealed" into something quite different.[82]

John primarily tells stories. But as Jesus speaks, his words flourish into conversations and discourses with all sorts and conditions of people, conversations brief and lengthy, conversations pithy and elaborate, but always *conversations.* Several times the conversations develop into discourses, but the conversational tone is

82. John Updike, "The Gospel According to Saint Matthew," in *Incarnation: Contemporary Writers on the New Testament,* ed. Alfred Corn (Lincoln, NE: iUniverse, 1990), 2.

always maintained. The Lord of language uses language not to lord it over anyone but to enter relationships of grace and love, creating community and bringing it to maturity in prayer—person-to-person conversations that include the praying presence of Jesus.

—

Saint John's gospel opens with this emphatically verbal beginning, repeating *Word* three times: "In the beginning was the *Word,* and the *Word* was with God, and the *Word* was God" (1:1). This Word, we soon find out, is Jesus: "And the Word became flesh and dwelt among us, full of grace and truth; we have beheld his glory" (verse 14).

The letters of John (he wrote three of them) likewise go back to the beginning and give witness to the apostolic experience of being convinced that this "word of life" (1 John 1:1) was Jesus, verified by what the Twelve heard, what they saw, and what they touched. Three of our five senses (seeing, hearing, touching) are employed in the verification (verse 1). This Jesus spoke the commands that resulted in a life of salvation from sin expressed in a community of love.

Each of the letters is shaped by a pastoral concern for people who are being upset and maybe confused by interlopers in their community. John knows his congregation and affectionately refers to them as "my dear children" (1 John 2:1, NIV). He has gotten word that they are being tested and challenged by competitors whom John refers to as antichrists, outsiders who are contentious and disruptive (1 John 4:3–5; 2 John 1:7). Take them seriously, John says, but not on their terms. Love is the only "weapon" that will be of any use against them.

The second and third letters are much briefer but still just as personal, and they provide direction and counsel in regard to these foreign elements that are upsetting and perhaps confusing the church. John is their pastor, and he is taking his vocation seriously, encouraging them to stick to what they are already doing so well.

And, finally, the Revelation to John presents the risen and present Jesus under the aspect of words: *human* speech. John gives "witness to the word of God and to the testimony of Jesus Christ" (Revelation 1:2). This risen Jesus Christ then identifies himself to John alphabetically: "I am the Alpha and the Omega" (verse 8). He is the alphabet, all the letters from A to Z, that is, the stuff, the vowels and consonants, out of which all words are made. Jesus speaks in such ways that the brokenness of the world and our experiences develop into a dazzling holiness that evokes worship on a grand scale, involving everything in heaven and earth.

And here is something that never ceases to astonish me. Pastor John of Patmos knew his Bible inside and out. The Revelation has 404 verses. In those 404 verses there are 518 references to earlier scriptures. But there is not a single direct quote; all the references are allusions. Here is a pastor who is absolutely immersed in Scripture and submits himself to it. He does not just repeat, regurgitate, or cite proof texts. As he preaches, the Scriptures are re-created in him. He first assimilates Scripture and then lives and preaches the Scripture he had internalized.

The Revelation is a thorough immersion in, and the last word in, what I think of as lived theology, which is often designated as spiritual theology. Austin Farrer calls it "the one great poem which the first Christian age produced."[83]

At first reading, Saint John's various books, written in three different genres, appear very different, but when they are read carefully and with imagination, they all seem very Johannine even though employing different writing styles (a pastoral *story,* pastoral *letters,* and a pastoral *poem*), giving a convincing internal unity that comes from the heart, mind, and soul of a pastor.

—

Language is the primary way in which God communicates. In the Scriptures the language is referred to in very physical ways. We hear the words, of course. We also see the words: "I turned to see the voice" (Revelation 1:12). We "chew" them (Psalm 1:2, MSG), we "taste" them (Psalm 119:103), and we "walk" and "run" in them (Psalm 119:1, 32). John in his Patmos vision was commanded by a "mighty angel" with a scroll in his hand to take the scroll and eat it (Revelation 10:1–2, 8–10). And he did. He ate the book, the word of God. He took it and ate it, assimilated it into his entire living body, not just into his mind, and then preached what he had taken in and digested.

We are part of a holy community that for three thousand years and more has been formed inside and out by these words of God.

—

83. Austin Farrer, *A Rebirth of Images: The Making of St. John's Apocalypse* (Eugene, OR: Wipf and Stock, 1963), 6.

What we pastors eventually came to recognize in John as a preacher is this: god-talk—depersonalized, nonrelational, unlistening, abstract language—kills. In "the land of the living," it is blasphemous, whether spoken from pulpits or across the breakfast table. Pastors can't be too careful in the way we use language, this sacred language, this word-of-God language. When we enter John's language world, we soon realize he was totally immersed in his congregations, their strengths and weaknesses, testings and difficulties. At the same time he was mindful of the political and economic world in which they lived, the killing and suffering and evil. And then, taking all this into account, with his incredible Spirit-formed imagination, he gathered his congregations into the great drama of salvation and provided them with an embracing story, clear instructions, and a dramatic poem that rocks with *amens* and *hallelujahs*. And not a cliché anywhere to be found.

My metaphor of choice for grasping what is involved in listening and meditating on God's Word is "eat this book." The metaphor achieves unforgettable prominence in the final book of the Bible when the apocalyptic strong angel, taking the cosmos for his pulpit, one foot planted in the ocean and the other on land, held the Scriptures in his hand and preached. He preached the words of God. The words coming off that page were thunder in the ears of Saint John. Impressed, he grabbed his notebook and pencil and started to write down what he had just heard. A voice from heaven told him not to write what he had heard but to take the book and eat it. The words in the book had just been voiced, taken off the page and set in motion in the air where they could enter ears. When John started to take the message he had heard—the rolling thunder of those sentences reverberating through land and sea—and write it down, he was stopped short. Why, that would be like taking the wind or breath out of the words and flattening them soundless on paper. The preaching angel had just gotten them off the printed page, and now John was going to put them back again. It's as if the heavenly voice says, "No, I want those words out there, creating sound waves, entering ears, entering lives. I want those words preached, sung, taught, prayed—*lived.* Get this book into your gut; get the words of this book moving through your bloodstream; chew on these words and swallow them so they can be turned into muscle and gristle and bone." And John did it; he ate the book.

I have used this metaphor for much of my pastoral and preaching life as a way of focusing on and clarifying what it means to have these Holy Scriptures and how the holy community has learned to eat them, to receive them in a way that forms us into Christian men and women created and saved and blessed by God the Father, God the Son, and God the Holy Spirit.

I later found a companion metaphor to the heavenly voice's "eat this book" in a poem by Wendell Berry. For forty years in a succession of novels and poems and essays, Berry has been reordering our Christian imaginations to cultivate totalities, to live life as a spiritually organic whole. In his poem "From the Crest," he works his metaphor of a farm, where we "bear the long, slow growth of the fields."[84] His work invites reflection on the form of Scripture and congregation as they give form to the Christian life.

What Berry sees in his farm as a form, I see in my congregation as a form. Think of the farm as an organic whole but with boundaries so you are aware and stay in touch with all the interrelations: the house and barn, the horses and the chickens, the weather of sun and rain, the food prepared in the house and the work done in the fields, the machinery and the tools, the seasons. There are steady, relaxed rhythms in place.

I did not grow up on a farm but did grow up in farming country and was often on farms and ranches. My father was a butcher, so we were often on farms buying and slaughtering cows and pigs and sheep. I am sure there are exceptions to this, but as I leaf through my early memories, I can't remember a farmer who was ever in a hurry. Farmers characteristically work hard, but there is too much work to do to be in a hurry.

On a farm everything is connected to something else. If you get in a hurry, break the rhythms of the land and seasons and weather, things fall apart. You get in the way of something set in motion last week or month. A farm is not neat. There is too much going on that is out of your control. Farms help us learn patience and attentiveness: "I am trying to teach my mind / to bear the long, slow growth / of the fields, and to sing / of its passing while it waits."

---

84. Wendell Berry, *Collected Poems* (Berkeley, CA: Counterpoint, 2012), 221.

If anything or anyone is treated out of context—that is, isolated as a thing in itself apart from season or weather or soil conditions or the condition of the machinery or persons—it is violated: "The farm must be made a form, / endlessly bringing together / heaven and earth, light / and rain building, dissolving, / building back again / the shapes and actions of the ground."

Both Scripture and the congregation are forms in just this way: a fenced-in acreage, whether of words or worshipers, of many different sorts and kinds, but all of them integral to the context of the words being read and the company that is gathered. We work in long, steady rhythms in which we participate but don't control. We meditatively enter this world of words and people and give obedient and glad assent. We submit our lives to this text and this congregation that is "endlessly bringing together / heaven and earth."

John of Patmos does this for us: encourages the development of a pastoral imagination that is adequate for keeping all the details of pulpit and sanctuary, parish life and congregational worship together. It is fitting that he be given the last word in gathering these kingfisher sermons.

Three writers have been of enormous help as Saint John of Patmos was developing a pastoral imagination in me. Austin Farrer's *A Rebirth of Images* is demanding, but more than anyone else, with the exception of John of Patmos himself, Farrer penetrates the workings of the devout pastoral imagination. Hans Urs von Balthasar in *Prayer* taught me to be contemplative in the company of Scripture and the congregation. Charles Williams, in his novels, poetry, and criticism, showed me the workings of the imagination as a means of grace and convinced me that an *exercised* imagination is essential to a full-bodied and full-souled life in Christ. In Williams's novel *The Greater Trumps,* one of his characters, Henry Lee, says, "All things are held together by correspondence, image with image, movement with movement: without that there could be no relation and therefore no truth. It is our business—especially yours and mine—to take up the power of relation. Do you know what I mean?"[85]

I think I know what he means, and I have made it my business to work at it as I have read, meditated, and prayed in the company of John of Patmos.

85. Charles Williams, *The Greater Trumps* (Vancouver, BC: Regent College Publishing, 2003), 41.

I

—

"Father, Glorify Thy Name"

ISAIAH 40:3–5
JOHN 12:12–30

We know that Jesus prayed. In the Gospels there are nineteen references to Jesus praying. It interests me that we are given only eight of the actual prayers that he prayed. My text for today is the shortest of the six, comprising four words: "Father, glorify your name" (John 12:28, NRSV).

This is prayed at almost the exact center of the Jesus story as John tells it. Through the first eleven chapters, John immerses us in the words and actions of Jesus, "the Word . . . made flesh" (John 1:14, KJV), Jesus alive. John means for us to take "made flesh" seriously. All of life, human life, is sacramental, a container for and revelation of the holy: the Word made flesh and blood, sinew and bone. Jesus, most emphatically, human.

The concluding ten chapters in John's gospel take us detail by detail into the story of Jesus's death. It opens with Jesus at a dinner hosted by his friends Lazarus, Martha, and Mary, during which Mary anoints Jesus's feet with perfume, an anointing that Jesus interprets as "for the day of my burial" (12:7). The next day, Palm Sunday, has Jesus prominently leading a crowd into Jerusalem for the Passover festival. The host of hosanna-singing people thought they were participating in the coronation of their king: "Blessed is he who comes . . . the King of Israel!" (verse 13). *King* is pretty heady stuff. The disciples had been listening to king talk and Messiah talk ever since they started following Jesus. Momentum is gathering. It looks as if it is going to happen.

And then Jesus throws cold water on all this overheated king talk by talking about his death (verses 23–25). He is their King, yes. He is their Messiah, truly. But not in the way they are thinking. In a very short time, they are going to hear him speak as a dying man, deliver his inaugural address as King from a cross.

Jesus has his work cut out for him. He gets his disciples by themselves and has a long, leisurely conversation with them (John 13–17). He starts out by washing their feet. He follows it up by going over, again and again and again, the ways in which he is King and Messiah and the ways in which they are going to experience and serve him as King and Messiah. Unhurried and patient, he completely revises their expectations. He then gathers it all up in a closing prayer.

The next day he is crucified.

—

The prayers of Jesus can never be isolated from the life of Jesus. Prayer is not a subject of its own. Prayer is not a specialist activity. In a symphony orchestra, some specialize in the clarinet, others in the oboe, others in the violin, and some in the trombone. But in the Christian life it is not that way. We don't have some who visit the sick, some who sing hymns, some who give money, and some who pray. In the Christian life we do not choose one aspect, get some instruction and training, and then specialize in what we like or feel we are good at.

Prayer is not something we pull out of the web of revelation and incarnation and then sign on to be prayer warriors. It is more along the analogy of breathing: if we are to live, we all have to do it. Although there are illnesses connected with breathing, there are no excellences. We don't single out an individual and say, "She is a great breather."

Prayer is woven into the fabric of life. Prayer is woven into the fabric of Jesus's life. The references to Jesus at prayer are part and parcel of everything else he does. None of his praying and none of his prayers can be taken out of context and studied on their own and then practiced as a thing in itself.

—

The link between the two parts of John's storytelling—Jesus's life and Jesus's death—is Jesus's four-word prayer: "Father, glorify thy name" (12:28).

Glory, in both its noun and verb forms, is one of the large, horizon-filling words in Scripture. But a dictionary is of minimal help in getting a sense of the compacted energy that radiates from its syllables. We need the entire story of Jesus as given to us by our four master gospel storytellers. And then we need that story backed up and filled in with the entire story of creation and covenant, in Torah and Prophets, Epistles and Apocalypse. We can't comprehend glory in bits and pieces. We need the Story from beginning to end.

I acquired a feel for the dimensions contained in *glory* from my pastor when I was about ten years old. He conveyed it in his voice, or rather his VOICE, in capital letters. He was Welsh. His voice reverberated from the pulpit through the sanctuary in full Welsh timbre and tonality. When Pastor Jones spoke the word *glory,* it began low and rumbling, like the sixteen-foot pipes in an organ. It gathered volume and resonance until it filled the sanctuary, the sound filling not only our ears but our hearts. Most people articulate the world in two syllables, *glo-ry.* In Pastor Jones it was multisyllabled, *glo-o-o-o-ory,* on an ascending scale of decibels and pitch.

I loved to hear the word and still do. Paul Jones, roaring the word into the lives of his congregation, made it truly Johannine. It was years before I learned the dictionary meaning of the word and even more years before I learned the fundamental place it holds in the biblical languages. But I knew its meaning: something magnificent was going on, was coming together, something that had to do with God and us in that congregation, even as we listened to Pastor Jones say the word. It was a word that gathered to a greatness all the bits and pieces of our lives into the wholeness and completion of Jesus's life. A resurrection word.

—

But however wonderful my early comprehension of *glory* was, it was quite without roots in my life. And as I grew up, it was roots I was after: roots as I went to worship and work, roots as I voted in elections and bought tires for my car, roots as I got cancer and had surgery, roots as I accumulated birthdays and anniversaries, roots as I wrote letters and read books.

The roots I am looking for are described in lines just preceding the prayer "Father, glorify thy name." These are the words: "The hour has come for the Son of Man to be glorified. Very truly, I tell you, unless a grain of wheat falls into the earth and dies, it remains just a single grain; but if it dies, it bears much fruit" (12:23–24,

NRSV). I like the way poet Maxine Kumin said it: "I put down roots and I put up leaf."[86] That is what I am after.

Jesus anticipates his imminent death. As I take in his words, I realize the roots of glory are in death and burial. This is going to take some relearning. It looks as if glory involves more than what I heard in the thunder that came from Pastor Jones's pulpit. It looks as if I have to let go of what I expected and enter a mystery.

Glory is what I am after. As it turns out, I am a slow learner. Glory is not just more of what I already have or the perfection of what I already see. Do I suppose the Christian life is my biological, intellectual, and moral life raised a few degrees above the common stock? Do I think prayer is a kind of mechanism, like a car jack, that I use to lever myself to a higher plane where I have better access to God?

The language of Jesus tells me something quite different: I become less. Instead of grasping more tightly, I let go. "Blessed are the poor in spirit" is one way Jesus said it (Matthew 5:3). "Those who want to save their life will lose it, and those who lose their life for my sake will find it" is yet another way (Matthew 16:25, NRSV).

~

It helps me to be patient in my slow learning to observe that it wasn't exactly a piece of cake for Jesus either. He introduces his brief prayer not with obedient assent but with a question: "Now my soul is troubled. And what should I say—'Father, save me from this hour'?" (John 12:27, NRSV).

It wasn't easy for Jesus to redefine *glory* so that it included loss, rejection, and death. It gives me breathing space in my prayers to know that it at least occurred to Jesus *not* to pray for this kind of glory but to pray for rescue from it. He considered praying "Father, save me from this hour." But having put it out on the table, he didn't pray it. He no sooner considered it than he rejected the possibility. To pray for rescue would be to reject his basic identity of his life as gift, his life sacrificed in love so that all could live saved. It would be a prayer that violates the very nature of prayer.

The prayer Jesus did not pray is as important as the prayer he did pray. That Jesus, who "in every respect has been tempted as we are" (Hebrews 4:15), did *not* pray "Father, save me from this hour" makes it possible for me also *not* to pray it.

86. Maxine Kumin, *To Make a Prairie* (Ann Arbor: University of Michigan Press, 1979), 7.

Because Jesus did it, I can do it: reject the me-first prayer, reject the self-serving prayer, refuse to use prayer as a way to avoid God.

First the no, and only then the yes.

"Save me from this hour"? No.

"Father, glorify your name"? Yes.

—

Maybe it takes a lifetime to learn to pray this with a pure heart. But as we pray and learn to pray, it becomes increasingly clear that we must let Jesus daily redefine the word *glory,* or we will miss it entirely.

The Greeks missed it. John tells us there were some Greeks in Jerusalem the day that Jesus prayed this prayer. They wanted to see Jesus. They were tourists in the Holy City, there to see him. They had heard about Jesus, heard about the glory, and wanted to see it for themselves. Cameras at the ready, guidebooks in hand, they approached Philip and tried to hire him as a tour guide (John 12:20–22).

When Andrew and Philip tell this to Jesus, he, in effect, dismisses them. Instead of posing for a photograph for the Greeks, he talks about his death. The glory that Jesus has been revealing in word and deed all his life is not a celebrity glory: "The hour has come for the Son of man to be glorified" (John 12:23). *Hour* here means "time to die." It is time for the Son of Man to die so the Son of Man may be glorified.

Andrew and Philip probably told the Greeks to go back home and take pictures of the Parthenon. The glory with which Jesus is glorified is not inspirational. It does not promote emulation. It is not conspicuous. It is not glamorous. It is not the sort of glory that is featured in glossy magazines and travel posters advertising sun and sand on the Greek islands. You can't take a picture of it.

—

We pray in the company of Jesus in order to learn this, to relearn the meaning of a word that has been corrupted by our culture and debased by our sin. Jesus is the dictionary in which we look up the meaning of words. We look up *glory,* and what do we find? Obscurity, rejection, a sacrificial life, an obedient death. And through and in and around all that, the bright presence of God backlights what the world despises and ignores, what *we* so often despise and ignore. Jesus's life and death come to a focus in this prayer and illuminate life, all of life, so that we drop to our knees and say, "Glory—that is the kind of life I want. 'Father, glorify your name.' "

Here is one more thing I don't want you to miss. This is the only prayer of Jesus in which we hear the Father speak. The striking thing is that Jesus and the Father are, as we say, on the same page. Jesus prays that the Father's name will be glorified. The Father answers Jesus: "I have glorified it, and I'll glorify it again" (verse 28, MSG). All three tenses are comprehended in the prayer: glory in the past, glory in the present, glory in the future. Anticipation of glory ends up as participation in glory.

Amen.

[Preached by Pastor Peterson at Christ Our King Presbyterian Church on May 5, 2013, the fiftieth anniversary of the founding of the congregation.]

2

"I Am the Good Shepherd"

EZEKIEL 34:2–5, 11–12
JOHN 10:14–18

It is while Jesus is having a spirited argument with his critics that he calls himself the good shepherd. Jesus has just healed a blind man (John 9). A most commendable thing to do. Unfortunately, he broke a biblical rule when he did it. He had healed the man on the Sabbath, which was against the Law of Moses. Some Pharisees, who were self-appointed as God's policemen, heard about it and examined the healed blind man, learned that Jesus had indeed done it, and then said it was impossible for anyone to heal on the Sabbath—plus the man was lying about having been blind. It was impossible. Sabbath keeping trumped everything. The Pharisees went to his parents and cross-examined them. The parents confirmed that their son had been born blind. The Pharisees were still not convinced and excommunicated the son from the synagogue.

Jesus and the Pharisees stood in contrasting relation to the blind man. A blind person is the classic helpless human being. He or she needs help to do almost anything; he or she needs to be led. A Pharisee was a leader in Israel charged with oversight of others. The Pharisees had leadership responsibility for any who needed help. Jesus was also a leader in Israel (although not officially acknowledged as one) and accepted responsibility for helping the blind man.

But notice how the Pharisees and Jesus cared for the blind man. The Pharisees treated him impersonally as a case study. They asked probing questions, testing his qualifications for being in the synagogue, the company of people accepted by God. When it turned out that he didn't pass the test, they threw him out. They were full of themselves, taking themselves very seriously and feeling the responsibility to keep the congregation pure: no sinners allowed. They understood their responsibility to judge, decide, and take the appropriate action. The blind man was just another case study to evaluate and pass judgment. Which they did.

In contrast, Jesus saw a human being. He saw need. He didn't ask questions about sin, parents, history, or prospects. The man was blind and obviously needed help. Jesus helped. The help in this case was healing, restoring his sight.

—

Then the argument started. What is the responsibility of one person to another? Is it to help him to be good, or is it just to help him? Is my primary response to another person to insist that he become good, to take responsibility to maintain law and order, morality and civility? Or is it to bring whatever help is appropriate? The Pharisees would argue: "What good does it do to heal a man's blindness if you do it in such a way that he is more of a sinner than before? The most important thing is the Law of God. The responsibility a leader has for another person is to enforce that Law. If you go around helping people without making sure they obey that Law, you are not in the long run helping them at all. What is better—to be blind all your life and yet be submissive to the rules and then go to heaven, or to have the gift of sight throughout this life but be indifferent to the rules and end up going to hell? Clearly it is better to be blind and go to heaven than to see and go to hell." According to the Pharisees' understanding, the man while still in the synagogue was righteous, but when he was healed of his blindness in defiance of the Law, he participated in breaking the Sabbath and so had to be driven out.

Jesus's response would be, I think, something like this: "What good does it do to keep the rules if a person becomes less as a person [blind!]? The important reality is the love of God, the compassion of God. The responsibility of those of us who are well is to share that love and compassion. If we are so intent on taking primary responsibility to get people to keep the Law without a passion for sharing love, in the long run we don't help them at all. What is better: to be perfectly right and never have a black mark against you all your days and be able to stand before God and say, 'You can't find a thing against me,' or to plunge into loving, caring personal relations with God and others, with all the difficulties involved?"

Clearly, it seems Jesus is saying it is better to be compassionate than to be right.

Jesus was compassionate. When the Pharisees learned that Jesus had healed the blind man on the Sabbath, they saw a major piece of their tightly regulated moral and social fabric being ripped apart. But isn't it better to be a person who could see brothers and sisters and God in a context of love and spend life being forgiven and restored in the moral, spiritual community rather than have it all be perfectly prim and proper but blind to loving and compassionate relationships?

This loving way is the scenario John places before us when he tells the story of Jesus defining himself as the "Good Shepherd." Those Pharisees would understand immediately what that meant. They knew their Scriptures. They knew Psalm 23:1, "The LORD is my shepherd," even as we know it. They also knew Isaiah's famous words: "[God] will gather the lambs in his arms, and carry them in his bosom, and gently lead the mother sheep" (40:11, NRSV).

And even more indicting, they would certainly know Ezekiel's words (Pharisees knew their Bibles inside and out): "Ah, you shepherds of Israel who have been feeding yourselves! Should not shepherds feed the sheep? You eat the fat, you clothe yourselves with the wool, you slaughter the fatlings; but you do not feed the sheep. You have not strengthened the weak, you have not healed the sick, you have not bound up the injured, . . . you have not sought the lost. . . . Thus says the Lord GOD, I am against the shepherds. . . . I myself will search for my sheep, and will seek them out. . . . I will rescue them" (34:2–4, 10–12, NRSV).

I wonder, how many of those Pharisees, after driving the blind man out of the synagogue, would go home that night and remember the shepherd in Psalm 23, the preaching of Isaiah, and most terrible of all, the angry words of Ezekiel and then realize they themselves were the shepherds Jesus was talking about? And maybe repent?

When Jesus identified himself as the Good Shepherd, could the Pharisees fail to recognize themselves in this Ezekiel prophecy even as the conflict was being played out before their eyes?

There are two specific actions that displayed the good in Jesus's shepherding: "I know my own and my own know me" (John 10:14) and "I know the Father" (10:15).

Jesus knows us as persons. He knows our names. He knows our needs. He sees us as wonderfully complex creations of the living God. He sees us having the imprint of God in us. We are not pawns moved around on a chessboard. We are not citizens being urged to vote in the next election. We are not defined by our places in the social system. We are each unique and infinitely worth knowing.

And not so incidentally Jesus trusts us to know him, to know God. Many leaders, maybe most in our world, are good leaders but don't permit the "sheep" to know them. If there is no mutuality in the knowledge, both knowing God and being known by God, it doesn't work. Jesus insists on our knowing him as well as he knows us.

The novel *Invisible Man* is currently being read by a lot of people. Ralph Ellison, an African American, is the writer. He convincingly tells us what it feels like not to be known, not to be seen. He begins his novel with these words:

> I am an invisible man. No, I am not a spook like those who haunted Edgar Allan Poe; nor am I one of your Hollywood-movie ectoplasms. I am a man of substance, of flesh and bone, fiber and liquids—and I might even be said to possess a mind. I am invisible, understand, simply because people refuse to see me. Like the bodiless heads you see sometimes in circus sideshows, it is as though I have been surrounded by mirrors of hard, distorting glass. When they approach me they see only my surroundings, themselves, or figments of their imagination—indeed, everything and anything except me.
>
> Nor is my invisibility exactly a matter of a biochemical accident to my epidermis. That invisibility to which I refer occurs because of a peculiar disposition of the eyes of those with whom I come in contact. A matter of the construction of their *inner* eyes, those eyes with which they look through their physical eyes upon reality.[87]

The novel goes on to tell of the terrible sense of isolation, of loneliness, of the extensive suffering that comes from being invisible to other people, from living in a world where people do not know your name or let you know theirs. Against this world, Jesus proclaims himself as the Good Shepherd who knows his sheep, and because he knows them, they also know him.

---

87. Ralph Ellison, *Invisible Man* (New York: Vintage Books, 1995), 3, emphasis in the original.

—

The second characteristic of the Good Shepherd is that he lays down his life for the sheep. In the complete passage of John 10, this is the dominant feature. Four times (verses 11, 15, 17, 18) it is repeated as being characteristic of the Good Shepherd.

The willingness of the Good Shepherd to sacrifice his life for the sheep is emphasized by contrasting it with the unwillingness of the hired shepherds to run any risk at all. When danger comes, they run. Wolves ravage the flock, and the sheep are scattered. Why should they put down their lives for a few ignorant sheep? The only reason for being with the sheep is to make money, and if that should be threatened, they would do well to run.

But Jesus, the Good Shepherd, was not dominated by self-interest. He was God's shepherd. He cared for the sheep to the point of laying down his life for them. He literally did this as he went to the cross and died on behalf of those he led. Maybe we forget this, but Jesus went to the cross out of no necessity. He could easily have escaped the terrors of the crucifixion, but he was interested in those he led. He was, *is,* interested in us. If he had refused to give up his life, he would have no longer been a *good* shepherd. If he had run away when the going got rough, he would never have any reason to think it would be worthwhile to think first of another, to put another's interests before his own. But the sacrificed life produced the resurrection life, and we have before us now the picture of the One who lives for others and, having conquered death, lives on in triumph and love.

—

As John writes the story of Jesus, his intent is that we should realize personally that this is what is intended for each of us. This is what it means to live a complete life, a good life. The story of the Good Shepherd is one of his best—my favorite, in fact.

As we grow and develop as persons, men and women of character and goodness, we are influenced, whether we are aware of it or not, by models, and we often assimilate these models into our everyday behavior. Childhood provides fertile soil for the formation of models. One of the models I assimilated when I was about ten years old was the frontier character Natty Bumppo, developed in the Leatherstocking Tales series of novels of James Fenimore Cooper: *The Deerslayer, The Last of the Mohicans, The Pathfinder, The Pioneers,* and *The Prairie.* I walked about ten blocks to school in those years, along a street that was lined with huge Norway maples in which, in my imagination, Native Americans were hiding. As I walked to school, I slipped from tree to tree, stealthily making my way silently and invisibly through the hostile forest, looking for them. I think now of what I must have looked like to the neighbors who saw what I was doing and undoubtedly wondered about this strange boy on his way to school.

I soon grew out of that model, but I often recall it. I now remember it in a very different context: the story John tells of Jesus and primarily the story of Jesus as the Good Shepherd.

And what I am imagining right now is that everyone here this morning—every teacher, every engineer, every doctor, every homemaker, every policeman, every tradesman—will leave here claiming Jesus, the Good Shepherd, as the model of how we are going to live our lives as good shepherds who become interested in the people around us as persons, not problems, not projects, not puzzles. *Persons* we will look to serve, to lay down our lives for. Too much to expect? Perhaps, but not too much to ask as you imagine the life of Christ the Shepherd being worked into the fabric of our minds and bodies.

Amen.

3

"I Am the Way"

PSALM 1:1–3
JOHN 14:1–7

My text for today, the Feast of Saint Thomas, consists of two sentences, each of the sentences spoken by Thomas in the presence of Jesus. The first sentence is a question; the second sentence is a prayer. The two sentences provide an inviting narrative focus for what we are doing today: the people of God at worship and the ordination of a pastor of God.

The setting for both sentences is similar: Jesus in conversation with his disciples. It is Holy Thursday, the evening previous to his crucifixion. Jesus has just told them, "I am going away to prepare a place for you. . . . I will come back and receive you to Myself. . . . You know the way to where I am going" (John 14:2–4, HCSB).

Thomas breaks in, "Lord, we don't know where You're going. How can we know the way?" (verse 5, HCSB). Jesus responds with the sixth of his seven great self-definitions provided in the gospel of John: "I am the way, the truth, and the life" (verse 6, HCSB).

Jesus is going away, and he is going to come back and get those who have been following him so they will be with him. A few sentences later he reassures them, "I will not leave you as orphans" (verse 18, HCSB).

Thomas misunderstands. He doesn't get it and tells Jesus that he doesn't get it. The word that provokes the misunderstanding is *hodos*—"road, street, path, route"—any surface on which you walk to get someplace. Jesus in essence says, "*You* know the road I will be taking; *you* know the *hodos;* you know the way."

Thomas is even more confused. He doesn't know the destination, so how can he know the road? Is Jesus going to Capernaum, taking the road through Samaria, headed north? Is he going down to the Jordan, taking the Jericho road east? Is he going to Bethlehem, taking the road south?

Jesus tries to clarify things for Thomas: "*I* am the way." Thomas takes him at his word. "Fine, but which road?"

As long as three years earlier, Thomas, along with his apostolic companions, had heard Jesus say, "Follow me." Thomas had taken him up on it and had been following ever since, following Jesus down the streets of Capernaum, across the hills to Chorazin, along the shores of Galilee, through wheat fields picking grain, into homes and synagogues listening to Jesus teach and preach. Three times a year they followed him for the three-day trek to Jerusalem to celebrate the great feasts of Passover, Weeks, and Booths. Thomas has been a faithful and obedient follower. He has followed Jesus up and down all these roads. He knows these roads like the back of his hand.

But when Jesus said, "I am the way," he threw a monkey wrench into Thomas's understanding. There was nothing wrong with Thomas's intelligence. He knew as well as anyone what a way, a road, meant. But there was something lacking in his imagination. Literalist as he is, he has a hard time with metaphor. Jesus is now using the term *way* or *road* not for something to walk on but as a way of life, a way of doing or saying or praying. But "*I* am the way"? Jesus is covered with skin, not asphalt. Thomas scratches his head: "'*I* am the way'? What is he talking about?"

Jesus is a master of metaphor and uses it frequently. If we are going to hang around Jesus for very long, we have to get used to metaphor.

Listen carefully. A metaphor is literally a lie. When we say that God is a rock, none of us signs up for a course in geology and takes field trips looking among rocks for Precambrian evidence of the nature of God. When Jesus tells us that we are salt, we don't go around collecting dandruff from our fellow Christians to sprinkle on our breakfast eggs. When Jesus tells Nicodemus, "You must be born again," Nicodemus in essence replies, "What are you talking about? Get serious. Say what you mean in plain language" (see John 3:1–4).

But eventually we catch on: a metaphor both is and is not what it says. And what it doesn't say is more important than what it does say. A metaphor does something that the precision of a definition or an explanation doesn't do: it insists we join the speaker and participate in the creation of a fresh meaning. Metaphor activates our imagination. We begin making connections, joining what we see to something that we don't see right before us, connecting the visible to the invisible. With the stimulus of metaphor, we develop an aptitude for dealing with all the interconnected visibles and invisibles inherent in reality. Metaphor is our lexical witness to transcendence.

There is more to everything than we can see or hear or touch or taste. And the largest part of that more is God in all the operations of the Trinity. The gospel is a joining of heaven and earth, and the Christian life becomes a patient and persistent invocation that God's holiness and kingdom and will on earth become as they are in heaven.

When we realize the way of Jesus is a metaphor, the term expands exponentially; it is the way Jesus talks and prays and heals and leads and forgives . . . and on and on and on. We throw away our collection of road maps and give our imaginations a chance to enter into the reality, much of it unseen, that Jesus is revealing to us.

The people of God—*us!*—are in continuous conversation regarding Jesus as the Way. If we are to get the most out of that conversation, we need to become proficient in entering into language, participating in the meaning, not studying it as if the nouns and verbs were laboratory specimens under a microscope.

I was driving with a friend not long ago on a spectacular mountain road near our summer home in a Montana valley. He had come to visit and wanted to see the country. As we drove through these glacier-cut mountains and across rivers and creeks, I was pointing out the peaks that Jan and I had climbed, named the profusion of wildflowers, identified a spectacular five-hundred-foot waterfall. He didn't say anything, and I looked over and saw that he was studying the map. I said, "You're missing everything! Look!" He replied, without looking up from his map, "I want to know where we are." My friend had reduced the *way* to a line on a map. He reminded me of Thomas.

That's why we need one another, pastor and congregation, not to study maps so much as to keep the conversation of the living reality going.

—

The second sentence Thomas spoke is a prayer. Ten days after that crucifixion-eve conversation, it is now a week after the resurrection, and Thomas speaks again.

The week before, the evening of the day of the resurrection, Jesus had appeared to his disciples. He blessed them, filled them with his resurrection Spirit, and set them apart to continue his pastoral, shepherding ministry. But Thomas wasn't there.

He wasn't there because he wasn't following Jesus. The other disciples weren't showing themselves all that well either. They were scared to death of the henchmen of Caiaphas and had bolted the doors. They were followers still, kind of, and so they at least were there. But Thomas wasn't there. When he saw Jesus dead on the cross, he knew that was the end of following Jesus. There was nothing else to it. If there was anything more to it, Thomas would require a map, a map for following Jesus—to see with his own eyes the holes where the crucifixion nails had been and to touch those holes, to put his hand in the spear-opened side, to have the crucifixion-become-resurrection all laid out before him.

Thomas had been following Jesus faithfully and obediently, watching each gesture and listening to each word. He hadn't missed a thing. At the cross he saw that the road he had walked as he followed Jesus had led to this dead end. And so he quit following. What would you do? There was no Jesus to follow, nowhere to go. Just a few days earlier he had heard Jesus say, "I am the way," but he could see with his own eyes that there was now *no* way. The way had ended on a cross and in a tomb.

But now, a week later, with his fellow disciples in that same room from which he had been absent earlier, Jesus appears again and blesses them again. He singles out Thomas for special attention and offers him a map, the profound map consisting of the crucifixion wounds in his hands and in his side. And Jesus asks him to believe.

This time Thomas doesn't ask questions. He prays. He prays a five-word prayer: "My Lord and my God!" (John 20:28).

I love this prayer. Karl Barth observes that this prayer occurs at "one of the peaks of the New Testament message." The prayer is a surprised exclamation that Jesus, so recently dead and buried, is alive and present to him. Thomas hadn't expected this.

He had no idea anything like this was involved in following Jesus. He thought all that was over and done with. But Thomas was not left to do life on his own. When the other disciples gave their witness that Jesus was alive again after his brutal crucifixion, Thomas had refused to accept it. He had been one of those people who had followed Jesus to Jerusalem. He had denied himself. He had taken the way of the cross as he had been commanded to do. But then he dropped out. He had seen with his own eyes that following Jesus was a dead end. He saw the nails go into Jesus's hands, fastening him to the cross. He saw the spear rip open Jesus's side and the blood pour out. He concluded—and who can fault him?—that it was all over. End of the road. No more following Jesus.

And then Jesus—was there. Thomas is all eyes. Jesus is gracious to him. He offers the holes in his hands and the gash in his side as evidence. And then the prayer bursts from Thomas: "My Lord and my God!"

Thomas's prayer keeps us ready for what comes next, keeps us alert to the Jesus who rules our lives as Lord and commands our worship when we are least expecting it.

It is obedience: "My Lord."

And it is worship: "My God."

No matter how much we know, we don't know enough to know what Jesus is going to do next or how he is going to do it. And so we ask questions, congregation and pastor together in conversation. And then Jesus shows up. Sometimes the congregation is the first to notice, sometimes the pastor. And we pray, in obedience and worship, "My Lord and my God!"

This is what we do, pastor and congregation together. We ask questions and we pray prayers. Stick at this long enough and the question "How can we know the way?" is trumped by the prayer, "My Lord and my God!"

Amen.

4

"I Am Leaving . . . I Am Sending"

PSALM 118:22–23
JOHN 16:4B–15

The story of the day of Pentecost is told in Acts 2. It is the story of the descent of the Holy Spirit on Jesus's followers with the result that the life of Jesus is now lived in them. The gospel text for today is a pre-Pentecost story, taking place fifty days before the event. It is the story behind the Pentecost story and, as many background stories turn out to be, is essential for understanding and then participating in the story that makes the headlines. John is the only evangelist to tell the story (John 13–17).

Jesus had arrived at his last night with his disciples. The disciples didn't know that Jesus would be arrested later that night and killed before their terrified eyes the next day in a bloody, mocking, humiliating crucifixion. And, of course, they had no idea that in three days there would be a resurrection. They didn't know this was their last night with Jesus.

But Jesus knew. And so he set about preparing them to continue what he had begun. They had no idea what was coming next. These unsuspecting, unaware disciples would in the coming months and years speak and do what Jesus had been doing; in fact, they would do "greater works" (John 14:12). But how?

How they did it is how we do it—by continuing to follow Jesus when we cannot see him. But be prepared for a surprise or maybe I should say a disappointment. For Jesus doesn't do anything attention getting, no dazzling miracle to remember him by, no riveting metaphor to keep his message in focus. But if he does not use miracle or metaphor—two things he is very good at—what's left? Just this: they will continue living the Jesus life and doing Jesus's work when he is not right here with them.

They've been eating supper together. Jesus gets up from the table, takes a basin of water and a towel, and proceeds to wash the feet of his disciples. Peter objects, but Jesus overrides him and continues the washing (John 13:3–11). And then Jesus begins to talk. He talks a long time. This is the longest conversational discourse of Jesus that we have reported to us. The disciples listen intently. Eight times the disciples make comments or ask questions, one-liners that Jesus weaves into the conversation (John 13:12–16:33).

Finally Jesus prays. As he prays, he gathers up the life they have lived together and fuses it into the life the disciples will continue to live, praying his life and work into an identity. It is going to be the same life whether people saw and heard Jesus living it or will see and hear Peter and Thomas and Philip living it (John 17).

And that's it. This is how Jesus chooses to spend that final evening with his disciples, preparing for the transition from Jesus present to Jesus absent. He begins by washing the feet of his disciples, down on his knees before each of them, getting his hands dirty with the filth of their feet. He ends by praying to his Father and their Father that what they continue to do will be congruent with what he has been doing.

The pattern holds: whatever we do in Jesus's name, we begin on our knees and conclude looking up to heaven, praying to the Father (John 17:1). Washing dirty feet and praying to the Holy Father bookend our lives. We can't live the Jesus life, we can't do the Jesus work without doing it within the boundaries that Jesus set.

But there is more, much more. Between the washing and the praying, there is the conversation. Condensed into a single Jesus sentence, the conversation is "I tell you the truth: it is to your advantage that I go away, for if I do not go away, the Advocate will not come to you; but if I go, I will send him to you" (John 16:7, NRSV).

The style of the conversation that prepares us for the Pentecostal continuation of living the Jesus life in the Jesus way is as important as the words themselves. It is a style that invites participation. Compare John's story style with the three writers who preceded him in writing a gospel, and you will see what I mean.

Matthew, Mark, and Luke each write the gospel story on the same pattern. The story line follows Jesus for three years or so of public life, most of it in Galilee, and ends up in a final climactic week in Jerusalem. Most of the action takes place during the three years in Galilee as our writers introduce us to what Jesus does and says, acquainting us with the various ways men and women respond to him: following, questioning, misunderstanding, recognizing God revealed in him, believing, and then ending with some hating and finally killing him.

They are all skilled writers and take us through Jesus's days with gathering momentum to that week of celebration, betrayal, mockery, rejection—and glory. In retrospect we can see that the main concern of all three writers is to get Jesus, and us, to Jerusalem and to that final Passover week, where the real action—suffering, crucifixion, and resurrection—takes place. They provide just enough narrative material to make sure we understand it is *our* and the *world's* salvation that is being brought to completion.

And then we open up Saint John's gospel. From the first line we know we are in a very different literary world than John's companion writers described. We find ourselves involved in a world of leisurely and extended conversation, discourses that expand and ruminate on something that has just happened (usually something Jesus has done or said), concluding with a long prayer that gathers everything up into a coherent whole. Unlike the pithy, aphoristic language that we are used to from Jesus, we are now in the company of Jesus as he takes his time, repeats himself, picks up a phrase and then drops it, circles around and picks it up again, like someone holding a gemstone up to the light and slowly turning it so we notice the various refracted colors.

Matthew, Mark, and Luke write like kayakers on a fairly swift-flowing river with occasional patches of white water—never in doubt they are going where the course of the river takes them. But John is more like a canoer on a quiet lake, drifting unhurriedly, paddling leisurely to take in aspects of the shoreline, noticing rock formations, observing a heron fishing in the rushes, sketching the cloud patterns reflected in the glassy water.

Halfway though John's gospel, in chapter 12, it appears the action might be picking up. Judas cynically criticizes Mary as she anoints Jesus. Palm Sunday euphoria trumps the plot to murder Lazarus. The crowd is aroused, responding to the thunder from heaven and Jesus's prayer. Jesus quietly disappears into hiding and then suddenly emerges, crying out in fragments an urgent apocalyptic. The adrenaline is beginning to flow.

Well schooled by John's canonical brothers, we, of course, know what is coming next. The real action—arrest, trial, crucifixion—will appear on the next page. We turn the page. But what is this? John abruptly interrupts the action and invites us into his longest conversational discourse yet (John 13–17). In my Greek Bible it is seventeen pages. The two longest discourses until now have been the Bread of Life discourse in chapter 6, which is six pages, and the Light of the World discourse in chapter 8 with five pages.

John is slowing us down. John is quieting us down. John is asking us to shut up and listen. John is telling us to turn off our cell phones, stow our PalmPilots, and pay attention to this story that we think we know so well. John is inviting us into the company of Jesus for a time of spiritual formation. John is getting us ready for the resurrection and Pentecost.

—

We easily pick up the drift of the conversation. Jesus says two things over and over and over. He tells his friends that he is leaving: "I am leaving the world and am going to the Father" (16:28, NRSV). I count fifteen times in this conversation in which, in one way or another, Jesus tells his disciples he is leaving them. The second thing he says, and this is also over and over again, is that he is sending them the Holy Spirit: "whom I will send to you from the Father" (15:26, NRSV). The Holy Spirit, also named the Advocate and the Spirit of Truth, is designated by name and by pronouns twenty-four times. Fifteen times he tells them he is leaving; twenty-six times he refers to the Spirit that he and the Father are sending.

Jesus is leaving; the Holy Spirit is coming.

Jesus is leaving. They are not going to see him again. But the leaving is not abandonment (14:18). He will not be incommunicado (14:13). He is not walking off, forgetful, distracted.

And then concluding the conversation, he pours out a long prayer, the longest of Jesus's prayers recorded in the Scriptures (John 17). The Holy Spirit is coming. This Holy Spirit will be in them, doing *in* them what Jesus did *among* them. The

Holy Spirit—God being present with us, revealing God to us, God within us—will make our lives and work continuous with Jesus's life and work. Just as God was present to them in Jesus, God's Spirit will be present in them for others.

The leaving and the sending work together, back and forth, back and forth. Jesus's absence from them becomes the Spirit's presence in them and to the world. Everything Jesus said and did among them is continued in what they say and do, what *we* say and do.

In the prayer this congruence between what they have experienced in Jesus's presence and what they will experience in the Spirit's coming becomes even more explicit. The conversation is rambling and unsystematic. This is not what we ordinarily think of as good teaching. But Jesus is not making things clear, smoothing out ambiguities; he is making things vivid, pulsing. No outline, no transitions. Definitions are lacking. What the conversation does is immerse us in the presence of Another, the presence of Jesus readying us for Spirit. We are soon listening more to who he is than to what he says. We are drawn into this seamless web of relational attentiveness, this leaving and sending, sensing within ourselves the pervasive, soul-permeating continuity between the absent Jesus and the present Spirit.

And there is also this about the conversation and the prayer: the conversation is very spare in imperatives, and imperatives are totally absent in the prayer. Jesus is not telling us how to practice what some call "spirituality"—how to do it. He is telling us how it is done. Spiritual formation is primarily what the Spirit does, forming in us the resurrection life of Christ. There is not a whole lot we can do here, any more than we can pitch in and work on the cosmos (the work of the Spirit in Creation), any more than we can assist Jesus in salvation (the work of the Spirit at Jesus's baptism). But there is a great deal the *Spirit* can do; the resurrection community is the Spirit's work. What we can do, and need to do, is *be there* to accept the leaving and the loss of the physically reassuring touch and companionship of Jesus. And then continue to *be there* to accept what is sent by the Father in Jesus's name. *Be there,* receptive and obedient. *Be there,* praying, "Behold, I am the handmaid of the Lord" (Luke 1:38).

A number of years ago we got a call from our son: "Mom, Dad, Lynn's pregnant. We're going to have a baby." Their first child. But more important, our first grandchild. Within days we were driving the two hours to Princeton Seminary, where they were students. Jan was excited, brimming with anticipation. But I wasn't feeling much of anything. We had had three children of our own. I didn't see why this was so special, and there were still six months before we would see a baby. Somehow this pregnancy hadn't penetrated my emotions. I felt dull, flat, routine.

Driving back home the next day, I complained of my lack of ebullience, which Jan had in excess. "What's wrong with me? Why don't I feel anything?"

Jan said, "It's because you've never been pregnant."

"Well, that's just great. So what I am going to do about that?"

She told me to build a cradle. When we got home, I went to the public library and found pictures of cradles. I decided on an early American hooded cradle, sketched out the plans, went to a specialty wood shop, examined the stock, and chose some Honduras mahogany. Most afternoons I came home to my shop an hour or so early from my parish work and worked on that cradle. I decided to finish it with applications of tung oil. I worked on each piece of the cradle with the finest grade of sandpaper, over and over. Then I went to fine steel wool, over and over. Each application of tung oil deepened the color. After several applications it seemed as if the wood glowed from within. I had spent time on each piece of the cradle, shaping it, holding it, rubbing it over and over and over. And all the time I anticipated the baby that would be in that cradle, over and over and over. Jan's prescription worked. I got "pregnant" by week after week of shaping that cradle, my hands and fingers working the wood, over and over anointing it with the oil that set the mahogany on fire from within, imagining the baby that would soon be swaddled in that cradle, praying my gratitude and anticipation for the life in Lynn's swelling womb. By the time the cradle was ready, I was ready, prepared to receive the gift of new life.

Think of Jesus's conversation and prayer as cradle building, the images and repetitions. The images: the continued life of Christ in us, grounded in the physical act of kneeling and the material stuff of dirty feet, a basin of water, and a towel (John 13); the life of Jesus being offered to the Holy Father who, we can be very sure, even now is faithfully answering Jesus's prayer (John 17). And the repetitions: Jesus's words working deep into our praying imaginations, over and over and over: "I'm leaving . . . I'm sending." The emptiness, the fullness. Jesus visibly leaving, the Spirit invisibly arriving: resurrection.

We Americans are typically impatient with this kind of thing. When there is something important before us, especially something like Pentecost, we like to set goals and develop strategies. But that is not John's way. He tells us a Jesus story. He takes us into the company of Jesus in such a way that we are formed into the way of Jesus, takes us into the room where Jesus is praying for us, "that they may be one, as we are one, I in them and you in me" (John 17:22–23, NRSV), a resurrection community.

Amen.

5

"Why Peter?"

PSALM 118:21–23
JOHN 21

Peter, for all his prominence in telling the gospel story, does not strike me as a very promising leader for people like us who need someone to step out and tell us how to follow Jesus, to provide insight and wisdom in being a Christian. Most of what Peter does and says in relation to Jesus, our Lord and Savior, is wrong. And not just a little wrong, but dead wrong. He was wrong at Caesarea Philippi when, after confessing Jesus as the Christ, he then tried to prevent Jesus from going to Jerusalem to his crucifixion. He was wrong on the Mount of Transfiguration when he tried to turn the glory of God into a tourist attraction for pilgrims. He was wrong at the foot washing when he tried to distance himself from the humility of Jesus. He was wrong in Gethsemane at the arrest of Jesus when he cut off Malchus's ear, thinking he could serve Jesus by using violence. I don't think I'd want him for my pastor.

That's why I find it interesting that Saint John, whom I consider the patron saint of those who follow Jesus, writes the conclusion to his gospel using three stories that feature Peter.

This Christian way of life is complex and demanding. And it is no less complex and demanding for those set apart to be the pastor to a congregation by preaching the Word of God and administering the sacraments, prepared to submit to the jurisdiction of the presbytery, prepared to kneel and receive the prayers of the elders and pastors and the brothers and sisters in Christ who have gathered here. No matter how prepared we are, we are *not* well prepared. All the same, John is a great help, and his three concluding Saint Peter stories provide us as good a text as we are likely to find for what we are involved in today in the ordination of our Peter Santucci, whose family name, he has informed me, means "little saint."

Picture John at his writing desk. He has just finished writing his magnificent gospel. Reading this book, we find ourselves in the company of Jesus, who is using words to create life in us and in the people we live with. We find ourselves in these scenes and conversations, and we determine to spend our lives following Jesus through thick and thin, wherever he leads us.

One of the serious misunderstandings that sometimes develops among people like us who worship and serve together in Christian congregations is that there is a spiritual world quite different from the ordinary world in which we make a living and have our babies. It is a struggle to keep our minds on God when we have taxes and diapers demanding our attention. And who feels like singing "This Is My Father's World" three months into a winter of Seattle drizzle?

But John will have none of that: God becomes flesh and blood in Jesus, moves into the neighborhood, and uses words that any five-year-old can understand, words like *light* and *bread* and *door* and *water* and *wind.* John shows Jesus getting us deeper into this world than we ever thought possible, not getting us out of it. Jesus is totally at home here, ranging from the wine and cake at the wedding festivities in Cana to the stinking corpse of Lazarus in Bethany. John tells us this quite incredible story in a slow, leisurely way, bringing in a large cast of men and women with their various responses.

All this is brought to a most satisfying climax in the resurrection of Jesus, as in swift succession Mary Magdalene finds the tomb empty, Peter and John race to the place to see what happened, and Jesus and Mary exchange poignant greetings in the garden. Mary reports the encounter to the other disciples; Jesus appears to them in flesh and blood—alive—blesses and commissions them and a week later does it again, this time with the earlier reluctant, unbelieving Thomas enthusiastically embracing the band of resurrection believers, joining them with exclamatory surprise: "My Lord and my God!" (John 20:28).

That's quite a conclusion, don't you think? After pages and pages of slow, spiraling, repetitive, relaxed, leisurely conversation, this sudden, dramatic change of pace brings us to the edge of our seats. Resurrection—wow! What is John up to? And why Peter?

Well, let's see.

John gives us three stories featuring Peter. The first Peter story takes place on a beach in Galilee sometime after that first resurrection week. The disciples had been ordained by Jesus to continue his work: "As the Father has sent me, even so I send you" (John 20:21). For reasons undisclosed to us, seven of the now eleven disciples are back at their old fishing ground, Peter having organized his friends for a night of fishing. (We're not told why four are missing.)

It seems like a total non sequitur. After their extended time—three years—immersed in the company of Jesus, the drama of those years, the adrenaline of the resurrection week, and all of it coming to a personal focus as Jesus breathed his own Spirit into them and ordained them to continue his words and acts, what are they doing back *fishing,* of all things? Why aren't they halfway around the world by now, speaking and acting in the name of Jesus?

Here is what I think was going on: whatever Peter and his friends previously imagined about the resurrection did not prepare them for what they are dealing with now. Resurrection, if you believe in it, has to do with the next life. It is something that happens to you after you are dead and buried and find yourself in heaven. But Jesus's resurrection took place on earth. And these first witnesses were not in heaven. They were walking the same old roads over the same old ground they had grown up on, talking and working with the same old people they had grown up with.

They saw resurrection take place *on earth.* With their own eyes they saw Jesus die on a cross. And with these same eyes, they saw him alive three days later, eating and talking with them.

It is now absolutely clear that resurrection has to do with *them*—on *earth.* My feeling is that this may have been even more difficult to wrap their minds around than Jesus's resurrection itself. Jesus was radically reconfigured and redefined by resurrection. Now *they* were being just as radically reconfigured and redefined by resurrection. The familiar concept of resurrection as life after death was totally recast as life "in the land of the living" (Psalm 116:9).

And so Peter led his friends out of the holy city of Jerusalem, the religious center, back to the country they grew up in, Galilee, their home and workplace. Fear may have had something to do with it, fear that those who killed Jesus might come after them next. But I think there was something other than that—an instinct for the local and the ordinary, a sense that if they were going to assimilate and live this resurrection life, they had to start out in the place they knew best and do the work they knew best.

I think that's why the seven former fishermen were back fishing that night. They needed an immersion in ordinariness, so they plunged into their old routines, the familiar workplace of sea and fishing boats and nets in order to experience and practice resurrection on *earth.*

As it turned out, they were not conspicuously successful during that night. Maybe they had lost their touch. "They caught nothing" (John 21:3).

Dawn breaks. Jesus is standing on the beach. The disciples, a hundred yards from shore, don't recognize him. He calls to them and learns they have caught nothing. He directs them to cast their nets on the other side of the boat. When they do it, their nets fill with fish.

John recognizes the stranger as Jesus and tells Peter, "It's the Master!" (verse 7, MSG). Peter dives into the water and swims to shore to greet Jesus, leaving his companions to the work of rowing and dragging in the fish. On shore they find that Jesus has already prepared a meal of fish and bread. Jesus is also back in Galilee, the territory they know best, the environment in which Jesus's humanity had been demonstrated so thoroughly. He calls them to the meal: "Breakfast is ready" (verse 12, MSG). The seven disciples, sweaty and smelly in their work clothes and slimy from the fish, eat a resurrection breakfast on the same ground where they have lived and worked all their lives.

—

The second Peter story is the conversation that follows breakfast. It is a single question but repeated three times.

Jesus's question: "Simon, son of John, do you love me more than these?"

Peter's answer: "Yes, Lord; you know that I love you."

Jesus said to him, "Feed my lambs."

A second time he said to him, "Simon, son of John, do you love me?"

Peter's answer: "Yes, Lord; you know that I love you."

Jesus said to him, "Tend my sheep."

Jesus said to him a third time, "Simon, son of John, do you love me?"

Grieved because Jesus said to him the third time, "Do you love me?" Peter answered, "Lord, you know everything; you know that I love you."

Jesus said to him, "Feed my sheep" (see John 21:15–17).

The Jesus questions and Peter answers occur three times. Questioned three times with the same question, Peter is hurt. Doesn't Jesus trust him? Doesn't Jesus believe him?

A week or so earlier, Peter was in the courtyard of Caiaphas while Jesus was on trial before the high priest. It was a cold night, and Peter and others were warming themselves at a charcoal fire (*anthrakian,* 18:18). Peter was questioned by other spectators in the courtyard that night about whether he knew Jesus. Peter answered three times with a denial. Matthew and Mark tell this story and add the detail that one of Peter's denials was accompanied by a curse (Matthew 26:74; Mark 14:71). Now, on the Galilee beach, Peter has just eaten a breakfast cooked by Jesus over another charcoal fire (the same word, *anthrakian*).

When the Galilee beach conversation started, Peter couldn't have known where it was going. But when Jesus put his question to Peter a third time, Peter's three denials the week before, while warming himself at a similar charcoal fire as Jesus was on trial before Caiaphas, pulled the memory of that awful night of shame into the present. So *that's* why there are three. The three Jesus questions on the Galilee beach reverse and redeem Peter's three denials at the trial the week before in Jerusalem. The three affirmations of love harness Peter into continuing Jesus's work—"Feed my sheep"—a change of vocation, no longer a fisherman but a shepherd following in the steps of the great Shepherd of the sheep. It is a remarkable story. Peter, the most conspicuous failure among the first disciples, is now forgiven, is restored to continue Jesus's work. Peter, for as long as he lived, never forgot the link between that night of denials and this morning of grace.

—

John continues his strategy of activating the Jesus life and ministry among us, Jesus's followers, with a third Peter story. This one follows after Jesus's command

"Follow me," which is repeated twice more (see John 21:19–22). This is the final command we hear from Jesus's lips in John's gospel.

This is significant. Just so Peter and those of us who succeed him in doing Jesus's work in Jesus's way don't get the wrong idea of what that means, Jesus doesn't say "Lead in my name" or "Lead my flock." He says as clearly, briefly, and emphatically as possible, repeating it twice, "Follow me. . . . Follow me."

There is a context that deepens our understanding of what is involved. Peter is told by Jesus not to have any illusions about what is going to take place. Jesus says, "You are going to get old and decrepit and will not be able to do what you want or go where you want. Someone is going to have to dress you and carry you around. And you are going to die" (see John 21:18). Sorry, Peter, following Jesus is not marching in a victory parade.

Peter knows by now that following Jesus means going the way of the cross (John 21:18–19). Too many times Peter has followed Jesus by doing the Jesus thing, but in his own way. He did it at Caesarea Philippi and at the transfiguration, at the foot washing, at Jesus's arrest. But this is now a chastened Peter, the restored and rehabilitated Peter: "Follow me" (John 21:19).

But Peter still doesn't quite get it. The third Peter story takes shape as Peter looks over his shoulder and sees John. Peter asks Jesus, "How about him? Is he also going to end up a tired old man and glorify God not with great achievements but in weakness and death?" (see verse 21). Jesus is sharp with his rebuke: "That's none of your business—*you* follow me" (see verse 22). Following Jesus demands our full attention. There is no time here to speculate on how others are doing. We are to keep our eyes on Jesus (see John 21:22). The minute we start making comparisons, we lose our focused obedience on Jesus's words and life. When we attempt to get our models of ministry from the celebrities of our culture, we obscure the uniqueness of this gospel life. When we start trading in a humble life of following Jesus for a celebrity life of leadership, we turn the Christian life on its head.

—

So, why Peter? Because as John concludes his gospel, he wants to make sure we understand how this glorious resurrection life gets lived out on the street by people like us, butchers and bakers and candlestick makers as well as by pastors and teachers and missionaries. We don't wait until we die to experience and participate in the resurrection life. And we start in our own neighborhood, with the people we have grown up with.

The second story involves Peter's change of identity from a fisherman denying Jesus in the courtyard of Caiaphas to a replacement identity of shepherd conferred by Jesus while eating breakfast around a charcoal fire on a Galilee beach.

The third story involves Jesus's insistence that Peter's place in the kingdom is to maintain his self-awareness as Jesus's follower (not leader) in the Christian community. The Christian life does not consist in achieving great things for God but in allowing Jesus to use our inadequacy and failure to rehabilitate us to a life experienced as grace and love and obedience. Peter's recovered focus on following Jesus to a sacrificial death, undistracted by what others might or might not be doing under Jesus's emphatic "Follow me," is basic for each of us. The Christian life is not about leadership but "followership," not about becoming more and more but less and less.

That's "Why Peter?" We can only live this resurrection gospel of Jesus in the way that Saint John has written it, by joining Peter in his embrace of the local and ordinary, by accepting the continuous renovating forgiveness of Jesus in our lives, and then by following Jesus without cultural detours or celebrity distractions.

Amen.

6

"See What Love"

SONG OF SOLOMON 8:6–7
1 JOHN 3:1–2

Five books in our New Testament have been ascribed to John of Patmos: the Gospel you are all familiar with, the Revelation of Jesus Christ that is the concluding book of the Bible, and a small bundle of three brief letters—1, 2, and 3 John.

The Gospel is John's pastoral account of Jesus's preaching and praying, and it provided John's congregations with the foundational story that has its origin in the Genesis creation and its completion in the birth, life, death, and resurrection of Jesus. Jesus, God in human form, who opened the door for all of us to become, in John's words, "children of God" (John 1:12). God in personal relationship with us, a Father. You can't be more relational than that. And children in personal relationship with a Father. You can't get more relational than that.

The Revelation is John's pastoral preaching that provided his congregations with the courage and hope to keep the faith in good times and bad, "in plenty and in want, in joy and in sorrow, in sickness and in health," as our prayer book has it. In Revelation, John provides us with a comprehensive imagination to embrace our entire lives as saved by God in Christ.

The Gospel and the Revelation are big books, extravagant workings of the holy imagination, giving us a feel for the largeness, complexity, and intimacy of the Christian life. The Letters are three fairly brief pastoral letters in which John writes to a small community of Christians who are having difficulty getting along with one another. He is helping them, showing and inviting them into the utter accessibility of what is involved in the Christian life. Three people are named in the Letters: Gaius and Demetrius in affirmation and Diotrephes as a troublemaker.

Imagine the Gospel and Revelation as magnificent mountain ranges, jutting high into the sky and stretching into miles of jagged horizon. And imagine the Letters as a small valley, carved out ten thousand years ago by a glacier, a valley now inhabited by seventy or eighty people who gather on Sundays to worship in a small church.

Everything John writes in his Letters is bounded by the world of the Gospel and Revelation mountain ranges, but the Letters have their own identity, not as another mountain range but a valley. This is a valley where people have homes and families, work and study and play, are born and die. A river runs along one side of the valley, and most days there is someone on its banks with a fly rod. Most of the people hike from time to time in the mountains, exhilarated by the good air and dramatic shapes and colors. The people love living in this valley. They can look at the mountain ranges any time of the day or night and be awed by them, feeling lucky to be able to live in such a place: inspirational, beautiful, healthy. On Sundays most of them pack a lunch after worship at Valley Presbyterian Church and climb into the mountains, giving themselves to the huge vistas and the mountain highs of so much beauty and truth.

But during the week, on the valley floor, things are not always so inspirational and beautiful and ecstatic. Sometimes they forget what they like and admire so much in the mountains, and they start talking and acting as if *they* are the mountains. And some of them, surrounded by so much beauty, act as if *they* are the beautiful ones and get miffed when others don't treat them as glamorous. Quarrels erupt, arguments develop, and people get their feelings hurt. Every once in a while five or six people get fed up and leave, climbing over a mountain pass to another valley where they are sure they will find a better class of people.

What's gone wrong in the valley? And more specifically, what has gone wrong in Valley Presbyterian Church? In John's Letters he is writing to people in trouble. What's the trouble?

They have no trouble apparently with the story of Jesus and none with the salvation of Jesus. The mountain ranges keep Jesus prominent on their horizons. We have to read between the lines somewhat to discern just exactly why this congregation is having difficulty in getting along, but as I was perusing it again this week in preparing for this sermon, it is clear that it has to do with love: the love Jesus has for them and their love for one another. The word *love* keeps cropping up all over the place. I counted fifty-one occurrences in the three brief letters.

These people know a lot about Jesus. How could they *not* know? Everywhere they look they see evidence. They hike these Gospel and Revelation mountains all the time. But they always return from their weekend hikes and picnics, bird and animal sightings, stories of weather and fatigue, and settle into another five or six days' routine in which they mostly have to deal with one another. You would think they would be so charged up with oxygen and camaraderie and beauty and Jesus-dominated conversation that they could hardly do anything but live magnificently.

But they don't. Why, when they come down from the mountains, do they have such a hard time getting along with one another? I think we could say that John in his Letters is describing a community trying to get along with one another in between telling stories of Jesus and experiencing Jesus's saving work in their lives. They are most aware of Jesus on the mountains, but somehow when they return to the valley, they manage to leave Jesus on the mountains.

So the Letters are about Christians getting along with one another, *loving* one another in the valley during an ordinary workweek with neighbors and spouses and children, jobs and responsibilities.

Why is love such a problem? Jesus, whom they have been hanging out with in such inspiring and energizing high-country conversation, clearly loves them unambiguously. So why does love become problematic on the valley floor?

Maybe this: they associate Jesus primarily and emotionally with the Gospel and Revelation mountain ranges. They first learned about Jesus on the mountaintops, and every time they are there, which is every week or so, they renew the old feelings. They can often be heard talking about what a great hike that was last week. They often describe it as a spiritual experience. Jesus is associated with ecstasy and beauty and endless sweeps of horizon.

But people don't live on mountain peaks. Back down in the valley, it's almost as if whatever they felt from Jesus or heard from Jesus had happened in another country. It wouldn't be, in the basic test for authenticity that the valley people use, relevant to life in the valley.

What is John, the pastor of these people, to do? In many ways he has a great congregation. These people love spiritual things. They love hiking in the Gospel and Revelation ranges. They know their holy-land geography inside and out. They carry topographical maps and can identify all the holy sites. And equipment. There is no congregation of Presbyterians as well equipped as John's: rappelling concordances, carabiner dictionaries, and all the latest in mountaineering technology.

But for all their Jesus-knowledge and Jesus-enthusiasm in the mountains, none of it seems to make much difference in the valley.

—

Pastor John realizes he has his work cut out for him. He strolls the streets, picks up on conversations on a park bench, drops into a local coffee shop and eavesdrops on the gossip. He notices they all use the name of Jesus a lot; *Jesus* is a key word in their vocabulary. That pleases him. At least they have been listening to his sermons. But he also notices the name *Jesus* only seems to come up in sentences that have to do with the big truths, the mountain truths. Dealing with Jesus usually means packing a picnic lunch and hiking five or six miles to a mountain pass. He asks one of his elders about the rumors he has been hearing.

"Thanks for asking, Pastor. But to tell you the truth, down here in the valley we have to get on with ordinary life. It is not a question about forgetting Jesus or not honoring him, but he is not the One we have to deal with right now. Jesus is magnificent, Pastor, and I believe in him with all my heart, but you wouldn't believe how tangled up my family is right now, a real mess with nothing magnificent about it. Don't think that Jesus is absent from my life, for those mountains are constant reminders of what he did and is going to do again. But for right now in this valley, I'm having to deal with a spouse who is acting contrary. You know what she is like; she's bent your ear plenty of times. And you wouldn't believe how rude the neighborhood has become since that Jones family moved in with their seven kids. And get this: I was down on the river the other day to do a little fishing with my son, and that filthy-rich old man Odegaard was there, fat and sassy, with his three grandchildren outfitted with the latest-model fly rods, showing off and making fun of my son with his bamboo pole. I hate that rich old tub of lard. You know, sometimes I just can't wait for Sunday so I can get up in the mountains for a little peace and quiet, climbing those Jesus Peaks and having a quiet time alongside Hallelujah Creek. By the way, Pastor, someone told me the other day of a prayer I could pray that is guaranteed to boost my salary and prevent cancer. Cancer runs in my family, and I've been a little worried lately. Would you teach me that prayer?"

—

So instead of teaching his elder the prayer he asked for, John asks the elder to call his congregation to a special meeting and gives them a refresher course on Jesus. And he focuses on their identity: God loves us, and we are the beloved of God. He begins like this . . .

"It seems to me that many of you have come to think that Jesus is God in the beauty and ecstasies of the mountains but that he isn't human in the way we are human. At the very center of the Christian gospel is the conviction that Jesus is as much human as he is God. He is as much with us in the valley as in the mountains. And the evidence is that he loves us and that we are able to love him—personal, relational qualities."

Pastor John of Patmos tells his congregation that the only Jesus he knows is a God-in-the-flesh Jesus. And he talks out of his personal experience. "This is the Jesus I ate meals with, walked around Galilee with, most emphatically touched, saw, and heard. He is as human as any of you are human." He is insistent that however glorious Jesus is, he is as human as they ever dreamed of being: "Jesus is involved in the mess of your lives, the dirt in this valley, your work, and your families just as they are."

John's rule of thumb for determining the truth of Jesus is this: "Everyone who confesses openly his faith in Jesus Christ—the Son of God, who came as an actual flesh-and-blood person—comes from God and belongs to God. And everyone who refuses to confess faith in Jesus has nothing in common with God" (1 John 4:2–3, MSG).

The basic test that John provides to clarify our mutual identity as children of God is to insist that Jesus is God in the flesh, fully participant in our history.

—

Pastor John continues: "We learn how to love, not by being told to love, but by being loved. Love is not built into our genes. A lot of very essential things about being human take place without our doing much about them. We breathe. Our heart pumps and circulates blood. Our sucking reflexes seem to be fully developed when we come out of the womb. We kick and wave and scream, cuddle and sleep and coo—all without schooling or training. But as we gradually develop genetically, other things come into play that require training and teaching: reading and writing, certain social skills, artistic and athletic competence, emotional and relational understandings, how to repair a transmission, how to program a computer, how to get to the moon. At the top of these learned behaviors, these achieved identities, is love.

"Everyone more or less knows this, but after the age of thirty or so, having failed so many times at loving and being loved, it seems out of reach, so we settle for a human identity that seems a little more accessible, like playing the violin or playing a ten-handicap golf game.

"I know that talking about love doesn't sound very practical. I can see you shrugging your shoulders and saying, 'Well, Pastor, I know you mean well, but I've tried it, tried it a lot, and it doesn't work. How about something a little more down to earth?' "

But Pastor John is unrelenting. "You know, this is about as down to earth as it gets. Remember what you learned that day on the mountain, that 'the Word (that means God) became flesh (that means Jesus) and dwelt among us' (John 1:14)? That is as down to earth as you can get. And remember that other sentence: 'For God so loved the world that he gave . . . ' (3:16)? Friend, you are the one he loved. You are the beloved. I'm not putting anything alien or ill fitting on you. This is who you are: loved by God. But being loved is not all there is to it. Being loved creates a person who can love, who *must* love if that person is going to be fully human. *Getting loved* is a launching pad into *giving love.*"

Pastor John is now warmed up and hitting his stride. "This involves, of course, a radical purging of our imaginations and self-centered habits that have accumulated like barnacles and parasites and grime around the word *love.* It doesn't exactly mean that everything you have experienced or imagined or even fantasized is dead wrong, but most of it is only a fragment of something larger, a single puzzle piece from a thousand-piece jigsaw picture puzzle.

"The whole story, the big picture on the box of jigsaw puzzle pieces, the picture of how God loves us, is laid out plain enough in Jesus, who now lives in you. It's the story of a 'beloved' (Mark 1:11; 9:7) who became the lover: 'For God so loved the world . . .' (John 3:16). Now you do it: love your sister, love your brother, love your neighbor, love your spouse, love tub-of-lard old man Odegaard. God loves you; Christ shows you how love works. Now *you* love. Love, love, love, love."

Amen.

7

"The Marriage Supper of the Lamb"

PSALM 23
REVELATION 19:1–9

John of Patmos was credited by the early church with writing a gospel, three letters, and Revelation, each quite different in style. But when looked at carefully, they have been recognized by many as providing a coherent identity of what John was about. I personally have recognized in them a mirror of a comprehensive pastoral vocation.

—

Here's a story that helps me understand why John's Revelation is so important to me. One October Saturday my wife picked up our seven-year-old grandson at Holy Nativity Church. Hans had been attending a class in preparation for his first Communion. They drove off, headed for a local museum that was featuring a special children's exhibit on gemstones. On the way they stopped at a city park to eat their lunch. The two of them ate while sitting on a park bench, Hans chattering all the while. He had been chattering nonstop ever since leaving the church. Lunch completed—his was a lettuce and mayonnaise sandwich, which he had made himself ("I'm trying to eat more healthy, Grandma")—Hans shifted away from his grandmother, faced out into the park, took from his book bag a New Testament that he had just been given by his pastor, opened it, held it up before his eyes, and proceeded to read, moving his eyes back and forth across the page in a devout but uncharacteristic silence. After a long minute he closed the testament and returned it to his book bag. "Okay, Grandma, I'm ready. Let's go to the museum."

His grandmother was impressed. She was also amused because Hans could not at that time read. He wanted to read. His sister could read. And he *knew* he couldn't read, sometimes announcing to us "I can't read" as if to reinforce our awareness of what he was missing.

So what was he doing, "reading" his New Testament on the park bench that autumn Saturday?

As it turns out, in this business of living the Christian life, one of the most neglected aspects in reading the Scriptures is reading them formatively and imaginatively, reading in order to live.

Hans on the park bench, his eyes moving back and forth across the pages of his Bible, "reading" but not reading, reverent and devout but uncomprehending, honoring in a most precious way this book but without any awareness that it has anything to do with the lettuce-and-mayonnaise sandwich he has just eaten or the museum he is about to visit, oblivious to his grandmother next to him. Hans "reading" his Bible. A parable.

A parable of the Scriptures depersonalized into an object to be honored. The Scriptures detached from precedence and consequence, from lunch and museum. The Scriptures in a park elevated over life on the street. A book-on-a-pedestal text buffered by an expansive manicured lawn from the noise and stink of diesel-fueled eighteen-wheelers.

Saint John introduces himself on the opening page of the Revelation: "I was in the Spirit on the Lord's day" (1:10). It is Sunday and John is worshiping God. Then he hears a trumpetlike voice: "Write what you see in a book and send it to the seven churches" (verse 11). When John turns to see the source of the voice, he sees Jesus.

If the first thing John sees in his grand vision is Jesus, the second is his congregations. It's pretty much what we have represented here among us as we gather in worship each Lord's day: Jesus and one another.

The most formative thing we have learned together in this sanctuary is the worship of God. And we learn more about worship from Revelation than from any other single place in the Bible. It is permeated by singing and praise, quiet and vigor, and our imaginations are stirred to recognize the invisible come into visibility in a relational community. All our senses are involved. We see things we never had eyes to see before. We hear voices that enter into and permeate our inner lives. The world around us comes alive with meaning. Everything means something. There are voices, pictures, animals, angels. And we are not just onlookers; we are participants. Worship is participatory. There are no bystanders. Something is done. We are involved.

It is easy to enter Saint John's Revelation. The emphasis on worshiping God is repeated. More than twenty times the word *worship* is distributed between the beginning and the ending chapters. In the center, there is a contrasting antiworship as people worship the Beast, an obvious representation of evil that includes the Dragon and the Whore. John is famous for his vivid and extravagant pictures.

—

I can still remember finding near the center of Saint John's Revelation a metaphor that grabbed my attention. It comes in the context of the gathering momentum regarding the mysteries involved in the conflict between the forces of good and evil. John sees a strong angel straddling land and sea, and in his hand he holds a scroll—the Scriptures—in which is written the "mystery of God" (10:7). A voice from heaven tells John to take the scroll. And then this: "I went to the angel and told him to give me the little scroll; and he said to me, 'Take it, and eat; it will be bitter to your stomach, but sweet as honey in your mouth'" (verse 9, NRSV).

The metaphor of eating a book is my favorite out of all of Saint John's well-crafted words. It means, of course, "Get this book into all the sinews and muscles and nerves of your body. It is not enough to get it into your head; get the book into your stomach and feet. *Live and digest* this salvation life!"

Saint John wasn't the first biblical prophet to eat a book as if it were a peanut-butter sandwich. Six hundred years earlier Ezekiel had been given a book and commanded to eat it (Ezekiel 2:8–3:3). Ezekiel's contemporary, Jeremiah, also ate the book of God's revelation, his version of the Holy Bible (Jeremiah 15:16). Ezekiel and Jeremiah, like John, lived in a time in which there was widespread pressure to live by a very different text than the one revealed by God in these Holy Scriptures. The diet of Holy Scripture for all three of them issued forth in sentences of tensile strength, metaphors of blazing clarity, and prophetic lives of courageous suffering.

We are always in danger of succumbing to the widespread setting-aside of the Holy Scriptures and replacing them with the text of our own experiences. We need authoritative direction in our actual day-by-day living for keeping the Scriptures in focus. These three rough-and-tumble prophets—Jeremiah, Ezekiel, and John, who were responsible for the spiritual formation of God's people in the worst of times (Babylonian exile and Roman persecution)—needed a word of God ready within themselves, capable of convincing their congregations of the gut-level necessity of acquaintance with God's Word. Yes, eat this book.

The most common misreading of Revelation comes from reading it as predictive prophecy, what is going to happen in the future. There are, to be sure, references to the past and implications for the future, but the predominant emphasis of the prophetic word is on the present, the presence of God among us in the circumstances of this everyday life. The Bible warns against a neurotic interest in the future (Deuteronomy 18:10–14).

—

Worship God. The introductory sentence in Revelation is "The revelation of Jesus Christ," not the end of the world, not the identity of Antichrist, but the centering and recentering act of each and every day: "Worship God." John did it himself in his Patmos exile and trained his seven congregations of Christians by writing and sending to them the Revelation to encourage them in their weekly assemblies. John's immersion in what he learned and practiced in company with Jesus is elaborated in his Revelation and then compressed in the command that he himself obeyed: worship God.

Worship recovers its authentic focus in Jesus Christ. It is complex work, more complex even than the brilliantly arranged sights and sounds, proportions and actions, numbers and animals in his poetic imagination. The act of worship gathers everything in our common lives that has been dispersed by sin and brings it to attention before God. At the same time, it gathers everything in God's revelation that may have been forgotten in our distracted hurrying and puts it before us so we can offer it up in praise and obedience. All of this does not take place merely in a single hour of worship. But faithfully repeated, week after week after week, year after year, there is an accumulation to wholeness. As Saint John's sanctified imagination, under the protection of inspiration, draws to a conclusion, the commands enable our practice: worship God!—yes, *God*!

I'm not saying that understanding Revelation is easy. John, though, is assuming his first readers knew their Scriptures. That is probably not true of us to the same extent. But I am saying that Revelation is not deliberately obscure.

The result of Saint John's theological work is a poem. If Revelation is not read as a poem, it is simply incomprehensible. The inability (or refusal) to deal with Saint John the poet is cause for most of the misreading, misinterpretation, and misuse of the book.

A poem uses words not to explain something and not to describe something but to *make* something. *Poet* (from the Greek word *poetes*) means "maker." Poetry is not the language of objective explanation but the language of imagination. It makes an image of reality in such a way as to invite our participation in it.

It is particularly appropriate that a poet has the last word in the Bible. By the time we get to this last book, we already have a complete revelation of God before us. Everything that has to do with our salvation, with accompanying instructions on how to live a life of faith, is here in full. There is no danger that we are inadequately informed. But there is the danger that through familiarity and fatigue we will not pay attention to the splendors that surround us in Moses, Isaiah, Ezekiel, Zechariah, Mark, and Paul. Saint John takes the familiar words and, by arranging them in unexpected rhythms, wakes us up so we see the "revelation of Jesus Christ" entire, as if for the first time.

It helps to know that the Revelation has 404 verses. In those 404 verses there are 518 references to earlier Scripture. If we are not familiar with the preceding writings, quite obviously we are not going to understand the Revelation. Saint John has his favorite books of Scripture; Exodus, Ezekiel, and Daniel are particularly prominent. But there is probably not a single canonical Old Testament book to which he doesn't make at least some allusion. Still, the life, death, and resurrection of Jesus Christ and the community of Christians living by faith in Christ are all assumed and are worked into the fabric of his poem.

These statistics post a warning: no one can hope to read this last book accurately who has not read the previous sixty-five. It makes no more sense to read the last book of the Bible apart from the entire Scriptures than it does to read just the last chapter of any novel, skipping everything before it. Much mischief has been done by reading Revelation in isolation from its canonical context.

—

Saint John's Revelation begins with seven chapters of nearly unadulterated praise, celebration, singing, and prayer. The first clue to what the book is comes in the third verse: "Blessed is the one who reads aloud the words of the prophecy, and blessed are those who hear" (NRSV).

Blessed is a word that connotes happiness. It is the word Jesus used nine times to introduce his Sermon on the Mount (Matthew 5:1–11). John of Patmos follows Jesus's example and employs *blessed* to provide a context of blessedness, happiness that seasons his vision with hope and good cheer. To maintain a connection between Jesus's sermon and John's vision, the word *blessed* is repeated eight times throughout what he writes (1:3; 14:13; 16:15; 19:9; 20:6; 22:7, 14). The blessings keep cascading into our lives. Hans Boersma comments, "It's like we're back on the mountain, sitting at Jesus' feet all over again, waiting for the perfect blessing he holds out to us."[88]

The vision of heavenly worship in chapters 4 and 5 is reflected in the hymn with which we opened today's worship: "Holy, Holy, Holy" (4:8). The vision sets the tone and is elaborated in the next two chapters as "a great multitude which no man could number . . . clothed in white robes," singing robustly around the throne of God: "Salvation belongs to our God who sits upon the throne, and to the Lamb!" (7:9–10). The sheer exuberance is expressed in John's vision of Jesus sitting on a throne in heaven, with twenty-four elders surrounding the throne, throwing their gold crowns high in the air, like football players throwing their helmets in victory or West Pointers throwing their caps to celebrate their graduation.

Soon there is silence in heaven for about half an hour (8:1). A lot is happening, some of it distressing. We need breathing room. We catch our breath as we are taken into a world where everything is wrong, which is expressed by using

88. Hans Boersma, *Sacramental Preaching: Sermons on the Hidden Presence of Christ* (Grand Rapids, MI: Baker Academic, 2016), 141.

unforgettable metaphors of disaster such as Wormwood (8:11); an army of locusts coming out of a bottomless pit (9:2–3) led by their king Abaddon, which means "Destruction" (9:11); troops of cavalry numbering "twice ten thousand times ten thousand" (9:16) riding horses with heads like "lions' heads, and fire and smoke and sulphur issued from their mouths" (verse 17). Then come the battle of Armageddon (16:16), the judgment of "'Babylon the great, mother of harlots and of earth's abominations' . . . drunk with the blood of the saints and the blood of the martyrs of Jesus" (17:5–6), and more. And after this interim of violence and blasphemy, using metaphors that express the worst of what humankind is capable, there is a magnificent thunder roll of hallelujahs (19:1–4).

—

It interests me that weddings play a significant part as John gives witness to the life of worship. In the gospel he wrote, John included a wedding story near its beginning (chapter 2). John had carefully organized his gospel on a framework of seven signs that give witness to the nature of Jesus's presence and work among us.

Then, in the final four chapters of Revelation (19–22), he picks up on this celebratory beginning in Cana and brings it to a vigorous conclusion: "For the marriage of the Lamb has come, and his Bride has made herself ready" (19:7).

I have always delighted in the parallel wedding stories that John uses near the beginning of his gospel and now in concluding Revelation as the angel instructs him: "'Write this: Blessed are those who are invited to the marriage supper of the Lamb.' . . . I fell down at his feet to worship him, but he said to me, '. . . Worship God'" (verses 9–10). Saint John loves weddings. Weddings play a significant part in his recapitulation of the life of worship.

This invitation is followed by the bride herself, "the holy city, new Jerusalem, coming down out of heaven . . . as a bride adorned for her husband; and I heard a loud voice from the throne saying, 'Behold, the dwelling of God is with men'" (21:2–3). A final mention of the wedding is generously welcoming: "The Spirit and the Bride say, 'Come.' And let him who hears say, 'Come.' And let him who . . . desires take the water of life without price" (22:17).

—

As Christ's salvation work among us is completed and as the New Jerusalem is established, there is this confirming but unadorned comment: "And its gates will never be shut" (21:25, ESV).

Never? Really? That is what the text says. Jesus doesn't want any of us to miss the joy.

Amen.

ACKNOWLEDGMENTS

I owe a debt of gratitude to the congregation of Christ Our King Presbyterian Church in Bel Air, Maryland. They listened with appreciation to my sermons for twenty-nine years, and their prayers were a substantial factor in what was preached.